ROBERT A. MARTIN

D0983147

The Journals of Thornton Wilder, 1939–1961

THE JOURNALS OF
Thornton Wilder
1939–1961

Selected and Edited by Donald Gallup

With Two Scenes of an Uncompleted Play,
"The Emporium"

Foreword by Isabel Wilder

Yale University Press
New Haven and London

Designed by James J. Johnson
and set in Caledonia type by Eastern Graphics. Printed in the United States of America by Vail-Ballou Press, Binghamton, New York.

Library of Congress Cataloging in Publication Data

Wilder, Thornton, 1897–1975.
   The journals of Thornton Wilder, 1939–1961.

   Includes index.
   1. Wilder, Thornton, 1897–1975— Diaries.
2. Authors, American—20th century—Biography.
I. Gallup, Donald Clifford, 1913–   . II. Wilder,
Thornton, 1897– 1975. Emporium. Selections. 1985.
PS3545. I345Z465   1985   818′.5203 [B]   85–3365
ISBN 0–300–03375–3 (alk. paper)

10   9   8   7   6   5   4   3   2   1

Contents

Foreword: Born to Read and Write

When I read for the first time the more than one thousand pages of the transcript of my brother's *Journals* that his literary executor had prepared—later drastically reduced to make the present book—I asked myself: "Do I recognize Thornton in this most private and sometimes painfully revealing search into himself and into various challenging aspects of his work?" That initial reading of his notations, covering decades of daily reading and writing and living at home and abroad, had been for me an experience running from joyful recollection of shared events and memories to surprise, even consternation at unsuspected states of mind. "Think again. Do I find him here?"

"Yes. Yes. I do!" In a flash I understood the importance of this stunning legacy. Combine these documents with the rich cache of letters written by him as son and brother, companion, author, teacher, friend (and friend, not least, to the stranger who so often beseeched him by mail or, without warning, knocked at the door with a bundle of troubles). Now add to these the original manuscripts (unfortunately not so numerous as they should have been because he had given away so many) and the published volumes in their various editions and foreign translations—a rainbow on the shelves. Finally top them all off with a vast accumulation of memorabilia, ranging from playbills, and reviews of his plays and novels, to photographs, medals, honorary degrees, even a painting or two and several pieces of sculpture. Here in abundance are the materials that make up the self-told story of the author. But Thornton could never have written a stereotype autobiography (as he himself confirms in Entry 575): the countless unavoidable "I"s, the repeated "me"s, the echoing "mine"s would have died on the page.

Instead, here in the *Journals* is Thornton Wilder alive in the innermost privacy of his thinking, of his struggle to communicate in his own way, and of his very being. He sometimes found the declarative sentence an unsympathetic means for expressing his thoughts because of his own spontaneous urge to pour out dramatic dialogue or story-telling narrative; but here it is tuned to another key. For the most part with seemingly effortless unselfconsciousness he set down urgent, forceful, and finely-honed sentences that cover hundreds of pages of manuscript and reflect a substantial portion of his life. Oh, yes, without a doubt, this was the man who had been the boy I had grown up with and, since I was almost three years younger than he, had known all my life.

The earliest of the diaries and journals in the Wilder papers in the Beinecke Rare Book and Manuscript Library belongs to 1912, with Thornton aged fifteen. The first entry in the *Journals* now published is dated February 8, 1939, when he was just two months short of forty-two. The span of time is a challenge to trace the journey of the boy to the man.

Things that led to wide consequences seemed to happen often to Thornton. Such an event occurred in early April 1906, when he first sailed to Hong Kong on the SS "Siberia" with his father, who was to take up the post of American consul general in that strategic port, his mother, older brother, and two younger sisters (a third sister was to be born later). Until this upheaval in the family's life Thornton had shared with his siblings a tightly patterned growing-up routine in a busy home in Madison, Wisconsin, dominated by a loving, proud —very proud—but anxious and overzealous father from the rock-bound state of Maine.

In those days the passage across the mighty Pacific from San Francisco's Golden Gate to the stunningly panoramic harbor of Hong Kong took a minimum of four weeks. But first there had been the wonder of the endless landscape of the American plains, with visions of sky-high mountains, as the train of cars snaked its way for days over the tracks of the Atchison, Topeka and Santa Fe to California. Next came the problem of trying to understand the vastness of the ocean. It was hungry; it would eat up the land and where would all the people go? To the bewitched eight-year-old Thornton the journey was mind-boggling.

My brother had boarded the ship very much looking forward to celebrating his ninth birthday on April 17th at sea. We children envied him this adventure. At last April 16th came, but the 17th did not follow: on that very day the ship crossed the International Date Line and the calendar leapt from the 16th to the 18th. How to explain that to a little boy who wanted to be nine years old?

Fortunately his disappointment was alleviated: another important "happening" occurred. He stopped to say good morning to one of a number of his deck-chair friends and was shown a volume in which she was writing. Each page was lined and blank except for the printed day and year. The book had a pretty green leather cover across which gold-embossed letters spelled the word DIARY. Nor was that all. The covers were held together by a gold-metal lock and, dangling on a yellow cord, was a small golden key. Thornton could only dream of a green-and-gold locked volume, but that very day he began to keep a diary, his equipment a stubby lead pencil and the smooth, heavy white blank pages of the elaborate dinner menus the grown-ups were given each evening. Yung Kwai, head steward of the children's table, supplied them to us as souvenirs. Every afternoon before tea in the lounge Thornton slipped down to the huge empty dining salon while Yung Kwai, now his special friend, dozed on fire-watch duty nearby. When the child's labors were over for the day, the two hid the pages under the green baize cover of an unused table in a far corner. The enterprise took on the heady suspense of a cloak-and-dagger conspiracy as the pile of word-covered pages grew. The afternoon before we were to land in Hong Kong Thornton let me go with him to collect what had become his treasure. The pages were gone from their hiding-place! Had they been found and thrown out as trash, or had they been stolen? Whatever its fate may have been, Thornton Wilder's first diary was written in April 1906.

By 1907, Thornton's passion for writing was already very much in evidence. I have described elsewhere how he "draped us and the neighbors' children in . . . cheese-cloth and coaxed us into declaiming his grandiloquent speeches." Thornton himself has told of his grandiose plans, only a year or two later, for various writing projects, notably "a carefully planned repertory for two theatres, a large and a small," where his longer plays would alternate with *The Wild Duck* and *Measure for Measure*, all cast "with such a roll of great names as neither money nor loyalty could assemble."

By 1912, the date of the first Journal among the Wilder papers at Yale, my brother, after several years of school in Berkeley, California, was back in China, a boarding student at the China Inland Mission School in Chefoo. The curriculum, designed to prepare for the Oxford-Cambridge entrance examinations, placed great emphasis on the classics. Thornton thus benefited by having his mind and imagination fired earlier than otherwise would have happened by the history and literature of Greece and Rome. There he began to learn Latin by himself (as he tells us in Entry 498), through studying the Odes of Horace. This classical bent was encouraged during his later student days at the Thacher School in Ojai Valley, California, at Oberlin, and at Yale.

We Wilders moved to New Haven as a family in 1915. When Thornton came home from Oberlin for the Christmas holidays, he lost no time in discovering the Yale Library, housed then on the Old Campus in what is now Dwight Hall. Transformed with excitement, he took me to see it. I was as impressed as he, and asked him: "Oh, Thornton, do you think you'll ever have a book in this library?" He answered, solemnly: "I've thought about it, Isabel; but I'd have to be about fifty before I could hope to write a book that would be good enough for Yale."

His interest in the classics continued to grow all through his undergraduate days, but by far its most important reinforcement came in the eight months that he spent, after graduation from Yale in June 1920, at the American Academy for Classical Studies in Rome. It was Mother who had arranged this. She had learned through George Lincoln Hendrickson, professor of classics at Yale, that the Academy had a few extra rooms. Thornton would enjoy most of the privileges of a Fellow, although without academic credit. Professor Hendrickson, who knew Thornton, wrote the necessary letters and Father agreed to make available the nine hundred dollars that the eight months would cost (the lira was very low at this time).

The thorough grounding Thornton had received at Chefoo guaranteed that he would make the most of that Roman interlude and, indeed, it bore fruit in his later work. But he was not permitted to forget that he would have to return to the United States—to reality, and to the necessity of earning a living. The final months in Rome saw a sometimes heated exchange of letters with our father on the delicate matter of Thornton's future. Thornton would have liked to look for work in a publishing house, a magazine office, even a bookstore (surely Father would not disapprove of his working in a bookstore?). Reluctantly, Thornton was getting ready to leave Rome to return to Connecticut and start job-hunting when Father's letters to him reached a climax with this cable:

HAVE JOB FOR YOU TEACHING FRENCH AT LAWRENCEVILLE SCHOOL LEARN FRENCH LOVE FATHER

Though somewhat tempered by the extra word *love* (which Thornton was uncertain whether to read as bribe, threat, or parental manipulation), the command was stark.

"Learn French"? Teach French! Thornton had a good reading-knowledge of the language (which, as he tells us in Entry 498 of these *Journals*, he had first begun to pick up from reading French gramophone-record catalogues) and already knew more French literature than many a young Frenchman of his age. He had a good vocabulary (and, again, the *Journals* demonstrate what a large vocabulary that eventually grew to be), but he could not conduct what he considered an acceptable conversation, and his accent was obviously not authentic. To *teach* a language, the grammar must first be mastered. Furthermore, to teach anything you must want to teach and you must know how.

Thornton paced several of the seven hills of Rome that night. At dawn he drafted a reply to our father's cable that gave expression to the resentment he felt at being treated like a child not capable of making his own decisions—a treatment all the more frustrating because our father had for years harangued him in person and urged him in letters to develop "character," to take on responsibility. But of course Thornton did not send the letter. What he wrote and mailed was:

Dear Father:
    What you ask me to do is very difficult, but I shall try to do as you wish this one more time. A graduate Fellow here knows Paris well and is giving me a letter to the head of an order of teaching nuns who specialize in tutoring English-speaking students [in French]. Also I've got addresses of some cheap *pensions*. The lessons will be about six dollars a day and I can live on two or less. I'm cancelling my steamer passage for two months. Have enough to get to Paris third class, and for about a week. Please send allowance to American Express, Paris.

In a letter *love* did not cost a cent extra: he wrote it in big letters and signed his name.

And so, for a few weeks in June 1921, Thornton Wilder was in Paris, unheralded and alone. His stay was even briefer than he had

expected because the nuns turned out to have more students than
hours for teaching them and, competing with all the young exiles de-
termined to live in Paris even if they starved, he could find no job.
Thornton had already written some sections of his "Notes of a Roman
Student" (later to become his first novel, *The Cabala*) and had
brought the pages with him to Paris. An editor of one of the many "little" magazines being published there in English wanted to print a selection, but when Thornton learned that there would be no payment,
he withdrew his manuscript. (The editor fled the city the very next
week, leaving his debts behind). To make the situation even worse,
Paris was in the middle of an unusual heat wave and Thornton's small,
airless room became almost uninhabitable. Imagine the enthusiasm
with which he received our mother's suggestion:

> Come back. I am told that in six weeks at the Berlitz School in
> New York, with concentrated cramming added to the considerable
> French you have, you will be ready to teach easily any high-school
> French class.

And so Thornton left Paris without having experienced the soirées at
27, rue de Fleurus and having been puzzled by the paintings then
hanging on the studio walls. It was only a good deal later—and in
Chicago—that he met Gertrude Stein (with what important results
these *Journals*, again, give eloquent and frequent witness).

Back in the United States, he dutifully carried out our father's
injunction to "learn French," and for several years afterward carried a
heavy schedule as an assistant house-master and full-time teacher of
French grammar and literature in Lawrenceville, New Jersey.

He had brought home with him from Rome and Paris many
pages of manuscript for the first novel and was somehow able to complete it after lights-out at the school and during weekends and vacations. When it was published in 1926, it was received with favor and,
indeed, praise. The encouragement afforded by excellent letters of
recommendation from his publisher and other friends persuaded
Thornton to apply for a Guggenheim fellowship. Much as he had
come to like teaching, he yearned to be able to break free and continue with his writing career. His failure to receive the hoped-for
grant was a severe blow. Our father, unwell and broken now from a
disease acquired in the Orient and fearful that his younger son was
facing the world with few qualifications beyond a slim first novel,
pressed him to carry through a long-made plan. Thornton, obedient

still "one more time," arranged a leave of absence from Lawrenceville and registered at the Graduate School of nearby Princeton University to work for a Master's degree in French literature and thus be prepared for a college-level teaching career. That is how he spent his first royalties from *The Cabala*.

Thornton's strategy was to please both our father and himself. He pursued the prescribed course of study with honest diligence. Although he had begun the year without a definite subject for a second novel, he showed me, years later, the exact spot on the Princeton campus where the idea for it came to him full-blown as he crossed a small bridge over a narrow flow of water that emptied into a lake. His academic marks were, alas, mediocre; but his book when it appeared in the fall of 1927 became a Pulitzer prize-winning novel. Its name? *The Bridge of San Luis Rey*. It reached an audience scattered, quite literally, around the world.

In Fargo, North Dakota (February 24, 1928):

Dear Mr. Wilder,
    I've read your book over and over. . . . I think the last paragraph is the most beautiful ever written. . . . I've learned it by heart.

In Adelaide, Australia (June 10, 1928):

Dear Mr. Wilder,
    . . . do you really believe that God sees the fall of a sparrow's wing?

In Boston, Massachusetts (September 1928):

Dear Mr. Wilder,
    I'm a woman fifty-five years old. My twin sister died three months ago. My husband is a good husband but he does not understand. I even think he has always been jealous of my love for her and now he gets cross with me for I can't always hide my grief. My children, too, though they are grown up and have children, do not understand. But from what you write about twins in *The Bridge of San Luis Rey* I know you do. How do you know? Please send me a few words in your own hand. . . .

The explanation was simple: Thornton knew because he himself had been born a twin. Like most twins the babies were premature and very frail. Thornton came first. The second child, perfectly formed and identical, was stillborn. Thornton missed this lost companion all his life. And his frailty at birth was to have a far-reaching effect. For the first six months he had to be carried on a pillow. At night, Father took his turn walking the floor with the tiny infant (protesting the failure of adults to find a formula that agreed with him)—an experience that certainly contributed to his over-protectiveness of his son all through the period of his growing up. He recognized Thornton's talents, but to him they had to be protected; to our mother they had to be fed.

The astonishing success of *The Bridge* did not spoil Thornton but, to a certain extent, it may be said to have ruined his life. As I wrote in the Foreword to *The Alcestiad*: ". . . it weighted [him] with a cumbersome bag of perquisites: honors, privileges, . . . balanced by loss of privacy and hazards to body, mind, and spirit." But it did bring with it as well its "dazzling opportunities." In 1932 came the commission from Katharine Cornell and her husband, the director Guthrie McClintic, to translate André Obey's *Le Viol de Lucrèce*; in spite of Miss Cornell and her doting public, the play was not a success when it was produced in New York. In 1937, the brilliant director Jed Harris asked Thornton to adapt for the actress Ruth Gordon a new English translation of *A Doll's House*; that was a triumph for everyone involved.

For his third novel Thornton had drawn once more upon his knowledge of the classical world and had set *The Woman of Andros* (1930) on the Greek island of that name. His fourth novel, *Heaven's My Destination* (1935), had been his riposte to the accusation from some quarters that he was refusing to deal with native American subjects. Crossing the United States on several lecture tours had given him the material that he needed in order to write it.

His third decade had started off at a high pitch, the continuing momentum of the twenties bringing together in a workable balance the four compelling interests that held his attention year after year: writing and the theater, teaching, reading, and music. He earned his living by the first two, and was continually nourished by the third and fourth. He had been a voracious reader all his life, and in several languages. And by the age of ten he was already crazy about music. For Thornton, music was not a small thing, to be accepted lightly or as an opiate. Mother knew that this interest must be encouraged. Now St. Mark's Episcopal Church, about two-and-a-half blocks from our Congregational church in Berkeley, had at this time what was for a small church an excellent organist and choir-master, and Thornton had discovered that a boy was needed to pump the organ when the organist practiced. During this period, even though it took at least eight weeks to receive an answer to a letter, Father, in Hong Kong, still in-

sisted on being consulted on matters, large or small, concerning his
children's education, religious and secular. But there wasn't time to
get his approval for this important step. Happening to meet the rec-
tor of St. Mark's, Mother dared ask if it would be possible for Thornton to be a choir boy. It all came together, and an arrangement was
made for Thornton to be excused from our Sunday School five minutes early so that he could dash over to St. Mark's, get helped into a
little white cotta (that our father would have thought *heathenish!*),
and march down the aisle singing joyously. Nine weeks later Mother
received from Father a wavering, not fully agreeing letter, but she
took no notice. That was where and how Thornton's familiarity with
and love for church music began. The organist appreciated Thornton's thirst for music and knowledge in general, and let him practice a
little on the organ. We have a beautiful little gold, harp-shaped pin
initialled "T. N. W." that was later given him for two years of perfect
attendance. He taught himself to read music and to play the piano.
(He tells us in Entry 725 that he got to know the sonatas of Beethoven
and Schubert through "fumbling with them" himself.) In later years
musicians were astonished to discover that they could talk to him as
to a musicologist. The publication of a book or the production of a play
drew him into the professional worlds of publishing and the theater;
teaching tended to bury him on the campus.

For, during all his activities as creative novelist and dramatist,
Thornton still remembered his calling as teacher. His former class-
mate at Oberlin and Yale, Robert Maynard Hutchins, having become
a very young president of the University of Chicago, had little difficulty in persuading Thornton, in 1930, to join his faculty. For six
consecutive years he found teaching two terms out of four a richly
rewarding experience: he enjoyed this commitment, gave it his best,
and said later that that Chicago period—although it was hard in a
number of ways—was probably the happiest of his life.

The year before these *Journals* begin, 1938, saw both an up and
a down in my brother's career as an American dramatist. In January
he made a veritable strike in the theater with *Our Town*, a play still
produced all over the world. Its success as a play matched that of *The
Bridge of San Luis Rey* as a novel and, exactly a decade after *The
Bridge* had won Thornton his first Pulitzer prize, *Our Town* won him
his second: he became the first author to have received the award for
two different categories of writing.

But before the year was out, in December, came the down.

Thornton wrote his play *The Merchant of Yonkers* for the famous
German-Austrian theater regisseur Max Reinhardt, whose career he
had followed over many years in German newspapers and magazines
with much the same detailed attention that these *Journals* show him
devoting to Lope de Vega and James Joyce. That Thornton had finally
met the great man and that he had agreed to produce *The Merchant
of Yonkers* was, almost incredibly, a dream come true. The high
hopes for the Reinhardt production made its conspicuous failure an
even more bitterly traumatic experience. It was the one time in my
brother's career when he was deeply affected and hurt by the public's
adverse critical verdict—and his suffering in this instance was for the
most part not for himself but for Reinhardt.

Of course the play did prove ultimately to be what Thornton
had hoped it was. In 1954, the text was reassessed and rewritten (and
again much of the story is told in these *Journals*), the transfer of
emphasis from the leading man—the Merchant—to the leading
woman—Dolly Gallagher Levi—reflected in the change of title to
The Matchmaker. With Ruth Gordon as its star the farce opened to a
warm reception at the Edinburgh Festival of 1954, was even more
successful when produced on Broadway the following year, and
reached still greater heights of public approval as the musical comedy
Hello, Dolly! With Carol Channing in the title role, it broke the record for that era for length of run for a New York production of a
musical.

Thornton once said of himself: "The most valuable thing I inherited was a temperament that doesn't revolt against Necessity and is
constantly renewed in Hope" (an allusion to Goethe's great poem
about the problem of man's lot, the "Urworte. Orphisch"). On another occasion he described himself in his young manhood as a "sort
of sleepwalker, not a dreamer but a self-amuser." He was never without a repertory of absorbing hobbies, curiosities, inquiries, and interests. As he grew older the habit continued but, rightly, became more
selective. His current interest—even when it involved writing—
often sprang from a sudden enthusiasm, inspired by a concert, lecture, play, conversation, or a book he had just read in almost any field
of world literature.

It was in the hope of attaining better control over his interests,
of "harnessing [his] notions into written paragraphs" (as he phrases it
in the very first entry of this book) that he undertook his Journal. I
think it was for Thornton not just a notebook in which he wrote: it was

more like a place to which he retreated. It had a door that he opened, entered, and closed behind himself, making an inside and an outside. He left the Journal carelessly around, on the desk, on a chair—I've often picked it up from the floor where it had fallen, slipping off the side of the couch, maybe. Thornton took no thought as to hiding it. He never told us not to read it. He talked of it as one did of a person, or of an animate creature.

Sometimes when we were lingering around the dinner table Thornton would say, "Gotta go and tell it to the Journal." For him I think it was also a form of companionship. Lope, Finnegan, Gertrude talked to him. He talked to the Journal; yet I can't believe it was completely a one-way conversation. When he used to write—oh, so long ago—in those handsome bound cahiers from which he would tear out fistfuls of pages to be discarded, he frequently would bring the remains to me. He was right: there was a lot of high-quality paper left. I remember once the mottled-paper covers were so beautiful they reminded me of a shell that one could hold to one's ear and hear distant surf. I thought to myself, Let's try this. It may have the pale echo of the Via Veneto or the wind in the pines of the Borghese Gardens or of Thornton's pen scratching or his voice talking to his twin. But, alas, I never caught a murmur!

Yes, to Thornton the Journal played many parts. And the proof, although massive in form, shape, and weight, doesn't register on any known scale—even the hyper-delicate kind that drive diamond-merchants wild.

Thornton frequently read to us-at-home his work-in-progress and letters he had written or received, but he never read from the Journal. How deeply I regret that he didn't "tell it to the Journal" on a more regular basis. Of all his fascinating insights into Shakespeare's plays, only the entry on Parolles (No. 763)—and one other bit of research not printed here—was set down. I am disappointed not to find accounts of his conversations with Gertrude Stein and many of his ardently defended (but perhaps not always so sincerely believed-in) theories. His own self-reproaches for not devoting himself more seriously to the Journal are recorded in several entries, and I suppose we ought to be grateful that he wrote down and preserved as much as he did. Certainly Thornton himself found the Journal invaluable (he compiled a rough index to its contents). That he did not destroy the entries we have indicates that he was willing that they should be read.

There are several notations, saved out from the present selection, that clarify Thornton's intentions in keeping the Journal.

11. NEW YORK, FEBRUARY, 21, 1940. On This Journal.

I began to maintain this Journal in order to discipline my thinking. . . . I had long noticed that my thoughts on some given subject (my judgment on some work of art and my attempt to give the reasons for such a judgment) ran into confusion or ran off the track or fell into a meretricious elaboration, which was able to bedazzle (yet trouble) the unthinking, but which left me with despair and self-contempt. . . .

My concern about my errors led me gradually to pay attention to "thinking" of others, particularly in conversation and lectures (since I seldom read anything but excellent books my observation of the "thinking" there was more in danger of leading me into the fault of misguided emulation), and I became aware that, apart from Gertrude [Stein], no one "thought aloud" very well. . . .

I soon came to see that the practice of reflection alone—even on the long walks which have provided me for twenty years with all that is my best in that very different activity, imaginative composition—would, for me, be fruitless. In my attempt to pass from the occasionally-permitted *aperçu* to a certain *suite* in my ideas I should require a more exacting method; and for that, written words would be necessary, written (1) for precision, (2) to prevent mere word-mosaic and self-deception, (3) to collect the notions into system, (4) to create a habit and a relation between thinking and writing, and (5) to collect from these records a reservoir of more codified ideas on which to base the judgments I am so often called upon for in conversation. . . .

My hope is that from these practices I may proceed to the ability to reflect without writing and build up the power of "unflurried" thinking in the thousand occasions in the daily life.

24. NEW HAVEN, MAY 21, 1940. On the Spontaneous Impulse to Write.

I have the instinctive habit-formed impulse, at any unoccupied moment during the day, to reach for a book to read: part intellectual activity; part habit; part evasion (*i.e.*, effacement of world around me, and self).

How important it would be if I could educate that impulse into a corresponding one *to write*. This Journal is an attempt at such re-education.

. . . It is not the same thing as "working"—. . . its color is likely to be liveliness and stimulation. It is more allied to conversation than to literature.

Its particular merits are that it exhibits the character of improvisation and disinterested absorption in its objects. It is far removed from the work of those who write a great deal for money, or ambition, or to further some single or allied causes. . . .

I do not have to rehearse in detail all the benefits of such a Journal as this (the practice of precision in ideas; the accumulation of an interrelated grammar of "reflections"—benefits increasingly clearer to me, not only in that ever-present burden, daily conversation): the chief is this (alas!) slow acquisition of the recourse to writing. . . .

441. SS "MEDIA," MID-OCEAN, MAY, 4, 1950. Of This Journal.

It seems to me that I now understand why I have always been reluctant to commit to this Journal a wide variety of matters which serve as the substance of most journals. Here are no descriptions, for instance, of the Holy Week ceremonies at Valladolid; no account of the conversations with the Max Beerbohms; of the weekend at Notley [Abbey][1] and the parties at Sibyl [Colefax]'s. Nor, for the most part, are there comments on the books I have been reading or the plays seen. This morning I have just finished Graham Greene's *The Heart of the Matter* and have been wondering why I feel no impulse to write down the many reflections that crowded into me as I was reading it.

My instinct has been right: nothing static may enter these pages (with the occasional exception of certain material which I transcribe here as sheer convenience—like . . . the Lope data; and occasional quotations from my reading). These notations are points for departure, not statements. This Journal . . . is my attempt to imitate what I take to have been the process of Gertrude Stein's "reflection."

To be sure, the view of Valladolid's celebrations started off many a reflection . . . ; in varying degrees reflections are set in march by a great many things about me; but I think I can distinguish those which contain the potentiality of extended subjective development on my part—hence material for this Journal—from those which after a short flight settle to rest. . . .

This Journal, then, is the repository only for ideas which are *moving* and *gathering*, which promise to reward me with greater extent and definition if I note them here, which are *snowballing*. The nearest I can permit myself to a static idea is to put down one which, as such, has just occurred to me and which by the very shock of its novelty gives promise of revealing its applications and consequences.

Since, then, I eschew all descriptions, all "book reviews" (save as they, like the notes on *The Wings of the Dove*,[2] lead to generalized feelings far beyond a mere review), I am able to guard myself against writing here for "show," for parade, for "audience."

This very Entry . . . illustrates what I am saying: it has cleared up a difficulty (my confused self-reproach that I had not here "expatiated" on the *Sehenswürdigkeiten* of these last months); it has refined an intention (the

1. The residence of Laurence Olivier and Vivien Leigh, situated halfway between London and Stratford.
2. See Entries 431 and 434 (February 25 and March 3, 1950).

purpose of this Journal); and it has added one new coral bead to that ever-expanding atoll: Why One Writes and What One Writes.

But there were times when Thornton had grave doubts as to the usefulness of the Journal for him in his *creative* writing. He expressed them, for example, in Entry 702. Hôtel Thermes Sextius, Aix-en-Provence, December 7, 1954. *The Alcestiad:*

> I think that the practice of writing into this Journal . . . the running accounts of my gropings, hesitations, etc. in the writing of these plays [*The Alcestiad* and "The Martians"], has been unwise. It enhances the element I have been calling the difficulties. . . . A method which is fruitful for the exact sciences (and perhaps for philosophy itself) is harmful for the play of fancy, for the emergence of the significant symbol; the developing symbol, like a many-antennae'd "nymph," searches, reaches, *tâte* wide fields of association in order to find its expression in image. To write down these *tâtonnements* incurs the risk of "fixing" too early and too concretely one of the passing phases and false attempts, thereby arresting the further ones.

Much the same attitude is reflected a year later in Entry 713. But the fact that he continued to use the Journal for this kind of *tâtonnement* seems to indicate that eventually he overcame his doubts: the "passing phases and false attempts" leading toward the late one-act plays are the subject matter of many of the Journal's last entries.

The invitation from Harvard University to Thornton to serve as the Charles Eliot Norton Professor of Poetry for the 1950–51 academic year came as a pleasant and flattering surprise. Moreover, the timing was right for him. The duties were clearly defined: a series of no fewer than four public lectures to be given over a mutually agreed-upon period of time, the subject chosen by him from his particular fields of interest. It was expected that he would reside in Cambridge during his limited tenure and arrange set hours for conferences with students. The lectures would be published by Harvard University Press.

This Norton Lectureship gave Thornton two opportunities for which he felt ready: a limited academic appointment with no teaching assignments; and the chance to write, under congenial circumstances, a book—one he had hoped some day to write, if only for his own satisfaction. Now under this commitment both the challenge of the book and the chance of finishing it would be greater. His theme would be the American literary heritage, the subjects of his lectures Melville, Whitman, Thoreau, Poe, and Emily Dickinson.

As a bachelor he was offered accommodation in a Fellow's suite in one of the University's residential Houses. He planned to move to Cambridge in early October and present his Norton Lectures during the first term, which carried into January. He spent several happy months preparing for "the pilgrimage to Cambridge." But then his well-made plans were shattered. Late in the summer, not long before Harvard was to open, Thornton received an urgent letter begging him to consider teaching a full undergraduate course on the novel. This would run parallel with his Norton series, but would continue through the college year. It was an emergency appeal and an immediate reply was requested.

Thornton later told an interviewer for *Time* magazine that the inscription on his grave would be "Here lies a man who tried to be obliging." And so now, almost as a matter of course, he felt he must accept this added, uncongenial teaching assignment. Of course he was honored—as any son of Eli was bound to be!—but even before he made the move to Cambridge, the speaking engagements for luncheons, teas, and dinners entered on his calendar—not counting the Norton Lectures—totalled fifty-four! The invitations had begun to pour in as soon as his appointment was announced (and Thornton groaned all through that year at the ever-present burden of having to answer these and all the other letters). He faithfully accepted most of the requests under the impression that this was a necessary aspect of the position that he was committed to uphold.

But he was rebellious at heart, and a hidden resentment grew against the price that Harvard was exacting. The feeling of being ill-treated was intensified when he arrived in Cambridge and found that his suite in Dunster House—unlike those of friends who were Fellows in the Yale Colleges—was small and not at all adequate for receiving more than a few students at a time: as he phrased it in a telegram to us in New Haven, there was "not even room for the bottle of blackstrap molasses." The respite of the Christmas holidays in the Florida sun helped to get him through to March. But then he collapsed with a slipped disk. He spent four weeks in the Massachusetts General Hospital, and several more recuperating in a wheel chair in a suite in a Cambridge hotel, where he could have attendants. Students came there to see him, along with the substitute teacher who had taken over his class in the novel. By mid-June he was barely well enough to accept an honorary degree and be the main speaker at Harvard's annual commencement ceremonies. Ailing though he still was, Thornton somehow managed to deliver a stunning, much admired address. (It was the time of the so-called "silent" generation, who were also a rising tide of restless, rebellious, unhappy youth.)

Thornton was a long time healing. The Journal tells of his struggle to honor his commitment to Harvard University Press and complete the book of his Norton Lectures. In the middle of that lecture year he had written:

491. COLUMBIA UNIVERSITY CLUB, [NEW YORK,] 9:00 A.M., SATURDAY, DECEMBER 30, 1950. Plan of Work.

[My colleagues X and Y] . . . have form—smooth presentational skill,—where all I have is bad logic, bad transitions, and every vice of incomplete circumspection and bad digestion. However, let me remain shameless: *du courage*; let me trust that I have some good ideas, and that the practice of discovering good ideas opens the channels to ever better ideas, and that with enough better ideas—real fruitful generating foliating insights—my presentational awkwardnesses will give place to something else: to my discovering *my* form, my way of expressing my notions. What that way will be I do not know; but it will not resemble what we see around us as the "critical essay," the "article."

And for all this, the Journal must serve as repository, as trial flight, as school of writing, as *four*—oven, furnace. Already I am immensely grateful to it. I shall never be a good lecturer; nor could I wish to be; nor can I now conceive what a good lecturer would be (if one really had good ideas that would be the worst use one could put them to, and appallingly damaging to the lecturer). But the fact that I do not despise my appearances at the new Lecture Hall is due solely to the fact that I knew more than I said; that what I said sprang from a *fumier* of thoughts and collected observations—not all of them assembled here but here partially organized and objectified, and here given the chance to grow and to extend themselves. The only interest of an idea, the only fun, the only reassurance, is its potentiality to reproduce itself, to reveal its own unexpected developments, corollaries, further relationships, its *Gestaltungstrieb*.

The book would have been easy enough to finish had Thornton been willing to allow the lectures to be printed as delivered. But he felt strongly that essays designed to be read should differ radically from formal addresses. He wanted them to be "both meaty and light." As he phrases it in Entry 722, ". . . I feel my instinct continually demanding of me those interruptions to the argument—the dramatic dialogues with the restive members of the audience, for example—

that prevent the book from being read and appraised as one more socio-literary treatise." He managed to recast three lectures as essays
for publication in the *Atlantic*, but planned further, even more drastic
revisions. The Journal traces the development of his ideas as to what
the Norton book should be, indicating that he thought of adding essays on both Hawthorne and Emerson (see Entry 596). I sometimes
try to imagine what "American Characteristics" (the title Thornton
planned to give the Norton book) would have been like, with its interpolated essays, interludes, and lay sermons printed, as Thornton
hoped they might be "in some *de luxe* edition," on pink or blue paper.
Thornton was certainly justified in suggesting that the book would
have been both upsetting to the reader and fun!

But the urge toward imaginative composition after the long period of criticism proved too compelling: the Norton book yielded to
various other projects: the Opera, *The Alcestiad*, the transformation
of *The Merchant of Yonkers* into *The Matchmaker*, and, finally, to the
various one-act plays whose gestation and development are chroni-
cled in a good deal of detail in these pages. It is a bitter irony that
"American Characteristics" was never completed.

As for "The Emporium," two scenes of which are printed here
for the first time, it was a point of pride to Thornton that not one of his
four major dramas is just an ordinary play: each requires that its readers bring to it an extra dimension. And in writing each one Thornton
reached out for help: his own "Pullman Car Hiawatha" and "The
Happy Journey to Trenton and Camden," one-act plays without plots,
were necessary preparation for both *Our Town* and *The Skin of Our
Teeth*. "The Emporium" was not finished because he never found
completely, in Kafka or Kierkegaard or Gertrude Stein, the outside
element to enable him to bring it all together. As he wrote of himself
(in "On Drama and the Theater"): "Some hands have no choice: they
would rather fail with an oratorio than succeed with a ballad." The
Journal demonstrates that both "The Emporium" and the book of the
Norton Lectures in the form in which Thornton hoped to be able to
cast them qualified without any question as oratorios.

Late one night at 50 Deepwood Drive (we called it "the house
The Bridge built"), I woke and, seeing light underneath my bedroom
door, got up and stepped out. There wasn't a sound in the house. I
looked down the corridor to Thornton's room. The door was open
and he was not there, but the downstairs lights were on. I walked

part-way down and saw Thornton in the living-room, walking back and forth before the books shelved against the west wall. These were books that had belonged to our parents, and he knew all of them well; his own were in his study upstairs. He was passing his hand lightly over the spines. He heard me and, turning, looked up. I asked, "Thornton, is there anything you want?" He answered, "No. I'm just looking—looking for a book that hasn't been written."

I like to recall that glimpse of my brother, one of the innumerable reels of the moving-picture of his life as I knew and shared it for more than seventy years frozen in the projector at that particular frame. So characteristic of him and of his outlook on life, it is reflected in his work almost from the start and to the finish—in the earth turning on its axis in the opening paragraph of *The Woman of Andros*, through the wheel-motif that he had introduced into "The Emporium" (see pages 325, 331, and 333), to the words he gave to Dr. Gillies in *The Eighth Day:*

Nature never sleeps. The process of life never stands still. The creation has not come to an end. The Bible says that God created man on the sixth day and rested, but each of those days was many millions of years long. That day of rest must have been a short one. Man is not an end but a beginning. We are at the beginning of the second week. We are children of the eighth day.

ISABEL WILDER

Editor's Note

In the manuscript materials left by Thornton Wilder—and now among his papers in the Collection of American Literature of the Beinecke Rare Book and Manuscript Library at Yale University—are various groups of diary and journal entries dating from 1912, 1916–17, 1922–33, 1939–41, and 1948–61, with two additional brief notes of 1969. Some entries before 1939 and after 1961 were destroyed by the author.

Most of the entries from the period 1912–33 are devoted to either daily events and engagements or early drafts of Wilder's writing. The entries of 1939 to 1941 (51 manuscript pages) and the major series dating from 1948 to 1961 (539 manuscript pages) are the source for the present selection, which amounts to rather more than one-third of the 1939–61 material. As a general rule, these exclusions have been made: most passages of introspection and self-analysis, including dreams; drafts of, and most notes for, published essays and lectures; most copies of material by other writers, including letters addressed to Wilder—for example, from Sibyl Colefax and Albert Schweitzer.

Although it has been my aim throughout to reproduce Wilder's manuscript exactly as he wrote it, I have done some editing: I have corrected silently errors of spelling or grammar and occasional mistakes in references; I have expanded most abbreviations and contractions, and have written out most numbers in the text; I have rectified many inconsistencies—for example, in the listing of elements in series and in capitalization; I have standardized the use of hyphens, quotation marks, and underlining to indicate italics, and have clarified punctuation. Wilder uses a series of dots or dashes to indicate hesitation, a search for the right word; I have substituted a series of four hyphens to distinguish such pauses from my own ellipses (of course retaining Wilder's use of three dots to indicate ellipses in quoted passages). Wilder uses square brackets and parentheses interchangeably; I have made them all parentheses—save in quoted material, and have used square brackets to indicate material that I have supplied, including omitted words, which are followed by question marks when they are not easily ascertained from context. Wilder marks his footnotes variously; I have indicated them by symbols (using the conventional series *, †, ‡, etc. when there are more than one footnote on a single page), identifying my own footnotes by arabic numbers from 1 to 9. Wilder uses quotation marks and underlining interchangeably for titles; I have used quotation marks for the titles of unpublished works and for essays, lectures, and plays published as parts of volumes, reserving italics for titles of works issued separately.

In a typical Journal entry, Wilder begins with a heading that includes the number of the entry in its given sequence, the place and date of composition, and a title indicating the subject matter. I have retained all of these, silently supplying the year in the dateline when it is lacking (beginning June 6, 1948, Wilder notes the year at the top of the Journal page), and adding bracketed title and elements of place and date when Wilder does not provide them. (A few entries are unnumbered, and the headings for the earlier entries do not include the place with the date.)

Wilder repeatedly makes it clear that he did not mean to use his Journal for first drafts of his writing. Of the entries that do have this character—for example, Numbers 557, 560, and 565 ("Alexander Woollcott"), Numbers 720, 727, and 728 ("The Life of Tom Everage"), and Number 770 ("The Care and Feeding of Lies")—other, later rewritings exist among the Wilder manuscripts at Yale. Wilder often continued his notes for essays, lectures, and plays in separate concurrent series; although some of these were subsequently destroyed, others still exist, like those for *The Alcestiad*, "The Emporium," the Norton Lectures, and the "Opera." An enormous additional quantity of notes on Lope de Vega (more than 1,000 manuscript pages) and James Joyce (more than 600 pages, plus hundreds of annotations in Wilder's copy of *Finnegans Wake*) are to be found in Yale's Thornton Wilder Collection.

DONALD GALLUP

The Journals of Thornton Wilder, 1939–1961

Delightful hour and a half with Desmond McCarthy yesterday afternoon. Very ashamed not to have been able to give him a better condensed outline of Kierkegaard's principle ideas. After reading with such enthusiasm the 600 pages of Lowrie's book. I must learn that I can only grasp and retain by putting the matter down in writing. More than that: can only hope and manage to receive ideas by harnessing my notions into written paragraphs.

Mr. McCarthy was very quick to see my difficulty in establishing a style for an Alcestiad. He suggested I look at Dasent's translation of the Icelandic epics.

It seems to me impossible that I could write any play in a realistic setting. Therefore my point of departure for a subject may very well arrive through a "vision" of a significant setting. For instance, in one-acters, I have been considering a Banquet-Table on a stage, with a banner or flag against the wall behind it; or one set piece like a hearth ("The Pilgrims.") The only exception to this would be a completely realistic play with a preposterous motive, character, or idea in the center of it: i.e. a real-estate agent who discovers that wings are sprouting on his shoulders.

Feb. 9. 1

Suppose I wrote The Top of the World and prefaced it with this note: "In this novel I have put into Julius Caesar's mouth words gathered from many authors in many different ages. The discourse to Catullus on nature is a paraphrase of Goethe's Fragment of 1806. The arguments on the immortality of the soul in the conversation with Cicero are from Walter Savage Landor and he in turn was indebted for several of them to Plato and Cicero."

The first page of the 1939–1941 Journal

The 1939–1941 Journal

FEBRUARY 8, 1939. [Desmond MacCarthy, and A Style for *The Alcestiad*.]

Delightful hour and a half with Desmond MacCarthy yesterday afternoon. Very ashamed not to have been able to give him a better condensed outline of Kierkegaard's principal ideas—after reading with such enthusiasm the six hundred pages of [Walter]Lowrie's book [*Kierkegaard* (1938)]. I must learn that I can only grasp and retain by putting the matter down in writing. More than that: can only hope and manage to receive ideas by harnessing my notions into written paragraphs.

Mr. MacCarthy was very quick to see my difficulty in establishing a style for an *Alcestiad*.[1] He suggested I look at [Sir George] Dasent's translation of the Icelandic epics.[2]

It seems to me impossible that I could write any play in a realistic setting, therefore my point of departure for a subject may well arrive through a "vision" of a significant setting. For instance, for one-acters, I have been considering a banquet-table on a stage, with a banner or flag against the wall behind it; or one set piece like a hearth

---

1. Thornton Wilder's efforts to dramatize the Alcestis story were interrupted by World War II. He returned to the project for seven months in 1945, and then put the manuscript away again until September 1953. See Entry 658 (September 18, 1953).

2. *Icelandic Sagas and Other Historical Documents Relating to the . . . Northmen on the British Isles* . . . (4 vols., 1887–94).

("The Pilgrims").[3] The only exception to this would be a completely realistic play with a preposterous motif, character, or idea in the center of it: *i.e.*, a real-estate agent who discovers that wings are sprouting on his shoulders.

FEBRUARY 9, 1939.   [*The Ides of March*.]

Suppose I wrote "The Top of the World"[4] and prefaced it with this note: "In this novel I have put into Julius Caesar's mouth words gathered from many authors in many different ages. The discourse to Catullus on nature is a paraphrase of Goethe's 'Fragment' of 1806. The arguments on the immortality of the soul in the conversation with Cicero are from Walter Savage Landor, and he in turn was indebted for several of them to Plato and Cicero."

1.[5]   FEBRUARY 1, 1940.   On Moralizing.

. . . There is a universal repudiation of moralizing; but for a thoughtful person it is as difficult to do as to receive. The diction of the moral life is saturated with two distasteful elements, truth and hypocrisy. The hypocrisy, as the old adage tells us, is a homage to the truth. The laws of morality are common knowledge, are truisms. They only live with force when they are applied to situations of crisis. The reason we resent preachiness is that it is tendered to us during occasions when we are in a state of complacency. It is a part of the practice of great preachers to prepare in the minds of their hearers, during the first portion of their sermons, such a state of crisis: the con-

---

3. An incomplete manuscript draft (twenty-two pages) of a play with this title exists among the Thornton Wilder papers at Yale.

4. An early title for *The Ides of March* (1948).

5. The first six entries of 1940 bear also canceled numbers from 312 to 317. No earlier entries numbered from 1 to 311 exist.

templation of mankind's *misère*. The brevity of life, the omnipresence of fallibility—against such a background they are able to introduce later the eternal truism.

The recurrent moralizing tags of the Greek tragic poets become understandable to us in the light of this rule. The atmosphere of the tragic performance has been lost to us—its solemn religious earnestness, its terrifying reductions of the action to the first principles of the passions, its air charged with the presence of supernatural beings. Under those conditions a character may say "Short is the life of man," or "Let me not be counted among the wicked," and the truism strikes upon the ear not only with the power of the truth but with the surprise of novelty.

2. **FEBRUARY 3, 1940.** On the Motion Picture *The Grapes of Wrath*.

While listening to a work of imaginative narration in which the suspense before good and bad fortunes is deeply engaged, we experience in our minds a double action. On the one hand we long to see a happy outcome, or at least an occasional happier event, in the series of catastrophes that befall the characters who have won our sympathy; and yet on the other hand, we wish a *truth*, we wish the implacable character of destiny to be preserved; we do not wish to be lied to even though it gratifies our concern. Consequently we are torn between our sympathies, and our respect for an objective truth. The "happy events" in the narrative must be introduced therefore with particular care: (1) They must conform to the rhythm of the whole work, that is to say, they must be in numerical proportion to the misfortunes; (2) They must proceed with the same proportionate degree of either sheer accident *or* logical preparation from the preceding circumstances; and (3) They must be presented with the same degree of specific detail and human-all-too-human imperfect texture.

In this splendid motion picture the authors made a number of mistakes according to these principles.

When the Joads, after a succession of unrelieved catastrophes arrived at the Government's Wheatstone Workers' Camp and suddenly found food, kindness, and promise of work, (1) The rhythm of unfortunate circumstance was too abruptly altered; (2) The discovery of this haven was pure unprepared accident, whereas the corresponding catastrophes had all had the character of inevitable consequences; and (3) The kindliness of the camp-director and the appearances of its inhabitants were stated in cliché "nice" terms without the degree of realism—warts, wrinkles, odd bony structures, imperfections—which had been adopted for the rest of the picture. (Several attempts were made to integrate this sequence of felicity into the grotesque prevailing tone of the whole: the humor of the younger children's first discovery of a w.c.; the episodes on the dance floor; but the mistake lay in casting Grant Mitchell—professional "kind-man"—as the camp-director.)

Although it is a rule that in a narrative where the catastrophes arrive as accidents the happy outcomes may arrive so, too—and such are most melodramas,—we might here have accepted the "happy camp" had the other laws been followed—an occasional reference to some more cheerful aspects of the community life of the caravan (the *Tendenz* works of proletarian authors refuse to concede the law that the human heart is unable to contemplate its misery for long at a time)—and shown us the proportions of a world where woe is not the exclusive color; and if the elements of the camp had not been all-roseate.

Hence: A happy narration is just as true as an unhappy one, for art does not record what the outside world is like, but what it is like to contemplate and to experience the outside world. Since in five thousand years no agreement has been reached as to whether the outside world is happy or unhappy, it is to be presumed that such an agreement will never be reached.

It would seem that tragi-comedy is the justest of all forms to record this mixed outer world, but the majority of masterpieces are cast as either tragedy or comedy. This is due to the intensity of the inner life and to the difficulty of assembling the details that will convey it. If a work of literature could juxtapose and amalgamate the outlooks of *Lear* and *Twelfth Night*, it might well fulfill the conditions contemplated, but the atmosphere of *Lear*—true to the intensity of a moment's inner contemplation of the outside world—requires the three hours' construction of a mood-building artificial succession of tragic details in order to convey the poet's inner sensation. This three hours is untrue to the variegated texture of experience; but it is true to the intensity of a subjective state.

A sentimentalist (and the pessimist is here included as identical) is one whose desire that things be happy [(or sad)] exceeds his desire (and suppressed knowledge) that things be truthful; he demands that he be lied to. He secretly knows that it is a lie; hence his emphases, his elations, and his heartlessness.

The great law of art is uniformity of tone; since it cannot record all experience, its fidelity to its chosen fragment of experience implies its consciousness of all experience as a similar though more variegated uniformity of tone. (To intrude into a work an unrelated tone is to imply that one is incorporating the "all," a presumption that speaks volumes on the author's inability to grasp experience's multiplicity.) Here lies the greatness of Jane Austen: her perfection in the small implies her comprehension of the large.

4. FEBRUARY 4, 1940.   Of Utopias and Panaceas.

Mabel Dodge Luhan has found a "wonderful doctor" for her sinus; she has found in Gerald Heard a writer who answers all modern problems; in psychoanalysis, after Yoga and anthroposophy, a covers-everything. This tendency to inflate a "good" to a "perfect"—as in the case of Mme. du Deffand's falling in love—is always, on one level, a religious vestige, and on the other a vestige of infantile life; and offers corroboration of Alain's insistence throughout *Les Dieux* that all religion (the notion of a Heaven, of One in Whom we can find security, of prayer, etc.) is the activization of our memories of childhood.

Nothing on earth (except mathematics?) should give us the sensation of seizing an Absolute Good.

The correction against such a perfection-image in the growing child does not arrive from seeing the father or mother or surrounding felicity broken up through misfortune or fallibility, but from self-knowledge: one should not acquire one's salutary disillusion from seeing the limitations in one's parents but from accepting them in oneself.

Hence (having in mind Mabel Dodge Luhan, Communists, Ad-

lerians, Californians, myself) in these panacea-moths one will find the
following traits: (1) The emphases necessary to those who are unwill-
ing to enter into a discussion; (2) The complete collapse when the miracle shows a crack; (3) The inability to be interested in anything else
while the spell holds, and the saturation of every part of their life's activity with the matter; (4) The sense of being "chosen," a sacred ves-
sel, with the egotism and coldness of heart that follows; (5) The eternal "personalization" of the idea, political belief, or cult into its leader
or the fellow members.

6. **FEBRUARY 16, 1940.** Of Sentimentality and Obscenity.

"No Irishman can have taste, save in an age of taste, and even
then but rarely" (Burke). Joyce's lapses from taste proceed from the
same disposition of his gifts as does his sentimentality. Time after
time he accomplishes great triumphs through the use of indecency
and through notations of tenderness, but occasionally he errs as completely with the one as with the other.

Taste in this sense does not depend upon a conformity with the
prevailing norms of emotional expression or candor—even of those
most intelligent contemporaries; nor, primarily, on the degree of
emotion or force behind the expression. It depends upon the extent
to which one feels the artist to be involved not as artist, but as person.
The author may be moved or violent as generalized medium, but not
as individual. It is the face of the specific "I" appearing in the work
that mars the communication.

This may be illustrated—in part—by the problem of the actor.

Should an actor convey to the audience that he is "really" ter-
rified or heartbroken or even amused, the scene in which he was
playing would immediately lose all illusion. Should a Macbeth convey
authentic terror at the appearance of Banquo's ghost, the audience
would cease to attend to the story and would follow only him, the actor, in his upset condition; and [in *Much Ado about Nothing*] should
Benedick really laugh at one of Beatrice's jokes, all the attention
would be centered on him, as upon a man experiencing an enjoyment
which has nothing to do with the inner action of the play. Acting is
not experiencing but describing and indicating a reality.

So all art has the passions and the states-of-being for subject matter; its function, however, is to contemplate them, to show them, and not to *be* them.

So in the realm of indecency the author may allude to and describe what he chooses so long as the reader is not aware of his (the author's) being himself involved—at that moment—in sexual emotion, or, if it be a scatological matter, in a state of ambivalent fascination-disgust. The same holds true of the emotions, as the works of Dickens so often reveal; the pity experienced by the author Dickens is superseded by that of the man—one man in London at one moment of time—Dickens.

(1) *Re Sentiment:* This repudiation which we feel has two grounds. (a) We dimly feel the incompatability of an artist's at the same time being engaged upon a piece of work and having the tears roll down his face for his characters' misfortunes. (Most artists weep at their work, but the tears are from nervous excitement.) Creating is making; it is positive; contemplating the suffering in the world is passive. Such artists, therefore, as the audience divines to be in a violent state of emotion about the situation are justly suspected of being shallow; their private "I" is offering itself the suspect luxury of an "individual's" emotion when their private "I" should on the contrary be entirely wrapped up in the exacting emotion-absorbing task of stating purely whatever aspect of life they have set themselves. (b) The emotion of a Mr. C. D. Forrester of Portland, Oregon, over the death of his daughter, his dog, or the soldiers of Finland does not concern the citizens of the United States, however sincere they are. If he were a great artist the expression of his emotion might concern us all, but not by reason of the object mourned, but by reason of the emotion itself in its expression. Neither the mourner nor the mourned is the subject of the work of art. So beyond counting are, and have been, and will be, the subjects of pity that to emphasize one example—either as object or as agent—is to offend [against] the law of proportion and to intrude an egotism. By art the emotion is raised to the plane of generalization and all mourners and all sufferers are included.

This is the meaning of my definition: a poet is one who realizes the separate existence of a million souls. Poetry is a language within the language that serves to describe de-individualized experience. A poet may say "I suffer," "I shall die," "I," "I," "I"—and we do not feel that some Ancient Mariner has taken us by the lapel to arrest our attention upon his own misfortunes in a universe of injustice.

(2) *Re Obscenity:* A different principle enters here.

Obscenity by reason of its roots in the instinctual life and by reason of its accumulated strength through suppression is so reinforced by such powerful drives that—far more than sentiment—it is likely at any moment to put artist and audience not into the position of considering obscene things but into a state of obscenity. Obscenity, far more than laughter or excitement or emotion, arouses a physiological and visceral reaction, and in those turmoils art has no room to enter. It is wonderful how Rabelais moved in this *épineux* realm. In such matters one is very quick to see the author employing obscenity to release drives within his nature—and often they are not themselves primarily sexual or scatological drives, but self-assertion or combative or toughness-protest drives—that immediately divert the attention to himself as an individual.

Here Joyce constantly errs. His cloacal obsession, like that of Swift, puts one constantly into amazement; and yet from time to time he can make magnificent material there, too. His sentimentality I must consider another day.

Obiter dicta:

Re Irish: As an Irishmen can only find his truth through contradiction to someone else's truth, so he can only find his force through infringement of the current norms of feeling.

Gertrude Stein said one day: "There is no such thing as abstract art; beyond a certain point it will always turn into pornography."

The music of Brahms is not for those who are combatting the presence of sentimentality within themselves. His is a losing battle. His harshnesses, his gruff passages in the lower registers, his bold jagged phrases in unison do not deceive us: . . . they are the marks of his trying to overcome his weakness. Even his . . . leaps of the sixth—as clear and honest an interval as there is—are invariably followed by a more than usually *Schmaltz* resort to the sequences that evoke self-pity. . . . I am astonished that I cannot find anyone to agree with me that the slow movement of the *Piano Quintet* is an open scandal.

I think that one of the reasons for the obscenity of *Finnegans Wake* is [Joyce's wish] to conceal its matter from his wife. There's no doubt that it is terrifyingly autobiographical; but there is only one person in the world J.J. would mind knowing it: Norah Joyce. Report says that she doesn't read his works and that she wishes he wrote things that people could understand. Yet putting two and two to-gether: the few uses of his daughter's name, Lucia, now insane; the poems about his children; that poem about love for a person whose name made him tremble with shame; the page that is certainly about the conversation and games and prejudices of his wife—couldn't that be the reason that the second paragraph would frighten anyone off and that the preposterous Wellington Museum and the Prank Queen story follow so soon after?—just to make sure that one person in the world would never by chance get as far as the Isabella-monologues? One reason.

[*February 17, 1940.*]

. . . Plentiful corroboration of Joyce's cloacal obsession: even the title of his book of pale little verses *Chamber Music* comes from that association.

7. FEBRUARY 17, 1940. On Religion and Psychoanalysis.

Every hundred years religion must suffer assault from a new en-emy, and each time—to the eyes of many—the blows seem mortal. *Les Philosophes* [in the 1750s]; then, together [in the 1850s], the at-tack on the Bible and on the origin of man, the latter reinforced by the whole scientific view of life. The new enemy will be psychoanaly-sis. It attacks in two places: the sense of sin, and the concept of [a] personalized agent behind the universe who can bestow security. Both concepts it traces back to the infantile life.

It is hard enough to answer the charge that conscience and the sense of guilt proceed from the praises and penalties laid down in in-fancy and their survival into later life without being told that they go back further still to a realm where the injunctions of moralizing grown-ups had not yet reached us: to the instinctive morality sur-rounding incest and the death-wish; and that the notion that the uni-verse contains a Being that is concerned to shelter and protect us, to grant us our requests ("if we cry urgently enough"), and ultimately to provide us a completely happy place comes from an age when we were fed, tended, passed gently from hand to hand, "dressed in white," in a place "flowing with milk"—that is, our first two years.

The *only* answer is to place God and right-and-wrong still further back in "the plan." The sense of security that an infant enjoys is *there* and could only be there because *there* that was the norm in the universe. The biological-physiological situation of the family does not derive its analogy from the beasts of the field but from the "Father-aspect" of God. The sense of having sinned does not proceed from the Oedipus complex, but from a continuous and accelerating consciousness in man that he is falling short of a series of perfection-requirements that were implanted in his soul before birth and which came from the order of the universe, from the nature of God. Man's falling short is early and powerfully made aware to him in the conflicts of the infant life.

If this is so I think the decline of the Church is due to the fact that even the hasty citizen has grasped that the emphasis has been placed on personal survival, on prayer as a request for an interference with cause and effect, on an immediate connection between "goodness" and conformity to current mores, and on sin as being (1) mostly sexual . . . and (2) linked up with the Crucifixion—our "murder."

The next religions that arise in the world will also undoubtedly draw their strength in large part from a slain-god myth and/or from a denunciation of the senses; but it may be assumed that in each successive "revelation" these emphases will play less dominant a part. The Crucifixion is still the most magnificent metaphor ever found for mankind's falling short of the perfection to which it might attain; but the Crucifixion's involvement in blood and murder reawakens the latent anguish of the infantile life and fills the inner mind with such vibrating nerves and such despairing self-abasement that the spiritual values can barely make themselves heard. The business of a preacher should be to divorce the specific dramatic elements of the story of Christ from the "educative" elements, and, like an analyst, ceaselessly turn the light of explanation into the dark pockets of over-emotional identification with the blood-guilt aspects of the story.

Obiter dicta: No wonder the Jews rejected the [Crucifixion] metaphor; their sense of guilt carries only one of those burdens: they loathe the flesh, but they are not killers. If it weren't for that element they'd have been the best of all Christians—as would the Chinese, too.

Like that other testimony to order and meaning in the universe, art, religion was communicated to the world by neurotics, and betrays its origin at every turn (look at St. Paul and Pascal and the Old Testament). But an artist expends his emotion also on wrestling with the technical problem of his craft, and the result is more often "pure." (It is astonishing that Bach in the *B Minor Mass* altered the world-wide canon of the Mass to introduce the adjective *altissime* before the *Christe* in the *"Gloria." Christus* has an *altissimus* all to himself a little later. Bach the "purist" of the religious artists!)

8. **[FEBRUARY 17 OR 18, 1940.]** Continuation of Entry 4, Of Utopias and Panaceas.

The marks that distinguish the "truly religious" from [the] "vestigial religious" [of Entry 4] are: (1) Assurance without over-emphasis; (2) Constancy throughout changes of leadership and betrayals or disappointment in former leaders; (3) Ability to extend attention to a diversity of other activities (including home life!); (4) An inevitable inability to regard themselves as good examples of what the cause or movement can do; (5) A more constant attention to the ideas of the party than to its representatives.

Obiter dicta: The principal fault of all modern movements is that they are full of impatience that the excellent results appear at once. The [First World] War shattered the historical sense of modern man; he forgot the centuries; it became possible for him to believe that advance is rapid: catastrophe is abrupt, so why not ameliorization?

Communism was designed by a Jew. Jews are not impatient. (Jews can pump themselves up into an impatience, but it is not a true impatience. It is doubtful whether Jews believe in the perfectibility of man, even on a millenary basis.)* Communism fell, however, into the hands of non-Jews, and look what has happened.

*(N.B. To consider: did the—do the—Jews await a Messiah?)

It is very Jewish that Communism describes a society in which every man is (1) patient, (2) a good citizen, and (3) willing to sacrifice a great deal of initiative for a security provided by an overruling force —the Government. That dream is very intoxicating—by antithesis—to the impatient, the unsocial, and the individualist. How fascinating, doubly fascinating, to those who feel themselves to be rulers is a state-plan in which there are no rulers.

Always returning to Goethe's words to Eckermann (October 23, 1828): "*Aber wissen Sie was? Die Welt soll nicht so rasch zum Ziele, als wir denken und wünschen.*" And Claudel's "The hardest thing for a believer to understand is the slowness with which God permits his plan to be fulfilled."

The Great War [of 1914–18], which should have made clear the slowness of the spiral-cyclic evolution of man—the five steps forward, four steps back,—on the contrary induced a luxuriant increase of the Utopia-tomorrow mentality.

9. **FEBRUARY 18, 1940.** Of the Chinese and Saving One's Face.
    (Also re the Japanese Efforts to Withdraw with Honor from
    Their War.)

A Chinaman is never dismissed from a position: he is always called away by reason of the sickness of an elderly relative of his family. He solemnly makes goodbye visits to the associates in the firm, who condole with him on this sad necessity. No one is deceived, but face is saved.

This necessity, like the Chinese politeness, arises from the crowded living conditions of China. Even more exacting than the city residence is the life in the village where the *gens* live in vast farm-units, bound together by narrow space, consanguinity, and collaboration. The rituals of politeness are barriers against intimacy, often saving-fictions of mutual deference and self-abasement. Courtesy is not only a sign-language that indicates that the persons engaged belong to a similar "stratum," are civilized, and can be trusted not to injure one another; but it is a ritual that effaces individuation from the participants and invests them with a generalized or typical character:

a Gallantry opens a door for Womanhood, or Youth admits precedence to Maturity. Ritual prevents people asking personal questions and the assumption is that it prevents them thinking personal thoughts. All women feel beautiful when a man rushes to open a door for them; every elderly gentleman feels wise and venerable when a young man addresses him as "Sir." So in close-packed quarters the Chinese try to save their soul by repelling their neighbors through the courtesy that depersonalizes. Moreover by failure one shames one's ancestors and one's descendants, which, in addition to other things that it says, is a Chinese way of saying this to the close-pressing urgently onlooking crowd.

But courtesy implies that all concerned are admirable. What becomes of the fiction when one has made a mistake or been found incompetent?

A new fiction must be created. The presence of onlooking neighbors plays a large part in our mortification over the failures we suffer. Our amour-propre is able to digest most of the mistakes we make in secret. In a country where the neighbors—and so many of their relatives—press closely about the unfortunate the mortification is many times greater.

But another element enters in.

February 19, 1940.

No country, not even America, is more given to moralizing than China. Over the empire hangs an atmosphere of copybook maxims of edifying and unattainable elevation. The examinations for government positions consisted for centuries not of questions and answers on economics or history but of essays on virtue and ethics. These essays did not even require the intellectual discipline of casuistry and fine distinctions, like those for the rabbinate or among the mediaeval schoolmen. All that was required of them was an exact memory of the classics and an elevated moral tone. Nowhere is virtue more talked about; and one result of this is that all qualities are "moralized." An efficient clerk is a good clerk, a virtuous clerk; an inefficient clerk is a bad clerk, *i.e.*, a wicked clerk. . . . The Chinese who has failed, then, suffers several degrees greater humiliation than one in a similar position in another country. The fiction to which he resorts deceives no one, but it permits the one degree of alleviation which is that the shameful fact is never put into words. Hypocrisy is the inevitable state to which a society must come in which the prevailing ethics is too lofty for human nature to live up to, and there is concurrently no pervasive doctrine of original sin or human fallibility. Protestantism has always been in this danger. It has paid much lip-service to the doctrine that all men are wicked, but it too often meant that all men who do not adhere to the strictest severities are wicked. Hence, the creation of the rebel-class, the scoundrel-hero, hence Lord Byron, hence the fact that all clergymen's sons are wild.

Obiter dicta: Since the social forms of courtesy build up a world where no one tells the truth, the unfortunate condition arises when one wishes to express true deference to [a] woman and true veneration for an older man. The forms have been so impregnated with their fiction that they can no longer convey that shade of meaning which is sincerity. They say in Paris that the expression *cher maître* is trembling on the verge of derision so often has it been abused. Similarly a mare is now called *dam*; *madam* has become *procuress*; so with *mistress*.

Since the forms of courtesy confer the character of being admirable on all who exchange them, no wonder the classes of society gaze upward in admiration and longing: up *there*, they are not only rich and leisured, but one has the impression that they are demigods.

12. **FEBRUARY 22, 1940.** Toward a Definition of the Novel.

In all the discussions that have arisen among book reviewers as to whether such-and-such a work is a novel or not I have never seen one of the principal elements of such a discussion stated: that the writer is permitted to tell an action which is not a historic action.

This element is included in Aristotle's definition of a tragedy in the clause: "the greater part of which is devised by the 'imagination'"; but though he knew such works as "The Melians" and *The Persians* where historical events were set upon the stage with what to the Greek mind must have seemed to be near to *rapportage*, Aristotle could not foresee where the truly difficult border-line forms were to occur, *i.e.*, in the autobiographical novel in the first person. In *The*

Persians the dramatist is clearly enough availing himself of the privilege to contrive a non-historical truth when he exhibits Atossa addressing the ghost of Darius.

The moment an author states dogmatically what a character "thought," what were his unexpressed motives, he is claiming the omniscience of the imaginative narrator and he removes his work into a realm that has nothing to do with the historians.

There is a truth of the historic fact in time, and there is a truth of the imagined, and the two truths can only be juxtaposed with extreme caution. So that the question as to whether *Tristram Shandy* or *Moby-Dick* be a novel is on that ground not for a moment in doubt. Any work of a given length in which the author asks the privilege of recounting the mental life of characters not himself is candidate for the category of a novel.

Objection: Certain novelists—in part Defoe, Jane Austen—refuse to avail themselves of the assumption of omniscience and their narrative records only such externals of the characters' behavior as could be reported by an outsider with ample means of collecting the facts from those involved. They wish their novel to have all the appearance of historic truth.

Answer: So fundamental is the distinction between these two kinds of truth, so imperative is it for the reader to know in which of these two realms he is moving, that the novelist—while gravely pretending that the happenings once took place—knows very well that the type of attention extended to a "historic" history is of an entirely different order and one which would inevitably shipwreck the effect after which he is striving. There have grown up a whole series of conventions which inform the reader that a fiction is being offered. For all its circumstantial detail, the opening pages of *Robinson Crusoe* announce themselves to be not veritable memoirs but fiction, no less than the opening pages of *Gulliver's Travels*.

The discomfort that arises in one during a reading of [André] Maurois's *Ariel*, and which inevitably takes the shape of an antagonistic "How does he know?" when Maurois attempts to report Shelley's unuttered thoughts, or even his protracted conversations, is an evidence of the fundamental importance that we know which "truth" we are confronting.

There remain two further matters necessary to such a definition: length and action.

Length: Even Aristotle confronting the same problem as to . . . tragedy—naturally refusing to descend to matters of approximate time-units—could only say "of a certain given length." Were one to venture a definition of a short story it is possible that a closer indication of length could be approached from the point of view of the degree toward which the recounted action (or actions) is developed.

Action: (This clause will be devised for the exclusion of such works as *The Sir Roger de Coverley Papers* [of Addison and Steele], *The Dolly Dialogues* [of Anthony Hope], etc., where there are both imagined characters and action in the strict sense of the word.) The novel will contain an action or series of actions . . . which will give the reader the sense of unity and of having been selected not for their historical validity but because they illustrate a central intention of the author fulfilled throughout the work.

It is this last clause . . . that requires now further examination.

15. MARCH 7, 1940. [John Van Druten's *Leave Her to Heaven*.]

I went last night with Marion [Preminger] to see the fourteenth and antepenultimate performance of John Van Druten's *Leave Her to Heaven.* The mediocre is less instructive than the good and the bad, but one observation arises: vulgarity cannot impersonate Vulgarity, and the vulgarity that transpires *à l'insu* does not serve to express the dramatic vulgarity required by the impersonation. The play treats of a former hotel-entertainer who by her third marriage has become a member of the prosperous upper-middle merchant class. She has an affair with her hot-headed young chauffeur, who kills her husband out of jealousy. She is represented as nobly in love with the young man (a love rendered unbelievable by the casting of the latter part in this production) and tries to assume the responsibility for the crime. He is hanged and she kills herself.

Miss Ruth Chatterton in the early part of the play offered some ingenious reporting of this woman's speech, faint traces of cockney and a series of stresses indicating the earlier background; but she became confused as to how to represent the sympathetic aspect of the woman and the validity of her love for the chauffeur. She could not see that the love and generosity of her character could also be expressed through the vulgar coloring; in such passages she became heroic-heroine-with-aristocratic-bearing—an attempt not aided by her short-legged figure, exaggerated *derrière*, and low bust.

Since the distinction between being a lady and not a lady still persists in America, and is particularly an element in the English plays offered to us, this difficulty continues to falsify the work of our actresses. They no longer regard the profession as representing a gypsy stratum apart from society, as it has always been in its best ages, and anxiously attempt to identify themselves with our leisure classes. There are a score of reasons whereby such an identification is preposterous, and the obstacles only render the attempt more obsessive. Hence their difficulty of representing on the stage the indications of all that is admirable in the category "vulgar": the spontaneity of loud laughter; the quickness of reaction against everything that is formalized compliment and mere convention.

One must have received one's acceptance of life as civilized repression between the ages of five and fifteen in order to be able to represent its opposite with appreciation. The reasons for the universal condemnation of this play were not what the critics said, dullness of the story, but: (1) The unattractiveness of the chauffeur, as played, prevented any credibility in the dignity of the heroine's attachment to him; (2) The lack of any magnetism in Miss Chatterton's personality (in spite of much skill), joined to unwillingness to play the aspect of her role which I have discussed above; (3) The author's attempt to make a last act of pathetic tragedy (the boy in his death-cell; the heroine's suicide) follow upon two acts whose selected details never rose above the genre of drama-crime + picturesque.

Obiter dicta: An actor is set apart from all other persons by: (1) The element of exhibitionism in his nature; (2) The degree to which he must observe and analyze in others and himself the appearances; (3) The passivity with which he is required to serve as canalization [of] the intentions of author and director; (4) The extreme degree to which his motor-mechanics become conditioned to the director's will and imagination; (5) The professional deformation by which his emotions must be trained to continuous stimulation and abatement.

16. **WILLIAMSBURG, VA., APRIL 10, 1940.** Faulkner's *Light in August*.

So much that is splendid, but finally swamped and defeated in the emotional steam, the drive to cruelty, the confusion as to what is good and bad, the mix-up that arises from identifying the strong with the good; and the gentle with the bad. The image of the South, crying out in self-justification and self-condemnation, and all twisted bitterness.

I am teased by one problem in it.

The surface is clear enough. The ambivalent hatred and adoration of the Negro; the impoverished Southern blood adoring the virility of the Negro. And the fatal envy-fascination of the Negro, which does not dare confess the envy-fascination, must take the indirect by-path of sadism: sexual envy becomes sexual sadism: the climax of the book is the castration of the half-Negro demon-hero Joe Christmas. Faulkner waits on that moment. He builds and builds the virility-hardness of Christmas, not by representing him as a sexual athlete, which would be too overt, but by rendering him and developing him hard under an unbroken succession of injustices and sufferings. Faulkner will not even allow him to be touched by the occasional alleviations of his misery; such as the attempts at kindness that come to him from his adoptive-mother, Mrs. McEachern. W.F.'s attitude to woman is armed neutrality—Lena's calm and fidelity and dogged search for her betrayer is a force dependent on her pregnancy; at times her characterization is about to advance to that of all-wise, all-possessing earth-mother, but always it falls short and she too wears an ominous character, as though, in Byron Bunch, she is Woman that uses and victimizes men. (Two of the women in the book, Mrs. Armstid, who is grudgingly kind to Lena, and Miss Burden, are repeatedly called man-like.) Note the close: Christmas's mutilator, a little military-adoring small-town fascist. He carries a gun, even under disapproval of the sheriff. Faulkner tries to make fun of him, but his admiration for that gun and that belief in order and punishment sneaks out, and finally Faulkner confers upon him the glorious act of the book: the mutilation of the Negro.

The puzzle is Hightower: ex-minister, betrayed by his wife, touched with two fanaticisms, flabby, obese, given to reading the "sapless, lustless" Tennyson. Even more painful to him than the disgrace of his wife and his expulsion from the Church was the letter he wrote to an institution for delinquent girls saying that henceforth he could now donate to them half of his little patrimony-income. All his conversations with Byron Bunch (so like those in the novels of Henry James, full of charged allusive indirect concern over how others will "feel" about what happens or may happen) are full of some vast emotion and moral weight disproportionate to the effect that these matters could ever have on him. I think that the answer to this is that for Faulkner Hightower stands a symbol for the South. Hightower's other fanaticism is an episode in his grandfather's life ("the most important day in his life, the only day he ever really lived, took place thirty years before he was born"): his grandfather was killed on horseback in a gallant cavalry raid, here in Jefferson, where he had come to burn up the store of General Grant. The other thing about Hightower is the implication of impotence. The delinquency of his wife is justified in one place by the phrase "he either could not or would not satisfy her," and W.F. goes on to say that his excitement about the grandfather's cavalry raid was the injustice or burden which his wife had to bear. The closing ferocious scene of the book takes place in Hightower's house, Hightower having done what he could to prevent it.

So the humiliation of the once gallant South is represented in sexual terms; the Negro's strength is perpetually before their eyes to remind them of their loss. All novels of the South (save *Gone with the Wind!*) must be lynching novels, like this: only so can the South enjoy a triumph; and the triumph must be not the killing but the emasculation of the Negro.

N.B. Christmas's paramour and victim was not a Southern white woman, but a Yankee. Even Faulkner could not bear to make her a Southerner.

N.B. There is something very adolescent about W.F.'s preoccupation with the sexual life of his characters: Balzac must tell the financial status of each of his characters; W.F. must tell how his spend their nights—and particularly adolescent in the recurrent necessity to inquire into how they *first* knew sex.

19. ST. AUGUSTINE, [FLA.,] MAY 2, 1940. On Faulkner's *The Hamlet*.

The tribe of the unscrupulous Snopeses gradually move in on a farm community and like locusts gradually possess the land; at the end of the book, having risen to power in Frenchman's Bend, they move on toward the larger town of Jefferson.

Everywhere the admiration for low cunning; more than that, the author's admiration for anything—unqualifiedly—that succeeds. The Snopeses gain their first foothold merely by terrifying the community with the report that they are barn-burners. W.F. is thinking of Hitler, but the larger demonstration seeps away in his more detailed illustration, and it is best that it does. W.F.'s admiration of virility has been absorbed into an admiration for "getting on."

Ratliff, the one admirable character, an itinerant sewing-machine peddler, watches, comments, reflects. He even does some kind deeds—incredible ones: his taking into his sister's home the wife and children of a Snopes who has murdered, the wife being a former lumber-camp prostitute; his restoring from his own pocket a five dollars which a Snopes had tricked from a farmer's wife. But at the end of the book W.F. turns on Ratliff, too, and shows him greedily digging for buried treasure (yet "Have I come to this?"), and shows him gulled by a Snopes.

This same motif we saw in *Light in August*. Though W.F. can surround the man of reflection with a temporary wistful prestige, in the end he must be immolated before some agent of force or cunning. Again the South's thin blood must prostrate itself in envy and admiration before any expression of action, however base.

But what curious reflection these men of reflection have: elliptical, wry, sarcastic, wrapped up in a super-subtle tangled syntax —W.F.'s fancy overwriting.

Devious—so is the method whereby even the facts of the narrative are communicated to the reader. In one passage we pass from the thoughts of a man being murdered to those of his murderer without transition. The *he* must serve both; the reader must return and reread a page and a half to disentangle the event. Surely this practice of indirection is related to W.F.'s insecurity in his emotional relation to his characters: he admires his "bad" characters but dare not avow it, and one small part of his mind despises them; he despises his "good" characters, yet wishes he could admire them.

The real immaturity in an author is the transparency with which he betrays this approval or disapproval of his characters—doubly immature when the approvals and disapprovals are thus mixed and impure—not because all ethical judgment is difficult, but because the author's emotional nature is at war with itself.

This is W.F.'s sentimentality: not only the uprush of emotional identification with the act of violence or guile, but the "messing up" of its statement, so that the admiration merely shows "around the corner"—as he thinks—but all the more overtly.

29A. THE MACDOWELL COLONY, PETERBOROUGH, N.H., JULY 6, 1940.
   "The Ends of the Worlds."[6]

Began my play on "The Ends of the Worlds," Monday, June 24, in the Veltin Studio.

The difficulty of finding a subject. During the last year subject after subject has presented itself and crumbled away in my hand.

Can this one hold out?

The difficulty of finding the right tone.

31. QUEBEC, OCTOBER 26, 1940. On My Play [*The Skin of Our Teeth*].

Here this week I've been writing the Second Act of my play, all wrong, and knowing that I was writing it all wrong. It presents problems so vast and a need of inspiration so constant that all I can do is to continue daily to write it *anyhow* in order to keep unobstructed the channels from the subconscious and to maintain that subconscious in a state of ferment, of brewing it. The wrongness of the present text lies in the fact that the scenes of the triangle situation and the family conversation are homely and realistic. It may well be that before I "bring them up" I will be obliged to bring down the portentous size and the furious energy of the present opening and perhaps of some of the First Act; but that I shall not touch until I've found ways of re-

---

6. An early title for *The Skin of Our Teeth*.

casting these intermediary scenes into moment-by-moment myth and a thing that one could call gigantism if it weren't also human generalization.

This attempt to do a play in which the protagonist is twenty-thousand-year-old man and whose heroine is twenty-thousand-year-old woman and eight thousand years a wife makes me see all the more clearly how necessary for Joyce it was, with a similar self-assignment, to invent a grotesque tortuous style of his own. Happier ages than our own could do it—or some aspects of it—in the purity of the lyric, the morality play, or in the relative simplicity of the *Prometheus Bound* and the *Oedipus*; but in this century and, above all, in these times, there has been added to the difficulty that of avoiding the pathetic, the declamatory, and the grand style. The only remaining possibility is the comic, the grotesque, and the myth as mock-heroic.

I have one advantage: the dramatic vehicle as surprise. Again by shattering the ossified conventions of the well-made play the characters emerge *ipso facto* as generalized beings. This advantage would no longer be mine twenty years from now when the theatre will be offering a great many plays against freer décors; the audiences will be accustomed to such liberties and the impact of the method will no longer be so great an aid to its myth-intention. (My play will be just as valid then, but what it has lost in surprise will be replaced by its prestige, by the audiences' knowing "what it's all about.")

The challenge that has been issued, then, by the accumulated weight from the previous act of the play's proposal to represent Man and Woman, and by the columnar moments already established in Act Two—the President's acceptance of his nomination; Mrs. Hobson's reminiscences on the history of marriage; Miss Atlantic City's outburst to the audience and, particularly, her closing consolation to her partner that men and women are "of straw"; the radio address to the other convening Orders; and the final storm and the cries down the theatre aisle (I have not yet been able to "realize" the scene of the Fortune-teller)—must be met throughout. The intervening material need not be as freighted with emphasis as thought, and should not be, but the theatric invention must tirelessly transform every fragment of dialogue into a stylization surprising, comic, violent, or picturesque. Here lies the increased difficulty over the writing of *Our Town*, where the essence of the play lay in the contrast between the passages of generalization and those of relaxed and homely tone.

Had I not all my writing life been convinced of the fact that the subconscious writes our work for us, digests during the night or in *its* night the demands we make upon it, ceaselessly groping about for the subject's outlets, tapping at all the possibilities, finding relationship between all the parts to the whole and to one another—had I not long been convinced of this I would have been the other night. Turning over the play in feverish insomnia, I suddenly saw that there, waiting for me in the structure of the Act, was a felicity, integral, completely implicit and yet hitherto unforeseen: since the Orders of the Birds and the Fishes were simultaneously holding their conventions probably nearby, how ready they were to have their representatives present, two-by-two, for the entrance into the Ark, which for months has been established as the closing moment of the Act.

A few more such revelations and I shall be building a mysticism of the writing process, like Flaubert's: that the work is not a thing that we make, but an already-made thing which we discover.

And yet how difficult it is—returning to the paragraph before the preceding—to restate those intermediary scenes. Even granted that my theatric invention could furnish an unbroken chain of strikingly novel devices, revitalizing representations of the material of our daily yet saecular life, how great is the risk that, placed side by side, these passages over-fatigue the spectator and finally stupify the attention, which through them is supposed to be gazing at the condition of life itself.

One's hand falls to one's side in discouragement; all one can do is to trust that the subconscious has foreseen that peril too; that the already written has circumvented it, and that I shall be permitted within the next months to read the solution of this problem.

33. [QUEBEC,] OCTOBER 29, 1940. On the Stage and Women.

All evening from under my window rises the sound of laughter, touched with hysteria. The men in uniform are parading up and down Dufferin Terrace and have found themselves companions in such girls as the mothers have allowed out. The girls walk up and down pretending to be very self-absorbed, and from the benches come the

overtures: "Commong dally foo ser soi?" Soon the couples are formed
and the laughter rises.

It reminds to be inserted into my play near the beginning and
at regular intervals, jokes about sex. Such jokes awaken the nervous
system, unlock a host of contracted centers, set a diffused humming
preparation along the receptive attention: prepare for the comic
spirit.

Laughter is not in itself sexual; but how closely it is allied to that
same censor that holds guard over all the confusions, the humiliations, and (to state the more positive side) the unspoken, unspeakable
gratifications of life. Most of laughter is the retaliation against the
inflexible Other of life, the adamant circumstance, texture, or accident, which neither our wishes nor our vainglorious will can alter.
(Here Bergson, as well as Freud.) Sex is a vast phenomenon, a maw
seldom pacified, never circumvented, and perpetually identified by
the subconscious mind with the refractory exasperating, not to say
unappeasable, character of external circumstance itself.

A laugh at sex is a laugh at destiny.

And the stage is peculiarly fitted to be its home. There *a* woman
is so quickly All Woman.

What more telling ratification could be found of my favorite
principle that the characters on the stage tend to figure as generalizations, that the stage burns and longs to express a timeless individual-
ized Symbol. The accumulation of fictions—fiction as time, as place,
as character—is forever tending to reveal its true truth: man, woman,
time, place.

And the operation of such an activity must be recognized: when
man and woman are regarded in their absolute character that character is pejorative: man is absurd; woman is sex.

It is no accident that since the beginning of theatre the actress
has been regarded as the courtesan. The usual explanations for this
are but secondary: the actress's private life as being incompatible
with that of the bourgeoisie; the professional deformation of the career that *aims to please*; the factor (imperceptible probably to the subconscious of the audience) that the succession of roles induces an
emotional instability in the performer's character. There is an element more significant than these: a woman appearing on the stage,
pretending to be someone else in a world all pretense, is revealing
herself as Womankind, and under conditions—however noble, dig-

nified, or even sanctified the role—which all too easily imply the more facile aspects of that condition.

Woman lives in our minds under two aspects: as the untouchable, the revered, surrounded by taboos (and a taboo is a provocation-plus-veto); and as the accessible, even—in spite of the mask of decorum and dignity-indignity—*inviting*. To maintain the first of these two roles all the buttresses of society and custom are necessary: the marriage institution, the prestige of virtue, the law, and custom. A woman on the stage is bereft of these safeguards. The exhibition of her bare face in mixed society, for money, under repetition, speaking words not her own, is sufficient. But far more powerfully is she delivered into the hands, into the thought-impulse life, of the audience by the fact that she is on the stage—that realm of accumulated fictions—as *Woman*, as prey, victim, partner, and connivance—that is, as bird-of-prey, hence attacker,—and as willing victim, that is, *piège*. Under those bright lights, on that timeless platform, all the modesty of demeanor in the world cannot convince us that this is not our hereditary ghost, the haunter of our nervous system, the fiend-enemy of our dreams and appetites.

(The above written while mildly drunk on a quart of Bordeaux.)

34. QUEBEC, NOVEMBER 1, 1940. Difficulties with My Play
[*The Skin of Our Teeth*].

The play seems—as it is being said of the Italian army in North Africa these days—to have bogged down again, halted in irresolution and a sense of lacking any vitality.

Undoubtedly, there is a real subject for a play there.

I seem to have lost it among misjudgments in manner, in whimsical digressions, and among a number of stated positions which are not real to me, which are insincere. For the present leaving out of consideration the Second Act, all of which may not *be real* to me, how about the First?

Yesterday and today I have been rewriting the opening of the First—not only as to manner, which is relatively unimportant, as that will come right when I have grasped with conviction the central intention of the Act.

This being the most ambitious subject I have ever approached (*sic!*) I am faced as never consciously before with the question: do I mean it? In this case, in what part or level of myself am I actually interested in such a problem (problem for literature, that is; hence, burning problem for the self) as the struggles of the race and its survival? Have I been "making up" emotion, and contriving an earnestness? Is that why my play has bogged down? (Only now as I write this note can I see that that is a misstatement of the question: it is like saying "if you could save a thousand Chinese by cutting off your right hand and leg, would you do it?" *i.e.*, indubitable and unrealizable; a concept graspable by the human mind only in the specific occasions that vitalize it.) No, it is a subject as real as any other, as dramatizable as any other. It is not so much that one might charge it with an emotion one hasn't got, as that one might charge it with a false pumped-up emotion—or an anemic emotion which ekes out itself in whimsical fancies. In fact, it's not so much a matter of emotion at all, as it is of seeing, knowing, and telling.

In so far as I see, know, and tell that the human race has gone through a long struggle (Act One) it is legitimate that I cast the consideration in the form of a modern man and his home; and precisely to avoid false heroics—in this time, of all others—that I cast it in comic vein.

My difficulties thereafter are three: (1) *Simplicity.* To state this is sufficient. With what dismay I see some of the passages I wrote this afternoon, passages which, under the guise of theatric liveliness, uprooted the play from its forward drive and introduced digression and inexpedient "color." My old dread of being "boring," my reluctance to trust to strong subject matter.

(I wish I could reread *Candide*—where the problem was not unlike—but though there are many French bookstores in this town, *Candide*, by reason of the Catholic censors, is unprocurable here. *N.B.* I think I should read Rolland's *Liluli*, too; I gather on the wind that that belongs to the same category.)

(2) *Working perseverance.* These two years of taking up subjects and dropping them, of desultory reading *as* an evasion from writing, of mixed activities have undermined what little collection-to-work I used to have. I particularly find great difficulty in fixing my mind on the play as a whole; that exercise *sine qua non* of composition. I seem only able to "flag the reluctant and tired horses of my

mind" to seeing instantaneously the whole play when I am out walking and have walked long and hard.

(3) *Inspiration without emotion.* This is the only phrase I can find to describe the moments when the material is really forwarded. The great danger these days is that when I do get "inspiration" it comes in tides of tears which not only are, as formerly, the legitimate tears of nervous excitement, but . . . bring with them the distortion of the material into a host of humanitarian, "pathetic," didactic directions which are not fundamentally real to me, but which are self-admiring or substitute self-pitying interferences.

Will these difficulties clear up?

I cannot say. I may say on my own behalf that the subject (and the treatment, which is the only way I could treat it) is indeed difficult; that, at least, I bring to it my sense of making the whole stage move and talk, and my characteristic style, which weaves back and forth between the general and the particular.

If I am bogged down, the reason is not far to seek: my mind's daily thinking for twenty years has not been of sufficient largeness to prepare me to rise to the height of this Argument.[7]

36. **MANOIR DE SAINT-CASTIN, LAC BEAUPORT, [QUEBEC,] NOVEMBER 1940.** On English Prose in the Nineteenth Century.

The English prose-writers in the nineteenth century were lacking in the essential characteristic of excellent prose and it is likely that, from the millenary point of view, their work must disappear. (? Works do not survive by reason of their ideas; with the exception of that minimal and infinitely gradual accretion of truly new ideas contained in the slow unfoldment of the religious interpretation of exis-

---

7. Cf. Milton, *Paradise Lost*, Book I, lines 22–26:

> ". . . What in me is dark
> Illumine, what is low raise and support;
> That to the highth of this great Argument
> I may assert Eternal Providence,
> And justifie the wayes of God to men."

tence, all the ideas in the world have been here since recorded time; they are common knowledge; what are generally called ideas are transient observations on the transient conditions of society; their deposition does not render a work immortal save as it is phrased in this characteristic which we are now attempting to define.) The virtue of prose lies in its movement, and the approach to its definition has usually been made through a discussion of its rhythms. This is indeed true, but discussion has too often rested there, with an appreciation of this or that author's musicality or cadence; and this resort to music as the analogical basis for excellence in prose has introduced a misunderstanding throughout the history of criticism. Musicality is an indispensable but secondary quality. Similarly, in attempting to define this quality, resort has often been made to an analogy from physics and it has been called "balance" and "proportion." The concepts evoked by both of these terms have their place in excellent prose, but neither is sufficiently inclusive, and both introduce connotations which are necessary to all the aspects of prose. Balance introduces the thought of judicious composure and abstention from extremes. *Tristram Shandy* is a triumph of sustained *kinesis*, but unless we push the meaning of balance far from its accustomed orbit and require it to describe an unrivalled tact in the maintenance of a uniformity of tone we could scarcely wish it to describe Sterne's novel. Proportion, with its emphasis on the regularity of the disposition of the elements, might well serve us save for the fact that like balance it brings with it a series of those moralizing implications from which few Anglo-Saxon abstract nouns are free and which have no place in the objective study of literature as an art. Moreover, both of these terms tend to imply an object at rest; the soul of prose is its movement. The analogy—as with every fundamental inquiry about mankind and his works—should be physiological. The movement or rhythms of prose have in common with singing the exigencies of breathing, and in common with dancing an element of covering this ground and then that, of encircling, of proceeding from this to that and yet again indicating the place left, of standing still after movement, and of resuming motion after arrest —all this in a far more organic and graphic sense than music, though it also, in a lesser degree, intimates such dispositions. Music and poetry incline to live the life of the voice; prose that of the body. I wish to call this central attribute of prose *kinesis*. The writers of prose in the nineteenth century were full of *kinesis*, but they were *akinetic*.

It is *kinesis* which is the great glory of the King James Bible.

That work has so long been surrounded with superstitious veneration that few have ventured to point out that throughout long stretches its ideas, in the temporal sense we indicated, are no longer valid, and that many of its most celebrated passages are meaningless. But books are not great by reason of the presence within them of their topical ideas, and many of the most treasured works of literature contain within them passages which are not today intelligible. Books survive through the fact that the truisms of every man's and child's experience are stated in language which contains an instinctively vital sense of *kinesis*. . . .

The light thrown upon poetry through the consideration of this quality would unduly extend this essay. I shall touch upon it briefly and only to clarify its presence in prose. Poetry may indeed give an impression of movement and of gesture. It too traverses a succession of ideas and sweeps them toward a conclusion; it too turns from one aspect to another, then back again. And conversely, prose borrows from poetry its characteristic power, which is the address. However, it is no accident [that] there are few epic poems in the world's literature, and that narrative poetry is a rocky territory in which many a flower has failed to bloom; that argumentative poetry, and the journal ode, the form which most implies *kinesis*, is seldom successful. We have but to consider the greatest ode in the language, Wordsworth's "Intimations of Immortality from Recollections of Early Childhood," to see that its greatness lies for us in its lyrical episode and not in its movement. It is still an open question whether the observation and frequentation of children inspire in us a conviction that the soul is immortal and came to us from a pre-natural state of bliss. The famous lines of that poem are more valuable to us as static assertion than as parts of a thought in development.

Conjunctions are the sinews of prose, or its wheels.

38. NOVEMBER 12, 1940. Some Victoriana.

Now that I am thinking of becoming a critic I see that this Journal (or another started for that purpose) should become the store of those secondary observations made in reading which otherwise cross the mind and disappear (or rather merge into that large shadowy cloud from which come one's "impressions" and "ideas").

I have been reading with much admiration for the first time Wilkie Collins's *The Woman in White*. There are some ripe illustrations of that Victorian cat-and-mouse game with morals, that having-the-cake-and-eating-it-too, which though a commonplace in considering them, may serve as an illustration I may someday wish to use. The book is deep in the most scrupulous moral refinement, "delicate sensibility," and yet:

(1) After we are allowed to think for a while that Anne Catherick is the illegitimate daughter of Sir Percival Glyde—himself the illegitimate son of "a married woman whose husband . . . had gone off with another person" (Modern Library edition, page 770), we find that no, she was the illegitimate daughter of our spotless heroine's father, Mr. Philip Fairlie, and a servant at a country house where he had stayed.

(2) This spotless heroine marries a man against whose character her suspicions have been aroused, and after telling him that she already loves someone else. We the readers forgive her this because she is obeying the dying wish of her dear father, whose judgment and advice had never been at fault. Later, we see that in this case his judgment was atrociously at fault, and are told (page 788) that besides being the father of Anne Catherick, he was "constitutionally lax in his principles, and notoriously thoughtless of moral obligations where women were concerned."

It is characteristic that religion is called in to make us swallow the goings-on contained in my catalogue (1) above. . . . But Wilkie Collins has introduced a series of moral *volte-faces* of his own:

(3) Three characters are de-sexed, perhaps I should say four. We are repeatedly told of the feminine characteristics of Count Fosco, recluse uncle of Frederick Fairlie; and the admirable Marian Holcombe is unmistakably first presented to us as man-like. Moreover the wicked Sir Percival Glyde: doesn't the author . . . try to tell us in as clear terms as his contemporaries permit . . . that he had no sexual relations with his wife (who is being saved by the author for a happy second marriage with the man she loves)? Moreover, though Sir Percival is for a time the putative father of Anne Catherick, and engaged in whispered suspect conversations in a lonely church vestry with her fascinating mother, . . . he was not interested in her.

It's all very unimportant save as it is still to be examined: the whole Natural History of the famous Victorian hypocrisy. And no less of the hypocrisy in reverse of the modern French, where *péché* is the real interest and *dignity* of life, and yet so reprehensible *by adjectives!!*

Obiter dicta: I think it can be assumed that no adults are ever really "shocked"—that being shocked is always a pose. It may as a pose go very deep, be believed in by the agent as a real emotion, yet be no deep spontaneous expression. Its true character contains a wide spectrum—from fear through self-esteem to envy. But its appearance is always the spectrum from incredulity (always insincere) through astonishment, to the assertion: "I would never do the [same] conceivably in a situation like that." A society like the Victorian that spent so much energy expressing itself as being shocked must have been either (1) immature, (2) insincere, or (3) so highly "pitched" to an idealistic interpretation of all human behavior that it had lost the power of realistic confessional self-appraisal. . . .

That it was (1) immature is out of the question: the Victorians were mature enough. That it was (2) insincere this very novel of Collins adds one more increment of evidence to that heap which is the love story in Dickens, [Thackeray's] Amelia Sedley [in *Vanity Fair*], *The Idylls of the King*—and the end of the reign.

The defense is (3): "Everybody else is—(seems)—so much more ideally constructed than I am that I shall in the first place make no sign of my humanity and secondly strain every minute to overcome it and this *by refusing to admit it.*"

Naturally the result of this was the safety valves: prurience and sarcasm. The reign divides itself into two halves, or rather into two-thirds and one-third. The last third: [W. S.] Gilbert and [Oscar] Wilde and [Aubrey] Beardsley and Henry James; along with . . . : Sherlock Holmes; the [Hawley Harvey] Crippen [murder] case; the Edwardian world.

"Moralizing is the assumption that the presence of evil in the world is each time an exceptional case." "Moralizing is assertion of one's own immunity."

All this is contained in the differences of the countries' geniuses in the words: *moralist* and *moraliste*; *morals* and *moeurs*.

39. MONTREAL, NOVEMBER 27, 1940. On Happy Endings, and the Pessimist.

Of the two worlds that we know, the external world of nature and the subject world in the mind of each individual, the former has a great advantage over the latter in the direction of being regarded as favorable. The majority of the catastrophes in nature, as seen from the point of view of men, are either: (1) Regular in their recurrence and regular in their reparation, like the nightly obscuration of the world and the arrival of Winter; (2) Exceptional in character, like the flood, the fire, the earthquake, and the destruction by lightning; or (3) Evitable through a deeper knowledge of nature's laws like the management of boats in storms, the predictability of weather, and the presence of illnesses in our organism.

Of these [three] the most important is the first. The fact that the sun reappears every morning and that the life of vegetation is resumed every Spring is written into the most intimate structure of our minds. Our sense of security that darkness and decay will be repaired implants in us a natural inclination to place our confidence in the universe; and the very fact that night and Winter are regular and predictable removes half of their terror. Regularity mitigates our sense of the tragic; it is no small part of man's consolation in the face of his own demise that almost all men die between sixty and seventy. Tragedy enters with the irregular, and the irregular is the exceptional.

In the realm of the subjective, however, many men have claimed that the preponderant character of experience is dark. Man's possession of consciousness has rendered his existence, considered in the whole, a misfortune. It cannot be claimed that, in spite of difficulty, he is unfitted to the natural environment, save in the brevity of his life and the inevitability of his death. But, except in certain periods of history, the prevailing judgment of men has repudiated the attitude that the inevitability of death is sufficient grounds to affirm that all life is in itself an ill. The significant pessimism in the world's testimony enters with the twofold charge that man's nature—expressed in his possession of consciousness—is (1) inharmonious in itself, and (2) incapable of giving or receiving a true satisfaction from its relations with other consciousnesses. This pessimism denies that there is any evidence for seeing that either of these ills is correctable.

There are no great works of literature that assert this pessimism. *Candide* excludes many of the satisfactions which some writers claim are to be obtained from existence, but Voltaire concludes that man can find a way of life that is a good, and to this way of life he gives the symbolic form of cultivating one's garden. The harshest picture in all literature of mankind's claim to a good is to be found in *Gulliver's Travels*; but the universal acceptance of that work has always seen that its passion and color accumulatively imply an immense homage to man: it is not man's unalterable disharmony that is being indicted, but the failure of man to take advantage of his possibilities of good. In classical and modern tragedy the catastrophe proceeds from an element of disharmony or imperfection in the nature of man, but the exhibition of this catastrophe is employed to light up the noble aspects of human nature; man's *good* is affirmed by man's ever present but partial ill. There is a large element of pessimism in Christianity, and particularly in its dogmatic development. The position that man is incurably wicked and can only be saved by supernatural intervention may well be taken as a complete negativism unless the doctrine of supernatural intervention be seen as an indirect symbolic statement of an element in human nature itself equally interpretable as purely human activity for finding his subjective and his social harmony.

It may well be that with the succession of time the pessimist who affirms a complete disharmony in his own nature and a complete disharmony in the social order (the insoluble problem of the mind at war with the body; and the incorrectable presence of the self-destructive element in the social group) will be examined for the physiological and individual mainsprings of his point of view. Pessimism is already seen to be the exceptional person's comment on the exceptional aspects of experience. That this exceptional comment is a deeper and "truer" judgment may well be invalidated if it can be shown to proceed from a point of view formed by an organism cut off from a large proportion of the goods of mankind. This does not mean that malady or neurosis invalidates judgment (in facing the whole problem it has been too often shown that the unwell and the extra-normal have issued the most affirmative declarations on the whole experience of man), but that a far more complete "natural history" of the maladies, neuroses, and impediments must be drawn up and analyzed in order to discover which ones dispose to positive and negative assertions, and how and why.

40. QUINTO BATES, AREQUIPA, PERU, MAY 23, 1941. Sketch for a
Portrait of Tia Bates.[8]

When I first knew her Mrs. Anna Bates was well over seventy
and had been forty years the famous, kind, roaring, strongwilled,
childhearted mistress of the best inn on the west coast of South America. She herself had variously reported her birthplace and the nationality of her parents; one would guess that the latter were American
with a dash of Irish; her early years were spent in Chile. Her husband
had been a mining engineer and she could tell wild stories of gaiety
and dangers of the "Wild-West" days of early Bolivia and Peru. She
had had two children—a son who died young; and a daughter,
through whom she was now a great-grandmother.
    She has a short stoutish body, generally swathed in neat sweat-
ers, feet which cause her some difficulty, and small ever-darting
hands. Her face, brick-red and brick-yellow, lit by a pair of candid
bright blue eyes, suggests at once that of an idealistic boy and that of
an old Cape-Cod sea-captain. It is forever in dramatic motion, rapidly
traversed by expressions of "wickedness," benevolence, haughty contradiction, tart scorn, and self-forgetting mirth. During the long
hours before lunch and dinner she sits uneasily bounding on a divan,
her family of guests about her, a scotch-and-soda at hand, keeping order; that is, shouting at the servants; preventing the guests' attention
from wandering; remorselessly nipping in the bud any ineptitude or
pretention that might crop up in the group conversation; and sustain-
ing the role she came into the world to fill: *raconteuse*, mother-pa-
troness, and historian of sixty years of opera-bouffe, tragi-comic,
epico-absurd adventurous life on the Coast. [With Tia Bates] endlessly groping for all but forgotten names of twenty nationalities, the
resurrected figures file by in endless procession, nabobs and failures,
revolutionists and servant girls, travelling salesmen and sailors. Beset
by both phlebitis and pernicious anemia, yet boiling within with a furious vitality and hunger for life, she effaces from any public view all
moments of fatigue, illness, self-examination, or even reflection. She
refers to herself repeatedly as "an old devil" and deplores her profan-
ity, which does not extend beyond a few *damns* and *hells* (she con-

---

8. Thornton Wilder admitted that "some reflection of . . . the generous heart and re-
sourceful mind" of Mrs. Bates may be found in Mrs. Wickersham in his *The Eighth Day* (1967).

fessed yesterday that she did not know the meaning of the hair-raising
Spanish oaths she resorts to when the servants exceed her patience);
she is nevertheless unexpectedly strait-laced. The gesture most characteristic of her is that when the laughter bursts from her at the climax of a story, with the fingernails of her right hand plunging into the
roots of her disheveled gray hair, and the fist of her left wildly pom-
melling her midriff, while her wicked blue eyes, travelling rapidly
from face to face, collect the homage of success.

. . . Her stories always arise from the subject discussed, are
never lugged in. . . .

The other thing that Tia Bates is famous for is her kindness.
This is reported—as such things are in our age—with an indiscrimi-
nating hagiographical effort that dilutes the activity in attempting to
magnify it. She is reported to have adopted and settled in life scores
—I was told *hundreds*—of children abandoned or orphaned by un-
fortunte gringos; to have "set right" financially and morally a host of
shipwrecked persons; to have refused payment from a large number
of her guests. The truth is even better.

42. **CHICAGO, 7:30 A.M., AUGUST 22, 1941.** [A Theory of the Novel
and the Short Story.]

Last weekend in Kalamazoo I set myself to trying to organize
. . . some of the notions that had occurred to me during the many discussions of my . . . classes[9] and so try to save something from the all
but wasted summer. Finally I found myself putting many hours into
the attempt, rewriting, crossing out, beginning again. . . . I started
out on the premise that imaginative story-telling reposes on . . . a
contract . . . established between teller and listener whereby the
teller is permitted to invent beings and circumstances and to know all
about them, *i.e.*, the Omniscience License, under the proviso that
such free invention will be justified at the close by the emergence
from the narrative of a generalized truth about experience satisfacto-

9. Thornton Wilder had taught three summer courses—translation, the story, and advanced composition—at the University of Chicago.

rily illustrated by all the selected details contained in the story. I then went on to catalogue the consequences that result from the assumption of omniscience in the teller. I then tried to define what the unifying and justifying "generalized truth" or "idea" was, and I became aware that the field bristled with difficulties and exceptions, from *Tristram Shandy* to *David Copperfield*: that the unification could repose on the personality of the author, on a mere chronological beginning-and-ending, or on a mere formal framework, or on the mere establishment of an emotional mood. I began again.

In the meantime I had wrestled in vain with the problem as to why the "idea" had to emerge from an action in the state of "reversal." It seemed to me, also, that I saw a difference that could enter the basic condition of narration through the mere element of length—that given mere extension one could induct the reader into the mere representation of "life" and dispense with the security furnished by the overruling idea. ("The shorter the narrative the more apparent must be the idea-reason for the collocation of its occasions.") Among the various concretizations that seemed real to me at the time I find the following: "The movement of a story is one of gradual narrowing of all its possible meanings and the condensation of its particular meaning, which emerges at the close with the character of unexpectedness." "The story-teller is under two allegiances: (1) To the generalized idea which is to be illustrated by the succession of its occasions; and (2) To the truth of beings and circumstances—human and animal nature, and destiny—from which the illustrated idea is to be extracted." "It may be that the modern audience is so habituated to loosely-cohered narrative that it can now find a limited satisfaction in the unrolling of event upon event and, arriving at the close of a story, feel no need of a unifying intention." . . .

I console myself with the thought that the stumblings may at least have prepared me for one good thing, a more ready rereading of Aristotle's *Poetics*.

44. NESHOBE ISLAND,[1] LAKE BOMOSEEN. VT., DECEMBER 2, 1941. On Act Three of My Play [*The Skin of Our Teeth*].

Again bogged down and frightened. Last month in New Haven not only did I tighten up Acts One and Two—I think I can say that with the exception of a short passage in Act Two they are finished, and good—but I wrote a "through" Third Act; but it is not right.

The employment of the "Pullman Car Hiawatha" material[2] is: (1) Dragged in indigestibly; (2) Insufficiently related to the surrounding material; (3) An incorrect statement of the central intention of the Act—is *that* intention, by the way, to be "save the cultural tradition?"—and (4) It smacks of the *faux-sublime*.

To go back to first principles: what does one offer the audience as explanation of man's endurance, aim, and consolation? Hitherto, I had planned here to say that the existence of his children and the inventive activity of his mind keep urging him to continued and better-adjusted survival. In the Third Act I was planning to say that the ideas contained in the great books of his predecessors hang above him in mid-air furnishing him adequate direction and stimulation.

(1) Do I believe this?

(2) Have I found the correct theatrical statement for it?

(3) Is it sufficient climax for the play?

Taking these in turn: (1) I do believe it. I think the only trouble with it is that *there* is the point where the vast majority of writers hitherto would have planted the religious note. It's not so much that I deny that religious note as that it presents itself to me only intermittently and in terms too individualistic to enter the framework of this place.

(2) The statement that the ideas and books of the masters are the motive forces for man's progress is a difficult one to represent theatrically. The drawbacks against the "Pullman Car Hiawatha" treatment are that (a) the Hours-as-Philosophers runs the danger of being a cute fantasy and not a living striking metaphor, and (b) . . . I cannot find citations from the philosophers' works that briefly and succinctly express what I need here.

---

1. Owned by Alexander Woollcott.

2. In "Pullman Car Hiawatha," published in the volume *The Long Christmas Dinner & Other Plays in One Act* (1931), minutes appear as gossips, hours as philosophers, and years as theologians.

At all events, I have begun work as usual by excision. Out go the "people who had died in the house"—we have had enough of the common men who preceded our Antrobuses. Out also goes, I think, the natural history, though maybe that might be useful, not as giving the arch of the natural world that surrounds us, but as making more easy the identification of Stars and Hours with Philosophers and Artists. Out go the allusions to the various calendars—partly because it is so difficult to choose *one day* to cite. Into the earlier part of the Act should go, if I can keep Hours-Philosophers, much more reference to Mr. Antrobus's books.

Couldn't the quarrel between Henry and his father hang on Henry's contempt for the books that had led his father astray?[3]

---

3. *The Skin of Our Teeth* was completed by January 1, 1942 and, after try-outs in New Haven and Baltimore, opened in New York at the Plymouth Theater on November 18, 1942.

The 1948–1961 Journal

[Thornton Wilder served with United States Army Intelligence from June 1942 until May 1945, being assigned eventually for duty with the Twelfth Air Force, first in Algiers and then in Caserta, Italy. His papers were lost in 1945, and journal entries made for the years 1942 through 1944 either disappeared at that time or were destroyed. No entries exist for the period 1945 to June 6, 1948, and the first extant entry in this series is numbered 406.]

406. JUNE 6, 1948. Of Success and Envy.

From a letter . . . , talking of writers who cannot write after having had one signal success: ". . . Success is paralyzing only to those who have never wished for anything else. Similarly, when the envious arrive at the position of being enviable their envy is redoubled and they become murderous toward others and whip themselves into being murderous toward themselves. It is one of the few blemishes I find in my beloved Lope de Vega."

407. HMS "MAURETANIA," EVE OF ARRIVING AT COBH, SEPTEMBER 21, 1948. My New Play ["The Emporium"].

Throughout the Spring, in so far as my absorption in Lope de Vega permitted,[4] I groped about for the theme of my next piece of

---

4. See Entry 408.

work—a play, a novel, or an original motion picture. I turned over some of the old themes, *The Alcestiad*, the Christmas pageant ["The Sandusky, Ohio, Mystery Play"], the pure detective story, the Horatio-Alger form, rejecting them all without much exploration. In May an elderly woman whom I did not know wrote me from Washington. She said that Dr. [Les] Glenn in church had recounted my "Empress of Newfoundland" story and thanked me for it. It did not then occur to me that it would serve as a project. I rejected it as I did most of the others as being sentimental. During my last week at home, however, I reread Kafka's *The Castle* with mounting excitement and, resolving to do a play of Kafka's atmosphere, the Newfoundland story suddenly slid into place as furnishing a possible framework for such a project. Dining alone with Mrs. [X] one night, I outlined such a play, combining it with the Horatio-Alger idea.

Now on board ship it has given me two nights of almost total insomnia and is in a fair way to determine itself as the next work I shall offer.

At present its state is as follows:

(1) An opening scene in an orphanage. A boy, aged about ten, has run away. Alarm over the countryside. Boy brought back. Superintendent and wife plead with him. His mutism. His whispered declaration that he wants to "belong." Dream atmosphere—they are and are not his parents.

(2) Scene Two. [The boy] Tom has been placed on a farm. Scene opens with wife holding lamp and calling to Tom hiding behind barn. Pleading that he will apologize to farmer in order to escape daily beating; the real resentment of farmer is that Tom will not call him father. (Night scene, but in this scenery-less play, lights are not lowered to represent darkness. The upheld lamp is not even lit, but understood as lit. Tom, mute and distrustful, stands in theatre aisle, advancing and retreating.) Farmer returns; whips Tom offstage. Tom attacks him; re-enters. Seizes locket about the neck of farmer's wife. Her treasure: a medal for faithful service long ago at the Emporium in the City. The beauty, wonder, and mystery of the Emporium.

(3) Perhaps Tom's first interview as applicant to work in the Emporium. Or boarding-house in New York: his efforts to get near to the Emporium.

Here disturbance at back of theatre auditorium: a patron has heard that this play had a prologue: it has been omitted this evening; he insists on seeing the whole play. It is explained to him that it is not certain that the prologue is by the author; [that] it was found one morning under Mr. [Arthur] Hopkins's door; that it gives the play a different meaning, etc. Patron insists.

Prologue. A nephew of either Mr. Fitch or Mr. Westman of the Emporium seems likely to inherit a high office in the store. The draught or potion.

So far is becoming firm.

Difficulties are: how to make Part Two—the effort to convey the Kafka-*Castle* character of the Emporium, Tom's agonized desire to belong to it, etc. —how to convey it as drama, and to do it without leaning too closely on *The Castle.* And how to prevent Scene Two of Part One from too closely resembling a scene from Faulkner's *Light in August*—Joe Christmas's flight from his foster-parents.

It may be that Part Two will take an entirely different turn: the story of a girl also burningly fixed on the Emporium. Alger theme of marrying the boss's daughter.

408. RMS "MAURETANIA," SEPTEMBER 21, 1948. The Lope de Vega Work.

Last Monday I arrived at my resolve not to bring the Lope apparatus abroad with me. I have now laid it aside for six months.

It will soon be three years since I first gave a second thought to the name of Lope. How many hours have I devoted to it since?

I have refused to appraise the time spent and shrink from appraising the time that remains to be given before an important book on the subject could be produced. So many of the hours are truly wasted—wasted in the sense that one has not yet discovered the several additional clues that would light up the texts. Yet it was just by such apparently unguided almost random juxtaposition of data that I discovered the pattern behind the *Peregrino* lists.[5] Had I been in possession of that earlier, what rapid progress in ordering and grouping I would have made while reading all those plays which I know I

---

5. Thornton Wilder had discovered that the apparently incoherent list of titles of his plays that Lope printed at the beginning of his novel *El Peregrino en Su Patria* (1604), is not so haphazard as it first seems. The titles there are listed—although with many exceptions— according to the manager *(autor)* to whom Lope sold them.

can ascribe to one or the other of the *autores*. Now I must read them all again.

I feel certain now that if I lived solely in the Lope plays and Lope biography (prior to 1615) for ten years I could: (1) Ascribe to most of the plays a date within a three-year margin of error; (2) From that chronology reveal a host of fascinating allusions between the lines; (3) Reconstruct a hitherto unguessed activity of Lope as *entrepreneur*, builder, and destroyer of companies; (4) Make clear the extent to which his plays were built for, around, and on actors, and were influenced by them.

The one question I cannot put squarely to myself is whether that book would be worth that time.

My fear that it is not worth it does not arise from a realization that the Lope studies interfere with or abort other plays and novels I might be writing. I have few enough of those to write, anyway; as interim work, the Lope studies on the contrary are excellent. My regret is that the Lope theory interferes with my pursuing other marginal curiosities as interesting as itself, "thinking through" a host of other notions that I might bring to a limited but real expression: observations on the style, the rhetoric, of Mozart and Beethoven; writing the "lost chapter" of a Kafka novel; finishing up the paper on an aspect of *Finnegans Wake*, on the Seven Sins against Shakespeare; really applying myself to Greek and probing the lost plays of Sophocles; devoting myself seriously to this Journal.

I had the bad luck to take up just such a discursive amusement and to strike a real vein of gold waiting to be discovered, one that yielded its treasure, however, only to long continuous application. Bad luck or good luck? The answer lies entirely in the realm of time and in the recognition of the brevity of life.

When I return in February I must devote solid months to Lope, then turn and review where I stand. Can a chronology really be established by this method? Is the close application continuously productive of real discovery? Or is the whole pursuit in reality a dangerous flight from the difficulty of thinking and writing?

409. RMS "MAURETANIA," SEPTEMBER 22, 1948. The Treatment of Scene in "Pluck and Luck" (Working-title of the New Play) [Later Called "The Emporium"].

For the first time I wish to use the Elizabethan scene, or rather the Lope scene: entrances up left and right; balcony back wall, with stairs to stage; perhaps inner room under the balcony.

And yet this treatment may be entirely impracticable because our stages within their proscenium arch are concave, from the audience's view, rather than convex, *i.e.*, because they are framed they will always look empty without settings.

For example, it will be difficult to indicate a scene-ending and the transition to a new scene. On the Spanish stage the actors made their exits at the closing of a scene and left the stage completely empty (this Lope indicated by a cross in the margin of his manuscripts). Every inch of the stage in all its bareness was completely in view; that bareness was punctuation, and the actors, entering for the following scene, broke a silence and filled a vacancy. On our concave scene, however, the audience will never be certain that an action has been completed, that a *time has been broken.* It will be necessary for me to go to unusual lengths to exaggerate these terminations and perhaps to devise a convention which indicates Change of Scene. And the two conventions which occur to me first, music and address to the audience (Lope's sonnet), are denied to me. (Suggestion: one of the stagehands who will be responsible for placing and removing chairs, tables, etc., might be directed at each scene-change to do a bit of sweeping the stage.)

Perhaps this bare stage will never be completely right within our theatre; nevertheless, although a compromise, I hope to wrest some signal advantages from it for this play. Foremost is the already proven suggestibility of the imagined scene. In *Our Town* that was accompanied by a studied resort to changes of lighting. I intend in this play to deny myself the aid of shifting lights. The challenge to the audience's imagination will be still bolder; it must be imperious. From the bone-bare staging I must derive the most imaginative of all effects, the incoherence and the absorbing intensity of dream-experience. This will be present mostly in Part Two, the Emporium scenes, with the Kafka mood, anguished groping, reading of signs; but the whole play should be touched with the unexpected and the disconcerting.

To consider: scene-change by placard.

410. **THE GRESHAM HOTEL, DUBLIN, WEDNESDAY, SEPTEMBER 23 [22], 1948.** Of "The Emporium" (New Working-title of the Play, già "Pluck and Luck").

Another night of insomnia, begoaded by the play straining to be born. This time I am well along in Part Two. Another "old idea": that of the person emerging from a long prison term, has coalesced with my theme. . . .

It is not impossible that most of the material that I've been thinking up during these feverish nights may turn out to be bad, but this is the way it's done. One becomes aware of the central idea of the play tearing around in one's head trying to find the clothes in which it must be dressed, or, rather, the concrete elements on which it must feed, picking up old motifs and rejecting them, or suddenly discovering that they will serve, modifying them to its purposes and then, with a rush, expanding them and exploring their unexpected possibilities.

412. **[DUBLIN,] SEPTEMBER 24, 1948.** Of "The Emporium."

Today I wrote the first halves of two scenes of the play. (Last night, after *The Doctor's Dilemma* at the Gate Theatre—and a little during it—I slept soundly.) . . .

It is going along all right, I think. I do not know what will happen when my inevitable "crisis of repudiation" comes.

There are changes to be made in these scenes [Two and Five], but I think that most of the words written today will stand. In Scene Five the audience must be thoroughly prepared earlier for the ambiguity in all dealings with the Emporium; . . . over the whole Scene [Two] must be thrown a veil of dream-action (as it stands now, it is abject realism).

I now see that the whole play can be set in six rectangular screens, just off white, man-high, shifted between each scene.

I went back and read portions of *The Castle*. How beautifully Kafka does it—but for the *re*reading. His book lives in its second reading, not in the conventional sense; you must know the middle of the book to know the beginning of the book. . . .

Of course, I should be frightened that I do not see my conclusion, but all writing is a Leap. And how carefully—in these nocturnal meditations—I obey Gertrude Stein's injunction: "Before you write it must be in your head almost in words, but if it is already in words in your head, it will come out dead." But having always "got" my writing on long walks I have learned to prevent its solidifying, its "jelling" in my head; always when the moment of writing comes it is ready for that moment's novelty, excitement, and surprise.

I do not know what my first scene can really be about. If Scene Two is every young man's relation to his home—not as the Oedipus relation, but as finding the security it offers to be no security—can there be something to be said about earliest childhood that can furnish me my opening scene?

I rather dread writing my Prologue. At this distance it looks "out of tune" and *trop voulu*. How can it be freshened?

413. **HOTEL RUSSELL, [DUBLIN,] SEPTEMBER 25, 1948.** Of "The Emporium."

A bad day yesterday. I attacked the Prologue, got quite a ways with it, and then recognized that it was all wrong. I still have no idea how I shall be able to manage, but after today's work I feel confident that it is there, waiting somehow, and can be done.

Today, in spite of a bothersome change of hotel just after lunch, I wrote Scene Four (The Employment Office) as far as Tom's "false exit." I finished writing the passage under strong emotion; it can hardly be as good as that, but I feel that it hits the tone and gets the stride better than any of the sections written so far. Vaguely during the morning I had said to myself that I would try that "employment interview" next; but I shrink from doing it. It presented itself then as a not very vital interrogation of Tom, based upon a few easily foreseen motifs and climaxed by his presentation of Mrs. Graham's medal. As I lay down to take a much-needed nap, I asked myself how I could start the scene, *i.e.*, establish the atmosphere of the employment agency. I

. . . thought of the Employment Office addressing a few words to a waiting queue offstage (last night Isabel and I stood so long in queue for Charlie Chaplin's "Monsieur Verdoux" that we finally gave it up); then suddenly the idea came of having the queue in the audience, in fact the audience itself. There was no sleeping after that and I got up and wrote the Scene.

Now the play takes shape and a new concern enters my mind. The play as it now projects itself will be all right, but it will have for me the drawback of being all about one thing: the baffling search for the Right Way. I am disappointed in plays that turn endlessly on one subject (*Othello* has always seemed to be for this reason less rich than the other tragedies). I would like to run some counter-motif into this one.

I now think the Prologue should follow the "Employment-Office" Scene. . . .

[Hotel Russell, Dublin,] the Next Morning.

Before I fell asleep last night I made myself face the fact that not only have I not got an ending to this play, I haven't even got a middle body to it. That note I made about wishing to enrich the texture with other interests was a projection of my uneasiness that by Scene Six, I should have exhausted even the primary interest.

What I dimly see is that Tom must go through the *noche oscura del alma*, the abysmal despair about the Emporium's concern for him, followed by his frenzied repudiation of all that the Emporium once meant to him; which leaves it to Laurencia to show that she "lives always in the Emporium" and to be unshaken by the fact that in any relation to the Emporium, human beings are always in the wrong.

414.   [DUBLIN,] SUNDAY EVENING, SEPTEMBER 26, 1948.   Of "The Emporium."

All day—except for a trip to the grave of Stella and her Dean [Swift], which I did not see—spent trying to find out how to do this; teasing the subject from every angle, and with only a faint glimmer of progress.

In Part One I establish the *Angst*—the wild homelessness that longs to "belong" in the Emporium; then in Part Two what is left to depict but the continuing *Angst* of those in the Emporium in their longing for recognition from those Higher Up and the incoherence of all responses from those upper regions? So I must find a mouthpiece for those who have "given up," who have renounced all attempt to establish themselves in [the] "A. and J." [Emporium] and who expend their *Angst* in crass self-seeking. . . .

Then what I want to write is love under the conditions of *Angst*. See the terrific paragraph that Kafka has given it on page 61. He is working in a medium so different from the drama, he can give himself those slow approaches, those muted subtleties from stage to stage.

The subject must be finally the liberty found in the *Angst*, the self-reliance that is the only answer to the bafflement, and then the lightest intimations that the Emporium approves the exploitation of one's liberty, however erratic.

A painful day—but a day which has just the color of my chief characters' inner state: the dragging search for the Right Way.

[Dublin,] 11:30, the Same Night.

After tea with Isabel I took a walk around the various greens and squares of the neighborhood and came back to write along the ideas that occurred to me during the walk. I have done the continuation of Scene Five (Tom has stayed in the Emporium after closing time, to his departure to fetch a glass of water for Laurencia). It's not well done, but I think I can tell a bad first draft that is unsalvageable from a bad draft that is "on the right road."

Tom, in my effort to make sure that he's not a "sensitive," has taken on a George-Brush color,[6] heightened by the old-fashioned diction from the Horatio-Alger framework. Is this wrong?

415. RUSSELL HOTEL, [DUBLIN,] THURSDAY MORNING,
SEPTEMBER 30, 1948. Of "The Emporium."

Monday morning I wrote the continuation of the scene between Tom and the Farmer's wife; Tuesday, the continuation of the first

---

6. Brush, the central character in *Heaven's My Destination* (1935), was described by Thornton Wilder as "a fella who not only had the impulse to think out an ethic and plan a life—but actually *does* it."

meeting of Tom and Laurencia. All going well; but the difficulties that lie ahead loom larger and larger. All must be thought through again at its most profound level; so I resumed rereading Kierkegaard's *The Theory of Dread*. So I took a holiday: the National Gallery (and especially the wonderful things in the Portrait Gallery); the National Museum. . . .

Now of the play:

Laurencia can go all lengths at recounting the bewilderments and "servitudes" of working for the Emporium because she never basically questions it; Tom denounces her; he wants the Emporium *his* way. Can such a "theological" divergence be made vital enough to "carry" a love story?

Would it help me, getting over the difficulties of the first two scenes, to place it in Pennsylvania Dutch country—the uncouth names, the dialect, the out-of-the-world, almost dim-wit simplicity? . . .

417. **GRESHAM HOTEL, [DUBLIN,] THURSDAY EVENING, OCTOBER [7?] 1948.** Of "The Emporium."

Yesterday I returned to the play again. I think I have the opening scene all right: the annual dance at L. P. Craigie's house.

Yet all sorts of things worry me:

(1) In three, four scenes I am using the address to the audience as though the audience were characters in the play: dancers at the Craigie party; applicants for jobs in the Employment Office; and (in a projected Scene Seven) customers in the Store. Apart from a few things like the scene in [T. S. Eliot's] *Murder in the Cathedral*, I can't remember any dramatist of quality who does this (of course melodramas have done it for courtroom scenes, for "theatre audiences," etc.). Is it valid theatre? and can it be employed as I employ it—casting the audience in a succession of roles?

(2) Oh, dear, won't the audience get tired of the very word *emporium* and the perpetual returning to it? Plays can turn on necklaces and legacies and crowns, but I begin to wince at this omnipresent *emporium*.

(3) The difficulty of using a store as a figure of the Absolute. The necessity for avoiding much reference to buying and selling, to the

very merchandise itself. The perils of a sustained metaphor are bad enough in a sonnet, but in a full-length play!

(4) All the time, for Arthur [Hopkins]'s sake, I keep thinking about limiting the number of actors. Hence, all my crowd scenes employ the audience. But, even then, the roster is mounting; and Lord knows how many I may have to call on for the closing section.

But my real basic fears—when I allow myself to admit of a fear—are that the whole thing may be a wild preposterous lapse of judgment on my part (and oh, how badly I can write!), and that I may not digest and compass a true ending. But *coraggio, coraggio!*

418. [OCTOBER?] 1948. Toward the German Lectures:[7]
The Theory of the Unique Occasion.

Metaphysically, man lives in a world of threats and ambushes. At any moment the Dreaded Thing may overwhelm him. (Develop.) This is true of him even in times of great political and national security. How much more is it true of such times as we are living in now. But in this discussion today we are not talking of man in his social and political relationships, but of the Human Condition in general.

Man's behavior under these conditions of potential catastrophe we know well: his resources against fears include: (1) Religion, which is finding a security for the spirit against evil; (2) Creation in the technics, which is the protection of physical man against evil (*N.B.* in their extreme expression the above two are incompatible—as the countries of the Orient, particularly India and China, are continually showing us); (3) Frivolity—distraction—*i.e.*, occupation so continuous that it excludes and evades all awareness of the potential catastrophe; (4) Art. Art hangs balanced in suspension between two resources: it both offers a flight and relief from dread by being as completely occupying as frivolity is, and it also, like religion, promises an escape from the insecurity of the human condition by offering a promise that there is order and relatedness in the world.

It is this double nature of art which particularly strikes us in the theatre. The audience desires that frivolity release [it] from presenti-

7. Lectures given at the University of Chicago Center in Frankfurt am Main in November and in Berlin in December 1948.

ments of evil, but it also desires that beauty which is the promise of
relatedness. In one sense all beauty is one; but in another sense we
know [that] the characteristic beauty of painting, of music, of lyric
poetry, of architecture can be distinguished. And the characteristic
beauty of the theatre arises from the representation of human lives, as
thousands of writers on the theatre have reminded us, of human lives
in conflict—in farce and comedy, in drama, and in tragedy; conflict is
basic to the theatrical vitality.

Development: hence audiences do and do not wish to "enter
into" a play which reminds them of the potential evil. They wish either or both the diversion (the self-forgetting absorption) and the
beauty (the assurance of relatedness), without paying the price of gazing at the possibilities of catastrophe.

The theatre has many ways of giving them this diversion-with-
out-dread and this beauty-without-pain: (1) It can give a beauty so
merely pictural that the audience can take escape into the fact that "it
is only a picture" (so last night at [García Lorca's] *Yerma*); (2) It can
turn comedy into comment, *i.e.*, not action but reflections upon action, bloodless puppets (and not symbol-marionettes), and tragedy
into melodrama, *i.e.*, blood is not really blood, but paint; (3) It can
represent the action as "unique occasion," *i.e.*, a precise moment in
the past, long past and over, a museum-glimpse into a passage in historic time.

(On rereading the above the next morning I find it all to be from
my old tiresome sententious self, but it has served as a point-of-de-
parture to plunge into my lecture.)

421. STEFFANI HOTEL, ST. MORITZ, DECEMBER 27, 1948.
      "The Emporium."

Yesterday a happy bit of work on the opening scene. But always
under the qualification that I may have to throw it all out, if the still
unclear main body of the play turns out to be something now completely unseen.

For, returning after this interval, I see that I don't yet know
how I can write this play. I haven't thought deeply enough. If this is
all I've got I'd better throw it away now. It has been wildly shallow in

me to think that the ticket-buyer in Row Q could ever understand that the Laurencia I have so far devised could represent the Knight of Perfect Resignation, or She Who Is Always in Abraham's Bosom—those to whom Faith is both self-evident and also hourly re-won; that Tom (henceforward, perhaps, called Daniel) could similarly be understood for several scenes as exhibiting the *Angst* before the Good. My concern is of course not with the spectator in Row Q, but with myself in Row Q, and as always any stupidity comes from the fact that I have not found the common-common way of stating these things —*i.e.*, of feeling them validly in myself; for if they are not common common they are not good enough for me. I have found them in books (in Kierkegaard), but if they are not in me (or potentially, with passion potentially in me) they have no business messing up my play.

During my walk to Pontresina today I saw a few things more clearly. We must see early Tom-Daniel's horrified repudiation of the Emporium, but see it as an attraction-repulsion. And we must see Laurencia as a fighter.

Oh, the difficulty of establishing the Emporium as the Excellent, as Gertrude [Stein]'s Human Mind,[8] and at the same time making it somehow fleetingly represent what centuries have called God —as the Other. Here I must clearly depart from Kafka's overstrained frustration, while still clinging to Kierkegaard. Kafka has overdone (but how valuably and in relation to himself how honestly) the impotence, the despair. That was the judaism, the Prague, the personal life in him. All, all honor to him. But just as he found an alleviation of man's benightedness in womankind, so he should have found another, another channel (to the Castle) in the work of art. Himself so sure an artist, but as though he were inventing art. (Note the references in the first volume of the *Journals* to certain perfectly achieved passages in Goethe's *Wilhelm Meister*. And note his treatment of [Alexander] Moissi's readings, of Else Lehmann in [Hauptmann's] *Der Biberpelz*—his analysis consistently destroying the work of art as object. His enmity to music, his failure to refer to painting, etc.) All to be explained as economy of energy: neurosis had drained him of all sight and hearing but that which could absorb passionately what was passing within him.

---

8. Thornton Wilder wrote an introduction for Gertrude Stein's *The Geographical History of America, or The Relation of Human Nature to the Human Mind* when it was first published in 1936.

423. HOTEL SPLENDIDO, PORTOFINO, JANUARY 15, 1949—SECOND CENTE-
      NARY OF THE BIRTH OF ALFIERI. ["The Emporium"].

During the last few weeks I almost lost my play several times,
totally lost it. Even now it may be lost, but today's meditations have
given it an extension of life. I now have the first four scenes (orphanage; farm; boarding house; department store), but that may be merely
dramatic vitality, not essential program. . . . It's all in the balance because I don't rightly see where I'm going from here. Certainly there is
a play there; whether it's a play that I can write is in doubt. All I can
say now is that my incitations to continue come from a reading of
[Léon] Chestov's *Kierkegaard et la Philosophie Existentielle* (*Vox
Clamans in Deserto*)—in French—and a brochure sent me from
Marburg.

Important is to note the way in which—after far-roaming explorations—one returns to a plan envisaged very early in the game,
but envisaged under conditions of high concentration. Later considerations have much altered the content of these developments, but
the ground-plan was established so.

425. [CLARIDGE HOTEL, ATLANTIC CITY, N.J.,] MAY 7, 1949.
      "The Emporium."

At least during the sketches these next few days to try another
attack: that all-out allegorical of which I have been afraid hitherto.

That it is a *Pilgrim's Progress*.

That it is the Decision of Hercules.

To balance continuously the Three Categories, the Bad, the
Good, and the Other.

Here the difficulty will be to find and to plant the mouthpieces,
the *raisonneurs*, of the "explanations."

I hate allegory, and here I am deep in allegory. Reading the
Wilhelm Meister these nights, without great enthusiasm I see a *Bil-
dungsroman* developing; the Herr Professor's introduction to the work
points out a moralizing schematic intention on Goethe's part, most of
which would have escaped me for the simple reason that I could not
believe that Goethe would have been so patent and unsubtle as that

—*i.e.*, at that level, allegorical schematization does not enrich his novel, it even petrifies it.

The Orphanage, then, is Childhood; it is the Family; it is the World into which the Child is dropped as an "orphan": it is neither Good nor Bad, but both. Its alternations between Good and Bad disorganize the Child, prepare the Anxiety, and hence prepare him for the claims of the Other.

The Farmhouse of Act Two is the Bad—the Bad all the worse for representing in Mrs. Graham a relapse from the Other. Mr. Graham [the farmer] is the Bad—*i.e.*, the Self exploiting itself under the guise of the Good. The difficulty will be to get this into the dialogue.

The difficulty of Scenes Three and Four will be to show how [Tom-]Daniel's thirst for the Other turns into hatred and dread of the Other—and most difficult to make it clear (*i.e.*, explain it) to the audience.

May 12, 1949.

No, I must have Daniel dread the Excellent from the first moment he comes in touch with it. He is the Horatio-Alger-success boy. He settles for the Good—and if I can manage it, I must show that in the beginning he is none too scrupulous about that—and finally frantically insists on the Good in order to drown out in his ears the claims of the Absolute. In Part Two the claims of the Absolute are seen to be poisoning any satisfaction he can receive from his adherence to the Good. *Today:* most important change: Laurencia is not resigning from the Emporium. Daniel meets her on the Square, as before; she is laboring under some injustice from the A. and J. [Emporium], but is far from wishing to resign. She obscurely, not the Emporium, is at fault. Daniel sweeps her off her feet and finally forces her resignation. . . .

This all brings a little aroused interest for me. These days I have really "lost" the play. Scared to death by the difficulty of following through on an analogy between the Absolute and a department store. Can it possibly be done?

So to attempt it I keep going back to beginnings: if there is a play here I must keep returning to its simple structural basis: the Horatio-Alger pilgrim. Where I get lost is in the over-refinements of allegorical spinning. And I think that the way I can pull it off will be by constantly introducing the atmosphere of dream—that is by offer-

ing on the one hand a real concrete story and by at the same time
"keeping it off the ground" through the irruption of bewildering, tan-
talizing irrational characteristics. . . .

426. HOTEL ARLINGTON, POTSDAM, N.Y., MAY 25, 1949. Goethe's
      "Die Geschwister."

I seem to have read somewhere that this little one-act play is
particularly prized as a sort of recondite treasure of the inner-inner
Goethe *aficionados*. Given the German mind, that would be bound to
happen in a Goethe work that is totally transparent.

The subject is: love coming into its own through cloudy and
imagined obstacles. Both obstacles are curiously chosen: Marianne
thinks Wilhelm is her brother; but what is Wilhelm's obstacle?

It is not his age, though Marianne is the daughter of a woman,
perhaps mistress, to whom he had been somehow unjust. The difference in ages is not touched upon. Yet take away the supposed
brother-and-sister relationship and this is one of the most frequently
used plots in European literature: guardian loves his ward and is
loved by her; their love only comes to light when her hand is sought
by a younger man. The obstacle seems vaguely to be that he will not
marry her until he has re-established his fortune; yet they are living
in the same house and she is plucking two pigeons for dinner. His obstacle is not doubt of her love. No, it is just obstacle, and acts as
though it were a sort of spill-over from the incest-taboo.

Now without this piquancy—very lightly touched, but strongly
latent ("*Welch ein Küss war das, Bruder*"!!!)—there would be very
little play. The charm of the play lies in the delightful characterization
of Marianne and in the incidental painting of *kleinstadt-kleinbürger-
liches Leben*—which in German is somehow far *kleiner* than corresponding *milieux* in Marivaux and Goldoni. Its charm surprises us, for
German natures and the German language in these genre-scenes can
never afford us what the Latins can. The Germans introduced the
middle classes into literature, but they still have not made them
pleasing as the Anglo-Saxons have. The brevity of the play spares us a
real descent into the *Spiessbürgerei*, as in the opening chapters of
Wilhelm Meister.

This play, then, is saved from banality by this *Hauch* of the

Forbidden. . . . Compare also *Wilhelm Meister*, Part One, where we have three women, very dear to our hero, wandering around in men's clothes, *die Amazone*, Theresia and Mignon; where Lothario cannot at first marry Theresia because her mother had been his mistress— later revealed as false.

What does all this mean? That Goethe (and his age) could not poetize the daily-daily life (exception: *Hermann und Dorothea?*) and the common man. It had to be *spiced* with the equivocal, or with the aristocratic, or with myths about the Devil.

But doesn't another unhallowed wind blow across this play?

It stands in close relation to Goethe's liaison with Frau (Charlotte) von Stein. The play glows with real ardor. Now the dead mother of Marianne in the play was Charlotte, and phrases from a real letter of Frau von Stein are introduced into the play as coming from the dead Charlotte. That is: Frau von Stein is identified both with the delightful impassioned young girl and with her dead mother. It's as though Goethe were saying: "I love you in both generations: *I love you as though you were my daughter by yourself*. Marianne is you, and Marianne's dead mother whom I wronged is you. And my love is so heady that I find it fascinating to picture it in a complex of brother-and-sister and mother-and-daughter and father-and-child relationships."

426A.   ASPEN, [COLO.,] JULY 23, 1949.   [Goethe's "Die Geschwister."]

Since writing the above, I have traversed the whole Goethe Convocation.[9] Conversations with our Goethe specialists---- It seems to be agreed that Goethe was psychically impotent until the Italian journey: that the whole liaison with Frau von Stein was platonic; that he had the *She-Stoops-to-Conquer*-of-Goldsmith situation—could only connect with a woman of inferior social class. This would indeed give rise to fantasies. But since writing the above note and learning these suppositions, I [have] read [Friedrich] Gundolf's commentary on "Die Geschwister": that it represents a beautiful floating *Keuschheit* that was a part of Goethe's sexuality. . . .

---

9. At the Goethe Festival, held in Aspen in June, Thornton Wilder had given an address, "World Literature and the Modern Mind," and had translated from German the remarks of Albert Schweitzer and from Spanish the lecture of José Ortega y Gasset.

Gundolf's note so struck me that I was willing to dismiss all my Notation 426 as misdirected nonsense. Now I return to it as pertinent. Goethe's genius is all sublimation and sublimation always entails a few fumes, not only of a "normal" animality, but of the Twisted —the price which must be paid for that very offense against nature which is sublimation.

428. ASPEN, COLO., AUGUST 25, 1949. "The Emporium."

All these months I have refused to enter notations here on the state of the play. I knew that they could give nothing but the backing-and-filling of a basically unclear progress. Their committal here would not help but would only discourage me further by rendering doubly apparent how little progress I was making. Tonight . . . I wrote the Prologue (for the second time, but without consulting the previous draft). . . . Yesterday, again on a walk, I decided to put the Member of the Audience on the stage.

The play is still far from written or even foreseen, but I feel that it is again in momentum.

429. HOTEL VIKING, NEWPORT, R.I., SEPTEMBER 28, 1949.
      "The Emporium."

Never have I had a work at once so far advanced and so far from completion.

I feel sure there is a true theme there; but I am as far as ever from seeing how this theme can be clarified in my mind and projected in a play. The theme as I turn it over in these daily meditations is perpetually presenting itself (that is, as I improvise scenes to illustrate it) in foolish debased easy moralizing terms. That is always its danger— that the Emporium represent itself merely as one's "better self," as the "ideal," as "creativity"—in Los Angeles terms.

And yet the passages read before the friends in Aspen—the Orphanage; the Graham Farmhouse; the Prologue; the scene in the Emporium—undoubtedly *went*. But where they go from there is still the mystery and anxiety they have always been.

Today, in a walk (to the point in Jamestown associated with the earlier visits here) it became clear that what was lacking was the statement of how [Tom-Daniel-] John saw the Emporium as cruel, as frightening, and as absurd. I devised a number of scenes which are not yet *it*, but which are getting warm. . . .

I must again remind myself that the feeling that I have made an advance these two days is the result of three things: (1) That I immersed myself in the play by working on the dialogue of some already stable portions; (2) That I dropped everything else to take a long walk; and (3) That I bent my attention not on the action of the play, but on the basic ideas from which it originally sprang.

430.   HAMDEN, [CT.,] NOVEMBER 6, 1949.   Faulkner's
Absalom, Absalom!

Cleanth Brooks having told me this is the best of the Faulkners, I have bought it and read it for the first time.

Written in quivering emotion and recounted, by refraction, by a series of narrators, all of them—except Quentin's father—in a state of quivering emotion, the book runs the risk momently of collapsing into ignominious absurdity. "Outrage" and "outraged" are the motif-words of the book and the author himself seems to be in a state of staggered outrage: that this vast iniquity had taken place in the land (the land whose other possession was the highest conceivable adherence to honor and pride and chivalry), and that the consequences of the iniquity were like the ancient concept of fate and retribution.

It has then the character of an "epic," the role of the supernatural being played by this operative doom. And the incongruity that ultimately saps its power is that we are all too aware that the author by reason of his state of quivering and outraged emotion is not capable of viewing the evils with that wide and removed view which alone can compass the actions of gods and men. It is as though we were hearing the fall of the House of Atreus told by a voice that was feverish and shrill, scandal-mongering-nosey, and a little prurient.

Just as *Light in August* trembled with anticipated horror and ecstasy toward the castration of a Negro, so *Absalom, Absalom!* does a frenetic dance about a finally impeded incestuous coupling of a white girl and her partially-Negro half-brother—having previously fainted with outrage at three miscegenations: Thomas Sutpen and the mother of Clytemnestra (*sic!*) Sutpen; Thomas Sutpen and his first wife; and Charles Bon and his New Orleans mistress.

The incongruity (the agitated narrator and the vast subject) betrays the author into grandiloquence. It would be rash to say, without having reread the others, that it is Faulkner's most grandiloquent book. This dizzying rhetoric rises to its most fantastic pitch when it approaches the subject of sex. . . . The one thing an author is not allowed is to look at the tragic background of life and the constitution of human nature for evil and absence of spirit *with surprise*, for surprise denotes that he is newly come from a conviction that it was otherwise. It is in this sense that Faulkner and the South are unequipped for tragic matter. They were first surprised that the North called them guilty; they are now surprised to discover that they *were* guilty, and with that comes the green adolescent surprise that the human race can be indicted for guilt. It is surprise, therefore, that takes pleasure—the wrong kind of pleasure—in contemplating violence and lust. It is at once consolation and absolution to cry out in horror, to say nothing of a sort of relish in the abasement.

But this is a notable book. It marches to the terrific climax of its closing lines:

"... Why do you hate the South?"
"I dont hate it," ... *I dont hate it* he thought ... *I dont. I dont!* ... *I dont hate it!*

The large articulated machinery of the plot does illustrate the motif that the institution of slavery set in motion its own retribution. The last lines are preceded by another theme, stated as though it were a baleful prophecy, that the descendants of miscegenation will gradually cover the country, and "conquer the Western hemisphere"— presumably as semi-idiots, like Jim Bond---- That such descendants are assumed to be idiots or incapables is the Southerner's assumption. There is a sneer at George Washington Carver in the book.

431. SS "VEENDAM," SATURDAY, FEBRUARY 25, 1950. The Novelist and the Assumption of Omniscience.

First, some statements from Henry James's preface to *The Wings of the Dove*.

H.J. is talking (Modern Library edition, page xxiii) of the ways that the actions and relations of the characters are successively recorded and rendered via the consciousness of his selected observers and participants—his centers, his reflectors, his plates. He as the author presents the weakest of all plates. His mere assertion of data in the novel has least power to convince or engage the reader: "It is as if . . . the impersonal plate—in other words the poor author's comparatively cold affirmation or thin guarantee—had felt itself a figure of attestation at once too gross and too bloodless, likely to affect us as an abuse of privilege when not as an abuse of knowledge." Having said earlier (page xxi): "From the moment we proceed by 'centres'—and I have never, I confess, embraced the logic of any superior process —they must *be*, each, as a basis, selected and fixed . . ."

We the readers are not assumed to "believe" the story save as it is recounted to us from the centers of consciousness of the engaged actors.

Yet these reflecting centers are not left to report what they see in their own fallible human way. These are not "monologues"—James is always there *reporting them*, in the third person, and, as it were, correcting them to an absolute truth. James hates Kate Croy as much as he adores Milly Theale, and Kate's view of things is carefully shown to us as detestable by the aid of H.J.'s discreet editorial nudging. This—and another device of his—is author-interference to a very high degree. Never was there a greater fuss-budget of a novelist, continually intruding his view of the case precisely under the pretense of withholding it. The other device is the intrusion of the speech in Sophoclean irony—the forward-looking prophetic statement of eventual situation. This H.J. employs under the sign of what he calls the "portentous"—having confessed in the preface that it is one of his favorite words and favorite practices:

[Milly (as though lightly):] "Ah, then let us hope we shall sound the depths . . . of sorrow and sin!" (vol. I, page 206)
[Kate (to Milly):] "Oh, you may very well loathe me yet!" (vol. I, page 308)
[Kate (to Densher):] "I verily believe I *shall* hate you if you spoil for me the beauty of what I see!" (vol. II, page 33)

All this is a consequence of H.J.'s passion. And what is he so passionate about? Several things, but all finally swallowed up in one.

(1) He is undoubtedly trembling with excitement about sex —the aspect of him which I have always called H.J.'s prurience. This

obsession manifests itself in James in different ways than in any other author, not least striking among them is its absence in situations where other writers would mark it. This comment should be reserved for another notation in the Journal. Here I only note Glenway [Wescott]'s remark of years ago that in James you must be prepared for an occasional substitution of one sex for another to explain some of the excitement in the novels; he instanced that in *The Golden Bowl* one should think of Charlotte as occasionally—as intermittently—a man.

(2) He is passionate about the American nationality. This anti-European pro-American crusade is carried on behind smoke screens of tact and dissimulation, but it is undoubtedly the second most important crusade of the book. . . .

(3) He passionately desires to exhibit, to praise, and to attest for the Right-Way-to-Be, and he is quiveringly indignant about the Wrong. This aspect of James would generally pass as moral fervor. It is our business then to decide just what are his requirements of the moral, the inquiry rendered particularly difficult by the fact that he seldom moralizes; this Right Way is exhibited as self-evident; he lays down no aphorisms and no sententious generalizations.

Borrowing categories from Kierkegaard we can ask whether his Right People are Knights of the Aesthetic, the Ethical, or the Religious Life (observing that his most triumphant exponents are generally women).

First we see that they are indeed not Knights of the Religious Life. All the burden of one's being Right rests on how one lives among other people. It is a world without God; and as always we see that it is so by the kinds of joy or exaltation which the Right Persons have, or strain toward. It is indeed a joyless book; but the two joys we wish for Milly are: (1) More of those moments of exalted pride when she knows that she has achieved inspired pinnacles of aid to others: when towards Susan Stringham and the great doctor Sir Luke Strett she has shown herself as reversing the situation: to Sir Luke, *she* is the doctor and he the patient; she is to comfort Susan, not receive comfort from her; these are triumphs of decorum and humane consideration; (2) Love—and no doubt is left that what is meant is passionate love—even with the Kate-Densher example before us of what an ultimately destructive thing passionate love can be. We all want her in Densher's arms, even though we know that Densher is not "a great man" in the sense that Milly is—and in more than the social sense —"the first young woman of . . . [her] time" (vol. II, page 176).

This is also a novel about sin, and very black sin. But the sins are not malice and hatred and the desire to destroy another's soul. Kate Croy "destroys" Milly (though not her soul) as a mere by-product of her need for material things. She commits what in this book [is] the supreme sin: she does not live for others. . . . It is also the sin of betrayal, but there are betrayals and betrayals. This is not the betrayal by gleeful hate, or revenge, or Iago's inexplicable will to do evil: it is merely that Kate uses Milly as an instrument.

And it seems to me that James is charging London (Europe) with this sin: the pursuit of material things leads Europeans to use people as instruments. This is turning the tables, indeed: it is in America's rush-rush for the Almighty Dollar that you would expect that sin to flourish.

Is Milly a Knight of the Aesthetic or the Ethical Order? That is the point: Americans don't know anything about the Aesthetic Order (even in the very high sense in which the term can be used—[Castiglione's] *Il Cortegiano*, a moment in eighteenth-century France). All the values of the beautiful are for Milly translated into the humane. (H.J. remarks how little culture she has: she tries to "read up" on Europe with Susan; in the National Gallery her particular favorites are the "English School." Note also, Mrs. Lowder is admired by us all and by James—she can be counted on for the Right Way; but James is merciless on the hideous "aesthetic" surroundings in which she lives.)

432. SS "VEENDAM," FEBRUARY 26, 1950. The Situation of the Young Girl of Eighteen.

Reading Søren Kierkegaard's "In Vino Veritas" (in volume *Étapes sur le Chemin de la Vie*, Gallimard, Paris, 1948), a symposium on women and love, I find a magnificent speech on the above subject (which for him, however, is the girl of sixteen): a girl when she is a child is given less attention than a boy; at the decisive moment, however, she suddenly becomes a sovereign; the men who approach her do so in real adoration; for her they feel prepared to die; she now lives in the world of the *fantasque*. . . .

The whole paper is extraordinary: it appears to be written *en jouant*, but is so opalescent that all colors are there—including S.K.'s perpetual self-justification for his failure to marry Regina and many a sharp lesson to and against her, poor girl. It resumes and adds further reaches to Stendhal's doctrine of crystallization and draws close to the point where Ortega ended his lecture at Aspen,[1] close that is to really treating of the closing words of *Faust* [*"Das Ewig-Weibliche / Zieht uns hinan."*]

Girls are invested with this power to drive young men crazy. It has not been sufficiently observed in literature that girls may be ecstatically in love, but young men do not drive them in this sense crazy. Young men are driven out of themselves; young women into themselves.

I see that I may have been wrong in that phrase of *The Woman of Andros*—on which I used rather to pride myself. Thinking of France, where every boy's initiation into love is through association with a woman considerably older than himself, I said: "Perhaps the maturity of a civilization can be judged by . . . observing whether the young men first fall in love with women older or younger than themselves; if in their youth their imaginations pass their time in hallowing the images of prattling unnourishing girls their natures will be forever after the thinner." *Une femme mûre* can civilize; she cannot irradiate, cannot provoke a man to invest her with that overwhelming ideality, which, in turn, both renders him creative and endows him with *"la conscience de l'immortalité."* (Or perhaps she can only do this for him, if his love is not gratified physically—which S.K. implies, and perhaps Goethe illustrates.)

This prodigious phenomenon—S.K. does not begin to discuss it essentially. Dante gazed at a girl of thirteen and before our eyes we see what it made of him ("and I resolved to say of her such things as had never yet been said of any woman"). It is as a projection of this force that she of the cathedrals and the crusades is both a mature mother and a virgin. The explanation may be either transcendental or psychological: the transcendental is still Plato's—that as the lover gazes at the beauty of the beloved, the God descends into his mind and speaks through his lips; the psychological is Vienna's—that the libido is the source of all intellectual activity. One is convinced there is a deeper law.

Remains the situation of the young girl. S.K.—still smarting

---

1. Ortega y Gasset's lecture at the Goethe Convocation in 1949 was titled "Concerning a Bicentennial Goethe."

over Regina's marriage to another—is very harsh on her. She has no faint understanding of the thunders-and-lightnings she has released in her lover; she takes it all to herself as food for her vanity. Even though she is exceptionally intelligent she will appear to be a *goose* viewed against the cloudscapes of ideality which she releases in a man. But consider her state ten years later, she who had dimly felt herself to have been empress and sorceress; . . . she had not known how she came by such powers, but they [had] seemed natural to her; now she does not know how she has lost them. She assumes that it was simply sex and youth—and so it was, but in categories she cannot understand. She has been "spoiled" (in the current sense of the word). In America—which makes an anti-ideal glorification of that young-girl ideality—the women over twenty-four are in a rage to recover those magics of which they feel themselves to have been *despoiled*.

433. SS "VEENDAM." MARCH 3, 1950. The Novelist as Omniscient, or All Writers of Imagined Action Proceed (and Expect It) on the Assumption That They Are Omniscient.

I am surprised to find that I had not committed to this Journal the reflections that occupied me at such lengths two years ago and which I have continued to worry ever since. They seem to me to cohere, but I cannot escape the feeling that there is a flaw in them somewhere, *i.e.*, that they are nonsense. I put them down here in order to see how they stand up under review and in order to add a new step in the structure, one which has occurred to me while rereading Kierkegaard.

Definition: A novel is a narrative (after Aristotle: of a given length, the greater part of which is furnished by imagination) presenting an action or a series of actions together with all such pertinent knowledge of the selected action as will induce in the reader the sensation of being omniscient relative to that action. (Vulgarly put: a novel makes the reader feel like God.)

Deductions: (1) The withholding of a piece of information pertinent to the action is a device to stimulate the reader's attention, but the device presupposes that all the information necessary for supplying the missing details is present in the story—hence present in the mind of the omniscient author. *Example One:* At the close of Tourgenieff's "A Nest of Gentlefolk:" What were Lavretzky's thoughts as he watched Liza hurrying by? What were her thoughts? We do not know. *Example Two:* Close of *The Wings of the Dove:* "But she turned to the door, and her headshake was now the end. 'We shall never be again as we were!'" *i.e.*, they did not marry.

(2) Knowing *all* about any one action presupposes knowing all about anything that has happened, or could conceivably happen. Hence all imaginative narration is a voluntary limitation of a novelist's omniscience. The author selects the limit at which, for any given work, knowledge may be regarded as pertinent or impertinent. *Example:* Jane Austen from unlimited knowledge selects the field of reference and the level of depth within which she will afford us information.

(3) The attributes of a novelist being omniscient are: (a) *Timelessness*: he knows the end of the story from the beginning, he can be in no suspense and can know no surprise; (b) *Passionlessness:* he knows all human existence; any joy or anger, love or hate he reveals will be a function of an ethical law not of a personal emotion; (c) *Sense of Order:* since his mind holds all existence, his selection of this limited number of actions from all actions will bear a relation and proportion to all happenings. Any disproportion in the ordering of the story will imply a disproportion in the ordering of the universe, both as idea and as mechanism. The presence of such disorder in a story will therefore imply that [the] author indicts the universe as deviating from a concept of order which he grasps. The result of this in literature will be an orderly expression of the view that the universe is in disorder. *Illustration:* Thomas Hardy's *Jude the Obscure* charges that events in existence arrive in invariably chaotic unrelatedness. The work is insufficiently mature to serve as a notable illustration of any principle, but it can be pointed out that Hardy is painstakingly careful (orderly) in presenting his view of disorder.

Obiter dicta: (1) The sole motive of the omniscient novelist is to arouse in the reader the emotion of omniscience.

(2) The intention of illustrating a generalized truth (or a moral idea) is an impurity in the novelist's function. It implies that, knowing all happenings, he selects certain happenings to illustrate a general proposition. Viewed on so vast a scale, however, every happening illustrates every general proposition, and to make any one happening illustrate any one general proposition is to twist, force, and distort the

web of pure happening. A novel is a total gaze—a *Schauen*—the limitation of whose totality is not for the clarification of an idea but for the clarification of experience. From this we deduce that there is another branch of imaginative narration to which the novel does not belong and which cannot lay claim to the omniscient assumption: this is the *fabulist's*, a purely human activity of didactic intention, and of confessed fallibility.

Now to the new contribution recently adopted from Kierkegaard.

It takes its place as Deduction 3(d) . . . [The] attributes of . . . [a] novelist . . . [being] omniscient: the novelist cannot write a novel which is felt to be an absolutely comic novel or an absolutely tragic novel. From his vast vista, human experience can only be regarded as presenting a synthesis of both.

Against the background of all human life every effort of an individual, by disproportion, is comic. Against the same background every defeat of an individual aspiration (in the light of an ethics which calls for our most earnest meditation) is tragic—tragic therefore as well as comic. To isolate one without the other is to be false to omniscience. It is at this point that Kierkegaard (*Etapes sur le Chemin de la Vie*, page 359 and *passim*) introduces his category of the *religieux*: "*Le religieux . . . présume la synthèse du tragique et du comique dans la passion. . . .*" *N.B.* also page 333: "*. . . la mort même du plus grand des hommes est une plaisanterie pour une Providence qui tient en réserve des légions d'anges. . . .*" *N.B.* [also] page 373: "*C'est ainsi aussi que dans la misère je vois le tragique en ce qu'un esprit immortel doit souffrir, et le comique en ce qui'il ne s'agit que de deux marks.*"

434. SS "VEENDAM," MARCH 3, 1950. Henry James's *The Wings of the Dove*, Considered in the Light of the Above Schema.

Preface: H.J. seems to have been aware that he had not succeeded in this novel. The preface is more than usually deprecatory: three times he uses the word *alas*. The reasons he gives for his disappointment are purely technical. He calls upon us to search for a "misplaced pivot" in Book Five and to deplore with him various foreshortenings in the last half of the book (glaring they are, for we are cheated of a proportionate description of what went on in the minds of both conspirators and victim during the crucial period of the Great Deception).

The operation of omniscience:

The prefaces of James continually return to this problem. In my Entry 431 I quoted his allusions to it from the preface to this novel.

The "centers" or "reflectors" are a dangerous compromise. He appears to resign his total omniscience by limiting it to a single character's knowledge. This procedure is, of course, itself an exercise of omniscience; but all novel-writing is a voluntary limitation of omniscience. James, however, does not truly limit: [Browning's] *The Ring and Book* and Molly Bloom's soliloquy in *Ulysses* are examples of how this is done correctly (as, in a totally different form, operating under different laws, are the Shakespearian soliloquies). James *reports* the viewpoints of his "centers," inevitably introducing thereby his knowledge of their thoughts and his ulterior comment on their thoughts.

Inevitably the shifting from "center" to "center" entails a vast amount of withholding information from the reader. This, too, if the "laws are obeyed," is a legitimate though very dangerous procedure. For when we have known a "soul" as well as we are permitted to know it in one crisis, it comes very near to being our right (this kind of knowledge being relatively profound by the author's selection and decision, and never proportionately obligatory) to know as much in the same "center's" relation to a later crisis. The author's refusal to accord us a continuous knowledge (at whatever level has been previously established) must therefore be justified by the rule I have given: "The withholding of a piece of information pertinent to the action is a device to stimulate the reader's attention, but the device presupposes that all the information necessary for supplying the missing details is present in the story." Let us concede, though with reluctance, that James has met this condition—with one important exception.

Now applying to James the list of attributes of the omniscient novelist:

(1) *Timelessness:* James offends against this rule in a very peculiar way. By permitting his characters to let fall remarks which we divine as prophetic, he betrays the fact that he, the author, is immersed in (aware of, delighting in) time-as-duration. We mortals, who do not know our future, may let fall remarks ten times a day which might be pertinent to our imminent death or our ultimate vicissitudes—but they are null, for *no one with knowledge of the future is listening to them.* James as novelist is indeed in possession of this knowledge of

the future and, as we have said, it is his purpose to inspire in us readers the sensation of omniscience; but this means of doing it is illegitimate, for it irresistibly affects us as *closing the gates upon the characters' freedom.* The novelist knows everything, but he does not direct everything. On the contrary he is passive; he is the gazer-at-life and the faithful reporter of an existence which he neither set in motion nor is able to alter nor arrest. The novelist is omniscient and ubiquitous; but he is not omnipotent.

(2) *Passionlessness:* James meets this condition—yet: it is sufficient to think for a moment of Tolstoi in the two great novels [*War and Peace* and *Anna Karenina*] to realize that James's partiality for Milly and his presentation of Kate Croy fall short of the absolute equanimity of Tolstoi's relation to his characters.

(3) *Sense of Order:* It is this order which is James's particular passion, and he has recorded his regret that he so seldom achieved it.

His self-imposed rule for order (disposition) in this book requires the use of these "centers of intelligence." Strictly speaking, then, we should in orderly fashion shift from center to center in such a way that we obtain "all that it is pertinent to know" concerning the action. At this point, however, another principle of H.J. intervenes . and makes havoc of his order. H.J. believes that we readers do not truly "believe in" the story when its elements are merely recounted to us by the author *in propria persona.* We only extend our belief when the actions, motives, etc., are conveyed to us either in action, in a "scene," *i.e.,* as he loved to say, *dramatized,* or when the information is relayed to us via the testimony of one of these centers. This is an admirable precept for storytellers, but disastrous as overruling principle: *whom can we believe if we can't believe the author?* (The confusion at the close of the book is increased by another fact: Milly is dying; H.J. does not wish to recount the details of her illness, nor her interviews with the principal characters. In the preface he congratulates himself that he has conveyed her greatness and martyrdom all the more beautifully by these elaborate indirections; he says he has treated her like a princess—rather, I should say, like an unexhibited icon. The result is so murky that we do not believe it. The selected "centers" are too "interested" to be adequate reporters.)

(4) *The Balance between Tragedy and Comedy:* Milly is a figure of both—of tragedy, as the victim of the purity of her motives; of comedy, because of the disproportion between her aspiration and the harsh facts of life, enhanced by the fact that she is long time a dupe.

H.J. will not look these conditions in the face; for him she is not even pathos, she is all tragedy, and the result (and it is sufficient to lead us toward a definition) is very near to sentimentality.

Obiter dicta: To what shall we ascribe H.J.'s failure to render his hero, Merton Densher, a living man? We should not be obliged to say that characters who are weak morally are weak artistically. The two young women in the story are infatuated with Densher, and there is evidence that H.J. is also. In the preface he speaks of his regret that space prevented his supplying the "quantities and attributes that should have danced about him with the antique grace of nymphs and fauns circling round a bland Hermes and crowning him with flowers." The discrepancy between such a potential description of Densher and the dreary petticoat-driven man in the novel is astonishing. If H.J. thinks he has given us grounds for so interesting ourselves in Densher, he has been blinded by infatuation and has sinned against our second attribute of the novelist.

About 1900 H.J. emerged from being a minor writer to being a very great one indeed. Inevitably, however, he brought with him vestiges of his long inferiority. His previous preoccupation may be described as: too thorough an identification with the received ideas of the customs and manners he was studying and recounting. He continually betrayed the fact that he was impressed, curious, shocked, indignant, and complacent according to the code of behavior adhered to by those about him. This can probably be explained in part by his *déracinement*—all voluntary *déracinés* (except Gertrude Stein!) live in a never-never land—and in part by his neurosis. It is this that gives to the earlier books the character of being related to tea-table gossip and dinner-table *racontage-pour-briller*. After 1900 he swept far beyond [this], but its musty perfume occasionally obtrudes—not because it is so largely about women but because it is so extensively *in* women.

436. HÔTEL DE L'ANGLETERRE, ST. JEAN DE LUZ, [FRANCE,] SUNDAY AFTERNOON, MARCH 26, 1950. A Look around My Situation [Excerpt].

. . . Tomorrow I go to San Sebastian for two nights; then two nights of *wagon-lits* to Granada.

This is then a Lope de Vega hunt, preposterous in many ways—its very absurdity being an indication of how deeply such researches now possess me. Preposterous by reason of the shortness of time now before me to accomplish anything; and by reason of the fact that I come armed with none of the letters of introduction and other aids which I could marshal. All that is a sign of the "irrational" character of the whole pursuit: I wish to pursue it in my own way; an independence which can tend to defeat itself; an appetite parading itself in the guise of an intellectual discipline.

We must take ourselves as we find ourselves, always hoping for some improvement but accepting the basic cast of the die. As a flight from . . . interlocking false situations I have fastened on Lope studies (they are impersonal; they are precise; they are mine own; they are related to great literature; they somehow express the "collecting instinct"; they "advance"). They not only obstruct my writing; they obstruct my very "thinking." They are like a banyan tree in my garden which saps all shoots save its own. Already they have robbed the life of "The Emporium" of whatever energy it possessed. (The death this week of Arthur Hopkins [the producer] removes whatever external pressure I had to pursue that.) Let me now, then, "rub my nose" in Lope so thoroughly that I can somehow get it out of my system. Then let me "rub my nose" in the American-literature problem for Harvard[2] so absorbedly that my "non-fiction" interests will be temporarily drained. Then and only then will it be possible for me to resume the theatre.

438. [HÔTEL DE LONDRES, SAN SEBASTIAN, SPAIN, MARCH 31? 1950.]
. . . André Gide's *Journal 1942-1949* . . . : A Few Notes.

Throughout this vast work, Gide never found the tone. Again the Doctrine of Audience supplies the explanation: in the earlier years he foresaw the publication; in the later, he deliberately published it, fragment by fragment. Hence it is subject to all the perils of autobiography, discursive essay, and journalistic diary without being

2. Thornton Wilder had accepted the invitation of Harvard University to give the Charles Eliot Norton Lectures in Cambridge during the academic year 1951–52.

able to derive a strength from the values of any one of those genres. It has the intermittent tension-in-depth of a confession without a confession's rigorously continued exploration (here the French revulsion from the subconscious plays its part); without an essay's requirement of building a construction upon an assortment of interrelated components; without a diary's fidelity to the multiple accretions of the daily life. It may be that this character of flicking-off, of touch-and-run, of never coming to grips with any one aspect of its proposal may be due to the . . . drastically expurgated text; but, even so, the evil goes deeper. It is not merely that Gide is constantly aware of the reader and . . . is "cooking up" his self-portrait for our benefit: . . . he is unable to be spontaneous. This is not insincerity in the sense that he offers an insincere document: . . . he has long since lost the tone of truth. The result is the saddest of all expressions: the sincere desire to be sincere of one who cannot be so. The occasional entries of a hair-raising candor render the confession all the more false: not only is their admission of senile lubricity accompanied by an embarrassing simper (related to the trivial coquetries of Thomas Mann in reference to his hospitalization in *Die Entstehung des Dr. Faustus*), but they do not emerge from a *fond*, an *ambiance*, in which such disclosures are in place. Here are *nugae* of literary criticism, infuriating in their casualness ("Remarks are not literature," as Gertrude Stein said to Hemingway); here are reports of life in a besieged and liberated Tunis—always stopping short of re-creation; here are reflections on the issues of the fates of nations—at the level of a provincial newspaper.

It is not enough to say that this must be condoned as the work of a septuagenarian uprooted from a hitherto easily cushioned life. Gide had proved himself as fighter and as prober. It is the latter end of a mind corrupted by: (1) An evasion of true autoscopy; (2) Literary bonzism—accepting the role which his public had thrust upon him; and (3) Failing to nourish that middle ground between his two chief intellectual activities: between crusade and bookishness; between carrying the banner for homosexuality, and a-theism, and the U.S.S.R., and bad government in the Congo—between all that and a palate-tasting of choice bits in La Fontaine, etc., etc. Note—of *Les Faux-Monnayeurs*—my sure doctrine that an artist is not suitable as central figure of a work of art—whence all the strained refinements of that work (and its predecessors!). . . .

. . . And like everything in the *Journal*—and always in a different way—that *son faux*. But not *faux* by malice or by servility or ingratiation: *faux* because Gide early in life *lost the true tone of voice*. All his vast intelligence is in *falsetto*—doubly tragic because his life is one long sincere effort to be sincere. One cannot even apply to him Cocteau's phrase: "It is not possible both to be and to appear sincere"; for one feels that his "sincerity" had long since retired into a cave way down in the depths of his being.

And the grave implications of all this for myself do not escape me.

Obiter dicta: I used to say that the one group of persons whom one cannot incorporate into one's life is that of the malicious; to these I now add those who are the enemies of themselves. These last are to be pitied, but ultimately they are clinical cases and should be handed over to the doctors. One is always thinking one can do something for them (one's sympathy proceeds from the very fact that one finds elements of a similar self-destructive operation in oneself), but their self-preoccupation is so intense that, however phosphorescently gifted, they cannot build, warm, love, nor benefit.

It is a predisposition to neurosis in infancy which awakens, spurs the intelligence—yes. With the passing of the years, the neurosis becomes conscious of itself, with two results: (1) The subject feels himself as "exception" in society; and (2) He is subject to the law of all neurosis, namely, that he burns to tell and burns to conceal his secret. All this we see written in enormous letters over the work of James Joyce. Now the dangers incurred by too diligent a *concealment* are—as with Henry James prior to 1901—a devitalized output, an intelligent but anemic façade-art. The dangers incurred by too urgent and courageous an *impulse to tell* are—as with Gide—that you tell, tell, tell, but what you are telling is not the essential but an *Ersatz* secret.

Shakespeare (and Goethe?) have shown the fortunate pattern under these predicaments: they turned that curiosity—that passion to explore into the *why* of their condition—*outward*. They asked of nature, of society, of the arts the questions that Gide spent so much time asking of himself (*L'Immoraliste, La Porte Etroite, Si le Grain ne Meurt, Le Journal*—to say nothing of the *opuscula*). The most beautiful example of this—in the sense with which mathematicians use the word *beautiful*—is the work of [Søren] Kierkegaard, where before our eyes we can see the questions he asks concerning his "thorn-in-the-flesh" expanding to questions . . . concerning every human being *existing*.

Where, in the development of a neurosis, that moment comes at which the attention turns from the self to the All, and hence to the self-in-the-All, and what force effects that all-important shift, who can tell? The self-destroyers are those who cannot make the shift, and their company is intolerable.

It is here that one could pass immediately into S.K.'s wonderful analysis of the variants of despair, which are, as it were, a reading of these very forms of "hard-pressed intelligence": the despair-through-weakness (the despair which is the absence of despair, unconscious of its relation to eternity); the intelligence-which-putters (so characteristic of great scholars and especially scientists—perhaps all scientists); the despair-as-defiance—those who choose despair—these S.K. calls the Demoniacs, who prefer to be themselves and all and only themselves: never to tell their secret, or to proclaim violently a secret which is not truly their secret (Baudelaire). And so on.

442. SS "MEDIA," FRIDAY, MAY 5, 1950. Project for a Novel:
      "The Turning Point."

During a partial insomnia last night the following project came to me and elaborated itself with considerable enthusiasm and not a few specific developments. It seemed that one could write a novel in short stories and fragments of narration representing actions from all places and ages—a sort of *Decameron*, except that the stories are of varying length, from four or five lines to that of a *nouvelle* by Kleist, and except that they would inevitably have the air of *pastiche*, an anecdote from the Annamese followed by a fragment of a Finnish epic or a modern newspaper clipping. The subject of this novel, however, would not be that which first presents itself: the life of Every Man and Every Woman presented in this manner; that would be very near to what has been done in *Finnegans Wake*. Here the subject would be: mind (first the mind of *l'homme moyen sensuel*, then mind that exceeds itself) exhibiting signs of idealization and self-probing; mind poisoning body and body overstraining mind; the "philosophizing" of life; the descent into despair; the anatomy of despair; here some stories of nihilism, of cruelty and obscenity (at its nadir represented by blank pages with the notation: "The stories here cannot be printed"); then the turning point—"one cannot reconcile oneself with life until one has passed through the valley of total negation"—stories of relative reintegration.

It is not the incidental perils here that frighten me; merely the major central peril of not knowing enough about the basic central subject: how the human mind *has* (in a few individuals) crossed that valley and how the human mind *must* (as a total social and cultural experience) cross that valley. But the central basic peril of every book is something one can never evade, short of retiring from writing; the lesser perils here are particularly inspiriting: the rendering of these *pastiches*, yet making them so easily and lightly that their sheer bravura becomes unimportant in the light of their service to the profoundly earnest intention of the book; and as always in the subjects which I propose to myself, the avoidance of schematization in the disposition of the elements.

Note the beautiful opportunities: to show how *homo faber* emerged—*i.e., emerges*, for this book transpires five thousand years ago and *today*—under the prompting of necessity, illness (by illness, I mean Thomas Mann's doctrine of the role of malady in all creation), and womankind; how the sense of sin was induced; the emergence of the "questioning"; the Sickness to Death—all this promises and alarms.

But how interesting that in a midnight's meditation I should have found a really new form for the *novel-in-impasse*, and one that could serve as vehicle for two of my compelling preoccupations: man seen in all his history; mind seen as a force struggling out of the biologic undergrowth—to say nothing of the secondary preoccupations: woman as instigatrix; narration as the means of depicting scientific process; and so on.

444. HAMDEN, [CT.,] JULY 6, 1950. Credo.

Went out alone to take dinner at Momauguin Beach, the once pleasing beach resort now a frantic catchpenny for the working classes. . . . The Sound: first the blues and grays of *nacre*; then the cirrus pink on blue; then dark, and the lighthouses of the coast. . . .

We human beings are in a universe that does not know we are here. The sunset deployed tonight was not there for my benefit and it had nothing to say to me beyond what I shall read into it. The family parties dining to my right and left had similarly gathered to enjoy themselves in Babylon and Carthage.

The universe does not declare to us that it is/was formed by love or by our mind; but it is easy to see why we could be led to think so. Nothing can reach us which is not the consequence of its physio-chemical process; everything can be seen, or dimly accepted, as included within its vast machine of law. This gives us the sensation of pre-ordained order—Consequence can always appear to be Pre-Or-dination. Christ mistook the Order of Consequence for the Order of Pre-Ordination and said "Our Father----" There *is* no father there of whom we can ask that he give us our daily bread, and no father there of whom we can ask that he forgive the harm we do to others. That harm is forever embedded in the flux; nothing can efface it in lives and in happenings. But the sea-worm developed some sensitive cells; these became the eye. All is development for survival. But the organs and the instincts develop pell-mell; they often war with one another; their headlong flight leads them into self-defeating channels. Sex leads on the one hand to aesthetics, and on the other to obsessive nest-building (and what a corroboration tonight: I got lost and drove through square miles of homes—the roof, the lamp, the children's room).

Is mind a development far in excess of its primary impulse toward survival and self-protection? Did we have to invent the railway train and the telephone in order to survive?

No. The drive towards intellection outstripped the problems which faced it. Mind leapt from the How to the Why. The drive of development which refined certain cells to the differentiated organization which is the eye is still at work. The human being is still developing new functions. What will the next faculty be?

Man for the last two thousand years has been in a green sickness as he prepares the next stadium. The next will be:

(1) The gradual subsidence of sadism: dog-eat-dog supplanted by rational adjustment. First, machines will do our cruelty for us. Already America is showing us this transition.

(2) Pan-sexuality—a regression or an emergence. Already we see that certain women are the *best men* and certain men are the best women. Male and female will always remain, but female will become clarified and released for its true function in the *Ewig-Weibliche*.

(3) Freedom from tutelage to that Coach and Giver and Picker-

upper who will somehow manage—however deep our inertia—so that "things will come out all right."

There are, however, two things to inspire our awe—though it goes against the grain to apply to them the old-old sorry word *religion*. They are that force which is the *Ewig-Wirkende* and which produced the eye, and the intellect, and which is now producing some new faculty; and there is the fact that all the complexity of the world has proceeded by law, from some unity. It is not an object of awe that the complexity is dependent on the first unity by a mere physio-chemical chain; nor that the result of that is that there is nothing conceivable that would not be "at home" in this causally developed machine which is the universe (it is not suitable that the understandable should inspire awe—admiration even at the highest pitch being of a different nature from awe). What is awe-inspiring (and here I see I am developing what I had only glimpsed in *The Ides of March*) is merely that it has happened at all. The incomprehensibility that surrounds our approach to how it began remains present in various degrees at every one of its manifestations, from a pebble to Mt. Blanc. (It is an aspect of the romantic fallacy that the incomprehensibility is *more present* in Mt. Blanc than in a pebble.)

455. **DUNSTER HOUSE, HARVARD, OCTOBER 10, 1950.** Kierkegaard's *Fear and Trembling*.

I have just finished rereading this book in a storm of admiration and yet feel like an idiot: I find nothing to say about it which does not sound like chatter.

If Faith existed, that's what Faith would be like.

The book is like some extraordinary piece of fiction—or like the propositions of the new mathematics: let us imagine that one and three make five; look what breathlessly beautiful consequences can be deduced.

All the more does it add to S.K.'s greatness that he continually pours out definitions, distinctions, ideas, grounded on premises which one cannot share, that are widely, deeply valid at so many other levels than those he primarily insists upon.

At present what occurs to me most is that the book is an elaborate and impassioned rationale of a man who feels himself to be "out-side the universal". . . . Just as the Middle Ages sharpened and devel-oped its wits (our wits) by wrenching from the mind a defense of a God-in-three-persons and a Virgin Birth, so S.K. pursued these brave and terrifying journeys to explain to himself and to Regina not *why* he couldn't marry her but *the situation of a man who, conceivably for sublime reasons, would have to break off an engagement with a girl.*

It is probable that the real situation was other: he had merely to write her a letter saying: *"Dear Regina, I suspect that I am impotent."*

What he *did* write in all these volumes is not a lie—not even an obfuscation; it is a presentation of a God-ordered world in which a man who so loved God and Regina would find himself in the situation of having to write (of having not to write) just such a letter.

In this book, more particularly, that little Copenhagen story is always present lurking in the wings; nevertheless, he also soars and plunges far above and below.

To anyone less a believer than S.K. the aspect of Abraham's story which presents a great difficulty is *how Abraham knew that God had commanded him to kill Isaac.* Yes, it is a datum in the myth; but unlike Calchas's similar order to Agamemnon,[3] we do not know how to "incorporate" it; we find no analogy for it in the promptings we know. ("God commanded Gauguin to leave his wife and children"; "God commanded John Brown to enlist the members of his family in an inevitably suicidal revolt.") For us all those decisions are not quali-tatively different from "God commanded Brigham Young to take sev-enteen wives." In a note Dr. [Walter] Lowrie [the editor and trans-lator] tells us that S.K. believed that his marriage was prohibited by a "divine veto." In the light of this is it not strange that the works are not more "strange" than they are? For generations they have been felt to be very odd, but, all things considered, they are singularly free of the more turbid fumes of genius, neurosis, self-absorption, and mysti-fication. Much of that he mediated into irony, humor, and crotchets. The only sign I find here of a momentary glimpse into derangement is a phrase on page 83: of Abraham's sacrifice: ". . . I have not much doubt that in the whole world one will not find a single analogy (ex-cept a later instance which proves nothing) . . . !!!" Yes, the context has sarcasm and irony and *yet* to what other writer would it occur to

---

3. To appease the wrath of Artemis by sacrificing Iphigenia.

so much as joke about his private drama as the sole analogy for the Biblical one he is presenting?

From that "religious collision" in his life, then, came this *aurora borealis* of ideas; came "the teleological suspension of the ethical"—probably an indefensible proposition, but which, thus stated, lights up the moral life of man like a meteor; came all these ways of saying that the Individual is more important than the Universal; and so on. . . .

472. **VIKING HOTEL, NEWPORT, R.I., NOVEMBER 4, 1950.** Toward the Fifth Norton Lecture: Melville's *Billy Budd, Foretopman* (Read in [edition published by] John Lehmann, London, 1947).

"Here ends a story not unwarranted by what happens in this incongruous world of ours—innocence and infirmity, spiritual depravity and fair respite"—so wrote Melville toward the close of his story. It is the sovereign statement of a collision in this incongruous world, superbly presented to us. Look and pass by![4] I find in it no metaphysical burden beyond the legitimate commonplaces of serious narration. Nor do I find that H.M. is engaged in demonstrating an indictment against the incongruous in human destiny or guiding us to a reconciliation with the human condition.

Within the accepted framework of those high commonplaces he is free to concentrate his interest on something else: on human nature and, particularly, the relations between men. Our principals are types, and so insisted upon; but each is given a deviation from, a coloring of, his type: Billy is Innocence and Spontaneity, to which is added—and so monotonously insisted on—his personal beauty; Captain Vere is Order, doubled by a temperament of reflection; and Claggart is Natural Depravity, . . . doubled by an aspect at which H.M. will no more than hint: he tells us Claggart felt envy of Billy's innocence and "fain would have shared, but he despaired of it"; "apprehending the good, but powerless to be it." Here we are directly in

4. Cf. the epitaph of W. B. Yeats, from the poem "Under Ben Bulben": "Cast a cold eye / On life, on death. / Horseman, pass by!"

Kierkegaard again: that demoniac dread aroused by presence of the Good.

But there is another step. Had Melville read Balzac? Is there a conscious reminiscence of Vautrin?[5] For the whole novel is filled with a sort of vibration of homosexual feeling and intimation. There is something uncomfortable about the extent to which feminine similes for Billy come to the writer's hand. . . . And as to Claggart's despairing envy of him, does not H. M. go to extraordinary lengths when we are told that after seeing Billy pass, "his eyes suffused with incipient feverish tears. Then would Claggart look like the man of sorrows. [!!] Yes, and sometimes the melancholy expression would have in it a touch of soft yearning, as if Claggart could even have loved Billy but for fate and ban." That contains something more than a demoniac nature generating destructive hatred in the presence of the innocent and the good. . . .

There are a number of aspects of this neurotic overtone that I leave for later consideration: . . . what I wish to say here is that it is very remarkable finally how little this element, though radical and omnipresent, harms this work or renders it "special." Two themes run their course. Innocence infuriates Depravity; Innocence is driven to murder by Depravity's machinations; Justice grieves at not being able to apply a justice which would take into account the provoked spontaneity of Innocence. The secondary theme is that the magic of Beauty strikes evil from the heart of the lustful and redoubles the anguish in the compassionate heart of the just. The secondary theme adds poignancy, color, and a wider though slightly stranger universality to the main theme, but without muddying or removing it—removing it into the realm of the merely curious.

Melville, however, almost lost his story through his own infatuation with Billy Budd. He almost *made him divine*—which would have robbed the story of its human poignance. There is a glory in the death of saints and of bright gods which we contemplate, which we re-stage, which we derive such benefit from that we wish them to die over and over again. That glory is out of place in this novel, as it is out of place in the death of Abraham Lincoln or in the death of [Lord] Nelson (meditated upon at length in this novel, pages 33–34). Billy is mysteriously born; and his Passion is all but hagiographic: "At the same moment [of his hanging] it chanced that the vapoury fleece

---

hanging low in the East, was shot through with a soft glory as of the fleece of the Lamb of God seen in mystical vision; . . . Billy ascended; and ascending, took the full rose of the dawn." . . . H.M.'s emotion is extreme, is overwrought; the magic of Beauty has almost murdered his story. . . .

473. **VIKING HOTEL, NEWPORT, R.I., NOVEMBER 4, 1950.** For the First Norton Lecture: The American Writer as a Speaker and to a Multitude.

Some books are written to be read by one imagined reader in an armchair.

Some books are written to be read by many imagined readers in many armchairs.

Some books are spoken to be heard by one imagined listener.

Some books are spoken to be heard by a group of imagined listeners ([Charles] Lamb).

Some books are spoken to be heard by a multitude of imagined listeners.

Most of the writers we are studying are *talking*. Their rhythms are of declamation, that is, to either the group of friends or the multitude.

We distinguish first the eye-books from the ear-books.

Almost all eighteenth-century English literature was ear-writing. Even Gibbon is auditory. The novel, however, inevitably introduced the words written to be read. It is extremely difficult to maintain the effect of spoken narrative throughout an entire volume. Dickens and Thackeray, like Fielding before them, introduce extended passages that have the character of conversational address; they may introduce *formulae* such as "Could you guess, could anyone guess how it came about?" and so on. But these devices had become conventions, vestigial mimeticisms; the manner of presenting dialogue, of introducing description, of analyzing a situation soon restores us to the printed page.

England had become a nation of readers.

But America was to retain for a long time the illusion of speaking and hearing a printed book.

The obvious effects which one would evoke as criteria for the spoken are not the principal ones, that is, invocations, rhetorical questions, interjections, use of the first and second person. In America as in England those had become, as I have said, conventions. One must look closer.

Reading is a habit and inevitably tends to assume that the material is [all] read at the same tempo. Hence, effects of emphasis must be arrived at by visual means. Adjectival clauses may precede the noun they qualify—and very effectively so—because the eye somehow steals ahead and all but unconsciously collects its subject—a procedure that would cause havoc in auditory literature. The written word may set up for the eye a far more intricate counterpoint of parallelism and qualification; the ear, naturally, may digest the same material but *spaced* more widely. The eye holds more elements simultaneously before it. Melville is more ear- than eye-man, but he was "formed" on much bad literature of both sorts and occasionally falls into atrocious passages of eye-fabrication. . . .

Some development like this may perhaps serve as an appendix for my discussion of the forensic in American literature. But it should ultimately lead to a discussion of the space-between-sentences in American writing.

478. DUNSTER HOUSE, [HARVARD,] NOVEMBER 15, 1950. Toward the Second Norton: Thoreau.

I finished writing the Thoreau lecture last night at two o'clock—always, as usual, excepting the concluding sentences. Since then it has seemed to me meretricious—and, to make it worse, meretricious in several ways. I reap now the whole harvest of my presumption in embarking on such a large subject—itself composed of this succession of large subjects—by [which I] mean insufficiently read, insufficiently meditated. The various developments with which I *enraisin* them frighten me—the American time-sense last week; tonight, the Wilderness, the American "disconnectedness." Are those (in my hands) not ideas but little grabby mauling of notions that completely elude me? As usual, last night, I ended up writing under strong emotion. *That* I no longer distrust so long as I have time—as I have this morning—to reduce it; nor am I greatly admonished by Mrs. [X]'s repeating to me that a professor had found my first [lecture] "evangelical." Yes, it's tiresome to sound evangelical, but I dread worse errors; if I could get the other aspects right the "evangelical" underpainting (given my subject!) would blend and make for an interest and a texture that would render it almost imperceptible.

Now let me pull myself together, reread last night's pages, and see what I've got.

Widener Library, [Harvard,] November 17, 1950.

I think it did come through all right—came through as a lecture, that is; not as an essay. And the reason for it was not "platform technique" nor the final day's revision, but *form*. And I'd like to think that this saving agent of form was there all the time but that I hadn't been aware of it. . . . The happy effect of form came precisely from the recurrence (as in symphonic structure, unexpectedly but patly) of the major themes. And now I know that I need not be afraid of long and apparently unrelated digressions because there is no gratification for the listener equal to that of discovering that the long digression prepares for a re-emergence *later* in closest relation to the principal subject of the discourse. So in this lecture I developed "Wilderness" and "American abstractness," "*Menschenkenner*" as general principles, only later to clap them squarely onto poor Thoreau in a kind of high coda. And looking back I can see that I accomplished much the same thing in the first lecture. Now I have two weeks before me for Emily [Dickinson]—two weeks divided between her and Whitman. (*Later:* This will be harder going when I come to write it as an essay. Such reliances on formal pattern are taken for granted in written work; they do not have the effect there, that they do in a lecture, of "bursting upon you.")

485. **DUNSTER HOUSE, [HARVARD,] NOVEMBER 30, 1950. A Letter.**

A Miss [X] had written me asking if she might send a "rare bluecloth binding" first edition of *The Cabala* for my signature—in fact for a "signed presentation inscription with a few lines regarding its inception." I wrote that I had a terrible time finding paper, cord, and post office, and wouldn't she like to bring it to my lecture on Emily

Dickinson, January 13, at the Poetry Center, YMHA/YWHA, New York.
     She wrote back on November 24:

     I am duly in receipt of your postal of the 21st instant, and, in reply thereto, beg to advise you that I have no interest whatever in the Young Men's Hebrew Association, or anything connected with the race in other than a fictional or historical relation.

Then a great deal of directions about the book, her sincere appreciation, and her "Cordially yours," and a postscript asking also for a photograph.
     I reply:

Dear Miss [X],
     The first sentence of your letter made me shudder so that I keep it by me all the time to remind me of how slowly the world is learning the lessons by which it must live and pursue happiness and attain peace. I need to be reminded of this continually—for the background of my teaching these young people at Harvard and Radcliffe. Although you would not wish me to, I thank you for this bitter remainder.
     Sincerely yours.

487. COLUMBIA UNIVERSITY CLUB, NEW YORK, DECEMBER 4, 1950.
     Toward the Fourth Norton.

     Returning to the declaration that no American had made a work of art until Henry James wrote his last three novels—with the possible exception of *The Scarlet Letter* and Poe's all too calculated artifacts:
     A work of art is distinguished by the visible restrictions which the artist had imposed upon himself. Form is accepted limitation.
     To the young artist and the artist in a young culture all such gratuitous self-impositions seem to be preposterous artificialities—and worse than artificialities: thwartings and gaggings of the spirit, of spontaneity, of emotion. (At the height of the Renaissance did Palestrina, writing the *Missa Brevis*, unlock his throat and sing "*Sanctus, Sanctus, Sanctus*, earth and Heaven are full of Thy glory"? No, he imposed on himself all the difficult laws of counterpoint in mode, and then to make it hard he based every musical theme on a theme in a previously written Mass by a French composer [Goudimel]—in a

vast mosaic—and with such totally unnecessary dependency as deriving from a jubilant *"Resurrexit"* the theme which will serve him a slow tender melody in his *"Agnus Dei."*)

The implications of form are: (1) The end is foreseen from the beginning; (2) Spontaneous emotion is ephemeral.

Now the literature we are discussing is all bent on the celebration of the spontaneous; and how understandable it is: in clearing a wilderness one does not lay out the geometrical gardens of Versailles—not only because one hasn't time, but because the landscape-gardening of Versailles does not arrange that you pursue the shortest distance to arrive at a given point, and it overwhelmingly denies that natural beauty in its natural state is beauty sufficient.

But all our writers were troubled by the intuition that Art—yes, artificiality—could fortify our spontaneity without diluting it.

That's where Walt Whitman comes in. (And, of course, in a different sense, where Edgar Allan Poe comes in.)

Walt Whitman wrote odes. An ode is the lyric at its extreme position of duration: it is the personal cry at the moment when it attempts to submerge the personal in the general.

Poe was right when he said that there was this limit to the length of a poem: our human concentration has its brevity—just as our inhalation and exhalation have—and poetry is precisely the maximum concentration of which the human mind is capable: not higher mathematics, not metaphysics, not music, not painting, but poetry.

Walt Whitman celebrated himself. . . . But he was perpetually trying to escape from the presumptuous assertion. He had his childish side—and some of its manifestations are a distress to us—but the glory is that he was constantly succeeding in saying one-a-million, one-all-of-us.

And that is what Art could have done for him.

It is ridiculous for us to ask [for] a different Walt Whitman than the Walt Whitman which we've got.

But we're not asking that he have written the deliberated stanza-patterns, rhyme-play, organization of the odes of Cowley and Wordsworth—. . . we are only asking of him as much as we can see him asking of himself. "When Lilacs Last in the Dooryard Bloom'd" is indeed an organized poem and foresees its end from its beginning. Its end is in the right place:

> Lilac and star and bird twined with the chant of my soul,
> There in the fragrant pines and the cedars dusk and dim.

. . . Yes, W.W. had heard the whisper of the claims of Art, knew that it could support and enlarge him, but he had that *American thing* which we have met before: *the staking everything on ecstasy.* . . .

Americans are impatient. And given the American problems of the first two hundred and fifty years, how understandable that is.

Benjamin Franklin played with prisms. He noticed that at the end of the spectrum magenta is always faintly suggesting itself. He adds: "I do not know why that is." Goethe quotes the passage. But Goethe with all he had to do—as occupied a man as even Franklin—sat down, quieted himself, foresaw the hundreds of hours that lay ahead, set up two sources of light, etc. [and wrote *Zur Farbenlehre*].

Emily Dickinson forever put off not only the day when she would select from the variants of a poem, the adjectives, the order of the stanzas of any given poem, but the day when she would indicate a grouping from among the poems—[and] destroy the scores that she would certainly not have wished us to see.

That's not impatience? No, but it's not patience, either. It's distrust of Art, the artificial. . . .

490.   DEEPWOOD DRIVE, [HAMDEN, CT.,] DECEMBER 20, 1950.
       Claudel's *Partage de Midi* and Love in France.

A New York producer journeyed to Cambridge to beg me to translate this play for the use of Luise Rainer. *Nenni, nenni, nenni.* He brought with him a nerveless translation made by an intellectual young couple. . . . Hence I have just reread the play, marvelling at how I could once have admired it and marvelling at the extent to which the old vulgar nonsense of the boulevard play irrupts everywhere in it—[Maurice] Donnay, [Georges de] Porto-Riche, [Henry] Bernstein, [Henri] Bataille.

Love in France is like love nowhere else. As I approach the hours of teaching *Le Rouge et le Noir*[6] (Stendhal being at once the

---

6. The death of F. O. Matthiessen, Professor of English at Harvard, in the spring of 1950, was one of several factors that caused Thornton Wilder to be asked to take over a class in the novel, involving intensive study of works by Cervantes, Stendhal, Melville, Tolstoi, and Dickens.

classic critic of this contagion and yet remaining one of its more ludicrous victims; this particular novel, however, not being one of the best places to study him on this matter), I feel the need to try and put in order some of my years-old bothers about it.

I used to phrase the problem this way:

France imports everything including its concept of love, and then Francizes it. *Amour* came to the French from Italy, together with their architecture, their comedy, their dress, and their desserts. But they live in a temperate climate and their sexual intensity is temperate and not at all Mediterranean; the French are logical and analytic and are constantly fearful of falling into situations which may render them ridiculous or abject—which passion precisely does and which does not greatly trouble the Italians. So, I said, the French (who had been very well adjusted to the cult of the Virgin Mary and had secularized it in the cool cult of the *Dame* or *Reine d'amour*) imported that intoxicating fever *amore* and the Northern Frog tried to blow himself up into the Southern Bull.[7] I will, I will, I will be a furnace of passion. This at once came into conflict with the French *amour-propre*, the French *bon sens*, and the French *ridicule*. And the result has been that sex in France has become a highly complicated etiquette or game: a simulation of passion continually controlled by variety, calculation, and several myths.

All this I still think to be basically true, but it is not sufficiently modulated. There are a number of things omitted from the picture. I place here a number of factors, higgledy-piggledy, hit-or-miss, hoping later to find their relation:

(1) France, the matriarchal country: the growing boy remains a boy as long as his (very long-lived) mother remains alive. Hence the mother of his children shares in his awestruck reverence for his mother. Hence he must arrange to attach a mistress who may represent woman-not-mother; but she herself after a year moves into the mother-orbit (the *pantoufle*-hour).

(2) The assumption is that no woman is secure from imperious passion. Any moment she may meet *him*; at once she becomes helpless, crumples up, subjugated. She then becomes a sinner, but a sinner is not a *bad woman*. Perhaps a *bad woman* can be defined as a *woman without maternal qualifications*. . . .

---

7. Cf. Aesop's fable of the frog who tried to blow himself up to the size of a bull, with a disastrous result.

Since women are at a moment subject to being overwhelmed by Imperious Love (the Devil in Mauriac, but the Devil is another face of God; Nature in most plays; God himself in Claudel—but see the long casuistries of *Le Soulier de Satin*), they are frail and fragile. But it's more complicated than that; they are frail, without will power before Passion, but that once granted, they are always powerful. In any situation, they rule, wreck, triumph, direct, coerce.

So from the emotional view of woman we pass without transition to the farcical—to the thousand plays about the husband *cocu* and the *amant trompé*.

The French mind is hard put to it to find the reasons why a woman attracted by a man should not go to bed with him. The Church's commandments? the marriage vows? conventional morality? family honor?—all the deterrents seem remote and pale from the moment that she feels the attraction; her knees turn to water; her will power swoons.

Columbia University Club, [New York,] December [20?] 1950.

This notion that a woman is weak as putty under the influence of Imperious Love is—to this extreme extent—peculiarly French and should be kept in mind. Its divergence from the Spanish is highly significant.

And yet there are several things to be said about *amour* that are important and greatly to be envied:

(3) The Frenchman makes an intensely *personal* love. The centuries-old cult of love is not friction; it is the personality of the lover taking possession of the personality of the beloved. And the drama results not only from the fascinating turning-points of male-nature in confrontation with female-nature—a glorious *accidenté* terrain in itself—but from this man confronting this woman.

This is the great contribution of the French *erotic* thought-world. And this would be sheer gain for the entire on-gazing world were it not considerably vitiated by the other concomitants I have mentioned. A French love-affair never loses itself in the typical and the general—save in literature and in stupid hands.

The Feminine *qua* feminine is always deliriously bewitching to a Frenchman, and each single woman brings to a Frenchman her individual fascination, her unique variant, to the cult of womankind which France has shed and dispersed above and among her growing boys in every generation. It is this very cult of the woman that has contributed to the demand laid on every young Frenchman to know as many [women] as possible and to know them in the realm where such knowledge is best assembled. Such a journey of adventure into the world of womankind would be all to the good were it not vitiated by less defensible co-impulses—particularly French male vanity, amour-propre. The Frenchman pursues woman after woman not only to enrich his connoisseurship in woman-nature but to *afficher* his huntsman's triumphs; *and* every Frenchwoman knows it. . . .

Hence, French amatory literature is pre-eminently burdened with the view that the relationship between the sexes is a war; that hatred is a concomitant of love; and that on the mattress itself a struggle for power is taking place.

Again our *Partage de Midi* comes to our witness, reflecting similar passages in countless plays—whose parallel in this sense it would be far to seek in Anglo-Saxon, German, or Italian literature. . . .

All the *amour* enquiry had better await another time.

491. **COLUMBIA UNIVERSITY CLUB, NEW YORK, 9:00 A.M., SATURDAY, DECEMBER 30, 1950.** Plan of Work [Excerpt].

. . . *Lope:* I shall be interested to see if I lose interest in this now that it's been shared and acknowledged and approved.[8] I suppose I ought to lose interest in it. I'm not likely to make any more dramatic discoveries; from now on—if I took up, for instance, plays from 1604–1608—it would be merely patient grad-student work. At all events during January I can only work on it during those seven days, January 4–11, when I shall be in Cambridge surrounded by my apparatus.

Palestrina: Maybe I have a good idea; maybe it's nothing: themes which Palestrina associated with the Virgin Mary (not merely formally but intimately) and which he introduced into the Masses

---

8. At the meeting of the Romance Section of the Modern Language Association in New York on December 28, 1950, Thornton Wilder had read a paper, "Aids toward Dating the Earlier Plays of Lope de Vega."

(even those not acknowledgedly based upon her motifs) precisely because she is only once alluded to in the Mass. Is the rising (and descending) triad of the *"Magnificat"* her Signature? Also is there a "lexicon" of themes held by Palestrina *in petto* which, originating from their obvious liturgical basis, recur to him in other connections for "symbolic" or allusional purposes? Preposterous though it is that I should enter this field—unacquainted with plain-chant, incapable of acquiring all one should know about the modes—nevertheless I think I shall push on into this a little farther. The best place to begin is to go back to the filiation: plain-chant *Audi Filia*; Goudimel's Mass based on it; Palestrina's *Missa Brevis* (did P. use portions of *Audi Filia* which Goudimel passed over? or did he *bring out* portions of *Audi Filia* which Goudimel had merely alluded to?); does *Missa Emendemus* use only that one theme from the *Missa Brevis*, and is there any particular reason for its use there? Since *Audi Filia* is a collect for "several Virgin-Martyrs" are there other allusions to that (or those) Feasts contained in the work? In the Masses on *"Je Suis Desheritée"* are there evidences that the (mighty secular) implications of the song are bound up in P.'s mind with the "abandonment" of the Virgin, etc.? . . .

492. DEEPWOOD DRIVE, [HAMDEN, CT.,] JANUARY 3, 1951. Stendhal's *Le Rouge et le Noir:* Preliminary.

The naiveté of authors asserting that at last they are writing the Truth. To the first edition (only!) Henri Beyle placed as epigraph: *"La vérité, l'âpre vérité. Danton."* I find quoted in Alain's *Stendhal* the following:

"Rome, 24 mai 1834. J'ai écrit dans ma jeunesse des Biographies (Mozart, Michel-Ange) qui sont une espèce d'histoire. Je m'en repens. Le vrai sur les plus grandes choses comme sur les plus petites me semble presque impossible à atteindre, du moins un vrai un peu détaillé. —M. de Tracy me disait: on ne peut plus atteindre au vrai il n'y a plus de vérité, en surcharge que dans le Roman. Je vois tous les jours davantage que partout ailleurs c'est une prétention. C'est pourquoi. . . ." (Quotation left thus suspended by Alain.)

The remark of M. de Tracy is important and the *vérité* of H.B. is indeed *âpre*; but assertions by Ibsen, Zola, anyone, that they are now for the first time penetrating into the True is of final value only to themselves—as a sort of tonic stimulant as they fashion their work.

The important thing is to ask: does their sense of communicating the True come from an immediate vision of it on their part, or from a rebound from or correction of some prevailing mode? I have talked elsewhere of the tiresome aspect of so much Irish genius—particularly Shaw's[9]—who because of the bellicose element in the Irish nature only discover what they think through the act of repudiating what someone else has thought. This makes for wit and energy as certainly as it makes for overstatement and personal ostentation.

The greatest expressions of truth do not have this air of competition with error. (Tolstoi, Jane Austen.) They keep their eyes fixed on the object as though the world were not loaded down with bad novels; they employ the current modes of novel-writing as though they found all the examples about them to be truthful.

Does H.B. in *Le Rouge et le Noir* indicate that he is out to annihilate the contemporary novel by calling our attention to the fact that he is being unprecedentedly truthful?

Yes, he does somewhat, but not distractingly so. Long tracts of the novel (in two volumes: Editions de Cluny, Paris, 1937. Preface and introduction by Henri Martineau) are an ironicization of *le roman reçu.* His use of clichés is a sort of sardonic bow to the *roman.* At one place it comes to the surface: describing the consummation of Julien's seduction of Madame de Rênal he says: *"Quelques heures après, quand Julien sortit de la chambre de Madame de Rênal, on eût pu dire, en style de roman, qu'il n'avait plus rien à désirer"* (vol. I, page 92).

Once one has remarked the astonishing effects that H.B. is able to obtain with extremely plain unornamented language (the famous style striving toward the Code Napoléon), a non-French reader must go on to be astonished at the extent to which the style is also frequently *enjolivé* and given to reflections of eighteenth-century-boudoir *mièvreries.* . . .

These phrases, however, are not used in irony; Julien's and Louise de Rênal's passion are not subjects for irony to H.B. In his

---

9. For Thornton Wilder's view of Shaw see his "George Bernard Shaw," printed in *American Characteristics and Other Essays* (1979) with incorrect date of composition—it should be 1951 instead of 1968.

eyes both these characters are *sublimes* (the great Stendhal word —his signature); even Julien's great mistake of playing the lover gauchely, as a duty, does not draw irony from the author, for H.B. is reserving young Julien for the great function of Italianate love. Nor is H.B. ironic about his *sots*; he hates them too forthrightly for irony. It is only toward this act of story-telling that he is ironic. . . . The fascination of the book (which is the fascination of H.B.'s nature) is that it is of emotion all compact, a hymn, a rhapsody which the author is trying to repress, to disavow, to "sit on," by attempting to recount it unemotionally.

Now the classic French way to be unemotionally involved in an action is to veil it in irony; but essential irony is denied to H.B. (I seem to remember that there is a great deal of irony in *La Chartreuse de Parme*—but are not Fabrice and La Sanseverina *sublimes?*) So he tries to disentangle himself from the impassioned involvement by his *âpre vérité*, by psychological analysis of a "cruel" nature. This merely means being stern toward those he loves. Even in the scene where Madame de Rênal, in remorse over her sin, sees Hell before her— which to H.B. must be a *niaiserie*—I hear no irony; that is merely his "knowledge" of how she would behave. And as for the lessons in cold calculation which Julien learns—those are stages in H.B.'s own life, or stages which he would have admired in himself; and H.B. does not hate H.B.

The astonishing thing about this "psychological" novel is, for us of today, that there is no inkling of a depth psychology. Here is the whole French constitutional repudiation of psychoanalysis. Julien, *tout court*, hates his father, and there is no mention of his mother. Louise de Rênal is an heiress, the product of her milieu, her reading, and her married life. Not only are there no ambiguities, no ambivalences, but there is no interstice whereby one can go beyond the author and insert them. The warfare between pride and passion (I am still considering only the first volume) is played within the realm of the rational, the totally observable.

Does this diminish the value of the novel?

Yes, it contributes largely to the sense that the book is an extended anecdote. In addition, it has its part in the increasing tiresomeness of H.B.'s hatred of the *sots*: it is a worldly book, and conduct is judged by how Paris (so constantly alluded to) would view the scene. Where the sublime characters have no mystery, the fools have none. Were it not for H.B.'s religion of spontaneous passion the book would be a mere *"Ecole de Parvenir."*

But I must wait and see how H.B. motivates Julien's attempted assassination of Madame de Rênal.

494. DEEPWOOD DRIVE. [HAMDEN, CT.,] JANUARY 18, 1951. The Poe Lecture: First Search.

Leaving aside one moment the question of whether or not Poe had a first-rate or a tenth-rate mind, let us inquire what kind of mind it was:

It was active. It does not even seem to have been subject to that predictable laziness of the speculative, inventive, "bright" type.

It was bold. One could have wished that, like Diderot's, it had ranged into a kind of "dry-run" nihilism; but that would have meant writing material which one could not publish.

Its curiosity (the greater part of its curiosity) was directed toward the morbid—and one divines that even E.A.P.'s attempt to describe, in *Eureka*, the beginning and end of all things was linked to his passion to understand the appalling disorders in his own nature. (One divines it from the fact that the overtures to his tales of horror constantly echo those cosmological speculations.)

It was in earnest. This has been much doubted and there are grounds for doubt; they proceed from the *magazinist* character of much of the work: the brisk adulation of nonentities; the mechanistic descriptions of the creative act, etc. But much in Poe must be read in the light of two things: his monetary necessities, and his resort to stimulants. Much that we attribute to bad taste, parochial culture, poor education, and shallow thinking should be charged instead to journalistic haste and to writing while drunk.

D. H. Lawrence thinks only of sex when portraying Poe[1]—at great length: Poe killing Virginia Clemm, and Virginia-Ligeia locked with Poe in a vast struggle of passion and will. There is no doubt that there was a serpents' nest of turbid eroticism in E.A.P.; but I should like to show that the intellect—as voracious passion—also drove and

1. In his *Studies in Classic American Literature* (1923).

harried him, and precisely as reaching out for order and air and explanation from the subterranean vaults (his recurrent image) of his nature. . . .

One does not demonstrate that a writer is great by showing how
remarkably he achieved a little artistic success through overcoming
fearful handicaps. But there is a greatness there. My business is to explain our sense of his greatness where so much of the material is obviously *manqué*. I am quite ready to acknowledge a greatness "in the
wings," *in posse*; we must, however, find it on the page.

Now to read [*The Narrative of*] *Arthur Gordon Pym*.

498. DEEPWOOD DRIVE, [HAMDEN, CT.,] SUNDAY NIGHT,
      JANUARY 21, 1951. A Spot of Work on
      Palestrina: *Missa Dies Sanctificatus*.

So . . . downtown to the Music School Library, which is kept
open on Sunday. There I sat and worked from five to nine—without
supper and without smoking—only stopping then because I could
feel that hunger was increasing the fatigue of my eyes. I went through
every one of Palestrina's *Mottetti* (every one in the still unfinished
Casimiri edition, which, God be praised, is in modern clefs), looking
for themes which Palestrina might have re-employed from work to
work. I was rewarded by finding one square to my purpose.

All such work as that—including the work on Lope—I do with
a most deplorable and wasteful lack of organization. For instance,
during these hours, I also collected first sketchy notes of the opening
phrases of some of the best known hymns of the Church, from reading
the *cantus* of his settings, the *Hymni Totii Anni*. These hymns I could
much more efficiently have found in some other volume, probably
then on the shelves about me. In the *long run* my search for repeated
themes, likewise, could best be done by attacking the problem with a
regular index on *fiches*. But no, I must go about these matters in my
own anti-systematic way. Perhaps, however, it is not so wasteful of
time and energy as it seems: I am alert to so many incidental things as
I go up page, down page. I learn these things not so much the "hard"
way as the discursive way; and not so much one aspect at a time, as
many aspects little by little, but simultaneously. It is thus that I shall
learn how to read neumes and how to recognize the modes and much
about the *fabrique* of this music. And this was the way I learned Latin

at the Chefoo School, beginning (so wastefully) with Horace's Odes; and this is the way I began learning French in Berkeley, from catalogues of gramophone records.

The tiny increment of today's acquisition was this:

The motet *Dies Sanctificatus*, like the Mass of the same name based upon it (and my whole interest is this problem of "based"), opens with a phrase clearly quoted from the *"Qui Tollis"* of the *"Agnus Dei II"* of the *Missa Brevis*. Where do the other themes in the motet come from? (The subject seems to me to be more important than any of the *Fachmänner* realize: How does Palestrina build a motet? What guides him in the selection of thematic material? Casimiri himself says that even the motet sequence on the Song of Songs is "based" on Gregorian themes. I don't think that's true. I suspect the motets were assembled from three sources: (1) Fragments of Gregorian chant; (2) Original themes invented for each motet *ad hoc*; and (3) Others chosen from the reservoir of musical themes floating about Church music and used in the "schools" and long since embedded in many pieces of music. It is these last that I am trying to collect, hoping that each one may be found also to carry its particular seasonal association and, even for the composer, its subjective association. And maybe it is one of these which I have now isolated.) . . .

Dunster House, [Harvard,] January 23, 1951.

Returning to Cambridge I find my text of the *Motet Dies Sanctificatus*. Stupidly I had missed seeing that the words of the *Motet* include the verset *"Haec dies quam fecit Dominus,"* and they are set to the very same theme but to a different contrapuntal arrangement of the voice-leading. The dates encourage us to believe that the *Motet Dies Sanctificatus* was written first (the volumes are separated by at least twenty-one years).

The text is: *"Haec dies quam fecit Dominus exultemur et laetemur . . . ."*

Is that verse—like *"Dies santificatus"*—a Christmas verse, or, as Protestants use it, merely a Sunday one?

At all events it possibly shows in Palestrina's mind an association with a "festal *dies*." If it turns out to be a Christmas verse I eagerly try to assemble a "background" for the other themes in the *Motet*—hoping to find them in an Advent context, and their possible occurrence in the Gregorian Antiphon. . . .

499.   DEEPWOOD DRIVE, [HAMDEN, CT.,] JANUARY 22, 1951.   Poe's
Eureka: Some Last Left-over Observations, Continued
from Entry 493.

. . . Is Poe trying to impress himself? Even if it could be proved
that the entire work is half-baked as physics and as metaphysics, is it
half-baked as *character?* Is Poe a trumpery fellow given to posing before us and before himself as a master mind and inevitably cheating at
it? No, he is truly *engaged:* the evenness of the style, the absence of
flashy diction, the clarity without condescension, the freedom (after
the opening) of conscious emphasis on the grandeur of his subject
matter, even the composure of the deliberate or implied allusions to
his own genius—all this reassures me that *he takes his powers for
granted* and does not feel under the necessity of reassuring himself.
Only in these last four pages where he announces that *he is God*
(conceding at the same time that so are we all) do we enter a new register: these probably spring from an anguished protest against death,
against extinction. The entire work preceding these pages may be a
tissue of ignorance, but it is not histrionic. It has the dignity of its
selfless application to its problem.

   Perhaps the chief thing to say about it is that it betrays an impressive urgency to find and express Unity. . . .

   It suddenly occurs to me that it may have been from this work
that Paul Valéry—who has written so large-mindedly about it[2]—
may have acquired his habit of underlining the guide-post phrases in
his prose.

   The American characteristic of *Eureka* is not that so brief and so
non-technical [a] cosmological treatise should have been written (rare
though that must be); nor that it should be written by one apparently
so limitedly trained for such a work; but that it should—the body of
it—be written in a tone which implies that the ideas are *self-evident.*
For an American there is no strain in the thoughts that project this
time and this place *toward* infinity.

   I presume that Diderot may have approached this type of speculation at some time. Even the idea of such pages by him throws a
light on Poe's; Diderot could not have sustained it long without re-
coiling from the audacity—he who had endless *audace* in re-invent-

────────────────────

   2. In his introduction to Poe's *Eurêka* (1923). The essay was reprinted as "Au sujet d'Eu-
réka" in his . . . *Variété* (1924).

ing our *moeurs*. Voltaire would have engaged in it only as polemics, though he could sustain a considerable gravity on great subjects. Lessing's flight would have stayed within the limits of the technical knowledge at his disposal. Only an American could feel that such a journey was natural—that is, was within the *rights* of any man— because vast simplifications are of this hemisphere.

Maybe it is one of the consequences of a protestant thought-world that any man has a *right* to explain the universe without being deferential to Authority.

503. QUEBEC, WEDNESDAY, JANUARY 31, 1951. The Growth of the Novela *Don Quixote*. Why the Manuscript of Cide Hamete Benengeli?

. . . Cervantes is inventing the novel while at the same time he is pretending to write a history.

But history and the novel are deadly enemies and are mutually destructive. When we read history we are furnished documents and objective data; the most we can do about them is to speculate concerning the inner life of the historical characters involved: we attempt to arrive at a truth *which we know we can never know*. The novel possesses and departs from precisely those truths; whether he is adequate to it or not, that is the novelist's proposal, his assumption, and the type of knowledge which is his stock in trade.

Now until Cervantes wrote this book there was no novel. There was the *récit*. What English word can we find for that? *Narration* covers any kind of account, historical or fictional. *Tale* implies a fictional narrative that is both brief and slight. Cervantes thought he was engaged upon a *récit* of which his models were the romances of chivalry on the one hand and the picaresque *novels* like *Lazarillo de Tormes* on the other.

In a *récit* one was permitted, by a mere convention, to furnish the thoughts, the prayers, the secret motivation of a character; but at most this was a rhetorical device; it was not there that the interest lay.

Cervantes shifted the interest; but he could not have done it had not the whole tide of the Western world's thinking been moving toward such a possibility. For the novel presupposes that the life of the mind is interesting because it is free. Cervantes's novel, like

Lope's plays, returns over and over again to the freedom of the will, the *albedrío*. It had long been one of the cornerstones of Catholic dogma; but even in religious thought there was as little freedom as in the social structure, as the Inquisition shows.

The field where everyman is most constantly aware of the freedom of his will is in the daily life, the thousands of minute occasions which fill every day and any day.

It is characteristic, then, that the first novel is also the first *récit* of homely things. The fact that it is a mock-heroic story throws this into a heightened light. The strength of the novel has always been that it is of the *intimate*: it reveals the hitherto unavowed truth that to any man his own toothache is more painful than the death of the entire Royal Family in one holocaust.

During the writing of *Don Quixote* Cervantes discovered that he could dare to write of humble beings as though *any person* could have for the reader the same kind of interest that the reader had for himself. The fact that that kind of interest can only engage us when we are conscious of another's freedom did not probably occur to him, although the recognition of freedom is the most outstanding of Cervantes's characteristics. Courage is admirable because it is chosen, idealism because it is uncoerced; Sancho [Panza] is most admirable because he is spontaneous.

Indeed, characters had displayed these qualities before Cervantes wrote; but heroes had been brave only by situation; rogues had carved out their advancement and peasants had been spontaneous on such given occasions as the structure of stories had dictated. Their actions were seen from without; all their actions had been viewed as reactions. In this first novel we move inside the characters; we are present at the springs of action. It is not the external event which justifies the narration but the life within the mind of the protagonists—as is shown by the Adventure of the Fulling Mills, where precisely nothing happens.

To read the first half of the First Part of *Don Quixote*, then, is to watch Cervantes discovering that the interest of a fiction does not have to depend on any external importance offered by its happenings—neither on surprise, nor suspense, nor novelty, nor complicated intrigue—the long consecrated structural rhetoric of narration.

This constituted a new freedom (just as it was so new a register—so new a mode of describing the human situation) and I think that Cervantes could not believe his good fortune. "Can it be possible that I am permitted to run on this way?" By the time he has reached the Second Part he is all at his ease; in the First he is continually pinching himself. . . .

It is not only for variety that he introduces the interpolated stories. He wishes to make sure that he is holding the reader's attention; and what better way than to furnish them the kind of thing which they have shown themselves as having previously enjoyed? Cervantes likewise had to make sure that he would make money by the book; the hurly-burly at the inn, the nocturnal visit of Maritornes, is in large part there to ensure it.

Rereading the book, for the first time in Spanish, I am astonished to see how much closer the interpolated stories and the "pastoral" episodes are to the main current of the novel; how Cervantes's "style" and the genius of the Spanish language itself can almost amalgamate apparently irreconcilable modes; but I find one passage where the author betrays an appalling concession to dead convention—and which serves to indicate to me how anxious he may have been as to whether his story was succeeding or not. It contains two speeches in which the characters inform one another of things they know already—that stupidest procedure of Victorian farces: chapter 13, two friends of the late Grisóstomo have brought his body to the mountainside for burial.

"*Mira bien, Ambrosio, si es éste el lugar que Grisóstomo dijo, ya que queréis que tan puntualmente se cumpla lo que dejó mandado en su testamento.*"

"*Este es,*" *respondió Ambrosio,* "*que muchas veces en él me contó mi desdichado amigo la historia de su desventura. Allí, me dijo él, que vió la vez primera a aquella enemiga mortal del linaje humano, . . . y aquí, en memoria di tantas desdichas, quiso él que lo depositasen en las entrañas del eterno olvido.*"

Why did that not set his teeth on edge—he, glorious master of the subtlest inflections of natural speech? Not only because until the very end of his life was he infatuated with the *pastoral* and the *caballería* modes—that one can understand, deplorable though it is. But this Marcela episode is not truly in the *pastoral* vein; it is half-and-half; and both preceding and following these two speeches his tact has managed to "entrain" us into accepting it even in the vicinity of the inerrable conversations of Knight and Squire. No, I take it to be evidence of Cervantes's "nervousness," that anxiety that what he is doing *may* be not only outlandish but *boring*.

Another example of this insecurity seems to me to be his repeated explanation—as to obtuse children—of his main *donnée*. As far advanced as chapter 18, he arrests the narrative to explain Don Quixote's delusion. . . . Now if the reader has to have that made clear to him on the sixtieth page of the book, that reader will have long fallen by the wayside; and Cervantes must know it; but he is working in such new fields that he cannot be sure of this secondary matter of being in relation to the reader. All he knows is that he is overjoyed by the new capacities, forces, which are pouring up through him, and only from time to time does he find himself uneasy and bewildered as to whether anyone else may share his enjoyment.

[Quebec,] the Next Morning

It was late last night and I was too tired after so long a siege of work to deduce the very consequence for which all that had been the preamble and the preparation:

Why does Cervantes feel the need of introducing (abruptly, at the beginning of chapter 9) his dependence on an Arab manuscript?

Why it was abrupt we know: to give mock suspense to the conflict with the Biscayan.

Why it was *there* we know: to open weightily what he thought then was his Part Two.

Why it was Arab? A deeper knowledge of all Cervantes's work would be necessary to answer that; although he says that the Arabs are addicted to lying and although he refers to this Cide Hamete Benengeli as a *galgo*, I suspect that he shares with Lope (here enter again his references to Abindarraez y Narvaez) a half-avowed idealization of the Moors. Were not the greater part of his sufferings in Algeria at the hands of renegades? Let us trace his journey up to this point, in respect to his sense of authority in writing the story:

He starts out by implying he is transcribing from a variety of historians. . . . These authors are twice reported as disagreeing among themselves. In fact the whole background of authority becomes more and more shaky. . . . Chapter 2 again invokes our several sources. . . . Thereafter he gives up all wavering and plunges into the preterite tense, which in Spanish seems to have a unique authority and finality.

Which of all the liberties which he was beginning to apprehend as the novelist's point of view astonished him most? That we must ascertain later when they have all come into possession. All we can ask now is: which struck him first and made him most uneasy? I think we have his own answer:

(1) That it was all in his own hands and he could do, in a new field, anything. The Romance-writers, to be sure, did, lavishly, a preposterous Anything; but the new field was that he could do anything in reporting the immediate life of every day. And that:

(2) He could extend himself into the most unimportant details of his characters' thoughts, behavior, and environment.

The evidence for this is found in his description of the kind of source he felt in need of when he went searching for the Cide Hamete manuscript: he wanted one like those which the Sages were accustomed to furnish for the Paladins: "*que no solamente escribían sus hechos, sino que pintaban sus más mínimos pensamientos y niñerías, por más escondidas que fuesen. . . .*" That phrase does not really describe the romances of chivalry: they went to enormous lengths, to be sure, and lingered long enough on certain types of details, even though all the details were unreal. A few pages later Cervantes is describing the woodcut on the new-found manuscript; it shows the Knight and the Squire and "Otras alguenas menudencias *había que advertir; pero todas son de poca importancia, y que no hacen al caso a la verdadera relación de la historia, que ninguna es mala como sea verdadera.*"

There is the crux:

Cervantes felt himself to be drifting out into the open seas—new seas—where you could tell at will the innumerable little humble unimportant details of real life and of the subjective life, and if they were true maybe they were not unimportant—at least oneself was the judge of that.

To do this he felt the need of support. Not the fiction that there were a variety of conflicting and fallible formal histories, but that there was one—one, observe, not written by a Spaniard—and one of a new kind, one, full of *menudencias*.

The first novelist stands where so many novelists have stood: bewildered at the possibility of telling life's truth as though it were to be told for the first time. And that links him to our course's second novelist—to Stendhal placing as epigraph to *Le Rouge et le Noir* the words: "*La vérité, l'âpre vérité*" (and Stendhal, on May 24, 1834, in Rome, recalling the words of M. de Tracy: "*On ne peut plus atteindre au vrai que dans le roman*"). And Cervantes's uneasy self-consciousness about any success he may arrive at in this furnishing of the "truth" links him with the misgivings of Stendhal, who placed at the end of his novel the words *"To the Happy Few."*

504. QUEBEC, THURSDAY NIGHT, FEBRUARY 1, 1951. Herman
      Melville: First Outlines, and Skeleton-Plan of
      The Confidence-Man.

Current criticism of American literature is full of *choses tues:* one would scarcely gather from it that most of the time Melville is an atrocious writer. Into some later entry I must bring samples of the many kinds of [the] falseness that is omnipresent in his work, not least in *Moby-Dick* itself. . . .

We confront a case which from one point of view has something in common with that of Emily Dickinson. H.M.'s concept of what literature should look like, should sound like, was fixed, arrested, *jelled*, very early, and all the impulses that arrived later in life from the reading of the world's masterpieces had to be re-assimilated in order to be integrated with this early and imperious model; and all these models were bad. *Pierre* is a very remarkable attempt to externalize an inner "being-lost-and-hunted-in-a-labyrinth"; but long passages of the first half could have been written by a soulful Richmond librarian, and many portions of the latter half by a sedulous imitator of novels about the doomed heir of the Vere de Veres.

But worse than the fact that many pages betray a crippling infatuation with bad models is the presence of false emotion and the evidence of H.M.'s appearing to have had a very ordinary mind. Both combine to make "Poor Man's Pudding and Rich Man's Crumbs" a howling exhibit of bathos; as is "The Two Temples"; as is the last half of "The Piazza." And long stretches of *The Confidence-Man* are not the biting indictments of human society which they obviously claim to be, but are immature sarcasms which even the talentless have outgrown.

All this must be said and analyzed before we get down to the great work [*Moby-Dick*]; and to show how perilously the great work came near to misfiring.

At the bottom of it all is an extremely disordered man, living in an age and environment which offered him nothing he could understand except the vastness of its life-engagement—and that he misunderstood. He was a man whose inner life, as [a] tormenting puzzle, so occupied him that he had little attention to give to the outer—hence the ludicrously bad ear for "conversation."

Nor must we forget that his recourse to the exploitation of symbol (his only salvation as a serious writer) took also the form of the sly and devious game . . . in "The Tartarus of Maids" and "I and My Chimney."

Now to *The Confidence-Man*.

The literary device is superb—that of introducing a concept as a succession of characters "in masquerade." The only thing that resembles it—and there, too, it has ended in failure—is that in Jean Cocteau's play *Les Chevaliers de la Table Ronde*.

But with towering stupidity Melville has failed to see what his subject is, and with ox-like obstinacy has continued to pursue his tiresome misunderstanding through all those flagging pages. Obviously, it is not, as so many commentators seem to believe, an extended satire on the doctrinaires and nostrum-sellers and hustlers of his time and of all times, nor even on the advocates of brotherly love and indiscriminate philanthropy. It is about Faith; like *Don Quixote*, it is about Faith. (Since this became clear to me I have returned to the book and examined scores and scores of its pages and have not found that word used *once*, synonym though it could be for the endlessly harped on word, *confidence*; it may be, and would be interesting to demonstrate, that Melville sedulously eschewed the word.)

Nothing of value can be done in this world without faith—from making an omelette to fighting the Civil War. That's true. And faith can be said to [be] affirming a confidence and acting upon it before *any* evidence has been supplied that the commitment is justified. That is true. Chapter 4 of *Don Quixote* (in which Cervantes probably had the worship of the Virgin Mary in mind) squarely expresses this "mental action" in novelistic terms: "Concede that Dulcinea is the most beautiful woman in the world." "*Señor caballero*, we don't know her; show her to us. . . ." "If I showed her to you, of course you'd be able to confess so obvious a truth. *La importancia está en que sin verla lo habéis de creer, confesar, afirmar, jurar y defender. . . .*"

All of this, and every time, in a score of illustrations, Melville exhibits always as faith in a *newly-met stranger*. Confidence in a newly-met stranger is certainly one of the exemplifications of faith, but it is the one which would least and last occur to most people. It is

true that the successive avatars of our confidence-man present medi-
cines, business investments, charitable causes, but always the emphasis is thrown on the confidence which men should feel toward a
fellow-man; and that is not Faith, that is Judgment.

I do not think it is difficult to see why Melville got entrapped in
this little narrow illustration of the problem of Faith. One, he was
afraid to so much as glance at the religious implications of the problem, though in the widest sense of the word *religion* that is what it
finally is. So he is thrown back on the social, the merely gregarious
implications. And those he cannot exploit because in the last analysis
Melville knows nothing about gregarious life. Time after time we
come up against this fact. We simply don't believe in Ishmael's "marriage" to Queequeg, nor Ishmael's worship of his idol; nor do we really believe Billy Budd's successive reactions to Claggett's persecu-
tion. All that comes from the same world in which the Merrymusk
family promptly dies as soon as their cock ceases crowing in "Cock-a-
Doodle-Doo!" That's the world ordered by symbolic images, and
Melville can do great things in it; but he cannot do them every time,
and in *The Confidence-Man* he seems to be powerless to set them
moving.

510. **WIDENER LIBRARY, [HARVARD,] FEBRUARY 16, 1951.** Toward the
Poe Lecture.

This is by so much the hardest of my tasks—not only because as
always I know nothing about it, but because I like Poe for reasons I
cannot explain. And my attempt to explain this *why* may lead me into
the most awful nonsense.

I think that the line I may take will be: that people don't read
enough Poe (out-staring the fact that I am a hypocrite in so saying)
and that when one has made the circuit of all Poe, every fragment of
Poe takes on a different color: that when one has travelled widely in
the Poe mind one returns to the stories of the horror-struck imagination and finds that their center of gravity is not what one first believed
it to be; and similarly with those of ratiocination; similarly with the
critical and cosmographical works.

That the mind of Poe is constantly present to us in the style of
Poe: and that the style of Poe is either controlled or uncontrolled. . . .

When it is uncontrolled we know that we are in the presence of Poe drunk or Poe under drugs: . . . bad Poe is not merely negligence nor journalistic haste nor half-baked vulgarity, but Poe ill. And in this sense bad Poe is not Poe and does not concern us. (All this referring solely to the prose; the poetry being an entirely different matter.)

That Poe is therefore a controlled writer of a very high degree of control. And that control is the subject of our interest and admiration because we can see that it is not merely a correctness and a lucidity—as with an Addison or a----Washington Irving, but it is *charged*, it is in tension: it is not only controlled but controlling: it is always imposing its order on passionate material, on vast and important material. Poe cannot bring himself to attend to anything less than Thrones, Dominations, and Powers.

Even in the few excursions we have into the light and the diverting—such as the *ortolan* of the "Duc de l'Omelette," and the little French *vaudeville* about the man who married his great grandmother ("The Spectacles")—their failure proceeds not from their banality but from the irruption into them of what we would now call *surrealism*, very badly managed though it is, the ghost of the Vast Irrational that shows its face in the daughters of successive generations who married Froissarts-Moissarts-Croissarts, and the sheer hideousness not of an old lady berouged but of the English she wrote.

We dare not say that Poe *always* maintained his control even in the material we have admitted as Poe, and occasionally we are confronted with bombast and bathos; but the greatness of Poe is that he insisted on confronting the most dangerous aspects of our human passions and the boldest reaches of our speculations about the human situation and that he forced from himself this style—which is the state of mind—of an objective gaze.

I am not interested in this charge that because he was the son of actors he was continuously and primarily histrionic. Poe did not summon up these horrors in order to be caught by us in a pose of fear, grief, valor, or brilliance: those who have read only "Berenice," or "Facts in the Case of M. Valdemar," or even "MS. Found in a Bottle" might think so. Poe is a real Lion-Tamer, not a Histrion among edentate beasts.

So I might begin the lecture.

Then go back and show the childhood. . . . Wherever we look there is horror.

Against a vindictive and mean-souled father a growing boy can straighten his shoulders; he knows his enemy, and his battle takes pride from the kinship—but Poe was not son, but dependent, and the Oedipus complex was atrocious not tragic; sordid not magnetic.

Mrs. Allan had to stand between these two—watch the terrific force of Poe's need to project his love and watch her husband's eyes on her: every movement of her love for the little boy augmented her husband's hatred for him.

If this young boy had not been the Intellect (writer and artist)—and intellects are not *made* by suffering; he was an intellect first—what would his story have been? I don't think he would have been a wastrel or a drunkard or an eccentric ne'er-do-well. I think he would probably have been a sort of Mr. Allan: a powerful mean man, charged with love and all the love poisoned at the source and destructive. There's a great deal of that around; it goes into business.

But in every degree of Poe's suffering a large portion of it went to fortify his mind.

. . . Maybe intellect is alone produced by suffering in infancy. But all wretched babies do not become intellects. The baby Goethe breaking the windowpanes. Anyway, Goethe and Poe became intellects and the forcing-house of intellect is suffering and the process is: to explain to yourself why you suffer. And that soon involves why people are cruel and why people are cold—why are people?—and once the momentum of questions is started *why* streams through the firmament: why does the sun rise? why does the ocean feel the pull of the moon? why do I ask why?

So we have Poe suffering and Poe inquiring.

And then we add Poe's impulses to cruelty: murderous thoughts—suppressed; but released (1) in dreams, (2) under intoxications, and (3) in writing.

Poe was a great criminal and whom did he murder? He murdered himself.

511. **WIDENER LIBRARY, [HARVARD,] FEBRUARY 16, 1951.** Edgar Allan Poe and Death.

I have never felt the knowledge that we shall die—the realization of it—to be a very real presence in many people. For most it is something they gradually learn as likely to happen to other people; to the young it has no more force than the all but preposterous notion that they shall some day have white hair.

It enters the consciousness of a few young people, however, in one form: not by seeing the dead, not by living among the dying, not by hearing themselves threatened with death by guardians or warned of it by clergymen; but by the fact of their hating someone. They learn death by force of wishing someone dead.

It is often said that love brings with it its shadow death; but that is so for the mature: to lovers it is increasingly clear that only death can separate them: hence all lyric poetry rings with the emphatic cry that death cannot, can *not* separate them.

The child Poe hated someone *to death* and then promptly felt all the burden of his guilt as assassin. . . .

So a pattern begins to emerge: the subject of Poe's stories is that *secrets will out.* . . .

Now I am almost ready to begin the lecture and to give over these notes.

So we have the criminal underground, where he is assassin.

We have the formation of the Intellect as analyzer, as safety-raft from the sea of anguish.

Now, as victim: Poe did not indict God, the "order of things," for the misery in which he found himself. He felt himself to be so wicked that it never occurred to him to put the blame elsewhere: un-til: until in the euphoric close of *Eureka*, he identifies God with him-self—God the Great Author, the Great Plot-Maker.

Now I must find some samples of the objectivity of his prose (which, of course, is not present in strength in the stories written in the first person—where he is dramatizing the victim not the detec-tive—and most of the stories are in the first person).

I can only glance at the literary criticism—only to emphasize the drive to affirm a unity.

Still, to be sure, I have not proven a high quality for Poe. This could still be a description of how a mediocre writer found his way to-ward his material. That question I must beg; nor have I for these notes aborded the central intention: what forms would the Investiga-tory Genius take in the United States?

513. COPLEY-PLAZA HOTEL, BOSTON, SUNDAY MORNING, FEBRUARY [18.]
1951. Toward the Greek Drama Lecture:[3] The Doctrine of the
Unique Occasion.

So I begin with three illustrative images of theatre experience:
the actor-spectator in a Noh play; the Capulet ballroom; the scandal at
the first performance of the *Medea*.

The Greek repudiation of the Unique Thing. The command
against portraiture in statues; even Greek erotic, where you loved not
so much the individual as the God-like mood which had taken possession of you.

All this I take to be also its opposite: the delirious appreciation
of each moment of consciousness, particularly when it is associated
with the high noon of youth and vigor. The one sin which cannot often be laid to the Greeks is *accedia* (Achilles sulking in his tent; the
reproach to Paris: "Spurn not the gifts of Aphrodite").

The unhistorical Greeks: their time-sense, therefore, so prepos-
terously different from our own—the frantic emphasis on the now;
the submissive acceptance of the great duration. And all between an
amorphous lapse—the treaty stone: "Athens will be at peace for one
hundred years from now"—and they forgot to affix the date! The vast
wheel of time not present to them as eternity, but as the uncountable
repetitions of crops and of star-movement.

All right—when then a thing happened, *i.e.*, happened *once* in
all time, it presented an absorbing problem.

It was the peculiar character of the Greek despair that the assertion of the self—the individual I—was both intoxicating and unimportant. (*Digression-illustration*: I have always felt that the murderous horror of the audience at the moment when Aeschylus seemed
to allude to the Eleusinian Mysteries and had to cling to the altar to
save himself, was not only that he revealed a cult-secret but that he
seemed to *allude to his private life*—so Aristophanes' ridicule of Euripides.) And the tragedy ran the constant danger of putting the emphasis on one moment in an individual life. So that every individual's
actions had to be freighted with as great an element of generalization
as possible: they were *hubris*, or they illustrated the moral laws reflected in the hereditary doom, or they were figures in a ritual cult.

---

3. Given to the Harvard Classics Club, Monday, February 19, 1951.

And if Philoctetes or Ajax or even Orestes begin more and more to press into life as individuals, you can always make the *unique moments* somehow more dignified, more *representative*, by giving them that weight of agony and that removal from the quotidian which is frenzy and madness.

But, of course, the converse is also true. Every representation of the individual as a unique person was ridiculous, was highly comical. I have always assumed that it was already excruciatingly funny to see a citizen on the stage: even before he spoke or moved you died laughing—at the towering disproportion between the High Platform of Theatre and one preposterous little Greek. Hence it is that the Old Greek Comedy entirely lacks those two things which have been the mainstay of theatre in every other age: the young leading man and the young leading woman. Leaving aside the whole matter of the fact that the Greeks—alone of all the races of the West—would not have been interested in seeing them fall in love, an admirable young man could not interest them because he would have been, as a stage figure, ridiculous. The Guard in the *Antigone* who must arrest the heroine is not an undifferentiated soldier, he is not even an undifferentiated messenger, he is twice ridiculous: once, because he is a dim-witted yokel holding that debate with his feet, and secondly, he is a man who cannot be conceived of as living in myth.

That this degree of abstraction could not hold is evident; as is the enormous scandal caused by Euripides' movement toward individuation and the approach of the New Comedy. Just as Pindar said that when money enters athletics the great thing which is Greece will be at an end, so Aristophanes cries over and over again: "When Euripides introduces the quotidian on the stage we will have degenerated from our fathers."

Now where in our thought-world do we get the feeling for the minute specifications of individuality, the acceptance of the interest and dignity of unique occasions?

From two things: (1) The Christian dispensation, whereby every individual is of vast importance in the eyes of God and, derived from it: (2) The doctrine of progress. No two individuals have ever been the same, no two happenings have ever been the same; but they are not haphazard in their differential: there is a relation between them all, and that is the forward movement of society. The death of Joan of Arc is a milestone. The repudiation of Falstaff is a tiny increment in the moral development of a prince. The plays of Chekhov are

plays about sloth—but they ring with a half-ironic, half-agonized assertion that the world will get better and better.

Spaniards: totally exempt from all tincture of progress. Every
soul repeats the apocalyptic drama of the universe. They love to see
the picturization of the repetitions of this vast drama. That is what ritual is: the reminder of the unchanging.

Actuality is what is left when possibility has emerged from necessity. Of the factors, each age feels the emphasis differently: the
ritual-minded emphasize necessity = the Greeks and the Spaniards:
fate and doom; the unique occasion is mere illustration of the general
invariant emphasized by terror or pity. Possibility = the modern
Western world: liberty and progress; the unique occasion tremulous
with what A. N. Whitehead called the injection of the teleological
movement of the universe into every moment of consciousness; etc.

(Well, well—that's not very good. I had hoped to move a step
forward, but my goaded existence has impeded it. However, let us
hope that the above remarks will be sufficient for the occasion tomorrow night. And now I turn back to Poe and to Cervantes's style.)

514. DEEPWOOD DRIVE, [HAMDEN, CT.,] FEBRUARY 22, 1951. Toward
Don Quixote: Lecture Six.

Oh, never again shall I propose to discuss *Don Quixote* before
listeners who cannot follow it in Spanish. Even reading in my Spanish
I feel moment by moment that I am missing its flower—especially in
the Second Part, where its intrinsic qualities strain toward an ever
greater refinement. What strike me now are:

(1) *The Germ Idea.* During the ten years that have elapsed Cervantes has been reassured: it works; this new thing the *novel* does enwrap, does engage readers. All his fears are unnecessary; no need of
interpolated stories, no fear (on the contrary!) that the conversations,
and particularly Sancho's "running-on" might weary readers. So he
launches out again largely—very largely—giving rein. He sees that
there is much more to explore and exploit in Sancho, but the Knight
and the *caballería andante* require a new note or a heightened value:
so he introduces a far more artful, intelligent, and colorful *provoker*
in the *bacheller* Sanson Carrasco. But Cervantes's meditations about
the subject have altered over the years. Part One dealt with the

spells, delusions, and illusions which circumstances can cast over us: "things" are not what we thought they were; events do not turn out as we hoped. Part Two will treat of the deceptions which human beings play upon one another, with or without intention. This is the book of *burlas*; but the *burladoras* are *burlardos*, over and over again. We are already astonished in chapter 11: Don Quixote comes upon the cart filled with actors dressed as Death, the Devil, the Angel. In Book One he would have been swept off into some frenzied fancy; here a few words of explanation suffice. We rub our eyes; he is amenable to explanation. But it is explanations that will henceforth be his downfall: Sancho has just explained that of the three *labradoras* one is Dulcinea. And this is followed by the Knight of the Mirrors: we are in for illusions motivated by mind: puppets, and Maese Pedro's monkey, and so on. With this new realm the criticism of the world becomes more searching, and we find:

(2) *Religion*. Yes, after long resistance I agree with Américo Castro.[4] Cervantes is not tilting face-to-face with the religious, *i.e.*, the Roman-Catholic, requirement for belief. He is "running" a parallel. I cannot make up my mind as to whether he is totally aware of it. It is so dangerous a game that it is hard to believe that he is unaware of it; and yet he might continually justify it to himself as a distinguishing between what is essential for belief and what is not. It should perhaps be noted that the asseverations of submission to Mother Church increase, yet note how apparently insignificant, how remote from essential doctrine [they are]. . . .

(3) *Conversation*. Ever more weight is thrown upon the conversation. *What they talk about* still flows inexhaustibly from knight errantry and the situations dependent upon it, but more and more it is *conversation of character*. Ever-shifting situations furnish new points of departure but are not the principal factor. Astonishing is the extent to which Cervantes deprives himself of the aid to a novel's conversation which is furnished by indications of gesture, glance, pause, and that *beat of time* afforded by an explanatory clause. All the more must he characterize by cadence and by idiosyncrasy. That he does this transcendentally I can see, but *what* I must be missing! We miss enough of such modelling in the scenes in Dame Quickly's tavern [in *King Henry IV*] (it is not enough to speak English); how much more

---

4. His *El pensamiento de Cervantes* (1925).

through my newly acquired Spanish. . . . Yet I am rich and happy enough with what I do get. . . .

But to teach it!

And I am not only talking of the *Tonfall* of the conversations. How the whole experience has renewed the realization that all books live by the *voice of their author*, that all books are *personality*. I'd rather not believe that's so; I'd rather believe that mind has no personality. But there it is: *Le Rouge et le Noir*—no paragraph is Flaubert or Balzac; and *Moby-Dick* is Melville, all too Melville.

516. DEEPWOOD DRIVE, [HAMDEN, CT.,] FEBRUARY 24, 1951. *Don Quixote*, Again and Again.

After a night's sleep and early breakfast downtown, I come back to warning myself to keep my consciousness always open to the Main Thing: a man mad about Perfect Justice, *i.e.*, perfectly insisting that there is a Perfect Justice—and perfectly insisting that the existence of Perfect Justice is maintained through the co-existence of Perfect Beauty. All that falls short of these two conditions is due to base enchantments.

Then to make this real to my class . . . I rub their noses . . . in the apparent relativity of all things, the *saleté* of life, of the limbo between hope, cynicism, and despair of Mrs. Hawkins, her shopping bag, and her three squalling brats.

When the Duchess asks Don Quixote whether Dulcinea really exists, the Knight must declare that "Only God knows . . . whether she is a creation of dream or not—she belongs to those things which a man cannot explore to the last realization." Yet these perfections must be, or Don Quixote cannot exist. And indeed he dies when he emerges into our "abject truth."

All this I must maintain in my mind and not allow myself to stumble, searching for smaller and merely literary needlework in the successive episodes. I must see how this concept so floods through Cervantes's mind that he does not have to erect systematic "variations" upon it: it hovers, it is the light in which the novel is played, it stares us in the face every moment that we see the Knight—so that Cervantes can produce episode after episode of varying degrees of epiphany—*spieland*—without imposing on his material the rigors that so tiresomely and literally I keep looking for.

521. [MASSACHUSETTS GENERAL] HOSPITAL, [BOSTON, MASS.,][5]
      GOOD FRIDAY, MARCH 23, 1951. Varia: The "I"-Narrator
      as Persona: Are Shakespeare and Dickens Honest
      Reporters of the Loathsome? What Is the Real Subject
      of *Great Expectations?*

Well, I shall start putting down some of the accumulated notions of these days and nights, *telles quelles,* insufficiently supported
and surrounded though they are, always reminding myself that this
Journal is not a collection of digested finalities but a technique for
stimulating idea-manufacture and for maintaining the momentum of
idea-production. —So:

(1) *The "I"-Narrator.* Hundreds of thousands must have read
Great Expectations without remarking that the Pip who recounts the
story is a very different person from the Pip who is its protagonist.
Pip-the-hero is quite a clear characterization: a humorless conscience-
ridden but likeable young man, nowhere near as contaminated by
snobbery as the narrative claims (therein lies a problem I must confront in a moment). Even the lapse of years, together with the acquisition of age and experience, cannot remotely cover the discrepancy
between Philip Pirrip, Esq. and the narrator of the book. Pip could
never have thought or observed the mixture of stylized fancy and realistic trenchancy that gives us the description of the trip around
Newgate or even the *"trockene"* observation underlying the portrait
of the lawyer Mr. Jaggers. In the same way, "Ishmael" of *Moby-Dick,*
the intermittently mawkish young man of Byron propensities, who
twice falls asleep on his high-perched watch, . . . is not the same
young man who furnishes us the incomparably clear, active, and zest-
ful descriptions of the various technical processes involved in the
sperm-whale fishery.

These discrepancies are illogicalities and as such can be

---

5. A slipped disk in March forced Thornton Wilder to spend four weeks in hospital.

counted blemishes. What shall we say of them? That the novel—
imagined life—is a form of such vitality that it can render such incon-
gruities negligible? Yes, but expressed differently: the blank check of
omniscience accorded to the imaginative narrator is so generously
large that we understand that the Dickens-mind and the Melville-
mind are the true narrators, and that the Pip-narrator and the
Ishmael-narrator are merely subsidiary fragments of it—temporary
and half-realized *personae* in whom we do not essentially "believe."

(2) Here is a large subject I can only "flush from the covey" now.
In literature don't even the great masters prevent us from seeing vice
as vice? This bewilderment arose while I was watching *Henry IV,
Part Two* (though it had been a bother to me for years: Sarah Gamp
[in Dickens's *Martin Chuzzlewit*] as a delight, rather than as a pesti-
lential dispenser of germs, dirt, and agony; Miss Bates [in Jane Austen's *Emma*] as an "observation" rather than as a social nuisance). The
new-crowned Henry V repudiates Falstaff not as a companion who
helped him waste his time and as an instigator of occasional dissipation, but as an enemy of the good and as an emblem of vice. But
where is the vice in those tavern-scenes? Vice is the destruction of the
human; its end is the loathing of others and the loathing of self; its
representation is reciprocal vituperation and the passion to degrade
others to the animal level. Its outward semblance is sloth, dirt, and
indifference to any activity above the animal. All that is glanced at in
the Henry IV plays (and I must promptly reread them), but its real
statement is covered over by charm, by dazzling word play, and by
the author's lending of his boundlessly supra-animal mental vitality.
Shakespeare simply *will not furnish the data of vice.*

Similarly in *War and Peace* Pierre whispers to the Masonic rhe-
tor that his besetting temptation is "women." Twice, Tolstoi thereafter tells us that Pierre falls into his old dissipations; but nowhere
does Tolstoi—with all those dimensions at his disposal—stop to illustrate, to dramatize, to real-ize this important element in Pierre's spiritual life.

Dickens and wickedness: the same thing—even of that passage
presenting Newgate as a flower garden.

Let's put it this way: most great writers (Dante a striking exception) will not release in force what they know of degradation; what
they do is to furnish intimations to the knowing, to those whose experience of life is capable of catching the allusion; they will not initiate

the innocent; for them (the innocent) the detestable and the loath-some are veiled in mitigations of the literary art.

(3) What is the subject of *Great Expectations?* G. K. Chester-ton, in a preface (Everyman's edition), reminds me again of how— just as many omnivorous readers read in order to stop up the springs of thought, frantically search for ideas in their reading because they are afraid to search in the only place where ideas may spring, in themselves—so certain writers use all that is flashy and immediately enthusiastic in their minds in order to spare themselves the more difficult *plongées*. These last are copious writers, and I think it can be shown that they belong to that curious company the diligent-lazy or the procrastinating-indefatigable. They write only by some outward propulsion (editorship; need of money; or the vanity of competition, clubs, and circles), and they write their paper in a whirlwind frenzy at the last minute before publication. In this preface Chesterton says that *Great Expectations* illustrates, in Pip, "how circumstances can corrupt men." Horsefeathers!

Pip, on Magwitch's money, becomes a gentleman, and he ne-glects to visit Joe Gargery's house by the forge. . . . Dickens in the Veneerings shows us what snobbery is; Pip's case of it is very mild in-deed and he affords us no illustration of corruption. He is an almost exemplary young man. . . . After a first revulsion from his convict benefactor he becomes a most tender companion of his last days. No, his sin is that in his heart he was ashamed of the rusticity of Joe and Biddy and that he did not regularly return to stay with them for the weekend. This Dickens deplores, but if Dickens were not in a cloud of emotion about something else, he would be quick to acknowledge that there is a limit to the gratification which can arise from the re-peated meetings of old friends who have become widely separated in station and in interests; friendship is fostered by the multiplicity of as-sociations, interests, and activities that are shared by both. Pip re-turning every fortnight to Joe's inglenook would have been reduced finally to mere gazing at Joe and Biddy in silence. And the same "re-duction to silence" applies to even whatever letters might have been exchanged between them.

What then is the subject of the book and whence comes the evi-dent emotion that is shaking its author?

The subject of the book is the effort of older persons to uproot young *protégés* out of their natural environment and to force upon them a life-pattern of the older persons' choosing. This Magwitch does to Pip and Miss Havisham to Estella.

Dickens's emotion is a transferred emotion, and I think it can be shown that Dickens may have been ruefully thinking of the change he had made in the life of . . . young Ellen [Ternan], his quasi-mistress whom he "set up" and at whose hands he met the whole sorry drama of all benefactor-*protégée* relationships—maladjustment, fretfulness, ingratitude, idleness, regret, bitterness, and frustration.

I shall not be able to lecture to my class on this novel; this will probably be the last time I shall consider it, so here I put a few notions that were beginning to form:

Dickens had had a fearful childhood . . . , so fearful that he wished never to look at those terrors again directly, picture them in their unrelieved atrocity. Yet he was too honest to expunge them entirely. So he built up an elaborate mechanism for glancing at them skimmingly, and that mechanism is *humor*.

Monsters are deprived of one-third their horror. I have shown to myself by an *explication de texte* how the reader—during the opening encounter of Pip with the convict in the churchyard—is subtly reassured that we are not face-to-face with the last horrors. And so throughout: Dickens longs for the Happy Issue to be accorded to all the characters he loves. He seems to be saying: "I have known cruelty and bestiality; I have been able to endure it for myself; but I shall do everything in my power—not short of a little lying, but as little as I can manage with—to ensure that these good people never know what I knew."

The last quarter of the book is almost totally devoid of the characteristic Dickens genius. He is busy showing how he can tie up knots and display an ingenuity in plot-construction: Magwitch is Estella's father; his lifelong enemy is Miss Havisham's faithless betrothed, etc. . . .

It is distressing to leave the book thus when there are so many other avenues to pursue—all that can remain is love and homage.

523. [MASSACHUSETTS GENERAL] HOSPITAL, [BOSTON, MASS.,] EASTER
MORNING, MARCH 25, 1951. The Norton Book: Shoots toward a
Description of an American Religion.

This notation will probably be otiose, but I wish to keep the
momentum going. It is the result of certain thoughts that came to me
during the night—came to me, however, in forensic form, as though
I were haranguing an audience, which is an unpromising way to arrive at anything.

It is in no small measure indecorous, however, that this passage
should be laid down now, on Easter Day, because it is about how
American religion will slough off all *anthropomorphic character*.

An American is a man who has outgrown his father; he needs
neither counsel nor support from any other man. Even in the daily
life about us fathers are beginning to appear a little ridiculous and annoying, and all their surrogates—presidents, senior statesmen,
sages, and so on—are as vulnerable to criticism as anyone else. God
as father no longer fills a deep emotional need.

Christus passus est. He was a contemplative whose slightest
emergence into a life of action brought down upon him a swift reaction of unjust retribution. He was exterminated.

Now the American is engaged in two things at once: enlarging
his realization of the multitudinousness of created things, and affirming his dramatic interest as a solitary individual. He is denied the recourse to identification with mythic type, as he is denied the consolation of feeling himself lodged and embedded in a social structure,
sanctioned by custom and rendered at once soothing and dignified by
being destined as his "lot" under God's will and the visible exigencies
of public order.

This American is alone, and no man-image can help him, deify
it though one may. This American is affirming his precarious individ-
ual-ity as a man, but the Christ-biography is far from being a projection of his *agon*. The American man is not contemplative nor an onlooker at experience, nor celibate, nor sacrificial victim of social
ideological forces. Least of all does he invoke in reverie a reversal of
operation of nature—a resurrection from the dead, a life after putre-
faction—as a compensation, a justification of his inability to harmo-
nize individuality and multitudinousness.

The Christ-story has indeed left its mark on the American
mind. Never has there been a people so instinctively conscious that

other people are also living (*scilicet*, other people are also suffering), but before our eyes we see the Christ-biography—in so far as it is held up before us as an adequate explanation of "what it is to be a human being"—being reduced to "prettiness and favor."

So we are back to Gertrude Stein: "In American religion there are no saints and no shrines. There is no Heaven because there is only 'up.'"

The American does not feel that the world was made for him: so that Nature and God cannot easily be thought of anthropomorphically.

Doesn't the man in the semi-tropical zone tend to feel that the *sun is shining for him?* And all those rites to persuade and to coerce the crops—don't they imply that Nature—though capricious and often reluctant—is there to serve man and, in fact, has nothing else to do?

The American—first as settler, then as colonist—learned (what Europe had already begun to separate from a theology Mediterranean-rooted) that Nature is not interested in furnishing anything to man; all must be wrenched from her or gained by foresight and unremitting work.

So Destiny is not a father and Nature is not a mother—and only a basically idle woodsman like Thoreau could indulge in lyrical states of gratitude to all-beneficent Mother Nature; and could despise his neighbors who wrestled with her.

So where can an American feel the Otherness—as giver, as connection between the individual and the Whole, as support in the search for self-explanation—not in nature, which is mechanism-process; not in anthropomorphic images of judge-father-atoner—where but in the life-force itself?

For that he is grateful; and that he confronts with an immediacy which has not been known in Europe, where it was veiled and confused in myth, in dogma, and in all that human-all-too-human personalization of nature. The American is grateful to Life not via the immediacy of his parents. . . . Nor is there a qualitative element in the fact of being-born. . . . Unfathomable it is; unrelegable (like the other aspects of nature) to mechanical process; and at every moment identifiable with every impulse toward quality—in love, ameliorization, art, etc.

So now, have I got anything here?

By excluding the classical explanation of the religious emotion as springing from the sense of imperfection, guilt, sin, suffering, need—have I been writing mere paper windmills? No matter.

527. [MASSACHUSETTS GENERAL] HOSPITAL, [BOSTON,] MARCH 29, 1951.
. . . French Individualism and Dr. Schweitzer.

To those who, in their fashion, love the French there is hilarious reading (be it said without disrespect to the great doctor of the Lambaréné) in Dr. Albert Schweitzer's paper on the difficulties of assembling in Paris a chorus to perform the great works of choral literature. We understand very well the difficulty that an unmarried girl would meet in engaging a chaperone to cross the city with her for attendance at evening rehearsals; the difficulty that a married woman would have in finding sufficient evenings free from that endless round of dinners among her relatives and those of her husband (*corvées* mercifully mitigated by the fact that the hostesses vie with one another to illustrate the glories of French cookery). But hasn't Dr. Schweitzer omitted an additional difficulty? When Madame Un Tel, known among her friends with many an admiring expletive as an accomplished musician, that is to say as a being set apart and initiate in recondite mysteries, when Madame has agreed to sing in a performance six weeks hence of Bach's *Mass in B Minor*, she feels she has already made a sufficient sacrifice to the Muses, in so effacing herself as to sit shoulder-to-shoulder among thirty other sopranos of dubious proficiency. She can read the notes; she can enter of herself into the last refinements of phrasing; for her, rehearsals are not necessary, and besides, given the presence of so many other sopranos, her absence will not be noticed; even at the performance it is scarcely necessary for her to raise her eyes to observe the conductor's baton. The French are very individualistic.

I thought that up at 4:00 a.m. and I think it's very funny.

March 30, 1951.

Received from Washington: "The President of the French Republic has conferred upon you . . . Chevalier of the Légion d'Honneur. . . ." So I suppose I must temper the above passage. . . .

535. HOTEL CONTINENTAL, CAMBRIDGE, [MASS.,] WEDNESDAY,
      APRIL 11, 1951. *Great Expectations:* The "I"-Narrator
      and the Novelist's Omniscience.

Let's try this again:

A reader knows—and must know—soon after beginning a work whether he is in the realm of the Imagined or of the Historical. (To develop this principle some day; special exhibit: the opening of *Robinson Crusoe.*)

If he feels that he is reading in the realm of the Imagined, he immediately concedes that all is "poetic" and that the novelist enjoys a permitted omniscience.

The "I"-narrative, then, is felt to be a fiction, a convention—a cut-off fragment of the novelist's total knowledge. [A reader] . . . will always feel that the novelist's mind lies behind, above, and below the narrating character's mind. He will even be on the alert for the novelist's adroit comment on, exposure of, the narrator.

The "I"-narrative may be called, then, one extended speech or thought by *one* of the characters in the work. It is understood that the novelist could, if he chose, furnish a similar and parallel narrative from any one of the other characters (which, indeed, is of frequent occurrence).

The "I"-narrative, then, is felt to be a fiction-within-the-fiction, a mere device, and the mind of the novelist behind it remains separate, and superior, and overriding.

Hence, since the work is in the poetic realm, the "I"-narrative is not bound to be a realistic presentation of the selected narrator's character or mental processes.

The analogy can be found in poetic drama. No youth of Claudio's type in *Measure for Measure* could be conceived of [as] having stated his case so richly—in so organized a form—as the great speech on the fear of death.

The concession on the part of the reader that in the poetical atmosphere of the Imagined Narration the supposed narrator may diverge widely from his characterization in the novel and may display powers far exceeding any limited human being's knowledge permits such phenomena as: (1) The discrepancy between Pip-as-character and Pip-as-narrator; (2) The passages in *Moby-Dick* where Ishmael records those soliloquies of "Captain Ahab, *solus*"; (3) In Proust, the

reconstruction of the inner life of Swann during the early part of the
love affair with Odette when the narrator was only eight years old.

What then is this "poetic world" of Imagined Narrative, in
which such divergencies from logic are permitted?

It has its counterpart in every man's daily life. It is a copy—an
extension—of the realm of our reverie, our imagination as we experience any twenty-four hours.

Every man at certain times in every day finds himself making
essays into omniscience. He attempts to reconstruct the motivation,
the inner thoughts, of his employer, of the members of his family, of
those to whom he is talking.

He even goes further than that: he takes flights into pure
fiction: "I wonder what a condemned man feels like on the eve of his
execution"; "I wonder what a kept woman feels like when she gives
herself to a great gross ugly lover"; or—as he reads today's newspaper:[6] "I wonder what a general like General MacArthur feels like
when, before the eyes of the whole world, he is removed from his
high post." All this reverie-life comes closest to the novel, however,
when his reveries are centered upon himself: "What kind of feelings
will I have when I am old—or if my wife died, and I were free—or if
I became a partner in the business?"

And this man—this non-artist everyman whom we are imagin-
ing—knows well that this truth he is trying to capture by the imagination (our picture of situations in life which are not yet, or are not to
our knowledge, historical situations) is most real when it is most independent of himself—less shaped by his wishes, more respectful of
those mechanisms of life which are not obedient to our ego-fantasies.
He is aware that he has outgrown the juvenile daydreams of "What I
would do if I were a G-Man" or "What I would do if I were a great
lover like Rudolph Valentino." He has learned that imaginative constructions are only instructive and rewarding if they are obedient to
the laws that govern that part of the world which is not our self-
gratification. With the result that when he attempts to reconstruct
the inner life of his employer or his wife, or even himself twenty years
from now, he learns that: (1) He must construct the situation, embody
it in a nexus of various and conflicting tensions; and (2) He must be at-

---

6. *New York Times* (April 11, 1951): "Truman relieves M'Arthur of all his posts; finds him
unable to back U.S.-U.N. policies; Ridgway named to Far Eastern commands."

tentive to those other persons (even including himself) in their *freedom*, in their inalienable right to behave otherwise than he might wish them to.

Everyman knows then, from his daily experience, something of the process that lies behind the writing of Imagined Narratives. And he is willing to concede that the presentation of an imagined situation involves two operations in the mind of the imaginer: the construction of the situation, and the observation of the act of construction; the flight of the imagination and the criticism of the flight, which safeguards the flight from too emotionally subjective a "wrenching-of-objective-truth."

This realm of the Imagined is "poetic," then, not because it is beautiful or gratifyingly contrary-to-fact, but because it is an attempt at the Real, yet is not real, and is at the same time precariously maintained by a serious attempt to be obedient to all the laws that govern the Real. It is all a "construction," yet a serious—even an indispensable—construction, necessary for life.

A Boston businessman learns that his mother is dying in Oregon. He takes the airplane to reach her. Inevitably he attempts to reconstruct what her thoughts may be. And inevitably he knows that he cannot arrive at the truth of what her thoughts are at that moment: her annoyance at nurses, her delusions under opiates and pain; yet he has no choice but to ascribe to her what *might very likely be* her summary of her whole life, her tender or reproachful thoughts toward him. And our businessman knows that his reconstruction of these attitudes in her mind is stylized, is poetic, is potentially true in essence though extravagantly erroneous in specific form. That is the Poetic, and that is all Imagined Narration.

Hence, even the man in the street has no great difficulty in conceding the apparent incoherencies in fiction; all the incoherencies are understandable in the world of the Poetic, for the Poetic captures an essential truth which no amount of factual narrative could ever assure to be the Whole Truth or the Essential Truth.

And with this I am back at a homely truism, which is always a pleasure when it arrives *unexpectedly*.

537. HOTEL CONTINENTAL, CAMBRIDGE, [MASS.,] SUNDAY,
      APRIL 15, 1951. Melville and the Novel.

I should like to delay for weeks the moment when I pull myself together to formulate any thoughts on this matter; to wait until my irritated rejection of *Pierre* has abated, as it has abated (though remaining a rejection) in the case of *The Confidence-Man*.

Both these novels are total failures. The more one sees the symbolic elaborations that went into *Pierre* the more one must acknowledge that ingenuity, struggle, attempted noble projects count for nothing, if there is no real maturity in the relation to a work of art.

What I shall try to do is to save from those two shipwrecks and from the indubitable triumph which preceded them [*Moby-Dick*] one observation: that Melville was struggling to find the new form of the novel: the novel which Joyce was to fashion, in which the hero is Everyman, and in which the totality of experience was to converge in that of the hero.

The Confidence-Man was wrecked by the smallness, the almost parochial *mesquinerie* of limiting the operation of society's deceptions to mere skulduggery and commercial and philanthropic fraud. Yet the remarkable thing in *The Confidence-Man* is the device of the Impostor reappearing in successive avatars. How magnificent this might have been—what counterpoint might have been afforded—had the range of Malice and Inhumanity and Guile been broadened from characterization to characterization; and what a field for the operation of the *vis comica*.

And *Pierre:* in the remote distance, through that appalling screen of attitudinizing unvivifying language, one sees a dim what-might-have-been: a vast morality in which the subjective element might have constantly charged abstractions with reality.

One reads the first third of *Pierre* with amazement: how could Melville have persisted so long in writing such cliché-ridden, uninspiriting yet excited stretches? The only answers—in rising scale of energy—must be: (1) An energy engendered in him by the sense that he is writing about aristocratic folk—his ancestors; (2) The self-deception that in Lucy and Isabel and his mother-sister, he is showing himself knowledgeable about woman; (3) The dark excitement aroused in him by the knowledge that he is approaching the subject of incest; and yet it is not incest that is really his agitation (for incest is a transference-excitement, a façade-formation), but other Unavowables; (4) The excitement, which should have been justified, that he was creating a new kind of novel: the story of Everyman in the situation where all psychic forces converge.

It was this last which led him into the error of his choice of style. Yes, such a novel would require a style of its own. The presentation of the hero would involve his doubling, his multiplication, his identification with innumerable men who had preceded him (here intermittently represented by *reminding* us of Hamlet, Christ, and Prometheus). His relationship to Family, to Society and Tradition, to Sex and to Honor and to Identity must be presented in ever wider and more varying symbols. And the balance must be maintained between one individual concrete man and the multi-form type-man.

Confronted by this task, Melville has chosen precisely the wrong style: he has chosen to overwhelm us with *his* emotion, *i.e.*, the rhapsodical; and he has chosen the style of public address, *i.e.*, the hortatory and compulsive, rather than the expository and the contained.

Scores of times I have pushed the book away from me, exclaiming that Melville has an incurably ordinary mind. . . .

And yet:

Remains *Moby-Dick*, and the whole fascinating problem of how so great a pyramid could be made with so many bricks which, taken individually, could be judged cardboard, but which *do* hold, shot through with strengths derived from the magnificent movement of the whole.

The weakness of the two later novels is not primarily a weakness of mind but a weakness of character.

Melville's character when he came to write *Moby-Dick* was screwed up to its highest attainable tension and—for once, given the most fortunate choice of subject—his very weaknesses played into his hand as strength. Thereafter, he chose subjects which he could not encompass. . . . In addition, some fatigue, some relapse into his complacent *stupidités* took place, from which only occasionally he emerged to compose a shorter narrative.

All his weaknesses are bound up with his dreary narcissism, his infatuated view of himself: all of his maladjustments are distinctions; he has been marked (by whom?) for woe; he has been distinguished (by whom?) for the role of tragic yet philosophical sufferer.

And all this springs from his anthropomorphic view of how

things happen. That is what so extreme a subjectivity does for an immature nature.

. . . I see in Melville, as in so many other writers, the ever-youthful surprise that there is evil in the universe. And, I must add, the unavowed self-righteousness of those who find none of this evil in themselves and who are therefore continually shocked and declamatory about its presence in others.

I must be so immured, indurated, in several points of view that I cannot understand what other people are talking about:

(1) I separate God from the physical and meteorological operation of the universe. I would never call an earthquake an "act of God," nor the birth of a defective child; nor any maiming or death in an automobile accident.

(2) The malignant behavior of human beings—even the Nazi operation of human ovens—I cannot regard as absolute Evil. I try in this life not to hurt a flea, but I am cruel to myself from a spring of cruelty which I occasionally exercise on others, and I find that I understand that cruelty in myself as separated from Iago's and the Nazis' *by degree only*, not by kind. Its presence in myself is not so absolute but it springs from just the *bad character* I am indicting in Melville: moral laziness, self-indulgence, self-importance—things for which I am furnished with the material for self-correction.

540. [HOTEL CONTINENTAL, CAMBRIDGE, MASS.,] SUNDAY NOON,
APRIL [22,] 1951. *War and Peace*.

So, in my distress, my downright physical annoyance, at [Melville's] *Pierre*, I again began *War and Peace*, which I had read in the hospital—up to the last chapters (which I think I have never read), where I ceased from very fear that Tolstoi was losing his grip.

Isn't my attack on *War and Peace* for the class simply that it's a novel by a man who believes in God? And isn't my line that, like Tolstoi, I am not to dare too narrowly to define what I mean—what he means—by that? Nevertheless, with all the difficulty of deciding how near to a definition one dares go.

And then to draw out all the stops of my omniscience-theory

and show what harmony exists between a belief in God and the act of imaginative narration.

And then to show that just in proportion as it is grandly right to think of the novelist's view as God's view—the awful rightness of it—so lies the pitfall of losing the novelist's mission entirely through too narrow a concept of God. Whereby hangs Sartre's essay on the dogma-fettered, dogma-crushed novels of François Mauriac.[7]

Then show how beautifully novels *can* get on without God.

That God is like a symbol one can insert into either sum in an equation without altering the correctness of the equation.

That were it not for a few intrusions of Tolstoi one could read the entire novel without being aware that Tolstoi is trying to express the omnipresence of God.

That the equable light which plays on all the human behavior in *War and Peace*—from the catastrophes of nations to the smallest events of domestic life—is made possible by Tolstoi's concept of God's nature.

Then the phrase occurs to me, with the change of one word: it is a terrible thing to fall into Tolstoi's hand. For Tolstoi's concept of God requires that a human being be thrown into the pestle of suffering life's extremest trial in order to reveal, yield up, acknowledge the God-relationship. Even in this longest of novels Tolstoi has not space to do this for all his principal characters; he does it for a few, but we have the sense that he could do it also for Mlle. Bourienne or for Vera or for Lieutenant Berg. Of all God's attributes Tolstoi expresses primarily God's impartiality, or, rather, God's unhurriedness—His interests will be served in the long run, on the large scale.

Whence comes Tolstoi's first and primary conviction that God overrules—from interiority or from historic perspective? He, of course, has both; but I should say that Tolstoi's conviction proceeds primarily from his view of All Society—otherwise we should have a "mystical" novel; what that would be like we can dimly see from *The Death of Ivan Ilych*.

I now see that I have all my life been an idiot about *Anna Karenina*—which came to such a bouquet of ineptitude in my conversation with Vivien Leigh about it: I have never had the faintest glimmer about that novel and now it is all to be reread.

---

7. "M. Francois Mauriac et la liberté," in his . . . *Situations, I: Essais critiques* (1947).

What would it be but repetition to consign to the Journal—to the class, that is another matter—all the consequences that flow from the God-interest of Tolstoi and the omniscience-theory?

From it proceeds the absolutely equalized attention to the specific detail throughout the narrative portions: every person, every nation, every moment in time is unique. Here there is no room for symbol—we are at the opposite extreme from Melville; no man is everyman, no man is type-man; each is himself in the God-relationship vertically, not in the community-relationship horizontally.

Hence comes also the passionless power: the inability of old Prince Andrey to communicate his love to his daughter Marya and that of young Prince Andrey to arrive at a human relationship with his wife Liza are terrifying; but not because they are a petrified determinism but because they are potential—they could have been reached in the freedom accorded to human beings; after the deaths of the Prince and Liza they continue, straining, bursting to reach their right due fulfillment. God's interest never flags: from Natasha's error (itself an expression of the passional life as a creativity) will come a glorious deepening of her union with Prince Andrey, just as he will have gained it from his error in his married life.

And what is God's interest but that these eating, serving, soldiering, limited human beings find their God-relationship in the natural human life?

In this, so far from classical and Shakespearian heroic, even in this book of warfare Tolstoi is not deeply concerned to give his "heroes" at war a feat of courage—though he is proud to praise the Russian common soldier. No, God will win the battles via the wisdom of the agéd Kutuzov and via something deep (and almost hidden from them) in the Russian people: Kutuzov is endlessly praised for not interfering with God's way of doing it.

For Tolstoi, the burning [of] and retreat from Moscow was "the central event of history." He can almost be heard saying with Themistocles: "It is not we who have done this thing." Yet Tolstoi is careful to say that no one lit the fires; they were the expected result of empty houses and bivouacking troops. But the more a thing is *natural* the more it is *supernatural*. (And note how he accords to his favored characters the adjective *natural*: Pierre repeatedly blunders with his naturalness in the drawing rooms and Natasha is the soul of spontaneous nature.)

Nowhere is this natural-supernatural identification seen more

clearly than in the great death scenes. Here Tolstoi insists on the clinical details of extinction, but a fierce blaze of the Other throws its
light on the past, the present, and the future—not as *mystique* (and
how he refuses all the ecclesiastical elements that might heighten
their spirituality), but as demanding that we ask the basic questions
concerning life and death. . . .

And all these deaths charge the book with life, irradiate it—not
as the deaths in the *Iliad* do (though Tolstoi was keeping his eyes on
the *Iliad*), by making us prize more highly the sense-experience of
living—but by making us prize the more highly the human relationships and depth one can put into them.

[Hotel Continental, Cambridge, Mass.] Later: April 23.

Have made my first trip to the Widener in seven or eight
weeks. Hobbled up to [the] SLAV [section] on the third floor of the
stacks. Read in [Aylmer] Maude, [Romain] Rolland, [N.H.] Dole—
together with their quotations from [E.M.] Forster and [Percy] Lub-
bock—and nowhere do I find anything like this concerning a religious interest. Nor do I find anything else, however, except a general
ecstatic fervor about "life-in-the-novel" tempered by a few judicious
reservations. Nor in a preface by Tolstoi—included in the Dole edition—do we find much more than a journalistic answer to a few criti-
cisms. One writer tells us that later, when Tolstoi was "converted," he
repudiated *War and Peace* and *Anna* as secular volumes—which (I
tentatively remark from my corner in ignorance) might be exactly a
sort of distortion of perspective whereby he would be remembering it
à travers Anna. Anyway my library-hunt merely recalls—as the
Lope-Palestrina-Melville-interests have: Be your own authority.

556. **DUNSTER HOUSE, [HARVARD,] SUNDAY, AUGUST 5, [AND TUESDAY,
AUGUST 7,] 1951.** Poe: How Literature Can Be Made out of
Necrophilic Sadism.

. . . The questions to be asked, then, are how so large a body of
violently abnormal phantasizings have been accepted, retained, and
often honored so widely for over a hundred years.

We cannot say as we do of *Oedipus Rex* and the more appalling

Elizabethan plays that they waken a sympathetic vibration in readers—at least this explanation will only partly serve. Even though we
concede that the sadistic element, and those [elements] which reflect
the oedipal and castration complexes may find a half-horrified half-
grateful echo, there are even more predominant strains of cannibalis-
tic, necrophilic, and impotence motifs which cannot be thought of as
eliciting so general a "recognition." In "Berenice" the [protagonist]
extracts the teeth—all of them—of his dead fiancée.

What's more, certain stories, like "The Assignation," should
long since have disappeared along with thousands of other horror
stories, for they are perfect nonsense as human behavior and are
presented with the worst trappings of a long since outmoded
romanticism.

Why have they survived and why—though reproved by many
critics—can they be said to be still in the canon of American literature? The question is all the more valid because "horror" stories continue as a valid genre and thousands have been read since Poe's, and
forgotten.

What name shall we give to the *fidelity* with which Poe recorded the promptings from his instinctual centers?

Expressed negatively we can say that he did not cheat, or he did
not interfere with them. He did not—like Hawthorne—impose
upon them moralizing constructions (no, not even in "Never Bet the
Devil Your Head," which he calls "with a moral").

He accepted the images of horror, he trusted them as self-sufficient. But in saying this we are also saying that he was *incurious* as to
their psychic meaning for him; he did not choose to probe further—
not even far enough to see that they dealt with a woman's body and a
man's. His powerful investigatory instinct stopped short before the
frightfulness of his subconscious.

Only when sex was not involved do we find him perhaps aware
—in "William Wilson"—of an allegorical interpretation. . . .

On the whole, . . . these stories were composed with an aston-
ishingly immediate submission to the promptings of the psychic life.
They were couched in the Gothic formulae, and one has the feeling
that had Poe lived in De Maupassant's time, he would have couched
them in the "realistic" mode—as "The Black Cat" is. But the mediaeval trappings are as deeply real to him as are the horrors.

What the world has acknowledged, then, is the "reality" of the
horror.

And . . . most readers derive pleasure from the horror, that is, "recognize" it, as they recognize the "imp-of-the-perverse" motif, and lend themselves to those portions they do *not* recognize through an identification within themselves—the necrophilic drive—because they are so obviously a reality to the author.

What arises from the pages is that Poe is not contriving and forging. Also he is not, on the other hand, merely gratifying his *velléités*. This is a distinction which it is difficult to establish: these are not merely emotional releases; these are not merely self-indulgent allusions to pressures, *Ersatz* acts. They are concrete representations in literature of authentic experience.

Poe's intelligence has had the daring and the concentration to see them, to embody them, and to separate them from himself. There does not hang about them any vestige of private pleading, self-justification, not even self-humiliation. "These things are so; these things I know," he seems to say.

This is what his intellect was able to do for him.

In the light of this, one can see that Poe's harping on the "unity" of a story—of a work—can be also read "honesty." He did not heap horrors on horrors to shock an audience, because his primary aim was . . . to tell a truth. (It is interesting . . . that when he did depart from unity . . . we are able—via psychoanalysis—to see that there is a deeper unity relating the disparate motifs than Poe himself could have suspected. He was faithful to an unconscious unity even when he thought he was infringing his own rule!)

Gogol is undoubtedly a greater writer, and "The Nose" is a greater creation in Poe's own realm; but "The Nose" lacks the crude force of Poe's stories precisely because Poe had no inkling of what he was dealing with. And compared to Poe, [E. T. A.] Hoffmann is continually heightening the horrors, painting the lily, and thereby attenuating the power.

For its relation to America: dare I say that the power comes from that aspect of the American mind which is abstract? That the abstraction did not feel the need to insert any mediational material? . . .

557. HOTEL CONTINENTAL, CAMBRIDGE, [MASS.,] AUGUST 18, 1951.
      Woollcott.

Have been spending some more time over the [Alexander]
Woollcott papers at the Houghton Library and am pulling myself together to write the spiel for the *Harvard Library Bulletin*.[8] Alexander Woollcott was born and spent a part of his youth in Phalanx, New
Jersey, that is to say, in one of the phalansteries founded by followers
of the social reformer [Charles] Fourier. By the time of his birth the
community to which his parents and relatives belonged had been
obliged to introduce many a compromise into the community's organization. The group of families living together in the long rambling
eight-room house no longer lived under a dispensation which included equal labor and equal earnings together with affording to each
an equal voice in the administration of a common effort. There remained at the Phalanx, however, the atmosphere of communal unity,
of contempt for competitive activity, of mutual forebearance. There
were a number of traits in Woollcott's character which would forever
have prevented him from being an exemplary member of a selfless
community, but there is no doubt that he so saw himself, and he
never ceased from attempting to build about himself a phalanx of like-
minded friends. To onlookers it seemed that the coteries in which he
moved were selected for caustic wit and conspicuous success, but
Woollcott's own description of them laid the emphasis, almost
fiercely, on their generosity and their spirituality. He was the prime-
mover in the launching of a succession of restaurants in New York,
designed as meeting places for this phalanx; he later took a large
house at Mt. Kisco in the hope that his friends would join him for a
visit without end; and finally—with eight others—he bought Neshobe Island in Lake Bomoseen, Vermont, and by might and main la-
bored to impress upon it the character, not of a club, not of a recreation center, but of an *agape*. Like so many Americans, Woollcott was
haunted by a sense of solitude which he strove almost frantically to
replace by an almost febrile gregariousness; and the gregariousness
that he sought was not primarily of talent or brains, but of the heart.
      All this marshalling of a social life was expensive: like himself,
the majority of his friends had become accustomed to a lavish stan-

---

8. This entry and Entries 560 and 565 are a first draft of the article, but it was not completed and was not published in the *Bulletin* until 1985.

dard of living. For long stretches of time he did not permit himself to recognize that he had ceased to conform to one of the principal tenets of Phalanx, New Jersey—a belief that virtues can flourish only under poverty. Toward the end of his life, however, he would be visited with grave misgivings. He would tire many of his friends with his never-consummated plans to disband his retinue and live in apostolic austerity. Yet he had been poor in his youth and he took good care that he would not be so again. "Alec's a Saint Francis," said one of his friends, "yes, a Saint Francis with a sound grasp of double-entry bookkeeping."

The Phalanx lived in an atmosphere of brotherly love. Woollcott did not regard friendships as things "which enter one's life," subject to the accidents of absence, preoccupation, and velleity, but as activities one maintains, cultivates, and defends. When he arranged a lecture tour, the cities in which he spoke were selected for reasons above and beyond remuneration: he spoke in Indianapolis because Booth Tarkington lived there; in Cincinnati because Dr. [Gustav] Eckstein was a professor at the University; in Chicago he would see [Robert] Hutchins, in San Francisco Kathleen Norris, in Los Angeles Harpo Marx and Dorothy Parker. Woe to the absent friend who had let too long a time elapse without a letter of a distinctly demonstrative character (mere facts were insufficient). Above all he delighted in giving and receiving presents. His circle strove with one another to offer him gifts of rarity, ingenuity, or of long preparation. Frank Lloyd Wright gave him a complete set of the Hokusai *Thirty-six Views of Mount Fujiyama*. Harpo Marx forwarded six jumpers or overalls, each in a different color and each having embroidered on the pocket a phrase in Greek or Latin (one of them no little startled Otis Skinner, who had to explain to his own that the sentiment was not exactly a thing to boast about). Lady Colefax sent him two extraordinary photographs of [Eleonora] Duse; Helen Hayes two majolica jardinières for the terrace on "The Island." And he, in turn, dispensed letters and first editions of Dickens, playbills of the historic matinée at Ford's Theatre, daggers that had belonged to Edmund Kean.

Woollcott would have wished to have had all his friends under one roof at one time. For him there was not necessity to see them one by one. But most of his friends had it in common that they were precisely very active, very deeply engaged elsewhere; so that correspondence was of great importance.

560. HOTEL CONTINENTAL, CAMBRIDGE, [MASS.,] AUGUST 20, 1951.
     Woollcott—Continued.

A selection of Woollcott's letters has been published[9] and has
given much pleasure. No reader could fail to see that each letter was
directed with a most unusual precision toward its recipient's interests and each reflected with high vivacity the traits of the sender.
Those are the marks of the born letter-writer and it is for those characteristics that letters are read long after their content, as events and
even as reflections, has lost consequence. Letters are the only form in
all literature, in all the arts, which reposes on the communication of
one to one. It is this condition which renders [them] the pre-eminent
vehicle for that aspect of life which is generally excluded from all literature except the novel: those innumerable trifles of the daily life,
that rain of trifling details, pleasing and vexatious, which falls upon
the just and the unjust and which is also an inescapable concomitant
of all human life. Letters are not necessarily a product of intimacy
(those of Walpole to Sir Horace Mann are not intimate), but they cannot be written by a nature which shrinks from or is afraid of intimacy,
for the unhesitating presentation of the self, in self-portraiture, lies
implicit in each letter. This was not in Woollcott's power. All his life
he had been engaged in constructing for himself a *persona*, a façade-
characterization, by virtue of which he was able to live with such
buoyancy and such intensity among his fellow human beings. This observation does not constitute a charge against him of hypocrisy any
more than it does against the many persons whom we meet who present to themselves and to others a similar *persona*. In the sense in
which I am using it (which differs from that employed so frequently in
modern discussions of poetic technique) *mask* is a coarse translation of
the word *persona*. Its assumption is involuntary; its owner can never
be fully conscious of its presence. It has already begun to become
fixed in childhood and is probably the result of some sense of depri-
vation or injury. Natures encased in *personae* can never join the company of great letter-writers, for the conveyance of the daily life, from
one to one, is only of interest to other readers when it is expressed by
a writer from his whole and undivided self. A *persona* invariably dictates vivid letters; it cannot confer a lasting value. The letters of

9. *The Letters . . . Edited by Beatrice Kaufman and Joseph Hennessey* (1944).

Lewis[-Carroll] Dodgson and Proust and Henry James are of this
sort,—as was probably their conversation. They were too obviously
fashioning what they said. The great letter-writers had, it is true, a
tragic or enigmatic element in their lives (only such writers could . . .
elevate the trivial to the realm of literature; only so were they able to
distinguish the trivial from the important)—[Horace] Walpole, Madame de Sévigné, [Edward] FitzGerald—but their sufferings had not
driven them toward the necessity of forming an *alter ego*. The
William Cowper who was cut down at the moment that he attempted
to hang himself in the attic is the same William Cowper who can en-
chant us with his account of the behavior of a Belgian hare in the garden or of his afternoon stroll through the village street.

Woollcott's *persona* was delightful, clamorous for attention, exasperating, sentimental, moralizing, and could have strains of rigorous moral elevation. It was not reflective nor pliant nor patient, nor
given to drawing fine discriminations. Its age—all *personae* are associated with the delusion of being of a fixed age—was about fifty—as
even his letters written in childhood show. It combined the elements
of being a kindly and indulgent uncle with those of being a willful,
crotchety domestic tyrant. Kind he was—and his correspondence
shows to what extent he was secret in his manifold generosities,—but
his *persona* required that he project himself as the arbiter of the
homely virtues, a sort of public statue of philanthropic responsibility.
He was deeply emotional, dependent on the expenditure and reception of affection, but his *persona*—constructed from some starvation
and some dread lest all affection betray him—drove him to a sort of
derision of the claims of the heart. His most affectionate mood would
find him addressing a letter to a friend with the words: "Dear Nausea." His prodigious wit had been schooled in invective—perhaps
the school of all wit—and his whole circle played the dangerous game
of couching their expressions of mutual regard in terms of derogation.
No wonder that almost all of his friendships were subject to intermittent coolnesses and occasionally to towering quarrels. He was occasionally unjust, and here also his *persona* intervened. To be con-
victed of error was not a relief but a mortification; the Universal
Uncle did not admit of progressive perfectibility. During the ten
years that he had served as dramatic critic of the *New York Times* he
had gained a reputation for caustic speech; a vivacious phrase from his
pen could all but cut short an actor's career. As he grew older, however, he became more careful of such damage. Of the character

founded upon his own in the comedy *The Man Who Came to Dinner*, by George Kaufman and Moss Hart, he said that the only aspect that he did not recognize as a reflection of his own was that of the hero's vilification of the servants. "I attack the weaknesses only of the assured and the powerful," he said, "not of those whose position prevents their answering back."

565. JANET [DAKIN]'S HOUSE AT AMHERST, MASS., SEPTEMBER 7, 1951.
Woollcott—Continued. . . .

The stage and platform are, as one would expect, magnets to all those possessing or in search of a *persona*. There one can impose a portrait of oneself that accords with one's needs. There are many men and women in conspicuous positions who receive no satisfaction from their celebrity, no added increment of confidence from the fact that millions agree with them; for them all achievement is solitary, and acclaim tends rather to heighten whatever they feel of self-doubt. Woollcott's role as an enormously successful broadcaster, however, permitted him to fashion his portrait to the finest detail. Now millions could join him in demonstrations of affection to those he admired; he instituted a series of supposedly "surprise" serenades to Jerome Kern and Justice Holmes, to William Allen White and to Ethel Barrymore. He could talk of Hamilton College to his heart's content and could interest an ever wider circle in the work of training seeing-eye dogs for the blind. Finally, in 1941, he was invited to England by the British Broadcasting Corporation to contribute to the famous series of "postscripts" to the eleven o'clock news broadcasts, and did incomparably well.

We frequently hear it said that no one writes letters any more, but Woollcott did not pride himself on being an up-to-the-minute modern. His *persona* was fixed as of about 1910; it attracted letters. From the vast numbers that poured in to him he made a collection of more than five thousand items which he bequeathed to the Harvard Library. They include the responses from the American and British public to his broadcasts and writings, as well as the testimonies to his warm yet rigorous concept of friendship.

From time to time scholars have offered to readers collections of letters addressed *to* an eminent figure. Sir Hugh Walpole, who gradually through life affixed upon himself a *persona* resembling that of Sir Walter Scott (who was so entirely without one); who built himself a sort of Abbotsford near the Scottish border, and who, launched upon the novels of the *Herries* family, bought the vast crates of the letters addressed to Sir Walter, and published two volumes of them. In France they have published *Le Portefeuille de Lamennais* and *Le Portefeuille de Victor Hugo*. To what extent can a man be described, be given—as we now say—a profile by the letters directed to him? The answer returns us to the question of the *persona*. Turning over the numerous folders of this Woollcott correspondence one is astonished to see the extent to which the letters are written in the "Woollcott manner." *Personae* have, as it were, a contagious force; they emerge in personalities (as the very word suggests) which are sensitive about personality, and even those for whom the immediacy of thought and emotion are alone important are drawn under the spell of personality. Their letters begin to return a sort of mimetic echo. Even Gertrude Stein, whose letters are generally of an unshakeable individuality, begins a letter to Woollcott with the words "Dear Papa Woojums."

567.   SS "VEENDAM," FRIDAY, SEPTEMBER 21, 1951.
   The Scarlet Letter.

I reread this story (with the greatest difficulty) after reading a volume of Hawthorne's stories in order to verify on this larger scale my observations on Hawthorne's *tempo*—the retardation he effects by loading the latter end of his sentences with matter already expressed or implied. The stories abound in this practice, by which he mistakenly attempted to achieve stateliness. I find that by the time he came to write this novel he had considerably corrected himself; instead he achieves a conscious slowness by . . . furnishing adjectives, verbs, and other forms *in pairs*—a practice probably derived from the parallelisms in Biblical poetry and all the literature that has copied it from there. . . .

My interest in this rereading was to make clear to myself wherein my memory of the novel made me certain that—in the sense that I have studied his contemporaries—it was totally "unamerican."

Hawthorne called this novel (in the last sentence) a "legend."

It is, and it is not, a religious novel. Certainly, all the principal characters are under the impression that they are engaged in a religious life. Their sin is not socio-ethical but religious; their (long-delayed) penitence is not primarily public confession and public suffering, but an effort to re-enter a right relation with God. . . .

Is it, for Hawthorne, a religious novel, or is it his description of the religious thought-world in which these people moved?

Though it is extraordinary how little God is named outside of the characters' directly recorded speeches and thoughts, Hawthorne in a very few places alludes to "Providence." (He alludes to God many more times, however, in contexts where he is reporting the attitudes of the characters.) . . .

The rarity of expressions of religious belief on N.H.'s part does not proceed from "mental reservation," I think. . . . Hawthorne took it for granted that the readers would assume his belief that adultery was a sin against God, that redemption meant "immortality," etc.

And yet: if Hawthorne had really believed that the issues of this novel were religious, all would have been stated differently. It is a novel of ethical preoccupation, and out of the author's hesitation between the religious and the ethical proceed all the elements of content and style which render the book so unsatisfactory. The fact that it is para- or pseudo-religious paralyzes the freedom of the characters; the fact that it is ethical—but not only ethical—prevents their appearing to us as fully mature persons.

Now, religion is passion or it is nothing; and religion places all ethics and all morals in a relative, in an unfrozen condition, or it is nothing. And Hawthorne's lukewarm and purely conventional attitude to this religion-motivated community has the most unfortunate effects: (1) It makes it appear that they, and he, are all talking cant, thereby rendering them all immature, all revolving in a hermetically sealed world of fixed, devitalized and stupid dogmatic positions; and (2) It permits him to shift from ground to ground—at one moment sentimental, at another intellectually cruel.

For Hawthorne, the basic sin which he claims to hold before our eyes is: resorting to the head rather than to the heart. Yet an obsession on his part is that sex is sin. But sex is nearer the heart than the head, and N.H. is at once entangled in a series of contradictions which make havoc throughout his book. Hester's affirmation: "What we did had a consecration of its own" is lost not only on Dimmesdale but on Hawthorne. Gretchen [in *Faust*] and Anna Karenina are broken by society and by their lovers but not by their poets; Hester is disavowed by her creator, who reserves for her only the cold justification that—had she been less "impure"—she might have launched a crusade for bettering the world's understanding of women. . . .

Hawthorne could have written this novel in secular terms (*Anna Karenina*) or in religious terms (Dostoievski); he thought he was writing it in religious terms, but his religious formation was without conviction or passion. He uses certain religious formulae as a vague background, as an enhancement of a sort of *faux-sublime*. . . .

It is from this unrigorous religiosity that the stylistic faults proceed. Hawthorne declares that he is writing a romance. He urges (page xiii) that the wise romancer will "mingle the Marvellous rather as a slight, delicate, and evanescent flavor, than as any portion of the actual substance of the dish offered to the public." Yes, such would be a legend and such a romance. But had he only recognized it fully, his choice had been made: this is not a romance nor a legend, but a full-scale story of the issues of the right and the wrong in God's eyes. A religious novel is precisely about the Marvellous, and every corner of it is invested with the rays departing from the Supernatural Center; the Marvellous, so present, only with difficulty admits of the co-presence of secondary appeals to astonishment or emotion. But Hawthorne on one level will have the fiend present in Chillingworth and an intimation of angelic qualifications (these are in irony; but imply their possibility) in Dimmesdale. And on a third level, the whole hocus-pocus of the contemporary superstition. . . .

This disordered supernaturalism leads Hawthorne into another chaotic emotion: Nature is possessed of a very operative intelligence. On rereading the book one cannot refrain from bursting out laughing at the opening of chapter 5. Hester comes forth into the "sunshine, which, falling on all alike," etc. Not in this book does it fall on all alike, for Hawthorne turns it on and off to serve his laborious symbolism; in chapter 18, entitled "A Flood of Sunshine," it falls on Hester (page 231)—"such was the sympathy of Nature." It is this omnipresent marshalling of a "sympathy in Nature"—the lowest form of the religious sense—which makes most clear to us how little a right Hawthorne had to launch out upon a religious novel.

These inconsistencies open wide the door to a world of bathos and sentimentality. . . .

Lastly, the didactic moralizing tenor of the work, supported by the sanction of this vague religiosity, reduces the characters to automatons. . . .

This is the blight of the doctrinaire novel: that it robs the characters of their freedom. It is bad enough that in such novels they are robbed of (our sense of) their future; in Hawthorne it is carried to such an extent that they are robbed of their present.

It is in this sense that N.H. is so unamerican. All is marked by a subservience to Received Ideas. He is not only describing a previous age, he embraces it. . . .

568. SS "VEENDAM," SATURDAY, SEPTEMBER 22, 1951. American Aspects of *The Scarlet Letter*, and the Unamerican.

What is unamerican in this novel is obvious.

In addition, however, it should be pointed out that it contains much that is instructive as to the negative aspects of the American character; it also contains some of the American traits in a wistful, starved, awkward, ill-digested state.

First, here is the famous New England conscience. The characters are bowed down and warped with self-reproaches; life cannot go on—because one has humiliated *oneself* through falling short of one's own expectation of one's own excellence (the wrong done to others is distinctly secondary). It might well have been after reading this novel that Whitman wrote his famous line about the cows who do not grieve over their sins.[1]

Second, the point at which conscience is most sensitive is sex. Dimmesdale's cowardice and hypocrisy hang on that. Chillingworth's overdevelopment of his intellect led to his "wrong" to Hester in marrying her.

Thirdly, penance is obtained by public penance, which indicates the extent that the sins were felt to be offenses against a social order. It is characteristic that when the situation is finally publicly aired, the three principals have no choice but to "go away"—two to death, and Hester to Europe. Pearl, that child of shame and sin,

---

1. "I think I could turn and live awhile with the animals . . . / They do not lie awake in the dark and weep for their sins," *Leaves of Grass* (1855), lines 683, 686.

marries a European title; as though Hawthorne would spare any American from taking over so grave a possibility of disaster. It is true that Hester many years later returns to Boston, but that goes to making our legendary atmosphere.

These three characteristics are not solely American—they are, however, deeply protestant, and they were to enjoy a large development in America.

The American elements in a starved condition are:

(1) The moral which, we are told, is to be derived—among many others—from Dimmesdale's life (page 295): "Be true! Be true! Be true! Show freely to the world, if not your worst, yet some trait whereby the worst may be inferred!"

This astonishing injunction sounds like some twisted echo of Father Mapple's sermon.[2] What does it mean? It is a monstrous variant on Be Yourself, and nothing else can be made of it.

(2) The curiously expressed confidence in the Masses of Mankind (page 143): "When an uninstructed multitude attempts to see with its eyes, it is exceedingly apt to be deceived. When, however, it forms its judgment, as it usually does, on the intuitions of its great and warm heart, the conclusions thus attained are often so profound and so unerring, as to possess the character of truths supernaturally revealed." . . .

That is the right tune distorted by being played in the wrong clef. Hawthorne is full of sententious remarks, often in the manner of the French *moralistes*, but most of them are either of doubtful validity or of a commonplace nature.

570. **HÔTEL MONTALAMBERT, PARIS, SEPTEMBER 29, 1951.** Anouilh, and the Woman in France.

Last night I went to Anouilh's *Colombe*, the great current success; tomorrow I shall go to his *Ardèle*, which I have been rereading; I have been reading his *La Répétition*.

Again, as in Entry 490 [(December 20, 1950)], I must try to arrange my thoughts on this matter; they are in a consternation. A Mlle. [X] came to lunch with me from the *Nouvelles Littéraires* (I

---

2. *Moby-Dick*, chapter 9.

dread what she may have chosen to print from our talk). To her I had to say that I was astonished at the low opinion of woman expressed in so much modern French literature. She agreed with me and put it down to the wide increase of pederasty; I claimed it went far deeper than that and that both phenomena may come from some common source.

Since lunch the idea has come to me that it is *the man who is constantly rendered ridiculous through his relations with women*, and it is *that* which is insupportable. Not only does the word *cocu* ring repeatedly throughout the Anouilh [plays], but Anouilh in *La Répétition* thinks it funny to apply it to a lover whose mistress is *soufflée* by another man; and it is a central situation of *Ardèle*, where a lover holds that kind of resentment against his mistress's husband (le Comte).

This may go far. A Frenchman hates a woman because she has replaced him by another, or will replace him by another some day. A Frenchman is furious that he is not the sole and exclusive man, for life, in a woman's life. And here we are back at the Oedipus complex.

But there is another point: thinking it over, isn't the role of *father of a son* a peculiarly awkward one in French literature? Has a father *dignity* in France? That is to say: in a matriarchal country doesn't a father play a role perilously near to the ridiculous?—*i.e.*, a father, the father, the male?

Everywhere I have been sounding off on my doctrine that America is passing from a patriarchy to a matriarchy, and have been pointing out all the strains and stresses that must result from such a transition.

Could France be preparing to swing from a matriarchy to a patriarchy? Is there such a law of the pendulum? What would be the signs of it? Certainly, the consequences of a matriarchy are now being revealed to their last preposterous limits. What comes next?

And all this is somewhat related to Gide's *Journal*, . . . whose latest instalment has just been published: *Et Nunc Manet in Te, suivi de Journal Intime* ([Neuchâtel,] Ides et Calendes, 1951). First, a memoir of his life with his wife, then some portions of the *Journal* which have to do with it—all of it so horrendous for stupidity and cruelty and on top of it such *mauvaise foi* in the telling that it's too abysmal to discuss. . . .

But—to return to the main contention: the endlessly surprising thing about all this is that at every moment one is struck on the street by the fact that the French nation is extraordinarily *saine*; there's no doubt about it. These so frequently unstable organizations are supported by the glorious common sense of their diet and by the superb mental safeguard of their egotism. Healthy they are, and right they are—from this point of view—to guard their self-centeredness. . . .

Post-scriptum: I'm always looking for proofs of my contentions in the syntax and style and choice of words of authors. There is one throughout Anouilh that betrays his whole anguished fury against womankind. In his case it is not necessary to seek out supporting evidence like this, but this telltale giveaway is there.

Throughout the plays the men, launching into invective against unfaithful wives or recalcitrant *partenaires*, charge them with carrying a menace or with over-evaluating a desideratum—and then they give the physiological location of the sexual parts. Over and over again: "*entre vos jambes.*" Somehow, in their minds that *nails* the insult and climaxes the humiliation.

But to be sure, rightly, that is no pejorative at all. It merely reveals that a physiological location has acquired for Anouilh all the emotional intensity of his nature. It's as though someone were to cry: "*vous m'avez giflé avec cette main* au bout de vos bras."

I hope that henceforth I can apply this kind of observation in a totally different terrain: in the stylistic problems of Thoreau and Melville.

575. HÔTEL LEGRIS ET PARC, FONTAINEBLEAU, [FRANCE,] OCTOBER 3, 1951. Memoirs: An Encounter with Gurdjieff at Fontainebleau.

For fun, I'm going to see if I can increase my memory by an exercise in remembering. Those who know me best have long been astonished that I have no memory for events and (until lately) a remarkable memory for literature and the arts. Naturally, the latter is remarkable only among those whose interest in those matters is, as we say, passing. I have always been certain that I would never write my memoirs; even going so far as to entitle that hypothetical volume "If I Recall Correctly" or even "I Don't Remember." It would be well if some day I talked to myself in this Journal about the reasons for my short memory. At various times in my life—usually during periods of a short and agreeable insomnia—I have attempted that experiment in auto-analysis which promises to reward patience with a total recall and I have indeed found that a not-overstrained concentration on the days, for instance, of my childhood in Madison or Hong Kong can disinter an astonishing amount of lost material.

In the case of such an episode as I am about to record, there is a second reason for its probable superficiality; that is, that I used to tell it, "expatiate" it for the amusement of others. The result of such recitals—the conversations with Freud; even those with Gertrude Stein; the meetings with the [F. Scott] Fitzgeralds—is that memory has petrified at once into a stylization. One ends by remembering not what happened but one's first account of what happened, deeply overlaid with the comments, deductions, and even moralizings with which one recommended it to the listeners.

This is particularly true in the present case.

I think these events took place on the trip I made about 1927, *i.e.*, writing *The Bridge of San Luis Rey*.

On the boat to Naples I found as fellow passenger a former student at Lawrenceville, [X], . . . [who] was not only well-born . . . but rich. He had flunked out of Lawrenceville and other schools, and then out of Princeton, had flung himself about in dissipation, and was just intelligent enough to experience something that could be called despair. I think I remember a walk around the deck in which he told me that . . . , having heard two years before of Gurdjieff's Institute for the Harmonious Development of the Human Being at Le Château des Enfants at Fontainebleau, he had gone there as patient, had passed a year, then gone back to the United States and was now returning for another year.

Gurdjieff's Institute was beginning to be well-known by reason of Katherine Mansfield's residence and death there. . . . There had been an article about it in the *New Republic* recently,[3] from which I used to retell the anecdote of some Scottish spinster of high degree (I called her the Honorable Angela Balfour). Gurdjieff had commanded her to climb a tree and fall out of it. "But I'd hurt myself, Mr. Gurdjieff!" "Yes, you fa' down; you hurt yourself; you no die." (This I used

---

3. The article (which does not contain the "Balfour" anecdote) was Carl Zigrosser's "Gurdjieff," printed in the issue for June 5, 1929. Thornton Wilder's meeting with Gurdjieff took place, in 1931, *after*—rather than before—the great success of *The Bridge of San Luis Rey* (published November 3, 1927).

to recount with my schoolmasterish comment that she had done nothing in her life which had not been reasonably explained to her—but
in a thin class-narrowed sense of the reason.) [X] told me that the
Master could speak all the languages of the world without having
learned them—merely by plunging in concentration into the reservoir of the memory of the race; that he had made and lost millions
—he was a Levantine, something about Russian-Bulgarian-Turk, and
had dabbled in wheat—and that he had never to worry a moment
about money: that he could *will* it to come to him. (This was all too
true: when later he came to New York and held his *Stammtisch* at the
Columbus-Circle Child's Restaurant, he was known to be in strait-
ened circumstances. This was explained as follows: here in France he
had made an error in his experiments in the occult; he had offended
the dark powers and been punished by some accidents; I think he
broke his back and at the same time had lost some of his magical powers.) [X] added that he was writing a book, the great book, that would
sell for five thousand dollars a copy; that once a week he went to
Paris, where he had a table at the Café de la Paix, to which his former
pupils came to receive guidance and instruction, and that once
or twice a year he held similar consultation hours in Berlin, Zürich,
etc.; that at the Institute the guests were waited on, at table, by his
many illegitimate children, mostly very beautiful girls (and girls they
were and mostly beautiful). [X] asked me, if ever I came to Fontainebleau, to call on him and promised that he would introduce me to
the Master. . . .

Many months later I came to Fontainebleau and to this hotel. It
was not until I had walked about the Park that I suddenly remembered [X]. I telephoned the Château des Enfants and asked him to
dinner. He was eager that I should be introduced to Gurdjieff the
next morning. I soon came to see that [X] was the tolerated fool of the
establishment. He was eager and devoted, but incapable of the high
gravity which so strangely alternated there with an element of buf-
foonery. [X] felt that my presentation as his friend would somehow
raise his credit.

Gurdjieff sat every morning on the *terrasse* of a café on the main
street of the town. He drank coffee and cognac and required everyone
in his entourage to drink them. He was engaged in translating his
book into several languages. For each language he had an amanuen-
sis, and each of these was a beautiful woman. So the next morning at

eleven I was presented to him. He grunted and directed us to sit down and have a coffee and cognac. He was in whispered consultation over his text with a very beautiful French woman. At last he turned his attention to me. I cannot remember his face, except that it was at once sly and jovial, arrogant and clownish. He looked like a very intelligent Armenian rug-dealer. He asked a number of questions, at each of which he laughed inordinately. He ordered more coffee and cognac. Then he began expounding with much laughter and many a clownish flourish:

"In the world, everybody idiot. Twenty-one kinds of idiot: simple idiot, ambitious idiot, compassionate idiot, objective idiot, subjective idiot—everybody one kind of idiot."

"Well," I said, "I guess I know what kind of idiot I am: I'm the subjective idiot."

"Non. *Il ne faut pas aller trop vite. Il faut chercher.---- Mais vous êtes idiot type vingt: vous êtes idiot sans espoir!*"

This insult did not offend me, even though he continued laughing uproariously. My reception of it seemed to please him for he turned to [X] and asked him to bring me to the Château to dinner on that or the following night.

I had begun to like him, and his eyes rested on me almost affectionately. He held his glass toward mine and said—barely able to speak for laughter:

"I idiot, too. Everybody idiot. I idiot *type vingt-et-un:* I"—holding his forefinger emphatically pointed upward, "I the *unique* idiot"—with convulsions of complacent laughter.

I think I must have forgotten some passage in this first meeting . . . for when I recounted it I used to add:

"My feeling about Gurdjieff was that he was driven to a desire to dominate souls and that he was very clever—so clever that he was lonely. In his loneliness his sole resource was to play with other minds, to think one step beyond the person he was confronting. Here he insulted me first crudely, then less crudely, until finally he put his finger on the point that would cause me most pain. That he did, but what it was I have now forgotten. During the progress of the insults, however, he said things of interest, and these he intended you to be attracted by, if you were worthy.

"The phrase here that I was attracted by was the category 'compassionate idiot.' I had not yet read Nietzsche; but I was ripe for a de-

velopment on the theme that pity and compassion were a weakness
—precisely I, who came from a thought-world where these words
held an absolute prestige." . . .

8:30 p.m.

Turning over these memories while walking, more and more
returns to me. I am going to shut them off now for a few hours—take
up my Emerson matter, then fix my attention on Gurdjieff as I fall
asleep. Again an experiment to see if the memory so prompted can
bring back matter during and after sleeping.

578. HÔTEL LEGRIS ET PARC, FONTAINEBLEAU, [FRANCE,] MONDAY,
OCTOBER 8, 1951. Memoirs II: Encounter with Gurdjieff—
Continued.

These exercises have indeed recalled much, but still it is the
"matter that I remember to have told". . . .

That night or the following, then, I taxied for dinner to the Château des Enfants . . .—a pretentious building of large wide façade,
which had formerly housed some rich philanthropist's orphanage. Before it, a large gravel terrace surrounded a circular flower bed. An automobile stood in the driveway and beside it Gurdjieff and a lady. I
was to sit beside this lady at dinner, she was from Des Moines or
Omaha, one of those sad beautiful ambiguous grass-widows, whose
melancholy gentleness seems to allude to the fact that life has been
unjust and unkind. (Later, in Zürich, I was to know two more of
them, similarly hovering about Jung's establishment.)

Gurdjieff greeted me with his buffoon joviality and introduced
me to the lady. Presently he said to her: "Smell him and see if he have
money." He sniffed at me. "Yes, I smell him. I think that he have
money." Relaxed laughter.

I still think this brilliant. He knew that I thought that he attracted people of means and (like Rasputin and [Frank] Buchman) obtained such a hold on them that they were eager to press their checks
upon him. That I suspected him of having done with [X]. Here then
he brought the suspicion out into the light of day.

Before dinner [X] brought forward another resident—a recent

Princeton graduate of old American family; I have forgotten his name but will call him Rogers. Neither [X] nor Rogers was a neurotic; perhaps . . . they were the sons of neurotic mothers whose action on them had resulted merely in sapping with their will any sense of relationship with the world about them, hedonists without narcissism. Rogers aspired to be a writer. He explained that at the Institute one merely continued "to go on doing whatever one was interested in doing." I gathered that there were no classes, but that from time to time one had an interview with the Master. [X] and Rogers showed me around the grounds. There were the flower and vegetable gardens in which they worked from time to time; the bath house, where every Saturday night there was a community bath, part dance, part party, part ritual; the room over the cow barn where Katherine Mansfield lived until her death in 1923. (I have since read that sleeping over a cow barn is an ancient "folk" cure for consumptives.)

Dinner was served at one vast table; there must have been twenty-five of us. Before each place was a bottle of cognac. I sat at the right of a man of about forty—a Russian-speaking Frenchman, I think—to whom Gurdjieff assigned me. We were at about the fifth and sixth places at Gurdjieff's right. I was told that many of the guests were simply destitute Russian refugees whom he maintained there. As it had been predicted, we were waited on by a corps of healthy pretty smiling girls of between thirteen and sixteen. The chief thing to remark throughout the dinner was that Gurdjieff was noisy, jovial, and clowning, and that all the guests were muted, meditative, and withdrawn. The woman from Omaha at my left explained that the hardest things that you experienced at the Institute were not the intimate interviews that you had from time to time with the Master but the periods—often weeks long—when he did not speak to you and did not seem to be aware of your existence. I soon noticed that the company's eyes were frequently turned on me: I was the new, the next person, who was to undergo the purgatory through which they were passing. They may well have turned their eyes on me, however, for Gurdjieff was constantly directing his attention to me. He constantly toasted me in cognac. He frequently asked my guide (I think I remember that they talked in Russian) what I had said to him. A great deal of cognac was drunk, for Gurdjieff would raise his glass and propose that we drink to one or other of the twenty-one categories of idiot. The principal dish of the dinner was a sheep brought in on a vast platter. Its head was still on, and it was lying in a bed of cooked fruits

of all kinds. It was good; I was light-headed with cognac and I was enjoying myself. Gurdjieff and I were the only happy people at the table. Here my memory fails me, but I know that at some point, ques-
tioned by Gurdjieff, I threw back an answer that was little short of
impudent, and that the Master liked it.

After dinner some five of us moved into another room that had a
sort of divan platform at one end. Gurdjieff installed himself on the divan and called for a kind of zither.

"I sing songs to you," he said. "When I sing in Paris, in Berlin,
it cost two hundred dollars. I give you two hundred dollars." I forget
the music and its delivery entirely.

Then he said: "I let you read my book. When my book published it cost five thousand dollars. I give you five thousand dollars."

For this I was put in charge of Rogers. Rogers was most particularly enjoined not to let me out of his sight while I was reading the
manuscript. Before we separated Gurdjieff asked me to come to the
bath party on the following Saturday night. I had been told that the
baths practiced at the Institute were of the Russian-Baltic-Finnish order and asked Gurdjieff how they could be good for the human system—since in nature it would not be possible to find conditions
whereby one could effect the immediate alternation of extreme hot
and cold water; and I ended up by invoking the development of the
human body during the hundreds of thousands of years before such
artificial conditions could be arrived at, and asking whether such an
appeal to natural conditions was not correct?*

Gurdjieff did not directly answer my objection, but my objection caused him a sort of ribald delight, which resulted in his crying:
"All Americans dirty. They take too many baths. All Americans dirty."
He pointed slyly at me and said: "You no square idiot, you *round* idiot." Rogers, [X], and I then went to a series of smaller public rooms
and I was given, in English typescript, the first prefatory chapter of
what was later called "The Tales of Beelzebub" (recently printed under still another title).[4] I was not greatly impressed; all I remember of

---

*This passage and several others I shall recount I had forgotten. After finishing the first
part of Entry 575, I took a walk. I set myself the task of trying to recall what took place. These
details slowly returned to me. But they returned not from a memory of the occasion, but from
my memory of what I *used to recount.* They are not the less true for that; but they are not true
recall.

4. *All and Everything,* vol. 1 (1950).

it now is a sort of allegorical fantasy resembling the parable of the rider governing two horses from Plato's *Phaedrus*. [X] and Rogers proposed to play a game of chess and, for some convenience of light or table, moved into the next room, leaving an open door between us. It was for this infraction of Gurdjieff's order that Rogers was later expelled from the Institute, told to pack his trunk and go.

This I heard later when I went to Gurdjieff to take my leave. The stormy dismissal was taking place. I assumed that Gurdjieff had made the rule to insure that I would not take notes from his text for purposes of plagiarism or ridicule. I said to him: "But Mr. Gurdjieff you could see *by my eyes* (*sic!*) that I wouldn't do anything with your book that you wouldn't like."

"No," cried Gurdjieff, "he no do what I tell him. He go!"

He then turned to me with bright-eyed invitation. "You come here and stay. You come three days, three months, or three years."

"I'd like to," I said, hesitantly. "But I can't come now. I can come in November." (I think I was probably going to the Salzburg Festival.)

Suddenly Gurdjieff put on one of his rages. I had already seen one during the evening. Perhaps it was the expulsion of Rogers, but my memory seems to tell me that there had been another. He rowed and lashed his arms about and stamped. "Not November, now! I no live November. I live *now*."

It was terrific and it passed as suddenly as it came. It was not a loss of control; it was a pedagogic emphasis.

He accompanied me down to the Gate House, where a porter was standing, a young Russian in a Russian blouse.

I proposed to walk home. "No," said Gurdjieff, "I send you home in car."

I protested that I liked walking, that I walked everywhere.

"No," he said, smiling at the Russian, who was to be my chauffeur. "He drive you to hotel. You no pay him. I pay him. I pay him—by showing him money." And he took a piece of paper money from his pocket and passed it before the eyes of the Russian. He grinned; the Russian grinned.

That, again, I think was bold and brilliant. Other people live by money; the relation of master and servant is regulated by money. Here we live by far more real values—so that we can even ridicule money in this way.

Naturally, I never went back. That enormous egotism could only establish its spell over crippled souls; but it was great fun to see.

All this is the exact truth, nor has the smallest thing been withheld. But I have got no pleasure from the telling. Would it have been a pleasure if I had been writing from a memory of it that had not been codified by previous relations? I don't think so. The sheer data—the abject truth—these do not interest me. History is for *Diener*-natures.

Isn't the reason for it that at fifty-four one has seen everything once and twice? A single example of charlatanism, astuteness, aimlessness—vary in detail though each may—no longer arrests the interest, which now lies all in relation, in the reasons for things. The interest of [X] and Rogers would lie in how they reached the Institute—how that kind of offered cure came to their notice, what went on in them. And [the] why of Gurdjieff is precisely what I had no way of finding out.

581. SS "SATURNIA," OCTOBER 30, 1951. Jean Genêt: *Oeuvres Complètes*; Volume II: *Notre-Dame-des-Fleurs; Le Miracle de la Rose;* and Two Poems. (Marie-Louise Bousquet tells me that Volume I—not out yet—will consist of Sartre's essay on Genêt; that this volume (Gallimard, 1951) was put out as a trial flight to see whether the police would suppress it.)

My acquaintance with Genêt began at Aspen. Saul Colin sent a copy of the English translation of *Notre-Dame-des-Fleurs*, bound in soft leather at thirty dollars—an edition which has had a most extensive circulation throughout the United States. I read the first thirty pages with astonishment and contempt, but was presently caught up into amazed admiration.

Now I have this French text,* which I must presently throw overboard.

First, a work of prodigious art, not only as brilliant writing but as establishment of tone, as *éclairage:* the oscillation between subjec-

---

*On the titlepage the title is written without dashes; on the top of every page, however, the hyphens hold. In the text the character is almost always given with the hyphens.

tive lyricism and the most detailed description of his world is managed with infinite resource.

Second, a work of unbroken artifice and ruse. As literature, all
livresque, all conscious; and as *tableau de moeurs* and as personal
document, all calculation.

Yet it is hard to imagine how this material could have been recounted differently unless it were by someone who was not "of it."
Sartre obviously copied a part of it in the first section of his tetralogy;[5]
but this is by an insider and that is the overwhelming strangeness of
it. The blurb says that *"s'il faut lui trouver un maître, ce n'est pas
Villon mais Rimbaud."* It may be Rimbaud for the poems—which
seem to me very bad and archy-artificial; but these novels have not
the authenticity of Rimbaud. No, the master is Proust—and for pages
on end the tone is Proust; and not because of the *moeurs* involved;
but Proust's is the rhetoric and Proust's the analysis of motivation
and, above all, Proust's is the guile.

Genêt had been burglar, then male prostitute (for males); as
new arrival at a house of correction he had had to pass the usual
ordeal—to be *violé*—by scores of the older inmates. And it happened that, this once in a hundred thousand cases, the *voyou* had the
endowment of a great writer.

Again the blurb says this is *"l'itinéraire d'un homme qui a visé à
transformer la malédiction qu'il subissait en salut."* Not *salut*. Out of
this abjection, forever inexpiable, he has built up a vast mythology, a
vast proclamative front; he uses the language of chivalry and of religion. These executed murderers are heroes and saints; much is made
of their "purity" and of the sublimity of their behavior before their
judges and executioners. And this transference of values won't work
—or will only work in so far as we watch its odd operation in Genêt's
mind. He makes no concealment of the fact—though at the same
time imposing on the images this idolatrous symbolism—that these
heroes are for him passionately desired sexual objects. He is attracted
by (1) their beauty, (2) their having committed murders (or
treacheries—an even more seductive qualification), and (3) their having been executed. To be sure "Divine" (who is given to betraying
"her" pals to the police) dies of tuberculosis, but Genêt will have [it]
that (page 13) *"Divine est morte sainte et assassinée—par la phtisie."*

---

5. Presumably *L'Age de raison* (1945), part one of his *Les Chemins de la liberté* (1945-
49).

But these canonizations do not work—or work only in so far as they throw our eyes back on Genêt—Genêt producing a trick and knowing that he is doing so. Here again the publishing blurb is wrong and is an impertinence: *"Jamais style n'a transfiguré d'une manière plus éclatante des héros de faits-divers; mais derrière ces héros . . . il y a l'évidence de destins aussi rigoureux qu'exemplaires."* Which is nonsense.

Genêt has read a great deal of great literature (he stole the volumes, beautifully bound, while housebreaking), but he also read— and describes with deep emotion—hundreds of dime novels of bandits, pirates, knights, and cowboys. And the heroes of these works were for him the objects of an all too literal, passionate fixation. The habit was formed: he is in an intense erotic relation with the characters of his creation.

It is his literary problem—and how conscious a literary artist he is—to make us accept his glorification and justification of his passional image—his habit, his necessity, his *malédiction*. This is what the Marquis de Sade set out to do also—with a far less dazzling literary equipment; but he pursued a different course: he tried to overtopple, first, our previous—our "normal"—preconceptions in regard to a wide variety of matters. De Sade, moreover, had a less difficult task, since there is a component of "sadism" in all passion.

Genêt engages, then, in every device which may establish himself in his own eyes and in ours as a "hero of erotic revelation"—every device except pathos. Proud he is, and the measure of his lofty pride is that he does not invoke pity. The material for such an invocation is omnipresent—especially in the second novel [*Le Miracle de la rose*] material for a conjoined horror and pity is omnipresent. The novels are immense constructions of special pleading, but that plea he does not enter: he is not the victim of early upbringing or neurotic deformation; not even the victim of an uncomprehending society.

A great deal of the time his plea is, as it were, presented in reverse: he insults us; he hurls obscenities at us—that is to show us that he is not bowed down with shame, he is not engaged precisely in pleading. The novels are very different; in *Notre-Dame-des-Fleurs* he reproduces at great length the life of these doll-like men—his people, his kind—showing them mocked by the populace, forced into a little world of their own. He is aware of (and underscores) the extranormality of it, but marks no scorn as he marks no pathos. Yet it has horror, too, and he knows it; but horror can exist with contempt which implies superiority in the onlooker. And here his "pleading" (his attempt to establish himself as a sort of moral hero) takes its most ingenious turn. He says that he descended into degradation for reasons one must respect:

[*Notre-Dame-des-Fleurs,*] page 51: ". . . *Je pourrais . . . confier que ce mépris que je supporte—en riant aux éclats, ce n'est pas encore . . . par mépris du mépris, mais pour n'être pas ridicule, pour n'être pas avili, par rien ni personne. . . . Que j'annonce que je suis une vieille pute, personne ne peut surenchère, je décourage l'insulte."* . . .

[*Le Miracle de la rose,*] page 210: There are no horrors in the world (he lists some) like ". . . *les quelques détails qui font du prisonnier . . . un réprouvé. Mais à l'intérieur de la prison, à son coeur même, existe le mitard et la salle de discipline d'où l'on remonte purifié.*"

Genêt, like Dostoievski, could have made us believe in this final purification and saintliness achieved through the conscious exploration of the last abjection, if he had not used his material constantly toward an erotic gratification before our very eyes. You can't both be purified by Hell and enjoy Hell at the same time.

But in one important passage he claims to have emerged from Hell: [*Le Miracle de la rose,*] page 206: "*Si j'écrivais un roman, j'aurais quelqu' intérêt à m'étendre sur mes gestes d'alors, mais je n'ai voulu par ce livre que montrer l'expérience menée de ma libération d'un état de pénible torpeur, de vie honteuse et basse, occupée par la prostitution, la mendicité et soumise aux prestiges, subjuguée par les charmes du monde criminel. Je me libérais par et pour une attitude plus fière.*"

Perhaps I have read these books wrong; perhaps that is what he shows us; but I think not.

Post-scripta:

But—as I have said so often on the platform—the secret of a writer's life is his search for the real Right Subject. Like Lawrence of Arabia, Genêt was (and more than Lawrence) a born writer. From earliest years he must have felt the life he led and the life about him as straining toward a state of literature. The ever-deepening horrors must have presented themselves to him as writable, transfigurable into a picture of themselves. With a sensibility like his he had no choice but (1) to kill himself (he tells of such promptings), (2) to become a saint,* or (3) to try for Dante's guerdon.

But one must not forget the constant gratuitous "self-indulgent" obscenity throughout. In the light of that it is almost with a smile one sees that France has to accept this painful situation: a great writer who exceeds the worst scabrosity of the Roman Empire.

How ironic a visitation. What a *fléau!*

583. SS "SATURNIA," THURSDAY, NOVEMBER 1, 1951. Emerson's Essay, "Experience," Paragraph 8: Explication de Texte.

For weeks now I've been tormenting myself with R.W.E.'s *Essays.*

I shall fight it out on this line if it takes me all winter. I feel sure that if I keep doggedly at this material the key will emerge.

It is not that I wish to demonstrate how bad a writer he is, but that I may from the phenomenon R.W.E. deduce the principles as to how each American (1) must be the founder of a new religion, (2) shrinks from the operation which is art, and (3) is an autodidact and a bad one, *i.e.*, is badly educated.

Then I wish to turn my finding back into my text at the point where I am analyzing the climacteric paragraphs of *Moby-Dick.*

Yes, this may take me all winter. . . .

If "Friendship" is the essay in which Emerson is most confused, embarrassed and contradictory, "Experience" is the one in which he lets us see most overtly all the latent distaste which his egocentric, passionless, and narcissistic nature felt for the world about him and for the role he is condemned to play in life.

---

*As illustration of this relation between extreme suffering and saintliness and as last illustration of his magnificent command of language, [*Le Miracle de la rose,*] pages 215–216: "*Ces condamnés à mort par toute leur vie—les relégués—savent qu'il n'est pour échapper à l'horreur que l'amitié. . . . après avoir assisté à la scène aussi terriblement fabuleuse que la menace coléreuse de Dieu au couple puni, oser vivre et vivre de toutes ses forces, a la beauté tragique des grandes malédictions car c'est digne de ce que fit dans le cours de tous les âges l'Humanité mise à la porte du Ciel. Et c'est proprement la sainteté, qui est de vivre selon le Ciel, malgré Dieu.*"

That almost persuades one. All Humanity has been cursed, is sinful, and is in dire distress. Wherein are these condemned young men much worse than their fellow mortals? And see—says Genêt—with what pride and energy and intermittently self-forgetting love they live out their lives, though immured, victimized and reviled.

He does not know that he contains these subterranean sources of distaste and, uneasy, he can always conceal it from himself by untapping his eupeptic nature, to which he gives the name of "sublime thoughts" and "divine intimations." Hence, the incoherence into which he is thrown; hence the odd doubletalk. . . .

. . . it is all undisciplined, slipshod—partly because Emerson cannot concentrate and partly because he is trying to be impressive by means of a willed indistinctness.

587. **COLUMBIA UNIVERSITY CLUB, [NEW YORK,] TUESDAY, NOVEMBER 6, 1951.** Emerson's Optimism (and America's).

Again there are so many things one has to hold in one's head at once—or at least . . . until one sees their relation to one another (and that seeing can only be reached at the moment they are all in one's head together at once; because if you get it wrong at the start you are apt to be wrong forever after):

(1) That when you discard a tradition-built God and start making up one for yourself, that new God will be a portrait of yourself. From which we derive: that when you discard a tradition-built interpretation of life-and-death, the one you will substitute for it will be fashioned after the traits of your own character.

(2) Your conception of the Good and the Beautiful . . . cannot be any higher than your conception of the Evil and the Loss (the Wasted and the Wronged and the Irrevocably Doomed) is low: your imagination's Bright is the counterpart of your imagination's Dark.

(3) A man whose reports of spiritual happiness are disconnected from his observation of happiness-and-woe in a total humanity is (as an interpreter) as useless to us as a man whose reports of spiritual woe are similarly disconnected. Nay, he is more so: for even he will acknowledge that his periods of happiness are only occasional—hence a report of woe comes nearer to reporting a universal condition.

Emerson lived for his moments of realization of the harmony of the universe. (The differences between his "moments of realization" and Thoreau's boyish "ecstasies" are instructive.) Those moments were so authentic to Emerson that he felt empowered by them to become the teacher and to instruct the world about the lessons he learned from them.

He had these authority-investing moments (1) first from the contemplation of nature, *i.e.*, landscape, (2) second, from meditations about total human history, as derived from reading—in the following order: the mystics, especially Sanskrit; Swedenborg; then the Greek poets; then the English poets. In other words, revelation came to him from woods, inland waters, wild life; and then from books. Glaringly conspicuous as lacking is the association with men and women. . . .

Emerson had so arranged his life that he was at a considerable distance from poverty, crime, vice, and squalor, and that chief aspect of evil as felt in most lives: the injury one has done to others (on which Tolstoi in that great scene makes turn the whole question of an after life). Emerson arranged his nature walks so that he had no occasion to confront the vast, the impersonal, and the overwhelming. . . .

Hence: Emerson selected the *Welt-bild* from which he drew his deductions. But first his own temperament had directed this selection.

I see that Van Wyck Brooks affirms that Emerson had known difficulty, poverty, and frustration. I doubt it; even if these conditions had been about him, they would have meant something different in that Boston air and, secondly, he would have been of too shuttered a mind to have taken them for such. He did not starve; he was not beaten; he was not—like Poe—hated. The death of his first wife? I can well believe he suffered; but he may well have *reached his resignation* too soon. There was no element of protest in him. He describes how the death of his son was not able to bring him to the feeling that he was coping with reality.

He was—to use a much admired phrase—sufficient to himself. And here we are back to our American individualism. That's what American individualism is: sufficiency to oneself. That Americans are also lonely and hence *in*sufficient to themselves is only apparently a contradiction: for they are sufficient to themselves without being able to make that sufficiency into a sufficiency to the whole experience of life which includes themselves.

Europeans are not sufficient to themselves: they must draw strength from all those dependencies on the social group, the environment, on religion, but on religion as it reaches them through its repetititions, agents, rituals, and concretions. They make for themselves a better sufficiency (to live by) from all that is about them; they make little effort to be sufficient to themselves: that only their great can do.

Emerson was sufficient to himself—and urgently admonishes us to be also; but he made a very suspect virtue of excluding a large part of the total human experience.

[Columbia University Club, New York,] Next Day.

Why, then, did the Americans split the role of evil in the world into the two aspects: Calvinist-bad conscience and optimism-humanitarianism (leaving our special-case Emerson to revolt against and airily discard the first)? Self-sufficiency drives to introspection or to externalization.

Theology—traditional with them—furnished the Founders with a grammar and technique for introspection. As one sees all around one today, introspection is self-stiflement unless one has inherited modes; there [is] no dead-end like self-exploration without a technique: hence the popularity here of psychoanalysis.

Emerson and most Americans threw away Calvinism and, with that discard, they saw that deep analysis of the self was directionless and wasted energy; so they turned to looking outward.

Emerson never tried to examine whence came his revelations, his divine promptings. It was enough for him to say: "I feel this; this insight slid into my soul."

588. **COLUMBIA UNIVERSITY CLUB [NEW YORK,] NOVEMBER 7, 1951.**
Emerson and the Lack of the Middle (or Emerson and the Counsel of Perfection).

It is too early for me to try to decide whether or not Emerson shrank from the contemplation of evil in and outside himself; whether it was a form of fear and anxiety, and guarding of a tender bruise, or whether he was the Insensitive Plant who was simply able to grow up unaware.

At all events, let us remember our Law: he who is not aware of evil in himself will not know what to do with it in the world about him. He may, of course, be much occupied with it (as Emerson was not), but it will be stupidly done (as reformer, as writer, for example); he will be impatient with it, exasperated by it, and, in many cases, will develop a hard cutting cruelty about it.

And there our second Law: he who does not know evil will not know good.

And here we come to Emerson's concept of the Good, the True, and the Beautiful. He will have them, he will urge them, only in their Extreme Condition. He knows no middle shades. . . .

Emerson creates his atmosphere of sublimity by . . . eliminating the mixed elements of good and evil: all of "Friendship" [is] written as though all those great concepts, Soul, Genius, Over-Soul, and Nature, were right there at hand for Mr. Smith and Miss Jones to work with, without cost or struggle. Emerson can assure you of this because he's got them, and (as far as his report goes) without cost and without struggle.

Genius without tears. Greatness without effort. . . .

590. COLUMBIA UNIVERSITY CLUB, [NEW YORK,] NOVEMBER, 1951.
American Individualism.

When lecturing I gave the examples of English, French, and Spanish individualism. I claimed that every country was individualistic, but each on a different terrain. And then I could not find a way of stating the particular type and area of the Americans'.

Now I have come up with self-sufficiency.

But as a word, a designation, it is not right. At first I see it as too positive; its negative would be better: *the inability to draw strength from any dependence.*

Am I, however, thinking only of the "sensitive" American? Those others—Westchester County—are certainly frantically engaged in justifying themselves to themselves through their belonging to the right crowd, and through their showing their money: a dependence, indeed. Which brings us back to the view I have so often taken that the American gregariousness is a real (but unrewarded, frustrated, and vain) attempt to create a belonging.

Shall I rest with the formulation that religion is the sense that one belongs—that it is right that one is here? And won't that serve for happiness also?

And *that* the American cannot have in any of the ways that the European has had it.

For a European even his sense of time—that it is a continuum, inexorable but a belt, a closely-woven belt—can be a "comfort." And even that [comfort] (to say nothing of place, environment, institutions) is denied to the American: time does not *support* an American, it is something he *fills*; time is neutral, it is not charged; time is at his disposal for what he can impress upon it.

596. PRINCETON INN, [PRINCETON, N.J.,] TUESDAY, NOVEMBER 27, 1951. Syntax and the Expression of Freedom.

I'm not ready to write this, but I'll launch out as best I can, to see what may occur.

Have been reading *The House of Seven Gables.* Yes, into my [Norton] book I shall insert two undelivered lectures: "Emerson, American All Too American," and "Hawthorne or the American Who Looked Back."

Allegory is the sorriest form of narration, but it can be done: Spenser and Bunyan (and one can see how they managed to escape its dead weight), Hans Christian Andersen and [Ferdinand] Raimund.

How is it that Hawthorne is able to remove the freedom from his characters?

All narratives take place in the past and the author's knowledge of what-happened-later constantly threatens to divorce the characters from their ignorance of the future, *i.e.,* their movement in freedom. This danger is multiplied many times when the behavior of the characters is imposed upon them in order to illustrate a moral truth. All that's easy to see.

The narrational stifling proceeds from the author's constantly insinuating a final descriptive judgment on them. They are condemned in advance to be that kind of person, and unless the writer is in love with freedom he will inevitably condemn them to a very narrowed "kind of person," to mere type. That is easy to see.

But what stylistic and syntactical modes will betray the author's refusal of liberty? It cannot be tense: Stendhal's preterite and Flaubert's imperfect both permit to Julien Sorel and Emma Bovary their freedom.

The answer somehow lies in description and in adjectives and adverbs. . . .

Again—these natures (Hawthorne's) believe in *essences*. It is
easy and very self-gratifying to make a judgment on an essence.

Last Tuesday I heard a very incoherent lecture by Jacques
Maritain on the Moral Responsibiity of the Artist. For the greater
part of it his dogmatic addiction had resulted in his refusing to think.
. . . But suddenly I heard him saying:

"There have never been in the history of the world—and never
will be—two identical cases of conscience. Each one is unique and
must be met in its existential [*sic!*—the word and association re-
curred frequently] situation." Naturally, since we had just been hearing about [morality] my thought jumped to Adultery; but Maritain's
thought, bolder than mine, jumped to Murder. I thought I would
then hear an extension into an infinity of potentialities of the classical
thirty-two situations in which it is permissible to take up arms without
sin. But again Maritain disappeared down a side alley of evasion.

Freedom in the human being does imply that no two situations
are ever the same. The belief in essences tends—especially in an
imaginative narrator—to affirm that persons are restricted within
types and situations.

And the way that an author betrays his disinterest in his characters' freedom is by insinuating his judgment—and this brings us back
to one of our categories in Omniscience.[6] But this [is] . . . a stylistic
criterion; I dream of enclosing with hard work a syntactical one—
with the hope of being able to apply it even to my page from
Moby-Dick.[7]

**602.   1440 NORTH ATLANTIC AVENUE, DAYTONA BEACH, [FLA.,]
FEBRUARY 11, 1952. Science Fiction.**

Waiting for Les Glenn at the airport I bought my first "science-
fiction" magazines, having heard much about the widespread and increasing cult of this kind of reading. . . .

It should be considered in constant relation to the other two
branches of mass reading: murder-mysteries and Westerns.

---

6. See Entry 433 (March 3, 1950).

7. In the first of the Norton Lectures (published in *American Characteristics and Other
Essays* [1979], as "Toward an American Language"), Thornton Wilder made a detailed analysis
of Melville's writing, using one page from chapter 133 of *Moby-Dick*.

It is being remarked everywhere that these last two "genres" have undergone a degradation: Westerns, which began as stories of action and fantasies that offered a contrast to the complications of big-city life, have tended more and more to appeal to sadism; murder-mysteries, that began by appealing to intellectual ingenuity, while at the same time arousing and allaying fear, have tended to exploit sadism and pornography (the latter deriving from an element in Dashiell Hammett, from whom came Chandler and now Spillane— three million copies in one year).

So far science fiction is addressed to activity of *exploration* alone. Even fear and horror are secondary—for the Martians, Vimps, Sluggs, and extraterrestrial races and beasts are carefully analyzed, explained—each having its novelty deduced from the physical conditions of its origin—in such a way that they are less objects of atavistic dread, vague "menaces," than objects of curiosity.

There have now been so many of these stories that the authors are hard put to it to "explore" every new type of enemy to human life. Already after reading eight of them, I find my appetite flagging.

The predominating theme is modes of life on the other stars. For the most part the writers seem to have outgrown or exhausted the invention of bird-like or five-handed or trunk-nosed beings. The emphasis is *how would they think?* The extension of space is correlated with the extension (by speculation) of modes of intellection; and the resolution of the story is how we—human *by mind*—overcame a different kind of *mind*. One story, here, takes place on our earth; a group of us humans has developed a mutant trait (editors discussing this literature talk of *mutant* stories as an important category of the art), they have *telekinesis* and have subjugated the rest of the earth's population to serfdom; the story shows how a secret resistance group finds a way to obtain *telekinesis* for all (the Teleks). In another story, the Aliens, from another planet, are enclosed in reservations; they have extraordinary powers and are apparently dangerous to us not by malice but by incomprehension; they talk English but unintelligible English; it's impossible to get in communication with them. All their values, interests, and reactions are different from ours. A beginning is found, and it is explained that they merely developed otherwise.

These stories are never surrealist; science is called on for an explanation of everything. In the constant search for novelty the authors go very far afield and some obtain effects of great interest and beauty. In one an Order stationed in Vega trains young men in the hundreds, thousands of stellar languages, so that they may serve as Translators (Heralds) for commerce throughout the Universe with the noble aim of introducing peace through commerce. Our young hero's library (of course on reels—reading has become conventionalized in these stores,—your microfilmed books are on reels, and a machine casts the image on the wall) includes: *Nicholson on Martian Verbs,* . . . *A Concise Grammar of Cephean* . . . ; but the story and its title ("That Share of Glory," *Astounding Science Fiction,* January 1952) turns on a phrase from Machiavelli's *The Prince:* "God is not willing to do everything, and thus take away our free will and that share of glory which belongs to us."

It is inevitable that this kind of story, so removed from the particularizations of our daily life, should tend to support itself by— should even require—general ideas and, without becoming didactic, story after story brings to clarity certain generalizations of moral elevation which would be out of place in murder-mysteries and Westerns.*

This enormous popular foliation will probably soon decline and decay; but it is certainly a deeply interesting phenomenon. It is the vulgarization of the scientific and technological concentration of the century. It would appear to stem from Jules Verne, but the passionate curiosity about mind constitutes a very real shift of emphasis.

The most important thing to notice is that it is not "frightened" literature. (. . . A specialist states that the golden age of the genre was 1939–49—that is, mostly before the atom bomb.) . . . The delight of exploration of space and mentality outweighs all the elements of dread, danger, and horror. Escape from this planet certainly plays a part, but the tacit assumption underlies all, that travel through deep space is imminent and that earth-humans will continue to be the norm. They will triumph, we are told, because the exploration of space will be constantly accompanied by an exploration of latent mental powers. The stories reflect a sort of pitying disdain for the backward twentieth century—such great and new developments are lying just around the corner.

---

*It should be noted that not infrequently science is the villain of the piece—that is, the story turns on a revolt against a world that has been overregulated by scientific developments. Science is but one exploration of the mind and mind must depose it to a subordinate position in the interests of life.

608. DEEPWOOD DRIVE, [HAMDEN, CT.,] FRIDAY, MAY 9, 1952.
Works in Progress.

Now I am indeed up to my neck in work and in unredeemed
pledges of work. Half of every week I go to New York to talk over this
"Chicago" (continually writing scenes for it, there and here);[8] the first
of the Nortons has been accepted by the *Atlantic* and the second (that
is: *a* second) must be readied for the August issue; I am overdue in
forwarding to the Academy my brief remarks for the Medal award;[9]
Oberlin wants some sort of advance material of the Commencement
address; in Cambridge at the [William] James's I read aloud my long-
promised guest-column for Leonard Lyons[1] and my piece on A.
Woollcott for the *Harvard Library Bulletin*,[2] but both must be
rewritten and pulled together; and, finally, I have promised a Lope
contribution to the Festschrift for Professor [S. Griswold] Morley.[3]
And in addition to all that, such stacks of unanswered letters.

The progress of the movie amazes me. We begin with a worth-
less story by Ben Hecht, throwing more and more of it away. Gradually in the conversations (Marcello Gerosi, Orin Jennings—Vittorio
[De Sica] does not add plot elements) something has grown. At intervals, not from enthusiasm, but from sheer distress at the story's unsat-
isfactoriness, I think of some new complication or "enrichment"; that
addition, in turn, dictates a new development. Could it be possible
that this is all right?—that the story is forcing from us its own true organic life? Might not this whole construction suddenly topple down

---

8. "Rain in Chicago," based on Ben Hecht's novel *Miracle in the Rain* (1943), was to have
been Vittorio De Sica's first American film, for Warner Brothers. De Sica himself worked, with
Thornton Wilder and Orin Jennings, on the adaptation, and eventually wrote a screenplay with
Dudley Nichols, but the project was abandoned. A film, "Miracle in the Rain," made in 1956,
was based on a script by Hecht and was directed by Rudolph Maté.

9. The text of Thornton Wilder's remarks on the occasion of the Award of Merit Medal for
Drama given to Sidney Kingsley by the American Academy of Arts and Letters was printed in
its *Proceedings*, 2d ser., no. 2 (1952), pp. 20–21.

1. Between June 22 and 29 and July 9 and 13, 1952, while Leonard Lyons was in Europe,
his daily column for the *New York Post*, "The Lyons Den," was written by guest-contributors,
including Herman Wouk, James Jones, Truman Capote, and Robert E. Sherwood. Apparently,
Thornton Wilder's contribution was not completed to his satisfaction for it was not printed as
part of the series.

2. See Entries 557, 560, and 565 (August 18 and 20 and September 7, 1951).

3. The projected volume was not published. Thornton Wilder contributed his MLA paper on Lope to *Varia Variorum: Festgabe für Karl Reinhardt* (1952).

about our ears as forced, contrived—a sort of cumulative over-self-persuasion?

The second Norton instalment presents a real problem since out of the six chapters we are to serialize only three. Shall I now "direct" the Thoreau chapter, as though it were a second of three, rather than a second of six? For this, I would have to cut out much of the biographical material and what would be left? The passage on Forest-Gods versus Desert-Gods; the passage on friendship and gregarious-solitude, which is already treated more generally in the first instalment. There must be the essay on the American time-sense, and that is not well represented by Thoreau. But none of the four others would fit the situation much better. I'd better do the Thoreau, making a sort of cuisine of passages robbed from the other chapters; only the Occasional Judicious will note a sort of "incoherence in application," and the whole will come out more correctly in the book.[4]

In the Medal Address I don't know what to say. It will be only five minutes long or less. I'll try and take hold of Gertrude [Stein]'s "decline of reality in an imagined thing."

The Lope paper is the most attractive. I'd like to do a mixture of a charming essay and a bit of erudition—a sort of [John Livingston Lowes's] *Road to Xanadu* (which I never read), dating one play, but weaving together many suppositions and half-dating a score of plays in the process. I think that I could start with Lope's forging the participation of Alfonso VIII in the Crusades—showing that it had not occurred to him when he wrote *La corona merecida* in early 1603, *i.e.*, he had not yet begun *La Jerusalén conquistada*; that work began late in 1603 when he wrote the "Epistola" to the Cantador—and then weaving in *El ejemplo de las casadas* (I have just found out today that when writing *La Jerusalén* he had no idea that a Moncada of Barcelona accompanied the King to Palestine) and *Los paces de los reyes*. So *El ejemplo* is posterior to *La Jerusalén* (published 1609 but finished 1605). Then, if I have time for it, the dating of *Los paces* involves Pinedo's company and the boy-actor. Fun, fun, fun; but I should have weeks of solitary work for it.

Now to go back to writing the movie. Late last night I wrote the first conversation, in the park, between Milly and her sergeant. Now

---

4. Three essays—revised versions of Norton Lectures—were printed in the *Atlantic*: "Toward an American Language" (July 1952), "The American Loneliness" (August 1952), and "Emily Dickinson" (November 1952).

I do a rewriting of a scene I did in Chicago—Milly's first meeting with the sergeant's family.

(*Postscript:* Later that night I realized that I could not continue writing the dialogue for Vittorio's picture. A number of reasons went into this decision which I had to announce to my Italian friends the next day and which caused them great consternation and distress. Although I had written a number of telling scenes, I saw that my nightly fabrications were purely synthetic; I was bolstering a story line which I would never have submitted myself. I could see that Vittorio's interest in the story inclined to presenting a Chicago—a loveless jungle of concrete—which represented his first superficial impression and which moreover he felt to be demanded of him by a small group of *aficionados* in Italy who were warning him in open letters in their newspapers not to be seduced from his "neo-realistic honesty" by the deceptive optimism of the land of "hamburgers and sanitary fixtures."

Moreover, another writer was in our company whose contributions in plot and dialogue, of abysmal conventionality and practiced facility, were appealing to my Italian friends; their basic taste had deserted them as they confronted the problem of picture-making in a new country and as they uneasily remembered that their script must be submitted for summary acceptance or rejection by Charles K. Feldman [the producer]. I saw being repeated the old story—the *dépaysement* of great artists thrown off their center in this country and finally mangled and rejected—which was the story of [Max] Reinhardt, [Elisabeth] Bergner, René Clair, [Julien] Duvivier, and [F. W.] Murnau.)

619.   COLUMBIA UNIVERSITY CLUB, NEW YORK, 6:15 A.M., JULY 15, 1952,
"LES GRANDES CHALEURS."   The Norton Poe Chapter.

"Poe had a very unhappy life."

How do you mean?

"Well, you can't deny, Mr. Wilder, that he was very unhappy most of the time—resorting to drink and drugs; living in awful poverty; seeing so often those he loved dying of disease. Of course, he lived a most unhappy life."

Who says so?

"I say so. Everybody says so."

Does Poe say so?

"Yes. Yes, often."

Does Poe say the experience of life itself is an unhappy experience?

"Well, now you [are] trying to involve me in some paradox of your own making. I affirm that Poe had a very unhappy life and I mean to stick to it."

The words *happy-unhappy* must always be handled with care.

Poe's is indeed held to be almost a type of the unhappy life. His life obviously was filled with causes for unhappiness. He did not escape occasions that filled him with grief, with rage, with a sense of suffocating frustration. Henry Adams was rich, healthy, surrounded by friends, and never lacked the admiration of men and women whose judgment he valued. Probably the central event in both men's lives was the loss of a much-loved wife. One has the sense, however, that Adams was a far unhappier man than Poe.

Is there a particularly American way of being happy or unhappy?

I said in the first lecture that American writers (nay, the American people talking) have been trying to give to the English language a "continuous present" even when they are talking of past events; that the preterite ("Poe had a very unhappy life") is always in danger of giving a wrong impression; it is a judgment delivered at the end of a continued action; it implies a determinism; and it robs those past moments of their once-lively orientation toward the future. . . .

The phrase "Poe had an unhappy life" tends to give the impression that Poe throughout his life was unable to believe that there could be any satisfactions, rewards, any "winning through" for him. And that is not true. That was true for Henry Adams and for Thoreau. They had not, however, reached the worst state, which is the loss of a belief in all possibility; they were merely in limbo—the loss of belief in the possibility *for them* of any succeeding. "The mass of men lead lives of quiet desperation"[5]—*i.e.*, they have lost the belief that there are to be any fair possibilities for them.

Unhappiness means loss of belief in possibility. Hell is the loss of belief in possibility. I avoid the use of the word *hope*, because I wish to insist on the *belief*.

When Goethe said that Homer's *Iliad* taught us that "it is here

---

5. The quotation is from *Walden*, chapter 1.

on earth our task to enact Hell daily," he meant that the *Iliad* showed us an Achilles *doomed* to die slaying a *doomed* Hector before the gates of a *doomed* city. It is somewhat ungrateful of Goethe to describe our life as an enacted Hell, for even at a great age he did not lose his belief in the possibility that he might derive rapturous happiness from his association with Marianne von Willemer, that he might still be given the power to complete adequately the glorious design of *Faust, Part Two*, and to be shaken by ever-new insights into nature's laws.

Poe finally destroyed himself. There is no doubt about that. The increasing frequency of his resorts to drink and drugs has a clearly suicidal character—but only toward the end. Intoxication had long been associated in his mind with an enhanced belief in possibilities of a happy issue. (I believe, in contradiction to his own statement, that he identified artificial stimulation with creativity—and what is creativity but the absolute conviction that one is about to make a thing that one can call good?) Poe was fascinated by the mathematical laws of probability. At what moment did he lose the conviction that whatever possibilities which might present themselves to him would all, all be ruinous? That would be [the] moment from which he could be said to be leading a very unhappy life.

I am juggling with the word *unhappy?*

Yes, the word is constantly unstable. But it can be said that all biography shows us that a life filled with unhappy moments is not necessarily an unhappy life. *Amount* never passes into *degree*.

623.   SS "AMERICA," SEPTEMBER 13, 1952.   Identity and the Little Dog.

Having used *ad nauseam* in the Nortons Gertrude Stein's quotation from the nursery rhymes of the image of the Old Lady and Her Little Dog as illustration of identity seeking corroboration, how surprised I was to find the following paragraph: *King Solomon's Ring*, by Konrad Z. Lorenz; Thomas Crowell Company, New York, 1952, page 127. Dr. Lorenz, a great authority on animal behavior, has been talking at length on the merits of dogs as pets; he ends up:

. . . In the almost film-like flitting-by of modern life, a man needs something to tell him, from time to time, that he is still himself, and nothing

can give him this assurance in so comforting a manner as the "four feet trot-
ting behind."

624. HOTEL BAUER GRÜNWALD, VENICE, OCTOBER 11, 1952.
My Situation.

. . . What oppresses me is the herd of obstacles in my path before I can return to my rightful situation. . . . the three reports for the
State Department. . . .[6] Unfortunately they take time. Here in Venice I sit up in a hotel room writing stuff which few will attend. . . .
Now Ruth [Gordon]—resolved like a lioness to stage *The Merchant*
[*of Yonkers*] in London—summons me to a week's discussion of the
matter, preferably in Paris, with Tyrone Guthrie. They have not yet
found a producer. The production may never come off.[7] Today I telephoned begging that the conference in the matter take place at St.
Moritz, where I dream of spreading my papers about me, and of at
last resuming this Journal and attacking "The Emporium."
Now to what is real to me:
I think I can and shall fall in love with the Norton book. Yes, I
can do that, but only with quiet, with long lazy days, with the growth
of that thing so central to it, the marriage of its content with its form. I
have told the Harvard Press that it is postponed for a year; . . . but it
is the right kind of postponement, because all the queer growth of it
can continue fruitfully while my thoughts are ostensibly elsewhere. I
never think of it, glance at it, without pleasure and without a teasing
promise of all the new beauties which I can cultivate in it. The difficult parts—the time-sense, and the profounder explorations—those
must await their own sessions of solitude. Even if it should turn out
that I am incapable of formulating such matters as the syntax of freedom, it doesn't matter. I can write a stimulating book and point out a
number of potential roads which others can continue.
As for "The Emporium," all that is as unclear, ultimately un-

---

6. Thornton Wilder had headed the American delegation at a UNESCO congress in
Venice in September. The General Report, written by him, was printed in *The Artist in Modern Society* (1954).

7. Thornton Wilder revised the play extensively and it was first produced in Edinburgh
as *The Matchmaker*.

clear, as when I entered the first notation about it in this Journal. Two scenes I have—solid and good. Only in these last days, and after reading it to Marion [Preminger]—whose judgment is radically sound always—have I seen that the Third Scene (that in the Emporium after closing time) is not right, is not *human*. But even in these dissipated days, moments have come to me in which I see how some of that material can be restated. . . .

. . . When I left America I whispered to myself that maybe it was for a long absence. Let me at least give such a proposal a chance to intimate its possibilities. No more *inclining* to this and that. Above all, this Journal as exploration in depth. Then the play. Then a movie. Then an opera libretto. Then a comic novel. All that as freedom—for play, for seeing what I can enjoy in the modest gift which has been given me. The pressures of reputation have always tended to make me figure as larger than I am. If I can figure larger it will be via the small—my note.

Maybe I must give way to Ruth and fly to Paris, but I must be stern thereafter—say goodbye to collaborations and go and hide myself. St. Moritz is right, though lonely. I have always hated heat. . . . In the Engadin I shall rejoice in the first snow and the following snows. I shall have no date-lines before me, and no promises. Let me see what I can do.

632. [HOTEL] BAYERISCHER HOF, MUNICH, NOVEMBER 26, 1952. Toward the Nortons: Some Economic ABCs and the Concept of Freedom.

Freedom is not a negative abstraction. It must always be used as having a specific content: freedom is the possession of the possibility of obtaining a given end.

Now in 1850 the conditions in the United States—limitless natural resources, vast unclaimed extents of land, the opening up of new industries—gave the impression that every man was free (*i.e.*, in possession of the possibility) to obtain that which he wanted.

But it was already a market economy: you got what you wanted by selling a product of your labor. You were *free* to select what you wished to produce and you [were] *free* to place your production before its eventual consumer. The freedom to produce what you wished was important because therein lay your personal satisfaction (your creativity, your expression, your "happiness"), and the freedom to sell was important because there lay your confidence that you could continue so doing (your security, your relation to the future).

Emerson's doctrine of self-reliance reposes on his assumption that this social condition was the normal state of economic life, rather than a brief transitional moment in the United States. It does not even occur to him to consider the economic background of self-reliance, so self-evident is it that he can at once transfer it to moral and psychological realms. Just as the happy blacksmith can be forever assured of making horseshoes for grateful teamsters, so can the Sage be assured of preaching self-reliance to grateful free men.

But all the time the market economy was developing toward forms that limited the citizen's freedom to select his product and his freedom to vend it. It went further: it established for millions exactly the *content* of freedom, namely: you were free *to make money*. And at the same time, it reduced the possibility of most men to make *much money*. Society took up the principle that if you made money you were a success, if you didn't you were a failure; they gave it a moral: the virtues that went toward making money were the primary virtues; if you were a failure, *i.e.*, poor, you were also unvirtuous.

Hence: the passion of Thoreau. He was defending himself against the charge of being a sinner—not only in the eyes of his neighbors (them he hysterically charged with being money-making sinners), but in his own eyes as well. He had to find a *content for freedom*. Obviously, freedom cannot be described as *the opportunity to do what you want*. He fumbled: he said freedom was the opportunity to live close to nature and the opportunity to discover the ends of man. (It was not even fundamental to him that freedom was the opportunity to teach those truths to others. What he really wanted was *freedom to be alone* and, it can be said, *freedom to suffer unobserved*.)

America has made classical the doctrine that every man is free to make money. It involves a great deal of self-deception; but there it stands. It involves harping on the highly exceptional life-stories of a few who rose from rags to riches (with its concomitant that all those who have not risen from rags to riches must confess that they lacked thrift, sobriety, perseverance, and, perhaps, honesty); and it involves harping on the immense value and benefit to all society of the commercial product and function. (This last doctrine was much aided by the contributions of science and the ever new technological inventions.) The unsuccessful or modestly successful man could console himself with several factors: (1) He might get rich any minute if he could pull himself together and be supremely virtuous; (2) He was engaged in—though modestly—a great and beautiful work: commerce and industry.

American satire has played with these legends, but never very forcefully, because Americans, including the satirists, really do believe them. Those who could not satisfy these requirements were obliged to take up positions of extreme revolt. There are three counter-positions: (1) The religious; (2) The artistic; (3) The bohemian (or vagabond hedonist).

Much American religion had gone far toward agreeing with the money-success viewpoint: it harped on the virtues that lie closest to such success. It had little to say about self-denial and humility, and it changed the very meaning of the word *charity*. . . . The American vagabond-hedonist recurs, often, but in the guise of the winning and childlike (*vide* the works of E. A. Robinson).

Now wherein is this different from similar attitudes in European countries from 1830 on? The Frenchman adjusted himself much more easily to competitive capitalist market economy. He has a content toward which he gains money, and the rewards are much the same whether he earns a lot or a little: he wishes to be *free to enjoy himself.* Much of his view of enjoyment would fall under the disapprobation of Anglo-Saxons, but not all: he too enjoys family life, gardening, fishing, etc., and perhaps far more consciously than we. Self-respect turns on being able to permit yourself a certain amount of pleasure. The English, too, have a content: they earn money in order to maintain a respectable and respected home life. Given the class-system this is possible at every income level and is rendered exciting by pretending to be just slightly above the level at which you live.

But both these *contents* of freedom are denied to the American: he does not put any importance in pleasure, and every American has all the respectability he can need.

What, then, does an American want?

[Hotel] Bayerischer Hof, [Munich,] . . . the Next Day.

Reprise: We are searching for what an American wants his freedom *for*, and we are doing it within the framework: What would he

wish to do with his money, if he were able to make the sum he aspires
to?

When we say that the Frenchman makes money so that he can
enjoy himself and the Englishman so that he can have a respectable
home, we seem to be saying that these are the sops—the *panem
et circenses*—that governments must accord them to render them
blind to the fact that they are wage-slaves in a system of unequal
distribution.

So far a large part of the mass of men are, indeed, content to be
wage-slaves. They are content to be so, if they are accorded their
pleasure-diversion or their respectable domesticity, however humble, because they: (1) Are afraid of responsibility and initiative*
(surrender is security); or (2) Find in themselves no promptings for
greater self-expression; or (3) Like the serfs of the Middle Ages, accept the religious and politico-social sanctions that direct them to be
acquiescent. All discussions on this matter seem to sum it up by saying that men want to be "secure," by which is meant: assured, at
least, of retaining what they have got—a label so sweeping that it
must be constantly re-examined. This "freedom from fear" in the economic world is constantly being colored by other factors. In France it
is certainly accompanied by "fear of being duped"—of being lulled by
politico-social lies into subservience.

633. HOTEL BAYERISCHER HOF, MUNICH, DECEMBER 1, 1952.
      My Opera.

      Today I sat down and sketched out plans toward the Opera.
Much fired by the enthusiasm and certain suggestions that Garson
[Kanin] made in St. Moritz. I bought a *cahier* and started a "Talk
without myself" about it in the manner of Henry James. Then after a
spell of that I started writing the dialogue from the beginning. Just to
amuse myself later with a view of what is discarded and what remains
from such a first *esquisse-esquisse*, I set down the first draft:
      "The end of the Second Act must be some grief, suspense, ten-

*Dostoievski said that all over our civilization are people whose supreme need is "to sur-
render as quickly as possible the gift of freedom . . . with which they, unfortunate creatures,
were born." Quoted by Harold Laski, *The Dilemma of Our Times*, George Allen and Unwin,
London, 1952.

sion which befalls a woman—a woman in love, a woman who seems
about to lose her singing voice because something has come between
her and the young man of the house. Either his parents have come
between him and the girl, or he has taken his new-found voice and is
praising another woman. Let us call our heroine what—coloratura or
light soprano—Irish? Patty. . . . And let us say that there is a second
woman—brunette—contralto or mezzo. Dare we make her a monotone? Our young hero is Edward. Edward finds his voice through
love of Patty, but then goes on to love Geraldine.

"This introduces a serious difficulty: we have to introduce two
girls—as for the first time—into the First Act, because we should assume that Edward has not met Geraldine before, though she is of his
class.

"Or we could open with tea—spoken: Mr. and Mrs. Edward
Hawkins Carberry and Geraldine. Edward II is upstairs. He is not
well.

"Mrs. Carberry announces the theme: music is life; the spoken
word is poor, pale, compared with music; prose is lifelessness. 'I go
through life singing.' Mrs. Carberry has to leave the room several
times. In her absence Edward *père* and Geraldine sing, monotone.

"Now we can't have any duplications. If Edward finds a singing
voice we can't have Geraldine find one too. Yet shall we have a man
—baritone—for Geraldine? A real singer? Shall we give her the Doctor in the house and make him a bass? Are we too crowded?

"Somehow we must crowd all this with deceptions, disguises.

"Edward *fils*, say, is the figure 'Prince-under-a-spell.' The Doctor plots to release him. Perhaps Patty is not a 'poor relation' as I first
thought but an importation of the Doctor [from Montana]. . . .

"It's all at Saratoga Springs. Mrs. Pettry [Carberry] doesn't
like to leave home, but she has brought Edward (the father is James)
to drink the waters."

Then I started writing the Act. Got to close of Edward-Patty
duet.

In trying to write entrance-aria for Patty—not couplets; not
ballad—I suddenly saw Gertrude Stein's problem and achievement:
not to furnish words, but the stuff-substitute for words. The rhymed
lyric would be quite out of place in this kind of opera: to stay always at
the verge of nonsense yet get the "feeling" of emotion and fancy.

To today's fragment I bring a sense of disappointment (it's all
too near [Eugène] Labiche and [Jacques] Offenbach—the large pos-

sibilities of the meaning of song and talk have drifted away into the sands of a "vaudeville") but I have hopes that as I work on it, *it* will teach me how to bring it into a more significant focus.

634.   HOTEL BAYERISCHER HOF, MUNICH, DECEMBER 3, 1952.
     My Opera.

     This whole thing may be rubbish and may come to nothing; but I put down some of the work notes so as to show myself later how it grew or how it failed. Yesterday was a bad day; after the first day's elation it all seemed to fall to pieces. Here are the notes. I then wrote no dialogue:
     "Such was yesterday's work. Disappointment that it's all dwindled to the dimensions of a Labiche-vaudeville. Back now to several graver features: the death-in-life that Mrs. Perry [Pettry-Carberry] spreads about her. All I have now is a snobbish garrulous woman. And always keeping a Second-Act climax in mind, trying to give some conviction to these people's 'being in love'. . . .
     "Perhaps the only way out—I have been twisting and turning over this all day—is to go still further into *vaudeville*. That is to say: the singing-silent idea is primarily a comic idea; it has connotations of gravity, too, but they could only last an hour. My business is to wring all the amusement out of it and gather a few moments of the graver aspects for fun. So let's try to see what further complications we can devise. . . ."
     That was yesterday's entry. A real block. I started today's work with the following notes:
     "A bad day yesterday.
     "Now to try again. . . .
     "We have a prologue in the Doctor's office with the mute patient, the singer Lucille. The Doctor 'talks' (only) when he has his coat on."*

---

*Notice, how part of my block—including my reluctance to envisage a prologue—proceeded not from "plotting" problems, but from an opera-idea difficulty. I refused to consider any material that required that my characters sing when the curtain went up. Singing must be introduced gradually and in such a way that the audience would begin to glimpse the relation between singing and *l'élan vital*. As soon as I got the idea that Lucille (now Anabel) can't use her voice, and the idea that the Doctor (though a very "singing" personage in my caste) doesn't sing when he's wearing a white coat—this problem was solved.

From there I went on and wrote the whole of the scene in the office—the Doctor-Anabel [Lucille]; and the Doctor-Mrs. [Patty] Hope. I may hate them next week, but I'm content with them now (content in the sense that when I rewrite them they can be built up to charm and fun). They still don't solve my problem of the Second-Act climax, but they make for support.

[Hotel Bayerischer Hof, Munich,] December 28, 1952.

(*Later:* These efforts collapsed—from their own apparent insurmountability and from the intrusion of other distractions in my life. Yesterday they began to resume. I think some new light has arrived which will be recorded in due time.)

635. **HOTEL BAYERISCHER HOF, MUNICH, SUNDAY, DECEMBER 28, 1952.**
A Hearing of Palestrina's *Missa Brevis*.

On the door of the Stiftkirche Sankt Cajetan, Theatinerstrasse, has been posted the music to be rendered at the more important services of the holidays. There are four-, six-, and eight-voice Masses by [T. L. de] Victoria and our *Münchner* Orlandus Lassus (after whom a café, a real *Nachtlokal* is named, down in the roistering Platzl). Today, Feast of the Holy Innocents, it was Palestrina's *Missa Brevis*. Although I must have read this to myself a hundred times, I had—apart from some totally unsatisfactory records—never heard it. The acoustics of the (full, but very cold) church were, strange to say, good. For the upper voices they were using women. Probably against liturgical usage, they sang the second "*Agnus Dei*," one of my favorite compositions in all music. Before the "*Sanctus*" and the "*Benedictus*" the organist played the first four or five bars!—as though, after the long pause occasioned by the ritual, to give the singers their note. The congregation followed closely enough to kneel or cross themselves at the "*Crucifixus*" in the "*Credo*."

I knew every note; yet often did not recognize them. A few passages were "better" than I was prepared for, than I had previously understood (the musical unity of the "*Sanctus*"), but most of it was far less a joy than in my readings. For one thing the men's voices generally afforded massiveness and volume at the expense of line: one seemed not to be hearing theme or imitation at all. Is that always true in this type of music—is it wrong to listen for the counterpoint too closely? Secondly, there was little range in dynamics; we were either slow or very slow; either forte, mezzo-forte, or piano. The *"resur-rexit"* did not pick up; the *"hosannae"* did not clamor, and the *"amen"* at the close of the *"Credo"* did not—those interlocking sequences in syncopation—declare an oh! so assured finality. I suspect that my relative disappointment was due not only to my lack of experience in listening to this kind of music (though one remains in a state of amazement that Palestrina's—and still more Orlandus's—contemporaries could follow throughout the year such contrapuntal intricacies). It was due in part also to a decline in vitality in European sensibility as a result of nervous wear-and-tear during the war and post-war years, probably combined with unbalanced nutrition. (Last week Hans Hotter sang the *Winterreise* [of Schubert]. In today's—December 28—paper it is highly praised, particularly the accompanist. In fact, the performance was notably lacking in accent, variety, eloquence, in spite of the singer's magnificent voice; all was uniformly elegiac. Even *"Die Post"*; even the cries of *"mein Herz, mein Herz."*) In addition, I cannot but believe that the choir's trainer and director is at fault. The two-soprano canon in *"Agnus Dei I"* got totally lost; the secondary voices frequently effaced the canon; and the canon's lines themselves effaced one another. Surely, [were it] sung with studious *legato*, the listener would distinguish the two simultaneous melodies.

Nevertheless, the hearing was an excitement and a pleasure; and were I to stay in town longer I would obtain permission to attend all the choir's rehearsals and find my way "into the interior" of all these works.

[Hotel Bayerischer Hof, Munich, Thursday,] January 1, 1953.

To St. Michaels-Kirche (*i.e.*, during repairs in the Bürgersaal) 8:50. Schubert's *Grosse Messe in As [dur]*—with offertorium, Bruckner's *Virgen Jesse*; but 10:30 in the Theatinerstrasse again: Cristôbal de Morales's *Missa Quaeramus cum Pastoribus*. Astonishing how from these two masses alone the ability to listen increases—oh, to pass a year with this choir alone!—and downright droll how coming away one finds oneself involuntarily humming in that style, inventing one's own imitative entrances, and bringing up the tenor line to cross an imaginary treble.

637. BAD-HOTEL ZUM HIRSCH, BADEN-BADEN, FEBRUARY 9, 1953. New
Play: "The Heir" [Later Called "Illinois, 1905"].

Yesterday I began a new play and have today all but finished the
First Act. I'm not excited about it and nothing may come of it—except the experience, which I hope will be very valuable.

Convinced as I am of what my theme is (and this experience of
Germany is making me surer that it is *the* theme of literature today) I
have been talking it and writing it and pumping it for two years. As I
grope for ways to infuse it into the "plots" that are "The Emporium"
and the Opera and the other projects, I become bored with it. In the
first place I have talked it too long; it is frayed by my forensic audi-
ence-directed emphasis; in the second place I came very near to writing it squarely in *The Skin of Our Teeth*.* What I have found myself
doing, then, these last few weeks is trying to marry that theme-idea
with one or other of the already-projected sketches; and at every turn
I find myself running into tiresome symbolism or *faux-sublime*. Those
Wilder stage-devices and that vast theme both need a rest. So I decided to *reculer pour mieux sauter*. Still struck with Hauptmann's
Die Ratten—the vast sprawling four-act genre-play, the total effect of
which is not dependent on any one of its plot-threads—I began to
meditate as to whether one couldn't do a similar picture of a milieu,
crowded with portraits and plots, of a Middle-West town—a Winesburg, Ohio–Spoon River play.[8] I knew that in the long run I'd have
to have an *idea* subtending it (*had* to, merely because I am I, not
because any theory of dramaturgy requires), yet noting how inadequately Hauptmann ties his play together (on the young dramatist's
inquiry, wasn't Frau John's death a *tragedy*?), whereby the whole of
Die Ratten becomes not only an ostensible thesis-play toward the
New Theatre, but an overtly submitted example of Hauptmann's the-
oretical views on drama.

So I started out, on a small plot-idea borrowed from a novel I
shall not name. The First Act has gone along rather spiritedly, and
has picked up on its journey another idea which I am afraid, however,

---

*In Munich Herlitschka [my German translator] made me go over some passages in "Pull-
man Car Hiawatha." I haven't read that play in fifteen years nor have I reread it all now; but answering his questions and looking at the text I was struck by two things: one, how funny some of
the lines are; and, two, how way back then I was writing *this very theme*. That is astonishing.

---

8. The reference is to Sherwood Anderson's *Winesburg, Ohio* and Edgar Lee Masters's
Spoon River Anthology.

may wreck it. My hero is turning out to be the Existentialist Man who, in words Camus quoted to me from Dostoievski,[9] is afraid that he doesn't hate everything enough. That could, indeed, furnish forth a play, but I am beginning to be afraid that it is too "hot" to permit itself to be expressed through a genre-tableau play. It requires that a whole play be articulated about itself alone.

At all events, it is fun working in the sheer naturalistic method for a change. And I think I have my Dakota hotel well established.

Nothing may come of it but self-discovery, and the temporary cleaning-out of my head of all those noxious gases—the by-products of the good ones which are my real work.

So tonight I shall go on and finish the First Act and see what I've got.

637A.   BAD-HOTEL ZUM HIRSCH, BADEN-BADEN, WEDNESDAY,
        FEBRUARY 11, 1953.   ["Illinois, 1905"].

Well, I've found its theme, and scarcely a word of the First Act will have to be changed. It's a play that's funny, and a little pathetic, and a little impressive. It was born of reading Harold Laski's (tired and flagging) *The Dilemma of Our Times*, and of Georges Simenon's *Le Voyageur de la Toussaint*.

It is about anarchists in Illinois in 1903! and I couldn't surprise myself more.

Reichsbahnhotel, Stuttgart, Saturday, February 14, 1953.

I got through the First Scene of the Third Act and then something began to block. I could make a pleasing Third Act, but I didn't see how I could make a big one. So I got a little drunk and some light began to come to me. And I started recopying Act One into another *Heft* (school children's exercise books that I buy in the local stationer's). And I reopen the Act with Mrs. Watson's calling on Carrie Nation and the meeting of the WCTU. And then I see that that makes counterpoint with Margaret's father's anarchism. The play is about the eternal movement of social betterment. Was that there in my sub-

---

9. See Entry 766 (May 5, 1960).

conscious all the time—this affinity between Mrs. Watson and the anarchists? The motto of the play is *"Eppur si muove."*[1] And how strange—that the play which began as a genre folk-play has found its way toward one of the subjects that so unfailingly moves me to tears . . . : the quiet absurd obstinate drive toward better things. Shall I dedicate this play to Jane Addams, to Dr. Alice Hamilton, to the memory of that breakfast at Hull House? My working title is now "Illinois, 1905." Have I the dates right? This is a play about [Eugene V.] Debs.

643. SS "AMERICA," FRIDAY, APRIL 24, 1953. George Büchner's *Woyzeck*.

Meeting Dr. [Kurt] Hirschfeld again in Munich, I expressed my doubts as to the advisability of ending *Woyzeck* with the Polizei's pronouncement ("it's a long time since we've had such a beautiful murder")—as they do in the Münchener Kammerspiele. Soon after, he sent me this book: Georg Büchner, *Woyzeck, nach den Handschriften des Dichters herausgegeben von Georg Witkowski* (Leipzig, Im Insel-Verlag, MCMXX). It consists of reprinting two sheaves of paper:

(1) Folio, seventeen sides: editor calls *"Entwürfe."*

(2) Quarto, twenty-four sides: editor calls *"Die Ausführung."*

(3) Quarto, independent leaf—two sides—containing the scene of the Professor-Doctor demonstrating to his students, and a brief scene: Idiot-Child-Woyzeck.

Woyzeck is still far from finished. The Quarto shows G.B. following the scenes from his first sketchbook Folio, expanding or compressing some of them and inserting new ones; it is not finished, however; it comes to a stop before the murder; the final scenes of the play (as given us in book and theatre) must be drawn from the early unrewritten Folio—and from the opening of the Folio, where Büchner (beginning at the climax of his play) has cursorily jotted down eleven scenes, before he starts to make sketches of the play "from the beginning, in order."

---

1. The (purported) words of Galileo: "Nevertheless it [*i.e.*, the earth] moves."

So what we read and see are about fifteen scenes in second draft, followed by eleven scenes in first draft.

What would I do, if I had the responsibility of preparing a workable text? To examine:

I think there is little doubt that the Folio sheaves contain Büchner's first notations of this play. He begins, as I say, with indications of eleven scenes including and surrounding the murder, then pulls himself up and starts writing the play from a logical beginning. (So in a sense we have three texts here.) . . .

[SS "America," Sunday,] April 26, 1953.

Beginning again:

(1) Büchner began by writing short scenes (even single speeches) all involving the climax of his story and the finale. There is no resort to the *Grotesk* (his own word . . .), but there is a recourse to the cosmic-sententious.

(2) Then Büchner says: "I am ready to begin at the beginning." Scene One:* Andres and Woyzeck cutting sticks. Woyzeck's hallucinations. Scene Two: Louise-Marie tending her baby is struck by admiration for the Tambour-Major; Woyzeck returns still full of hallucinations. Scene Three–Eight: The Street-Sideshow: full of burlesque, which coincides with and parodies the cosmic pretensions. Scene Nine–Eleven: Three scenes that prepare the Inn-Dance. Scene Twelve: Woyzeck and the Doctor: lunatic grotesque against Woyzeck's simplicity until Woyzeck "meets" the grotesque with his hallucinations. Scene Thirteen: Doctor, Captain, and Woyzeck: the idiotic grotesque of the Captain and the Doctor taunting one another; enter Woyzeck; Captain sows the seeds of Woyzeck's jealousy. Scene Fourteen: Woyzeck threatens Marie. Scene Fifteen: Marie's prayer.

(3) Büchner is now . . . at the climax of the play and can use the sketches with which he first began to write. So—taking a *Heft* of quarto size—he again begins the play from the beginning.

And at once he gets into difficulty. He opens the play with the scene we have called Scene Thirteen—Captain and Doctor taunt one

---

*The numeration of these scenes is arbitrary. We are at the mercy of the editor's divisions.

another. He wishes his "frame" to be the idiocy of those in authority. But he must stop short at the place where—in the earlier sketch—Woyzeck enters, because it is too early in the play to show the Captain sowing the seeds of jealousy in Woyzeck's mind: Marie has not yet met the Tambour-Major. The scene as it stands not only does not mention Woyzeck, it is a static bit of genre-grotesque. Six pages later Büchner will write the scene that will correctly open the play (and with which Alban Berg opens the opera), *i.e.*, Woyzeck shaving the Captain. In production, however, producers open with the scene of Woyzeck and Andres cutting sticks.

Büchner then rewrites (copying from his first Folio sketchbook in succession) the cutting-sticks and Marie-Child-Her Neighbor-Tambour-Major scene.

Notice what G.B. does in amplification. Andres-Woyzeck: almost the same number of speeches. The "line" is a little tighter, hence the tension greater: Woyzeck is very near madness. The Marie scene: almost the same number of speeches. Again Woyzeck's hallucination-speeches are reduced, but none the less appalling. . . . Marie in the earlier scene had one of the theme-phrases of the play, "*Ach, wir arme Leute*"—which is now taken away from her to be given to Woyzeck in two later scenes.

Büchner does not now recopy the sideshow-scenes; he merely writes down: "*Buden. Lichter. Volk,*" which sufficiently shows that he does not regard this as a final draft. In a moment he will use, however, the students-and-apprentice speeches of the *Buden* scene to fill out the Inn-Dance scene. He goes on at once to another scene between Marie and Woyzeck. Marie has met the Tambour-Major and received the present of some earrings. Büchner is full of bold omissions and transitions, but in a later draft he would certainly have amplified the meeting between Marie [and the] Tambour-Major: what we read and play now is a Draft-One scene inserted into a Draft-Two text, none of which is a definitive Draft Three. Yet the writing is powerful, is glorious. Büchner, with Marie and her earrings, is rewriting the jewel scene from *Faust* and knows it; Louise-Marie no longer bears also the startling name of Margarethe. This scene and the two which follow it (the shaving scene, and a Marie-and-the-Tambour-Major scene) are new; after them G.B. will return to follow the scene-order of the earlier text.

Büchner is under powerful inspiration, yet some of his most magnificent phrases were already in the earlier draft: those incandescent speeches of lubricity or bitterness:* the *Nachbarin* charges Marie with the ability to see through seven leather "*Hose*"; she says to her child: "*Bist doch nur ein arm' Hurenkind und machst deiner Mutter Freud' mit deim unehrliche Gesicht. Sa! Sa!*"

Now we get from Woyzeck a ground-theme of the play, "*Wir arme Leut'!*" But in what a speech! He is disturbed by jealousy—the earrings—but he says (and where did Büchner get this immediate plunge into the domestic genre?): "*Was der Bub schläft. Greif' ihm unter's Ärmchen der Stuhl drückt ihn. Die hellen Tropfen steh'n ihm auf der Stirn; alles Arbeit unter der Sonn', sogar Schweiss im Schlaf. Wir arme Leut'!*" . . .

All this level of the play is revolt: of the trial of the historical Woyzeck Büchner is making a picture of the humiliated and the oppressed which is itself an indictment. Why then did he add to Woyzeck's miseries by making him the victim of a crazy doctor's experiments?†

Because Büchner does not believe that the social order—neither class nor invested authority—is responsible. The tyrants are higher up. The oppressors of this world are mere idiots and zanies. Their very malice has not sufficient stature to be reckoned as moral responsibility. It is the universe itself which is crooked, which is "*sinnlos*"—hence the Grandmother's fable.

Thérèse Giehse, teaching actress, who played that sole-one-speech role of the Grandmother—and journeyed all the way to Venice to play it—told me she thought this was the greatest tragedy in the German language. It has another claim: it is the greatest fiction of the "Absurd." It maintains three axes with extraordinary justness:

(1) A human story, self-enclosed, searchingly explored. Note that Büchner meets Goethe not only in the jewel scene, but, in Marie's remorse in two scenes, he confronts Gretchen's prayer and torture by the *Böse Geist* . . . and her Bible-reading and prayer.

---

*I stole one from *Dantons Tod* and put it into *The Skin of Our Teeth* [Act Two, speech of the Fortune Teller, page 65]: "Stick out your tongues. You can't stick your tongues out far enough to lick the death-sweat from your foreheads."

†The Doctor's experiments are an invention of Büchner's, though in detail Woyzeck's hallucinations were taken from the records. The historical Woyzeck had had a similar experience previously with two women, by the second of whom he had had a child. Woyzeck testified that "the change in his *Gemüt*" began after the second betrayal. Such motivations are too natural and normal for Büchner's purposes.

(2) The "cosmic" relations: even the fools are pressed upon by the relation to all. . . .

(3) The reduction of the human misery and the human aspiration to a passionate insistence on the Absurd.

Yet the play is unfinished. In his second draft Büchner had reached the moment before the murder: Woyzeck is handing over his possessions to Andres. (How Shakespearean is this: he finds some hymn-verses that belonged to his mother: *"Mein' Mutter fühlt nur noch, wenn ihr die Sonn' auf die Händ' scheint.—Das tut nix."*

648. HAMDEN, [CT.,] JULY 16, 1953. *Finnegans Wake.*

Paid a call yesterday on Adeline (Mrs. Francis) Glasheen of . . . Farmington, with whom I have had a long *F.W.* correspondence. I had renounced that drug and had given her all my apparatus; she has entered into correspondence with two addicts in England. At her house I saw [J. S.] Atherton's paper on the Koran in *F.W.* [and his] . . . lists of songs (and *all* of [Thomas] Moore's *Irish Melodies*) embedded in *F.W.* . . .

The wonder grows. All kinds of wonder. But the chief one today is the extent to which J.J. so constantly leans on a book: he must find a place in *F.W.* for *every one* of Moore's melodies, together with the name of the old tune it is sung to; he must find a place for *every one* of the *sutras* of the Koran; he must introduce every figure in the [Lewis-Carroll] *Alice* books. It is understandable that he must find a place for every constellation, every element in the physical series; every color in the spectrum (over and over again); but this passion for all-inclusiveness applied to Moore! That one should have to know in such detail Boucicault's play *Arrah-na-Pogue* and Wills's *A Royal Divorce*!

It is characteristic of our time that every serious work must attempt either a cosmology or a basic metaphysic. The presentation of a fragment of experience is no longer possible, so worm-eaten or eroded do all the scaffoldings of thought and custom appear to be.

But what is hard to see is that Joyce and Pound use such bits of flying straw or odd-shaped bricks to build their Hagia Sophia— *Arrah-na-Pogue*, and the career of a minor *condottiere.*

With Joyce, however, it represents a sort of honesty: he doesn't only use what he has read ("library-read"); he uses what he has lived with: the student at Clongowes and Belvedere went annually to Boucicault's play and was enthralled by it.

But it is a sign of impoverishment that Joyce's point of departure has been so often from the written word. Life—and his life—is always pressingly there, but it reaches us through that refraction. As Kafka's does not; as Proust's does not. Mann leans heavily, too, on erudition and on the parody (or imitation) of antique styles.

This is not the same thing as saying that they employ myth-figures: Ulysses, Faust, Teiresias, Semele, etc. They draw not only upon the myth but on the literary tradition of the myth—which reaches its most astonishing exemplification when Pound [in his Canto I] lovingly gives us a Latin translation [by Andreas Divus] of the *Odyssey*.

Books—writing-men—feeding on writing-men.

And, of course, in all this I am thinking of myself.

649. HAMDEN, [CT.,] JULY 20, 1953. Whitman and the Breakdown of Love.

Just as I've been thinking—as a concern laid upon me by the months in Germany—of the "lowered temperature of the planet," the cooling of hearts—suddenly I seemed to be overwhelmed by accounts of neurotic woe. Last night [A] again transported to the hospital and undergoing more blood-transfusions; [B] a total wreck; [C], who seemed the soundest fellow in the world, writing [a] euphoric letter from his psychoanalysis; [D] confessing to a dead end and asking my suggestion of an analyst; [E] writing that his wife tried to kill herself—and more and ever more.

Now let us not be afraid of clichés. Of most of these persons I know the life story. It's easy to say (and it's they who say it) that it all has to do with sex; they are not able to make "harmonious sexual adjustments." But it has to do—more deeply and first—with love. (One can talk all one wants about the libido element in parental and sibling love—yes, but one falls into the danger of overlooking the sheer emotional devotion which is a qualitative difference, and must be continually recognized as such.)

That all of these friends were not afforded in infancy a sufficiently affectionate environment is true (and not contradicted by the fact that one of them has been all but asphyxiated by a devouring mother: *her* affection to her son was an ego, an amour-propre, compensation for deprivations elsewhere, and the little boy must have been perfectly aware of its impure origin).

Starved of the environment of love: hence forever after exhibiting so greedy and omnivorous an expectation of love that no affection they *receive* is adequate, and (what is worse) their affection for others is not truly love but a demand and command to be loved. (I am more and more willing to agree with certain authorities that homosexuality is negative—that it is, even when apparently aggressive, a submission to solicitations. These solicitations are not necessarily those coming from the outside; they come from within also, from an exorbitant need for tenderness, *i.e.*, to be valued by another.)

I am now ready to alter my views: man, such as he is, has no choice but to believe, to insist on believing, that the world is grounded in love—love as affection. Which brings us back to the main premise of Christianity. The human soul must feel that it is loved. Are there certain superior persons who are able to rise above this? Two classes: the complete scientist, and the saint-philanthropist. There I get back to my old theory: the scientist is one who has decided that he'll have nothing to do with the whole painful business of the heart's pulls: he plunges into a heart-free world called objective truth. The saint is certainly the unloved lover. The saint *is* loved, but that is not [his] aim, nor his consolation; in fact it bores him. (That may well read: "No personal love extended to me will ever equal the extent of my need, so I have given up expecting it here on earth," etc.)

All this takes on a new character in the New World: what is the American's love-object (unsavory, dreary is all the terminology for these things)? Yes, a woman. But as we saw that an American does not fix himself upon a concrete sense of place (one place, my own), and submit to one situation in society (that station to which God and the social order have assigned him) and correspondingly does not feel himself enclosed in one moment of time—so his erotic emotion is capable of a wider focus than the European's, not as polyandry, but as sublimation. Not even as homage toward the general abstraction *femininity*, either. He has unfocused affection to dispose of and cannot find durably any object. This is combined with his independence to take a certain autoerotic color (as in Thoreau and Melville—not, I think, Poe). Can there be a strong autoeroticism without narcissism? I seem to feel some distinction there.

Does the American sublimate easily? Yes. But the term *sublimation* is misleading: it implies only a *higher* transference of the sexual drive. The American sublimates into business, into infatuation with celebrities, into philanthropies.

All these "broken-winged" about me had such a need to be loved that they were unable to start the movement of loving.

Walt Whitman's object of love is certainly an imagined companion. Biographers may name this or that streetcar conductor, etc., but certainly the "love-poems" do not give the impression of having been addressed at a given moment to a given person. They are the most abstract love poetry one can remember; even more so than the mass of quasi-pastoral verse—"To Phyllis," "To Chloe"—partly because they are constantly wavering between an address to one camerado and an address to all camerados, and then, in addition, go on to build a theory of state-government on "love."

The very amorphousness of Walt's love-object is proven by the fact that the poetry was so easily adapted by readers to their own needs and experience, *i.e.*, "we must be more frank about sex and more proud of the body" and "we should join together in a communal pool of affection."

Well, this is only a first skirmish with a deeply complicated subject. . . .

651. COLUMBIA UNIVERSITY CLUB, NEW YORK, JULY 23, 1953. Alma Mahler-Werfel on Freud.

Called on A.M.-W. yesterday. We drank champagne in her beautiful apartment. Conversation basically impossible, because of her deafness and my inadequate German. She is filled with stereotyped crotchets: anti-Freud, anti-Kafka, anti-Karl Kraus. *Au fond*, she has the ineradicable Viennese anti-Semitism ("Have I not been lucky with my Jews?") and, in addition, by attacking these figures she feels that she is exalting and rescuing from any comparative judgment her favorite (once *their* close friend) Franz Werfel.

"No, I have never seen anyone who has been healed or even benefitted by psychoanalysis; I have seen hundreds who were ruined by it.---- All geniuses are sick, but the sickness is closely interwoven with the genius: I do not believe they should be *nivelliert*; they would just come out from the so-called cure as banal men.

"I knew a man. He was a Guards officer and in a duel he killed another man. This left a *bloc* in his mind and he lost the power to perform certain manly functions----you understand me. He came to Freud for treatment---- It turned out that he could only perform these functions in Freud's house. So Freud gave him his house key" —(presumably to bring his girls into the house). "In the end, by the way, he killed himself."

That story is "very Vienna." It has all the air of having been passed from one teller to another; and it is certainly untrue. It was recounted with the particular kind of emphasis of someone trying to sell a dubious piece of goods. With all its charm Vienna lived for generations on the bug-eyed gratifications of tendentious slander.

653. HOTEL CONTINENTAL, CAMBRIDGE, [MASS.,] SUNDAY, JULY 26, 1953. Continuation of [Entry] 649: Whitman and the Breakdown of Love.

. . . Let us not be afraid of clichés, nor in our groping afraid of falling into nonsense. Can I say: that in our time the faculty of loving is being replaced by the craving for being loved? Moreover can I say: that in a patriarchal age, one *loves*; and in a matriarchal age, one waits to be loved? And that worst of all is the age of transition between those two ages, when the sole pattern is the avidity to be loved? All I dare say at present is that there are five in my immediate acquaintance who are in shipwreck or approaching shipwreck from an omnivorous chaotic demand on love, in whom there is scarcely visible the faintest evidence of a power to love, who repel love by the self-centeredness of their demand. . . .

How sincere is Whitman's command to form a society of lovers? . . .

As Gertrude Stein was always saying: "The difficult thing [in 'thinking'] is to hold so many things in one's head at one time." Here we must keep in mind, also, the concept (the "tacit assumption") of all these struggling unloving-lovers relative to the universe in which they live. Do they feel themselves to be living in a loving cosmos, an indifferent cosmos, or a "rejecting" cosmos?

Nature is obviously kind to the contemporary American. To the pioneers nature was kind and cruel. One acquired one's establishment with unmitigated effort. Unmitigated?—no, surely. Nature seemed at least collaborative; at most, quick to reward one's efforts. Was I wrong (in the Thoreau chapter) to mock Thoreau's phrase: "Nature is crystallized goodness"? Yes, I have a right to mock that in Thoreau because he is unable to surround it with sufficiently high-wide-and-deep vision of all that Nature embraces. . . .

These unloving demanders-of-love are spoiled children who want in perpetuity the being-loved condition of infancy, and the being-loved situation in which American protestantism presented the cosmos. "God is love; God is father"—these phrases constituted a cosmic environment which broke down.

Which broke down first: their inability to love the totality in which they live; or their inability to love a human being?

655. MACDOWELL COLONY, [PETERBOROUGH, N.H.,] AUGUST 2, 1953.
["The Emporium."]

Here begin a series of notations toward a continuation of "The Emporium," which later, I shall or shall not bind into this Journal as a group *hors-série.*[2]

658. PETERBOROUGH, [N.H.,] FRIDAY, SEPTEMBER 18, 1953.
The Alcestiad.

Last Monday evening to interest poor [X], I recounted the first act of the *stehenbleibende Alcestiad,* and ventured some material that might go toward its closing scenes. That started me off, and since then I have used a part of each day to "turn over" the play. Specifically, I have been probing . . . —*i.e.,* modifying the given legend—to see in

2. These notes were not made part of the Journal but exist among the Thornton Wilder papers at Yale. They extend to twelve pages and date from August 2, 1953 to June 17, 1954.

The play was never completed, but the two scenes that Wilder found "solid and good" are also among the Thornton Wilder papers at Yale. They are printed, along with Entry 655 *hors-série,* as appendices to this book.

what ways I could make it express the incommensurability of the human and the divine, the ambiguity to which all human reading of a divine would be subject. Could I mould the story in such a way that it left in doubt whether the Supernatural had spoken to men or whether men had had sublime promptings which they immediately ascribed to the Supernatural?

Soon I saw that: (1) We could reveal that the Nurse (long after?) confesses that she invented the story that she heard Apollo in a dream teaching Admetus how to yoke together a lion and a boar. Under the pressing urgency of persuading Alcestis to marry Admetus, a few hours later she *lied*. Nevertheless, as she points out, Admetus did the feat; the miracle, made possible by his love, did take place. (2) I can sow doubt that the Five Shepherds include Apollo: might it not be merely a wise and beneficent stratagem of Delphi to ennoble the mountain country by pretending such a visitation? (3) And today I got the following idea: Why was Admetus dying in Act Two? Because he had been struck in anger by one of the Five Shepherds. But it was five or six years after Act One; Apollo's one year on earth was over, but all *Five Shepherds* had remained in Pherai. Where was Apollo? He must have *invested* one of the shepherds. Did Admetus punish the shepherd who had struck him? No,—because he *might* have been the man who had housed the God.

Now we are on the highway to some very beautiful possibilities. You never know where Apollo may be lurking. Especially is this clear to Alcestis. Was it Hercules who brought her back from the dead? (In Act Two we make it perfectly clear that Hercules shrinks from no task but that one.) No, it was in the summer solstice and Hercules undertook the task only because he knew that Apollo loved the House of Admetus and these were the days in which he was closest. So to Alcestis's eyes, Apollo *invested* Hercules on that journey. In fact, we may intimate that they were companioned by a Third Person.

So we come to the Third Act. The son of Admetus and Alcestis returns to Pherai to kill the usurping tyrant and to regain his throne. To murder the tyrant. But Alcestis, widowed and a slave, will not have her son kill the tyrant, though the tyrant had killed her own husband and though he fills the land with his injustice and crime. As the Act develops, the tyrant seizes the young man to kill him; the young man has his stratagem ready to kill the tyrant. Arrives Teiresias (again!) from Delphi with the message: "Let no man be put to death in Pherai, for Apollo is again in the land." (This is no news to Alcestis, who has come to see Apollo everywhere.) The tyrant, in his uncouth way, entertains a cult for Apollo and is proud to rule a country singled out by him; he is ready to see the possibility of Apollo's residing in the young man he has captured; the young man springs his stratagem on the tyrant and overpowers him, but he cannot kill him, because the tyrant *may* be Apollo. And what then takes place in a wicked and ignorant man when the bystanders suspect that he is Apollo?

This bristles with difficulties—not least of them the fact that Alcestis herself is not in the center of the stage—but it does show how the metaphysical quizzing, the maybe-yes-maybe-no, may be continued into the last Act. To digest.

661. [CASTLE HILL HOTEL,] NEWPORT, [R.I.,] NOVEMBER 4, 1953.
A Telecast.

I went tonight to my favorite bar ("Ann's Kitchen") and again watched the television—and was overwhelmed by what I saw. Eliza Bishop Lipstick and Rouge presents a program called "This Is Your Life." A retired schoolteacher, Miss Anne Lou Babcock of the high school (thirty-five years there) of a town in Michigan I never heard of (White Falls?—something like that), comes up from the audience. . . . Her beauty, dignity, sweetness, and her composure under astonishing surprises are a large element in what follows. Photographs of her parents; of herself as baby, young girl, young woman; of the schools where she successively taught. Then people suddenly appear from behind a curtain: a beau whom she had not seen for thirty-five years; her sister; a sergeant from World War I who had known her when she ran a canteen in France; a member of the first class she had taught in this high school in 1907; a famous baseball player and his wife whom she had somehow brought together; a woman judge whom she had once advised; and finally the president of the student body in the last year of her teaching. This ended up with the view of the audience, which contained one hundred former pupils now resident on the West Coast—out of the ten thousand who had been her pupils.

Why was I so strongly confirmed in my sense that this is the greatest country in the world?

Not because of the technical marvel of what we were seeing; nor the lavish expense of the dozen persons flown to Los Angeles for the occasion; nor the radiance of the Cinderella-come-to-the-ball climax: Miss Babcock surrounded by these *revenants* and this apotheosis, and presented with a movie camera and a Mercury car ("In the name of a million teachers in America, we present you . . .").

Wasn't it that though it was all happiness and homage, it was not really felt as exceptional or surprising? There was no condescension. In this country a similar focus could be turned on so many thousands. Miss Babcock was not rich nor highborn; she was merely admirable in her function—so *there was no one above her*; she filled the picture; she was not lifted up from obscurity; nor, as center of attention, did her elevation obscure anyone else's place. In other words: in relation to one person's life, the emphasis was correctly placed—better than it would be in any other country.

662. HOTEL LA CONCHA, KEY WEST, [FLA.,] NOVEMBER 17, 1953.
  The Alcestiad.

. . . So it came to me that after a new opening—the conversation between the bat-like Thanatos on the ground and Apollo on the roof of the palace*—the way was open to introducing Apollo *incognito* much more specifically into the First Act, and into the whole play. So now I can break up the too-long-dialogue between Alcestis and the First Herdsman by having Apollo himself take part. Yes, when the Five Herdsmen are introduced by Teiresias, there is Apollo in his golden armor† among them, but obviously to the eyes of Admetus and the others he is as dirty and travel-stained as his companions. From this new direction—Apollo on the roof and Apollo among the Herdsmen—I gain a great advantage for my central idea, but I run my play into the greatest danger in relation to another idea.

What I gain is a way of stating dramatically—through Herdsman-Apollo's conversations with Alcestis and Admetus—the difficulties that a god meets in trying to communicate with mortals; "a man who is too closely approached by God receives a scar"; a god's efforts

---

*And after I had written this scene—in Newport—I suddenly recalled that in one of the Greek tragedies there is such a dialogue—and isn't it precisely in the *Alcestis?*

†(Later, the same day:) No—I cannot have him in his "divine" clothes, but I can have him recognized by the audience.

to mitigate the *terribilità* of his sympathy. What I lose is this: this play is in motion to say that the gods do not exist at all; that a god-like [force] presses upon the universe but . . . we can never be certain whether it is without or within. All that was supernatural in this play —so I planned it—was to be so ambiguously stated that it might be interpreted as a projection from the subjective layers of the principal characters. Yet *now*—there as an all-too-objective fact is the over-guiding, over-brooding presence of Apollo. This "danger" I had long foreseen, since it is already present in the legend given as a datum. Yet I had hoped to play with Apollo's presence as Herdsman and Her-cules's restoration of Alcestis in such a way that they might have a "ra-tional" interpretation.

If I cannot find a theatrical way of throwing doubt even on this visible participation of Apollo in our action I am writing a *mysterium* which assumes the personified divinity. And such a play I do not wish to write. These recent developments in the conduct of Act One make the play more and more brilliant and less and less meaningful; and I will end up with real baroque *Kitsch*. Then these days I shall devote myself to finding ways to restore to this Act the puzzling ambiguity.

I cannot conceal from my diary that I have also been driven, urged, to introduce another dimension into the play. Something in me is bored with writing a "beautiful" saint's legend: all must be wider, newer, crazier. The only device that has yet occurred to me is to introduce a company of twentieth-century archaeological trippers surveying under a guide the site of the palace at Pherai. They are in-visible to characters of the ancient action and vice-versa. The *cicerone* makes his spiel: "Ladies and gentlemen, please stay together in a group.---- Here, it is believed, was the palace of Admetus.----" etc. Very near to ostentatious triteness as this is, it might be admitted, if I found still one more irruption of later time, or *other* reference, to add to it—so that a coherent incoherence could flicker all over the play.

And oh how I wish that the tone of the play could be of high comedy—lyrical, diaphanous and tender—just because it threatens so to be sententious and didactic.

664. THE KEY WESTER, [KEY WEST, FLA.,] TUESDAY, DECEMBER 3, 1953.
Gogol, Russian Humor, and the Consciousness of
a Vast Universe.

Rereading *Dead Souls** I have been struck by a humorous device which I call the *excessively specific in non-pertinent situations*. To be sure, we are accustomed to this in the conversation of old ladies—the classic example being Miss Bates in *Emma*—the *enchaînement* of details introduced through free association. In their case, however, we understand that the far-fetched details are *relevant to them*. In this novel they are embedded in an obviously intellectually controlled exposition and their presence does not denote that the author has a silly and incoherent mind; why then do we laugh?

In the style of Defoe and in Flaubert we are also given details of the highest particularization which are far from being necessary to our knowledge or even credence. These are a device of realistic writing; they are attempts to convince us that the narrative is absolutely factual: the only reason for mentioning such apparent irrelevancies is that they were so; no one would have dreamed of contriving them.† To some extent Dickens imparts vividness to his characters and places by conferring upon them certain singularities; but the singularities are so harped upon and developed that the intention becomes obvious; the singularity takes the center of the stage; the irrelevance by force of insistence becomes an operative factor—that is to say, a relevance.

Gogol's "irruptions of the impertinent" have another character which renders them irresistibly droll and which lends them a philosophical character. Aesthetically, they convey a sense of the innumerability of persons and objects in the world, but they reach us in the category of irony: "Millions of people and things in the world are now in existence; isn't it laughable that I isolate *this one*, for truly a man would be driven to despair if he attempted to catalogue the most tiny fraction of them all."

But the strangest part of this in Gogol is that one is continually

*Modern Library, 1936. Translation by Constance Garnett, which one divines to be deficient in agility and surprise. Must get Nabokov's book [*Nikolai Gogol* (1944)] and compare his rendering of certain passages. *Query:* Did Gogol (1809–52) read Dickens?

†As all liars know. So the tall tales of Davy Crockett, etc., go in for the most grave-faced minute specification in order to support the credibility of a whopper.

reminded of Homer. Homer's formal similes are constantly doing the same thing: the simile exceeds its formal function of indicating a resemblance between two appearances; it burgeons into specific details which are not relevant to the comparison and which occasionally run counter to it. "As when a woodsman fells a tree on a rocky height" (this is me improvising) "and the crown of leaves falls with a mighty crash upon the ground, and the woodsman rejoices *knowing that his dear wife and children will have fuel for the winter months and bright flames will leap on his hearthstone*—so fell mighty Theognis." Outer circles of life are forever pressing upon the narrative for admission. In Homer the effect is not ironic because the details that have been drawn into the image are not highly specific; given one more degree of singularized specificity they would strike us as incongruous ("incongruous" because we say to ourselves: "If you're going to pause to recall such freely-associated details as that, you will never end, for there are millions and millions of them open to your reach at that degree of relevance"). . . .

The very first paragraph of the novel gives us a character who never appears again:

. . . Moreover, just as the chaise drove up to the hotel it was met by a young man in extremely short and narrow white canvas trousers, in a coat with fashionable cut-away tails and a shirt-front fastened with a Tula breast-pin adorned with a bronze pistol. The young man turned round, stared at the chaise, holding his cap which was almost flying off in the wind, and went on his way.

Are we to be given everyone who looked at Tchitchikov? The breast-pin of everyone who looked at Tchitchikov? We smile at Gogol's impudence; but we get the point. Gogol's hero is very nearly an Every-russian (and so joins that company of [Joyce's] Bloom, Earwicker, and Kafka's K.—the hero of the novel of the future); and the more a central figure represents a universal, the more the author must construct an ambiance which furnishes indications and intimations of everything, everywhere, everybody and everyhow.

Hotel Ambos Mundos, Havana, [Cuba,] December 17, 1953.

Lately I have been reading *The Brothers Karamazov.* So far, in six hundred pages, I have not found one "gratuitous" detail (though there is one society lady who babbles with them). (*Query:* Do I not remember seeing somewhere that André Gide, writing about Madame de Sévigné, picks some bold adjectives—that is, adjectives that serve as metaphors but from which the conjunctions implying metaphor have been omitted—and says of them that they show the "Dostoievski touch"?)

I say that this kind of irrelevance gives the effect of drollness. It says that out of the billions of things that are present in the world surrounding my selected story-subject, I introduce, *without reason*, this *one*. And with that "one" the door is for a moment opened to all the others. It is droll because it is incongruous, disproportionate, and unmanageable. Hence, it could barely find a place in a tragic presentation of life. The tragic emotion, although it is subtended by a sense of tragedy in all living, can and must express itself in a specific instance of catastrophic event for one person or group of persons. These sufferers must be for a time isolated from all the other sufferers in the world and in the world's history. The sympathetic emotion we feel for one mother who has lost her son is not the same emotion that we feel in contemplating all the mothers who have lost their sons.

667. HAMDEN, [CT.,] MONDAY, JANUARY 18, 1954. Time-Sense: Baroque, Renaissance, and Other.

Working on the preface for the ANTA décor volume for Rosamond Gilder.[3] (Why do I say yes?) Trying to find an expression for my long-held convictions that a bad theatre is a theatre out of phase —a play infused with an outworn time-sense—I have been driven to put together loose characterizations of some of them (by loose, I mean what the architects and painters call "mock-ups").

My one on the Greeks isn't very good, but it must serve. I use the old story of the shattering effect on the first audience of *Medea*:

"Time and circumstance seem to have presented themselves to the Greeks as an advancing block, foreordained, indivisible, and inescapable. Such is the concentration of the moral and ethical vision in a Greek play that the events seem to take place in a world where *nothing else is happening*. One might say of them: 'Where God's eye rests is the center of the universe.' No wonder the characters wear masks. Could anything be more remote from our modern feeling?"

---

3. The projected book was not published. An incomplete manuscript draft of the essay exists among the Thornton Wilder papers at Yale.

Now for some free-swinging: .

In the baroque age life is seen as a constant succession of metaphors; the event in our daily life is understood as (*i.e.*, is like to) a
type-experience in the world of fixed religious and social patterns. A
man's relations to sin, merit, love, honor, the family, the king—all
are viewed as a metaphor, therefore as doubled. Hence, if the experience in our earthly daily life is felt to have its high abstract counterpart, the burden of interest for the men and women of the baroque
age was directed toward the timeless and unvarying element in the
equation. The earthly event was but illustration; it was absorbing and
passionately experienced, but it lost importance as a "unique occasion." The door was thus opened to every improbability, coincidence,
and hyperbole; in Spanish drama, girls, dressed as men, rose to be
conquering generals; and parents discovered their long-lost children
in the most preposterous situations. Since the attention of the audience was fixed upon the patterns behind behavior, the mere quotidian anecdote that illustrated them acquired from the patterns the
character of being "outside time." Events transpired in succession,
but where and when was of little importance. The thought-world of
the baroque age did not arrive in England until several generations
after it had engrossed the western Mediterranean world; but there,
too, time and place were secondary to the interest in character and
circumstance. (Think of the mentality of an audience before whom
every scene—whether it was laid in antiquity or in ancient Britain or
in a country a thousand miles away—was always played in its "modern dress"; what an incuriosity about time and place!) Here, we are in
full Renaissance, where after the Middle Ages the attention is directed to freedom, enterprise, and self-reliance. Here, too, there is
an appetite for improbability and coincidence, for the more exceptional a crisis is, the more it brings into play the intoxicating freedoms
of the will.

Well, I hope I've started a train that will be useful to be in the
Norton[-Lectures] book also.

I seem to see that time cannot be thought of save in relation to
one other coordinate—time and place; time and circumstance.

[Hamden, Ct.,] the Next Day.

Let's chivvy this a little bit farther:

The Greek drama takes place in a world where nothing else is
happening. "Where the eyes of the gods rest is the center of the uni-

verse." Racine and Corneille took over this single-action world, too, but from another compulsion—they secularized it: "Where a king or queen is on the stage, that is the center of the world." (Very clever, Thornton.)

The Elizabethans delighted in indicating that many other things were happening in the world, but what was happening on and off stage was that a great many people, rightly or wrongly, [were acting] in fulfillment of their character—and the most interesting thing in character was its initiative: its boldness in freedom.

The baroque theatre, principally represented by the Spaniards of the Golden Age, also was aware that a great many things were going on at the same time in the world, but the events were in "metaphor" to type-patterns.

The nineteenth century was aware that many things were going on but each presented action barely illustrates anything beyond itself. It is sufficient for a play that it be a "slice of life." It is characteristic of them that their plays did not center on any abstraction: not on "fate," the message from the gods; not on sex, not even on the passions, though they walked the stage; but on property or money, and on social position, *i.e.*, reputation: [Dumas *fils's*] *Camille*, [Pinero's] *The Second Mrs. Tanqueray*—even [Ibsen's] *A Doll's House*—turn on matters that reflect a social situation.

669. HAMDEN, [CT.,] FEBRUARY 27, 1954. Poe, Death, and Telling the Truth.

A letter from [Thomas J.] Wilson of the Harvard [University] Press has stirred up in me a little sluggish eddy of remorse about the deferred Nortons. For two days I have been putting Lecture One in order. All I can say now is that it has much profited by the cold storage. I still occasionally read myself to sleep with Thoreau (no longer the *Journals*, though), bewilderedly asking myself why I admire the books. My admiration for them is real, but the only grounds I can find for it so far are aesthetic: the prose and its rhythms and their perfect adaptation to the content. The eternal idiosyncratic exaggeration of his ideas and their remoteness from "life" prevent me from taking them very seriously: he is an odd awkward immature fellow who writes beautifully. I suspect that something was awakened in him by the Latin language; it does not emerge as latinity, so deep has been the digestion, but it has the quality.

Today I took a walk to think about Poe—and Americans, all the things in Poe that are not American. It was they that killed him, just as it is the things that are not American in Thoreau that gradually sapped his strength. The chief thing in Poe that sets him apart is that he was a criminal, he was filled with murderous thoughts. Americans are not sadists.

All children (I was going to say little boys, but the Niagara of autobiographical material by women writers these days shows that we must include little girls) generate death-fantasies. . . . We learn to know the fact of death truly—*i.e.*, inwardly—through our wishes for the extinction of others.* This is universal, but Americans have very little of it. Why? Because of the "kindness in the American home"? Because, on the whole, the American parents have themselves no sadism; they must constantly curb and rebuke the child (which arouses the "murderous"), but it does not *interest* them to cause pain, humiliation, and despair, though inevitably that is what they must frequently do. It's not that they rebuke sweetly, tenderly, and reasonably; they do it mechanically. . . . What becomes of the American child's murder-fantasy? It turns in on himself; or is converted into the more abstract forms of business competition, social leadership, etc. . . .

Poe "unamerican" as an assassin, but very American as a truth-teller: his strength is the unimproved candor with which he reports his fantasy-life—he refuses working up the material into moralizing, etc.

To whom and to what end does the American tell the truth? The ethical injunctions of protestantism? Not primarily: prevarication springs from two sources, only subterraneously related. Outwardly directed, it is an instrument to succeed; inwardly directed, it is a means of escape. Prevarication as a means of winning is particularly induced in those in whom social obstacles seem to be legitimately insurmountable: guile is the resort of the oppressed and disbarred. Inevitably, the Slavs expect guile and practice it. The French live in terror of being duped—of being made to appear ridiculous as duped

---

*[*Later:*] I see in today's (February 28th) [*New York*] *Times Book Review* the motto of Simone de Beauvoir's novel *L'Invitée* is from Hegel: "Each conscience seeks the death of the other." At the close, the heroine murders her (female) house guest.

(hence the enormous literature on cuckoldry). Those who live in fear of being duped know all about duping. . . .

Lying, like gambling, flourishes in situations where you despair of winning by honest effort. Guile was induced, then, under a society in which the awards were apportioned on some other basis than merit —that is, feudalism.

Americans are not liars. Was it because nothing drove them to it? The English are truth-telling, but they do not object to the convention which is compliance in fictions. And why were they known throughout Europe as citizens of "perfidious" Albion?

Americans are not liars. How are we to dispose of: (1) The charges against "us puritans" of hypocrisy,* and (2) The early relish in skulduggery?

670. HAMDEN, [CT.,] MARCH 1, 1954. Poe: Obiter dicta.

Taste. Those who enter upon a reading of Poe must be prepared beforehand to abandon all fastidiousness in one realm: the description of imagined visual objects. For reasons we know, his imagination had need of flamboyant imagery. He certainly cultivated waking daydream and finally cultivated it with opium. His imagination, no more than that of most of us, could not furnish him images other than those he had already seen in picture books, theatre, etc., and his repertoire of images was that of the deplorable taste of his time. His head was filled, like the bedchamber of Ligeia's widower, with Gothic-Druidic-Saracenic lumber. Even Ligeia's face, we are told, was Greek-Hebrew-Persian.

Whenever Poe *remembered,* his descriptions were admirable —as in that of the English school in "William Wilson." But the remembered and the near could not feed his imagination when it was heated. In fact, his censor, his inner censor, would not have permitted his early stories to rise to the conscious level had their background been in any recognizable world. "Berenice": the teeth chopped out of the corpse, nay, the revivified corpse—which has so much to say . . . to anyone with even the most cursory reading of psy-

*It was precisely Poe's death that Mallarmé laid to the *mensonge* of American hypocrisy.

choanalytical material—could not have been envisaged in Baltimore, where it was written, *circa* 1831. Of it, Poe himself said (to [Thomas W.] White, April 30, 1835): "I allow that it approaches the very verge of bad taste—but I will not sin so egregiously again." He declares (though he is writing to the purchasing editor) that it originated in a bet, but goes on to point out that stories of that order were in wide demand in England and America. But he was talking of taste in matters of subject, not of décor. . . .

It is generally thought that education will preserve a man or a milieu from falling into bad taste; but education has nothing to do with it: it can bring the very pitfalls from which it is reputed to preserve us. Winckelmann, Lessing, Diderot, Renan, Ruskin—all enormously educated—had their lapses, tracts, and shipwrecks. (Diderot *on* Greuze is worse than Greuze.) Taste is like sinlessness in the Bible: let no man say he has it, lest he fall.

Bad taste arises when a group admits to its canon one or more exotic elements too hastily. England and America at the beginning of the nineteenth century had run through all its post-Palladian motifs and were in need of fresh imagery. They turned to the Middle Ages, through German Romanticism and the Orient. Chippendale had admitted *one*—the *chinoiserie; Empire*, already Greco-Roman, admitted the Egyptian. Poe's age flung itself into too many. But America is, precisely, the syncretic country; will it found norms of taste from what we are now calling "modern," or must it wait until it has digested all the art forms of human history?

N.B. The problem of taste arises also when we come to Whitman. . . .

671.   HAMDEN, [CT.,] MARCH 2, 1954.   Poe and the Lack
       of the Middle.

Poe, to the extent that the inner and outer turmoil permitted, rejoiced in cerebration. He had two escapes, one, sinful; one, beatific: dream-fantasies and pure cerebration. The former were not only about death, but re-enacted an obsession about a return to a second death by stifling in the grave. . . . Poe's great sin was not primarily drink or drugs—*they* ministered to it: it was daydreaming. He seems to have insisted that his were "sleeping dreams," but by practice he

had been so attentive to them that they had risen to the almost conscious and unusually rememberable level, and could be called daydreams. . . . Dreams were about the dead, and the final end of them
was the horror of being buried alive.

Without his obsession on death, Poe would have been released
to an extraordinary fulfillment of his other obsession, the potentialities of the mind toward mastering life. He was removed from the
American stream by his cult of death; he was in the vanguard of that
stream in his sense of immensity and the scientific approach to it.

What he lacked was any faculty for interesting himself in the
Middle, in the operations that constitute an adjustment to the immediate and near, to earning a living, to organizing the present. Even
into this, however, he flung himself repeatedly in his attempts to
found a magazine. . . . This no little contradicts an earlier project (October 18, 1848) of building a "cottage . . . of strange, weird, and in-
comprehensible yet most simple beauty. . . . Not *too* far secluded
from the world," however.

We are back at Gertrude Stein's distinction between human nature and the human mind. Poe strained to pull himself out of the mo-
rass of the sex competition, self-assertion, vanity, and pride—seductive and despicable—into cerebration and ideality. This is the very
basis also of his *Erotik*. Never has there been such an incoherent mixture of images that combine the fiercely passionate and the pure. . . .

We have heard sufficiently of his redoubled attraction to women
from the moment he knows that they are beyond his physical possession; now to turn to his resort to cerebration. Was his interest in
astronomy a dilettantism designed to impress us and himself?
Eureka disproves that: competent or inept, it was a self-forgetting
absorption. . . .

But that leads us into a big subject.

672. HAMDEN, [CT.,] MARCH 2, 1954. Poe and the Living Corpse.

I wish I knew what *symbolical* meant; but I shall use the word
just the same. Poe is not interested in ghosts. . . .

. . . He is not interested in ghosts, because he cannot conceive
of the *really dead*. The living are galvanized corpses—there are no
other.

Now enters necrophilia—the unavowable subject of "Berenice," the subterranean image behind all these unembraced dying
heroines. In necrophilia one does not embrace a *totally* inert "dead
body," but----one faintly conscious, so weak that it cannot hurt
you—a toothless one, so to speak.

All that side of Poe is appalling and pitiable beyond words. This
is the extreme picture of Gertrude Stein's category "human nature."
No wonder he reached out of it to cling to the human mind. Yet,
contemplating it, one is filled with admiration that he could and did
put down these fancies without superimposing upon them the pallia-
tion and lie of allegory and moralizing.

Here then was this black ground always underlying Poe's life
and thoughts—this deeply non-American frequentation of death. Its
force is derived from its complexity: he is preoccupied with death for
a variety of reasons. It is what saves so large a part of the work from
claptrap and convention, at a time when all writers were harping on
shrouds and charnel houses. In so far as he can be said to reflect the
"Gothic," he has outlived all the others.

674. **HAMDEN, [CT.,] MARCH 4, 1954.** Toward a Theory of Twentieth-
Century Symbolizing (Norton: Little Essay on the Emerging
American Religion).

. . . *The world has no meaning save that which our consciousness confers upon it.* And by "our" I mean not a collective human consciousness, but that of each separate existing mind. All those objects
in the universe exist without having any meaning. Existing without
meaning—let us not even call that existing.

So we have the next step: *consciousness brings the world into
existence.* Any consciousness, or only a superior consciousness?

Oh, any consciousness. But the ordinary consciousness, ha-
rassed, bound by fear in self-consciousness, brings its world into being in fits and starts, living largely in the memory of the few brief
occasions when the world was thus invoked, and on borrowed testimonies of others concerning the world that *they* had brought into
being.

There are several vehicles for this operation of bringing the
world into existence: art, music, literature.

Now we have readied Hölderlin's verse: *"Was bleibet . . . , stiften die Dichter"* (all that remains—in the endless flux of appearances—is established by the poets . . .).[4]

Now am I not almost ready to go on and write this as a section of the Nortons—either as "interlude essay" before we do the last group, Poe-Whitman-Melville, or as an interpolated essay in the middle of the Poe? I mustn't "write it" here, or it will go dead on me when I finally feel myself to be really writing it *in situ*. This Journal must never present itself to my mind as the "last writing" nor even as the "first draft of the last writing." This Journal is mere *remuement* and circling around; the moment the *writing* comes into sight, I must stop.

And from this point I see the next developments: the denial that these ideas are atheism; the reason why the American, because of his apprehension of immensity, brought these things to birth—the symbolic writing being of a new sort, not the romanticist's finding a symbol of an inner feeling, but the symbol presenting itself to the poet as a way (the only way) that that inert outside could be invested with meaning. Etc.

A pretty good day, I think.

675. HAMDEN, [CT.,] FRIDAY, MARCH 5, 1954. Lope de Vega and the Abencerraje Problem: The Date of *El Sol parado*.

Had a little Lope skirmish lately. An idiot at Columbia University ran up a theory, on the basis of a bastard [text of Lope's *El] Peregrino [en su Patria]*, that the . . . list of plays [in the introduction to the 1618 edition] was really . . . [the] list [in the first edition], —*i.e.*, written by 1604. He came near to convincing the Spanish Department at Columbia and the editors of *PMLA*.—Well, what fun for me. For the principal thing I got out of those thousands of hours of Lope is that I am the authority on the *Peregrino* lists. This Mr. [X] wrote me about his discovery. I wrote back: "Dear Mr. [X], You are crazy as a coot." And sketched my reasons. Then I share all this controversy with [Courtney] Bruerton and [S. Griswold] Morley. They write Columbia and *PMLA*, giving their reasons, bibliographical. But

---

4. From his "Andenken," first published in *Musenalmanach für das Jahr 1808.*

I hold up my sleeve the quick simple sledgehammer blow to the nonsense. What fun—to possess with finality what you know.

This Lope skirmish induced me to take a day off. . . . I reopened my Lope-world. My next diggings there will be the . . . plays sold to [the actor-manager Nicolás de los] Ríos. So I attacked *El Sol parado*.

Now a secondary subject in that play is that the *villano-bobo-gracioso* Campuzano makes the vow to go to the shrine of the Virgen de la Peña de Francia. The play is early—Morley-Bruerton [*Chronology of Lope de Vega's Comedias:*] 1596–1603. How early?

We have several plays that contain material on allied themes —plays whose dates we know, or can be fairly certain of.

Lope wrote a play *El casamiento en la muerte*, on the subject of what happened immediately after the battle of Roncesvalles. It was also called *Roncesvalles*, and appears so in the *Peregrino* list. . . . In it Lope *contaminates* for the first time . . . the relation of Bernardo del Carpio to that shrine. This play—a document tells us—was offered by Manager Ríos to a town for performance in June 1597. Bernardo del Carpio is associated with the shrine. Lope is a Carpio. . . . Lope in the years that follow will intermittently advance his claims to being a glorious Carpio—which will lead to Góngora's derision. Lope attaches himself to Carpio's car, and Carpio's car is attached to the legend of the Shrine of the [Virgen de la] Peña de Francia near Salamanca.

(1) Now in the play *El Sol parado* this Campuzano makes a vow to go to the shrine of the Peña de Francia. The Virgin appears to him twice and reminds him of his vow. There is no mention of Bernardo del Carpio, Lope's new obsessive pretension—hence the play was written before *El casamiento en la muerte*—June 1597, and before that date.

(2) In *El Sol parado* we see a Moorish *galan*, a romanticized Moor. He is of the Gazul dynasty. His name is Gazul. There were a number of these wonderful dynasties; ultimately, the most gallant, tragic, and glamorous were the *Abencerrajes*. Lope wrote a play about them. In it were mentioned the Gazules. The play is *El remedio en la desdicha*, October 19, 1596. Thereafter the Abencerrajes and their tragic end will leap into Lope's mind whenever he mentions the noble Moors in Spain. There is no mention of the Abencerrajes in *El Sol parado*. So the play was written before October 1596. Morley-Bruerton say it was 1596–1603. I feel it is 1596. Might it be earlier

than 1596? Not likely, but that awaits my study of Lope's relations with the House of Alba, which is mentioned in it.

All this is very important. Because I wish to build up a sequence of the plays Lope wrote for Ríos. When I can get that right, a lot of other things fall into place.

Years ago I started this whole deplorable hours-and-years-consuming thing in order to know more about a few masterpieces of Lope—not Lope's vast oeuvre,—about *La Discreta enamorada, Peribáñez, Los Comendadores de Córdoba,* and a few others.

Well, I'm getting warmer. *Los Comendadores* is of 1596. Does the use of the phrase *"el sol se pare"* (*Acad.*, XI, 281a) in *Los Comendadores* confirm the supposition that it was written after *El Sol parado?*

Work, work, work. There's lots of work ahead. But I'll get it. I'll be master of that field. I'll write a book finally that will align those plays side by side. It will give me a wonderfully smooth satisfaction.

677. **HAMDEN, [CT.,] MARCH 13, 1954.** François Mauriac: *Ce qui était Perdu; Les Anges Noirs (Oeuvres Complètes,* Volume III—with *Le Noeud de Vipères*—Bibliothèque Bernard Grasset, Chez Arthème Fayard, Paris. Date at the back: 1950. *Ce qui était Perdu* appeared 1930; *Les Anges Noirs,* 1936; *Le Noeud de Vipères,* 1932).

It's easy enough to express one's indignation at these novels (and at the later ones of Graham Greene): the *délectation* in concupiscence that lies so hypocritically close beneath the surface of the reprehension; the artificiality with which F.M. constructs the traps of sin into which he hounds his poor characters; the abuse of coincidence in his *finales*; the sentimentality, the sugared holy water which bedews his prose when he has occasion to draw near the altar or the rosary or the company of his priests (of whom we are so often told that they were *chastes*).

What struck me this time was something else:

The subject of these works is sin. It certainly is. And what sins particularly agitate the writer? *Ce qui était Perdu:* drugs, . . . homosexuality (implied, . . .), suicide, incest and adultery. . . . *Les Anges*

Noirs: murder, seduction, blackmail—everything implied . . . ;
adultery . . . ; and subtending them all what Mauriac himself calls
matérialisme, by which he means the passion for acquiring money—
which plays the whole role in *Le Noeud de Vipères*—and the neglect
of "God."

Let us concede sin, without attempting to define it, and concede a wide range of it. The geographical, cultural distribution of sins
has yet to be made: from Leviticus to the Code Napoléon; and from
the New Testament to the novels of Mauriac.

We find ourselves at once in the problem of "essence": the assumption that there is an essential crime as against the crime-in-situa-
tion. Crimes are posited as "essential" in two categories: the social
convention, or law; and the religious convention, or the higher morality. And both find themselves at once in contradiction, each with the
other.

Murder is a sin, yet soldiers are encouraged to murder. Murder
is justifiable in self-defense. So there is a whole gamut from justifiable
to reprehensible murder; from admired murder to regrettable but
necessary murder to perhaps unjustifiable murder, to reprehensible
murder to heinous murder. Religion allows of the gradations, also.
Yet the kind of mind that is formed by living in "environment" (and
the end of this series of reflections is to relate Mauriac and Greene to
the European dense-population feudal-inheritance thinking) tends always to erect essences: to inject finality and authority into a concept,
and thereby to inhibit the mind from examining the particular occasion of murder—and murder is nothing but a succession of particular
occasions. This process of erecting essential categories is related to
the millenary formation of the Western mind, the ascription of final
authorities to kings and priests and conceding magical, unexaminable
qualifications of rightness to them: the mind, too, is governed by
Principalities and Powers.

These novels teem with illustrations of the contradiction into
which the adherent of such essential thinking is driven. First, the
yawning gap between the good and the bad: everybody is deep in sin
except the priest or the saint. . . .

The Mauriacs ensconce themselves in a set of received ideas:
the Seven Deadly Sins. *There* they are authoritative—dogmatic ethics are their throne,—from there they project their cadres of human
behavior.

Now note: The twentieth century flows like a river—it advances the assumption that each occasion of behavior is unique.* The word *murder* does mean to put an end to the life of a human being; it is a word of description and is inevitably surrounded by associations of rightful horror and reprehension; but each of the millions of murders which take place annually must be thought of as taking place under the sign of and participating in the nature of an ethico-religious essential category "murder." This distinction is not based upon any effort to palliate or even to "understand" the motives of each separate murder; it is part of an effort which should continually be in process to refine the language, to introduce gradually the same distinction as regards an enormous amount of such usages.

Note: Well, well. I see that I have not yet been able to make clear to myself what I feel but cannot express. All the above has been an effort to *surprise* out of myself a further step of definition in this feeling.

Hotel Algonquin, New York, March 15, 1954.

When I began this aborted train of thought, I wanted also to trace out another. To show that Graham Greene and Mauriac and the later Julien Green, writing from a dogmatic point of view, inclined so easily toward the criminal novel. (Mauriac boasts in his fatuous preface to Volume Three that he could have rivalled [Georges] Simenon—a passage I shall transcribe for Georges, if he does not already know it; and Greene was himself a writer of crime stories before he was struck down by *la grâce.*) Isn't it precisely because one cannot make one's points in our time on sin-viewed-as-essence save by stating it in its most extreme and horrendous aspects?

God is a king. As he is a king he is also a judge. Judges of necessity work in essences: justice and crime. Mercy is an irregularity, a violence operated on justice. This is clearly expressed by the observation in popular Catholic life: one pleads with the Virgin to sway her Son, who will then use His influence to deflect His Father. The greater part of prayer has always been the effort to make Absolute Wisdom *change its mind*—the most revelatory illustration of the anthropomorphic character of Western religion.

---

*I remember my astonishment at hearing Jacques Maritain declare—in his lectures at Princeton a few years ago, that "no two murders are alike." The dilettante *existentialiste* who will not permit himself to draw the consequences.

Shouldn't I have introduced into my train of thought yesterday (I mean: wouldn't it have advanced me better) that the erection of essences is an example of misplaced concreteness?*—It is the propensity to treat a complex of *vital* force as though it were a thing—something objective, in arrest, circumscribable. Murder—that thing. (Yes, yes—that's right. Now where do I go from there—except to reread Sartre? Doesn't he make a long development of Jean Genêt's being a thief because society and himself objectify the category "thief"?)†

678. HOTEL ALGONQUIN, [NEW YORK,] TUESDAY A.M., MARCH 16, 1954. My Opera.[5]

Last night Louise Talma and Marjorie Fischer came to dinner. The best jazz and bebop places were closed as of Monday night, but I took the girls to their substitute offerings: jam sessions at Eddie Condon's (he was playing) and Nick's. Music not very good, but just the same, the real thing; besides, it was early: that stuff doesn't activate before 2:00 a.m. I had resolved to offer Louise my Opera; I told her about it. She is entranced. She gets a sabbatical next year. So I have been turning over the plot structure again, and some subsidiary ideas.

We have two men and three girls. Who's going to hitch up with whom? . . .

Now, if we . . . have Montana-Patty meeting Edward *fils*, and Bella [Edward's sister] meeting some suitable (surely, highly unsuitable) man—the action must be laid in some public place; and then we're in for a different kind of opera, damn it. Just as we'd be if we staged a scene at the Bachelors' Cotillion. This is a small-theatre opera, isn't it?—to make its point about speaking and singing? What I *would* like, however, is that we could go back to the Nestroy type of

---

*This is a phrase of Alfred North Whitehead, I seem to remember. . . .

†Yes, and of course this problem must be even more central to *Portrait of the Anti-Semite*. How curious are the very ways in which I have appropriated—or, in this case, not appropriated but set aside for later rumination?

---

5. For earlier references to the Opera see Entries 633–34 (December 1, 3–4, and 28, 1952).

play with many scene-changes, but that one cannot ask of the modern theatre (and this play could not stand either *entre*-scene pauses, nor *entre*-music). *Peccato, peccato!* Otherwise I could have a scene of Edward encountering Patty, Bella meeting Canfield, etc. But I don't want a flock of subplots: I want complications of the main plot.

Now for a notion—playing on the spoken-singing idea: won't we have a scene where Miss [Anabel] Leclair is called upon to sing? And she sings, say, the opening of "*Voi che sapete*," accompanied by a piano on the stage. But since singing = talking in this opera, she doesn't sing it at all; she makes her mouth go; her listeners *on the stage* hear it as singing, but we don't hear a thing; and Louise writes jolly orchestral counterpoint to Mozart's melody.

Oh, what an awful lot of work still ahead. But there's certainly something there. I've been getting some lovely ideas for the Doctor's office: the Nurse Mrs. Watkins, most matter-of-fact speaking character when she's in uniform, crosses the stage in street-hat and coat at the end of the office day, and is at once a singing character. She whispers to the Doctor to give her his white coat, because tomorrow's laundry day; and he gives up his white coat and at once becomes a singing character.

Hamden, [Ct.,] March 17, 1954.

Remember in this kind of plotting to work backward from the climax. The climax is certainly a moment when someone who has been a speaker becomes a singer, or someone who has been a singer becomes a speaker. Preferably both should happen at once. . . .

. . . it is not only about how some people acquire, through love, a "singing voice," but how our Doctor plans, dangerously intrigues to bring them into the state of the singing voice. He does not identify it with love; for him it is merely to release them from boredom. At first I was doubtful whether I could furnish a credible motivation of Mlle. Leclair's masquerading as Montana-Patty—but all I have to do is to make very emphatic our Doctor's accumulated exasperation at the number of patients who have been expressing themselves as "bored to death": he is at the limits of his patience. As he puts it, he is beginning to fear that he is getting to be bored to death. . . .

But now I see that my groanings over the Opera must not fill up my Journal, so I'll set aside a *cahier* within the *cahier* for the Opera alone and call it Entry 679.[6]

680. GIDEON PUTNAM HOTEL, SARATOGA SPRINGS, [N.Y.,] MARCH 20, 1954. Madame de Sévigné. . . .

. . . Naturally, when I went to New York last week, I rushed to the French bookstore in Rockefeller Center to see whether the *new* edition of Mme. de Sévigné had come in. It was there,* and Mesdemoiselles de la Libraire had not got around to notifying me of the fact, though I had left my name and address long ago. I had hoped that we'd have had an edition on wide page and good margin, but no! it's an edition conformable with the other classics of the Pléiade series. So the paper's glossy and spongey and I can't make notations on the margins.

What is new?

Much and nothing.

This is merely the first volume . . . , from her first letter to her tutor Ménage (*circa* 1644, *agée* 18 *ans*) to a letter December 29, 1675 —her age, *circa* 49; she will die on my birthday, April 17, and almost on an anniversary—1696. There will probably be two more volumes. This first is 1198 pages long—the first 93 pages of the introduction will not have to be repeated.

From this glorious rediscovery of the ur-text what have we gained? (Judging only from this first volume, but many of the *restored* letters come from the sixth volume of the Capmas manuscript where the text presents the most *inédits*.) What have been deleted have not been the *chroniques scandaleuses* of the Court, primarily, but the effusive protestations of affection for the daughter. There was already a mountain of those. Do the new ones alter our understanding of the picture? Yes,—one must be ever sensitive of the point at which *quantity* may pass into *quality*. We always knew that there was

---

*Madame de Sévigné, *Lettres, Tome I, 1644–1675*. *Edition nouvelle comportant de nombreux fragments inédits et restitutions de textes, établie avec une introduction, des notes et un index par Gérard Gailly*. Bibliothèque Nouvelle Revue Française de la Pléiade, Dijon (1953).

---

6. Destroyed February 1955. See Entry 706 (February 22, 1955).

a frenetic element in the adoration of Madame de Grignan. In differing ways all the commentators have made their relative adjustment to it. Now it is an amazing, a flamboyant datum.

And by sheer degree, the datum becomes an absolute: we are in the presence of this situation, a superior soul in bondage to a mediocrity.*

Mme. de Sévigné's epistolary art is but a pale reflection of her capabilities. This is not aesthetic genius—or not only an aesthetic genius. This is a multiform genius which had no outlet. She had business-management; she had statesmanship; she had an infallible eye for combinations and especially for *men*. Even in this first volume she is trying to save her daughter from the havoc and ruin into which the prodigious situation of the de Grignans fell. She—the mother—is as good as the de Retz and the d'Hacqueville.

But she is not only a practical genius. She is a woman, leading a suffering, woman's life. Is she also an artist? There is never a sign of it. Her joy in Tacitus (so akin), in La Fontaine (so akin)—I swear on ten Bibles that there is no sign that she is writing to annex posterity's honors. She knows that the contemporaries are taking relish in her letters (that fascinating story of the request for her letters on *la prairie* and *le cheval*); that did not *deflect* her. Why not? Because she was only interested in the present. She could not envisage a world other than the present. The effort to engage her daughter's attention saved her from the other peril—the effort to engage the attention of aftertime.

Her masterpiece is—as every masterpiece is—a wrestling with the angel, immediately present. This new edition makes it even more glaringly obvious: the letters were primarily for the daughter: after the first separation from the daughter she literally cried her eyes out. But by 1675 Madame de Sévigné can no longer cry her eyes out—she has too many *powers*. Yes, the fixation on the daughter is always there, and returns overwhelmingly in the late afternoon; that one can never overlook or deny; but from time to time Madame de Sévigné is unfaithful to her daughter. "Alas,"—as she herself might put it—"I am also seduced by the world at my doorstep, by the impassionating presence of life itself". . . .

*To study: Mrs. Edith Wharton and Walter Berry.

*[Gideon Putnam Hotel, Saratoga Springs, N.Y., March 21,
1954.]*

(Here I interrupted what I had been writing. . . . I had been led
on to too many cocktails with Monty Woolley; and coming upstairs after dinner, launched out into all that incoherent rubbish. It continued
on to a further page, which I have destroyed. . . .)

It was nonsense to say that Madame de Sévigné was in bondage
to a mediocrity,—but the point is important. Mme. de Grignan can
be regarded by us as a mediocrity only in this relation: her defects
were redoubled in this relation; her advantages were diminished in
this relation.

In the first year after Mme. de Grignan's departure for the
South, Mme. de Sévigné went about frantically collecting compliments for her daughter. One doesn't collect compliments for a person
who is already the loved admiration of a community. Mme. de Grignan was a profoundly spoiled girl, self-sufficient and arrogant, who
had no friends. Mme. de Sévigné had no rivals in her daughter's
heart, or we'd be well aware of it. But there was the husband—already twice a widower. The marriage was a satisfactory, perhaps even
a happy one. Mme. de Sévigné did not—could not—ever completely understand that. So here is the diagram:

(1) The fixation on the daughter.

(2) The consciousness that the fixation on the daughter was ex-
cessive. This had two consequences: (a) her sense that it endangered
her religious life. . . . And (b) her arms-length relationship with anybody else. This commitment of her soul and imagination prevents her
feeling a deep reality for anyone else. This is apparent to us first of all
in the relation to her son.

(3) Hence, she is thrown back into a situation wherein she must
continually live a lie: she must violate her true judgment and force
herself to believe that her daughter is an incomparably superior being; and she must force herself to put a high value on the friends in
her circle.

In bondage to an Inadequate Belovéd. The secrecy and the
loneliness of it.

Think of all the ways in which Mme. de Grignan is *foreign* (to
put it charitably) to Mme. de Sévigné's judgment. Her extravagant
mismanagement of her finances; her tactless behavior to her official
and unofficial visitors; her acquiescence in an annual pregnancy; her

taste in reading, both serious and recreational (Mme. de Sévigné begs her, please, to *finish* Tacitus, the History of the Crusades, Josephus; in conversation and literature Mme. de Grignan scorns *histoires* and has a grudging and even disdainful view of La Fontaine). She will not reply to her mother's enthusiasm for the devotional literature of Port-Royal, nor her mother's delight in Tasso and Ariosto.

The relationship with the daughter did not make Madame de Sévigné a great writer—that organization lies in the backward of time, and was polished by a superb education, her two great *maîtres*, Ménage and Chapelain (page 314). But this secrecy and loneliness and this requirement to construct a Prodigious Lie that her daughter was the Paragon of Virtues and the North Star of Taste taught her to manipulate the language. All is dextrous, sinuous, ingratiating manipulation. Where is the "real" Madame de Sévigné? We shall never know. Once in a long time, it leaps out of the scenery. It hovers about us *in suspension.* If we had the letters to the Cardinal de Retz and to Madame de La Fayette, what would we find? Authenticity—sovereignty? Or the whole sequence to the Abbé d'Hacqueville—the letter of June 17, 1671, page 310, is like nothing else; but that was written in frantic crisis, and does not turn upon *him* and the *writer*, but on the stark terror that Mme. de Grignan had ceased to write her mother.*

It is exaggeration to say that the letters of Mme. de Sévigné are one long *comédie.* But the *cadre* was a false position. Her vitality, her eye, ear, and mind had their adventures; time after time they broke through the requirements imposed upon them by the necessity of courting the good opinion of Madame de Grignan; but basically the great letter-sequence is an adaptation, an editing, of Mme. de Sévigné's potentialities.

And if this Niagara had been directed to her son? All would have been gayer and wittier, but the energy would not have sprung from passion.

So the question should be asked in another register: had the de-

---

*Note that that ever-recurrent terror never took the shape that in a smaller degree besets the rest of us—that something she had written had offended her daughter. That evil she did not need to fear, for all ten million words are one long reassurance, flattery, accommodation. Mme. de Sévigné knew to a millimeter how far she could go in advice, in scolding, in concern. To be sure, she often feared that she bored her daughter, but even that boredom, as well as the tentatives toward advice and correction, were surrounded with clouds of adulation. Not only the mother but all Paris and Brittany are *pâmés* with admiration of Mme. de Grignan.

votion been directed to the son: *then*, the letters would have been even more the glory of letters.

681. GIDEON PUTNAM HOTEL, SARATOGA SPRINGS, [N.Y.,] MONDAY, MARCH 22, 1954. Madame de Sévigné [—Continued]. . . .

She has been reading the enormous novel *Cléopâtre* by La Calprenède (she had been induced to reread by her son), [and the *Morale* of Nicole] . . .

Each person to a different degree has a need and an appetite for exercising the faculty of wonder. Mystery and the marvellous surround us; but the consciousness of their presence haunts some people more than others. The forms of the Catholic religion feed this need richly; but Madame de Sévigné could not deeply imbibe them there. She was a humanist. She was possessed by a powerful and mysterious passion; that was an object of wonder. She was naturally absorbed in the painting of high passions and that she could not find to the degree necessary for her in *La Princesse de Clèves* nor in the *poésie galante* of her time. Strangely enough she could not, or would not, see it in the society about her,—though if she had lived to read the *Mémoires de Saint-Simon*, she would have been caught up into astonishment at the pitch to which he ascribes the passional life of her neighbors. So with what self-forgetting delight she assimilates it in Tasso, in Ariosto (a little cooler), in the History of the Crusades, Tacitus, Josephus,—and in these grandiloquent novels. Moreover, she had lived through the Fronde and among the friends dearest to her was a *grande âme* who conducted himself epically then—the Cardinal de Retz. Early in life her imagination had been opened to the heroical grand style. . . . It is this *échapée* into the sublime (explaining also her preference for Corneille over Racine) which permits her (I am remembering Gertrude Stein's remark about Horace Walpole) to describe trifles without descending to the trivial. . . .

In the presence of great works of art our admiration or disparagement must find reasons for its existence. And most of these reasons are beside the point. We praise and blame for the wrong reasons, with the wrong reasons—from the woman who disliked Rubens because he painted the fat behinds of so many fat women; [to] Glenway Wescott, who didn't like Beethoven because of all those "abrupt louds and softs"; to professors who admire Shakespeare because his psychology is so "true." A painting is primarily a demonstration of the effects obtainable from affixing paint to a surface; its relation to the world outside the canvas is secondary. So the letters of Madame de Sévigné are a triumph of medium, —and her self-portraiture, her adjustment of the content to the recipient, the thoughts and events she communicates are secondary. This isolation for our discussion of the medium is something different from the old distinction between form and content; it is a third element to which even form is subservient. Mme. de Sévigné's medium is the voice speaking—the voice speaking as distinguished from the mind functioning. She had an exquisite faculty for marshalling words into the numerous modes of which they are capable in converse,* but music has laws of its own far more subject to form and mistakenly introducing into the discussion of this medium certain associations of auditory harmony, sweetness, or force. Auditory her relation to medium was, but auditory in a more fundamental sense than is expressed by the word *musical*; it is auditory in the sense that one would recall the sounds of wind in a forest of pines or that of surf or [of] a train heard in the distance. Madame de Sévigné's medium is an alembication of the sounds of thousands of voices talking. Even before we attend to what she is saying, we hear this *tone*. Her means are long words and short ones, long phrases and short ones, interjections, accents, inversions, cadences. Just as the iambic pulsed in Milton's mind before the words of a verse presented themselves; just as the spectrum pressed upon Titian's imagination before he dipped his brush, —so the resources of rhythm and syntax lay like a clavier before her, but *her* clavier. The usages of a singularly accomplished society had long prepared a wide range of effects, but all of them and more she had made most singularly her own.

It is by mastery of this medium, then, that she is the transcendant letter-writer, and we are not saying sufficient when we praise her for her wit or narrative skill or vivid observation. It is insufficiently remarked that those qualities themselves "ride" on the cadence of phrasing and on the happy adjustment of syntax. One could select a paragraph of a letter and substitute nonsense words for the words most significant for the sentence's meaning and still be aware of her skill as a writer; but one could not delete words from it, not (not most of all) those many words which seem at first glance to be no major elements in the success—the innumerable "*ma bonne*," the omni-

---

*(*February 1956, after reading fifteen comedies of Goldoni:* Goldoni had this quality too.)

present qualifier *"fort,"* the attack on a sentence with *"Voilà ce que c'est que. . . ."*

683.   JANET [DAKIN]'S HOUSE, AMHERST, [MASS.,] MARCH 27, 1954.
Robert Frost's Birthday.

The dinner last night. R.F. had received the honors of a similar dinner the night before at the Waldorf-Astoria; told me he hadn't slept all night; told the guests that he didn't read much about himself, but that when he did read about himself, praise or blame, he couldn't sleep. "Lines that cost the critic three minutes to write, cost me a whole night's sleep. I ask myself if I write like that" (*i.e.*, is he as great or as negligible as they say?). I seem always to have missed taking into account this extreme vulnerability to comment of poets and writers: Virginia Woolf's diary; Gertrude Stein, asked by Virgil Thomson what a writer wants most, is reported to have flung up her great hands and cried, laughing: "Oh, praise, praise, praise!" Should I take this into account in all writers? Is there something about the word that separates *its* writing artist from the painter and composer? R.F. was undoubtedly thinking of fame in the afterworld. He ended up by saying he hoped he had left "a few poems that you couldn't get away from." They were pebbles—hard, worn down. The quizzical sententious Diogenes-monologue was better than usual last night, in spite of his fatigue. He likes the role, and here were eighty persons, selected by him; some had come a distance, one from California, the [Gordon K.] Chalmerses from Ohio, etc.

Too big for friendship, too small for apotheosis: the evening really wasn't right; none of the speeches were right (mine, deplorable —the same old over-emphatic incoherence—but it bores me to rehearse the reasons again). What saved the evening was—we hoped —that he liked it. But the fact that he liked it was not an expression of the greater part of him, but of that part—the Lion-visitor at campuses—that was his way of earning a living.

It's my business to think through the ways in which I can see him and his work as representative of the American traits. But I'm all too near, and, besides, at this moment I'm still tasting the quinine of my discomfort at my more than inadequate contribution.

I once said to Bob Hutchins after a sermon he gave in the Chicago chapel: "You did fine, Bob." He replied: "Don't hurry me. I shall think so tomorrow." I don't wish to find that issue; nor the issue of self-justification in grievance against the factors stacked against me. The thing to do is to turn my back on it and think of other things. I used to think that all we did well came from our effort to compensate for what we had done badly. I no longer believe that: though it may apply to life and relationships, it's too earth-bound to apply to art.

Is there any country in which such an eighty-years-festival-homage would have been achieved correctly? It is an occasion for formalism, the forms concealing the pressure of all that cannot be spoken. Forms and humor. Shaw would have made a great noise; Freud was absent from his; Bergson's would have been borne forward on academic pomp.

Frost read us a poem he had written recently.[7] From his farm's door many a night he had reinforced himself by looking at Sirius. One night a dog, errant or rejected by a home, slips by his knees and lies down by his fire. He brings it food and drink. Beautifully exact descriptions of the dog's behavior throughout. In the morning, it slips away. Was it a return visit from Sirius? I couldn't get the whole import of the poem, but it looked to me as though it directly contradicted what I had been saying about his view of nature "and the stars" in my poor little bungled speech a quarter of an hour before. "All is symbol in poetry," he said. Yes, but a symbol is a lariat; formerly it has been sufficient that the lariat enwrap and bring to its knees a passing fancy, a fragment of a fragment of experience. There is something about the pressure on our minds today that demands that a symbol be a mode of stating the All—only so can it be a growing kinetic action of the mind. All symbols less than that are static metaphors: "Look here, upon this picture, and on this, . . ."* It is these facile quasi-symbols that permit poets to flirt prettily with big ideas, and then draw back leaving them unexplored, un-wrestled-with—giving at one and the same time an air of philosophical thinking and of discretion, modesty,

---

*In writing this I went to the shelf to verify the phrasing in *Hamlet*. To myself I said: "Where will I find the Closet Scene?" But the book had opened at the very page. So while Frost was reading from his poems to us the other night, having difficulties with eyesight and with the index, he suddenly said: "Here the book has opened at the very page I was looking for---- That's never happened before. One might think there was a special significance in that; but best not----" then mumbled some words. He *skirted* a mystique, then rejected it; but he should not have even skirted it.

---

7. "One More Brevity," published in *In the Clearing* (1962).

and of knowing more than is told. Frost and Housman and Hardy are full of this. The later Yeats is not. . . .

684. HAMDEN, [CT.,] MARCH 29, 1954. Norton: Religion:
The Next Step.

Before I begin: driving along . . . from Amherst to . . . Newton, the pleasing idea came to me that I might ask the Harvard Press to print these "interpolated" essays in the Norton book on pink or blue paper. This would so help the reader to see that they are a progression, links in a chain; that they can be reread separately and, especially, consecutively. That would also—a little, though not very much—release me from a good deal of organizational repetition and from those devices of reminding the reader of certain positions we had arrived at earlier.

The pink sections would be:

In Lecture One: Essay on a Certain Disconnectedness in Americans, Part One: Place.

In Lecture Two (Thoreau): Essay on the Differences between the Gods of Great Space and the Gods of Vale and Glade.

Later: Essay on a Certain Disconnectedness in Americans, Part Two: Time.

Later (before Poe?): Essay on the Emerging American Religion.

Later: How to Tell a Paragraph by an Englishman from a Paragraph by an American.

Wouldn't such a device be helpful and attractive and properly upsetting to certain readers—and fun? It would also be expensive for the publishers. So now to our muttons:

The chain of argument: America was founded by those who repudiated authority (king, father, custom); the sense of the aloneness of the individual unaided and unsuppressed by authority was enhanced by the vastness of the land and the multitude of beings; these mental attitudes increased in them the sense that experience is a process of making: place, time, and destiny are *to be made*; the objects about them are separate, self-developing, hence without any other emotional relation to ourselves than that which we may impose upon them by thought.

Literature (and thought) is then the conferring of meaning on "process."

The next step for which I am now searching is this: that under these conditions every exercise of thought is a thought about the whole. *Gloss*: In the authority-founded world the Whole was already taken care of by dogma, doctrine, and tradition. Hence, thought was free to occupy itself with this or that fragment of experience. That is no longer possible.

(*Digression*: Note how surprising it is that I arrive at this position by this train of thought, and find myself at a position which I had arrived at by another—namely, that the central figure of the superior works of our literature is Everyman, and that for some time that will probably remain the literary objective. I arrived at that by saying that the multiplicity of lives and occasions, present and past, in the modern mind is so enormous that the anecdote concerning individuals in situations which are only intermittently recurrent can no longer arrest for long the attention; the only thing that can arrest the attention is the archetypical.)

Now, the next step after that is difficult. By what means does the mind express the Whole? The answer is: by symbol-making.

Caveat: Remember, remember to give all this kind of exposition out in the field of immediate "accessible" thinking—do not let me wander into semantics or into [I. A.] Richards's field—which are none of my business and which I know nothing about. When I read them I am cowed and despairing—brow-beaten, I call it. I believe that one can legitimately pursue these subjects in a realm which is everyman's and I get comfort from the pages where Gertrude Stein doing it—able though she was to skirmish in *their* fields also—says brusquely, "These are ordinary ideas. If you please these are ordinary ideas." I want mine to have a kind of self-evidence so that there is no need to glance to right or left at all the knotty problems that a Richards can discover in Coleridge. And for me to be unalarmed by such difficulties I must digest my line of argument so thoroughly that the statement does have the air of being "ordinary ideas."

It is an ordinary idea, then, that the mind (the modern, the American mind) gazing out at nature and circumstance is constantly occupied with the Whole. I'm not sure what I mean by that—or rather I feel sure that has meaning but I don't see all the steps that make up my assurance. Anyway, it leads right into the problem of symbol-making.

685. HAMDEN, [CT.,] MARCH 30, 1954. American Symbol-Making.

Now let's try again. Let's assume—synthetically—the characteristics of what an American-made symbol would be; and then see if we can find the operations that would have been set in motion to make it; then try some samples from Poe or *Moby-Dick*.

(1) Such a symbol at the moment of its appearance in the *Dichter*'s mind would be a way of "figuring" to himself the totality of experience. *Because* the American sense of vastness and multiplicity forces upon [one] continually the need to create formulations of the whole.

(2) The picture elements in the symbolic representation are not subject to (*i.e.*, selected by) the conscious rational intelligence, and once present to the American are not so developed, *because* he, having freed himself from tradition, authority, inherited patterns of thinking, is in a position to recognize and trust images and concepts that associationally present themselves to his mind from feeling and intuition.

(3) The American symbol has no $\tau\varepsilon\lambda o\varsigma$ other than its self-contained truth for the writer. It is not produced and developed for purposes of illustrating a moral generalization (allegory, parable), nor for the aesthetic pleasure of the orderly presentation of a parallelism (rhetoric), *because* the activity of stating a truth is not primarily a social one—for gratification, edification, admonition, or even instruction.

(*Pause:* The American symbol then is cosmological, extra-rational, and non-tendentious. Isn't there one more factor which I need here? Something that leads to the thought that since this symbol is cosmological and is not under any pre-established orderly mental pattern it is the whole work—being not an illustration of some fragment of the Whole. But this is too difficult and I must leave it for a moment.)

Obiter dicta: Now every work of the imagination is a construction of symbols. There is no operation which is not either description (which includes analysis) or symbolization. (Mathematics employs symbols, but is not symbolization, but description. Is that right? Here, I am straying over into that territory which is not mine, but it won't hurt me to blunder about there from time to time.) Every work of the imagination is a construction of symbols. Let me therefore eliminate some works which are not of the order of this American symbol-making.

The Divine Comedy, Pilgrim's Progress—the journey, controlled by rational schemata (very undreamlike dreams) and controlled by its moralizing intention. *Faerie Queene, Paradise Lost* —about the Whole, but tendentious and so composed that they expect, even require, a constant *translation* or paraphrase of their presented action into other terms, into definite limitable abstract ideas. This observation shows us that the "American" symbol is not reducible or representable in any other terms than itself. *Othello, Romeo and Juliet*—not symbolic representations of the Whole. *Hamlet*—ambiguous. *King Lear*: a symbol in our sense? Very likely. Probably *The Brothers Karamazov* also, though weighted down with foreign matter. "The Rime of the Ancient Mariner"—almost; is the tendentious aspect essential?

Well, now, I think I've made some progress. And I think it all has to do with Poe, and throws light on why he has played so great a part in the French intellectual's understanding of himself. *Eureka* is the great example; it is not an exercise in description, and Poe did not re-title it a poem in order to escape the criticism of the professional astronomer.

So we're back where we started from. The American not only attempts to make a whole thing (a thing complete in itself, which everybody does) but to include the Whole in each of his wholes, or at least to form a whole which is open to the Whole.

696. CALEDONIAN [HOTEL,] EDINBURGH, AUGUST 1954. Walter Scott and a Restored Balance.

I did something rather odd (for me) tonight. Our play, [*The Matchmaker*,] after brilliant notices in Newcastle and good ones here, also got some sour ones from visiting London critics. Text revisions daily—which have taken all my free time. Tonight after taking Isabel and Tanya Moiseiwitsch to *Ariadne auf Naxos*, [I] took them also to our local chic supper [place], the Pompadour Room in this hotel. At another table the Kanins were entertaining Michael Redgrave. As we left we all stopped at their table a moment. Ruth [Gordon]'s face was ravaged (the [text] alterations of these weeks have been extreme) and she mentioned a minor cut in the text as so harmful to her role that she could "give up her part." She had so threatened a week ago and two weeks ago. Michael—an old friend—made no obliging sign to me that he had received any interest from the performance. (The Strauss opera had ended so early that our trio had dropped in for the last Act at the Lyceum, and from the back of the dress circle I had been able to see that the ticket-buyers had sat through two and a half hours and were still sending out volleys of responsive laughter.) After taking Tanya home I returned to the Caledonian and to the Kanins' table.

Now Michael is a great star of stage and screen, but I had seen that, for reasons I could guess, he had thrown Ruth's confidence in the play (and with fulsome praise, too, of her own part in it) into blackest despair.

So I sat down, asked for a whiskey and soda, heard a moment of their despairing mood, and said:

"Now listen: none of us are fools. We know—Ruth and Gar[son Kanin]—that there's lots wrong with this production. We know that every production is an approximation, but we know too that lots of people are getting----etc., etc., out of it. But now, Michael, there is something destructive about your approach to things, every now and then----"

How often in life I've known that the moment had come to say something like that and I've not said it. That thing in me that is not so much (though it is also partly) timorousness, but which is also so much *indifference*, a resigned acceptance of what Gertrude Stein called our *human nature*. Yes, Michael, who had heard and in part participated in the surprisedly joyous response of the audience to much of the play, had gone to the supper with the Kanins and had insidiously made a catalogue of the elements which were not right (harping—as a star—on those which were and are so limiting to Ruth's assumption of the central star function).

But what I'm talking about is my astonishing *ad hominem* to Michael. And how did he take it? A moment later he mentioned that his secretary in London had mailed to me his dramatization of Henry James's *The Aspern Papers* (which we had talked about at luncheon, two days ago) and added: "That thing you said about my destructiveness, I don't know where you could have gathered that, but we'll take that up some time together." But [he] was without alteration cordial to the end of the session.

Yes, I had opened his eyes. Hell, I would never have done it for its own sake. On this occasion I had to, merely to defend Ruth's confidence in her relation to the play.

But I never do that kind of thing. I see such traits but I never speak up. I have long, long since accepted—beginning with self-knowledge—my knowledge of how others are behaving.

But I have white hair; I look like a judge; I think like a judge—a thousand things would be righter in my life if I *lived* my age and *lived* my mind. Michael's reaction showed that I had touched a truth; he wasn't feeling wronged, nor even exposed—he was "refreshed,"—someone had said something he knew at once, that he must have often talked over with [his wife]. . . .

Oh, it's my father's hand still on me—casting over my social relations not the pale cast of thought, but the pale cast of an inhibited deference to an unexamined undiscriminating "niceness" toward everyone.

And where did I get this moment's manly candor? From reading these nights the manliest of books—the *Journals* of Scott's last years—the sublimest pages, which it would never have occurred to him to think sublime, so long had he lived in the high equable weather of his own mind.

More: After Michael left, I went for a last drink to the Kanins' apartment. The air had cleared. Ruth had replaced in their proportion the things that had upset her—raised during their dinner with Michael to calamitous ignominy and failure—and Garson, with his superior good sense (which so often needs aid from outside), had material to restore the balance.

698.   ATLANTIC HOTEL, HAMBURG, SEPTEMBER 6, 1954.   A Play for Edinburgh ["The Martians"].[8]

Absurd though it is to report here, I am considering an invitation extended to me by Ian Hunter, director of the Edinburgh Festival, to furnish a play for their next summer for their "problem hall" —the Assembly Room, high council chamber of the Presbyterian

---

8. The play eventually furnished for Edinburgh was *The Alcestiad* (in an earlier version), produced there in August 1955 as "A Life in the Sun" (not Thornton Wilder's title).

Church, where *Macbeth* is now being given. He took me to see it
—pew-like rows of seats rising on three sides of a central platform.
The fourth side they had walled off, a balcony, and podium to make a
back wall for Shakespeare's tragedy, but that also could be utilized in
some other way.

The absurdity lies in my having already before me so many
unfinished projects, and the consciousness of my increasing inability
to carry through a project in a prolonged effort of concentration.

But I have promised to write Mr. Hunter by November first.

My first fancies turning on this matter played with the idea of
making a play in the manner of Aristophanes on a subject in the field
of "Science Fiction." To steal from [Eduardo] De Filippo (*La Pauro
numero uno*) the *donnée* that a man will not let his daughter marry
because the world is about to come to a cataclysmic end. He [Herbert
Bostwick] gathers his family about him (this is not in De Filippo) and
goes to a cave to await the end—and there slides into his front yard
the flying saucer. There are many perils: that which overwhelms me
now is that I see no other basic moral to be read in this than the one
already supporting *The Skin of Our Teeth*. But I do see some admirable fooling.

The "basic moral" that does present itself to me as capable of
supporting some kind of play is the one which I have been tearing to
tatters in these speeches of mine: that many of the problems which
seem insurmountable to us in our present world would find their solution if we could bring ourselves to face them supra-nationally. Always returning likewise to the long-aborted "The Hell of the Vizier
Kabaâr". . . . But that turned on revenge-pardon. (So [it is] revived in
my mind each time I return to this country or, as recently, hear and
read the British on this country—the difficulty, impossibility, of urging constructive co-existence without appearing light-mindedly to
condone or ignore the fearful past. Yet how sharp I have become to
hear the vibration of all the ignoble reasons for desiring revenge on
the part of these noble patriots. And how quick to hear on the part of
my "finest" Jews, together with their abhorrence of viewing *one* German, their glimpse of a peace for themselves if they could "think" all
Germans.)

Could this be expressed by Part One of my Martian play?

Some first fancies:

(1) A space-ship is being fitted out. It is fairly certain of landing
on another star, but certain of no return. A number of gallant men

have volunteered to board it—*i.e.*, man *might* survive up there. But what we need is the continuance of man—*i.e.*, child-bearing women.

(2) The Martians creep out of their flying saucer and expire before our eyes, babbling. The babbling is taken down on a tape-recorder and later deciphered.

(3) A *richissime* woman comes to offer all her money to our hermit—for any cause he would name—if he would lend his daughter to the Martian journey.

(4) *Title:* "The Bats." "The Martians."

Oh, the pleasure of feeling about me the Aristophanic stage— the perpetual counterpoint of the little, tiny, absurd, gross, specific, and the large scene supported by the large idea. How naturally the lyrical arises from the shock of those extremes.

The man in his cave. His wife's sister comes to visit. He refuses to emerge, but shouts from behind the cave-curtain. The two women wrangling on the forestage about food, about the daughter's marriage. The press photographers. The descent from the ceiling of the iridescent, cellophane "saucer"—the little men (coming up a trapdoor).

699[A].   HOTEL MONOPOL-METROPOL, FRANKFURT AM MAIN, SUNDAY NIGHT, SEPTEMBER 19, 1954. The Edinburgh Play ["The Martians"].

. . . Even these days—and what overweighted days—I keep looking at the subject of this play in stolen moments. . . .

The new elements in the play:

The Martians want to receive permission to immigrate to this earth. Up there they have no war, sex, taxes, worry (bewitched delight of our hermit). They have no passions. Without war one cannot know peace, etc.

Scene of contemplating a rose—a girl.

The police arrive and arrest them. Have they any weapons? No, but of course they can kill anyone at will. How? "We can, but we don't know how we do it." *Police* (fearsomely): "We don't believe you. Kill that dog!" *Martians:* "Why? It has only a thousand years to live." *Police:* "Well, kill this ant." *Martians:* "A living thing? You may kill us, we will not kill an ant." *Police:* "Then will you kill a rattlesnake?"

Oh, I think this play can go far. . . .

[699B.]   HÔTEL CAYLEY, 4 BOULEVARD RASPAIL, PARIS, THURSDAY,
    SEPTEMBER 30, 1954.   The Edinburgh Play ["The Martians"].

At Berlin I told Binkie [Beaumont] the outline as I see it so
far—he bewitched: at once saw Helen Hayes—which is perfectly
right—and jumping ahead, could see that no usual theatre auditorium in London could house it—began building plans around his
bomb-gutted Lyceum (?) next to the Globe. . . .

On trains—and when falling off to sleep—I "invite" portions of
this play. I now have the opening. Dawn—bicyclist milkman and
newspaper boy. Mrs. Bostwick emerges with two pails. Flashes from
the photographers. She inveighs against. Interview demanded by as-
sorted women's magazines, etc. I must take care that *she* does not run
away with the play and become the mouthpiece for all the material.

New and important, too, is Herbert [Bostwick]'s line of invective: leaving the earth because parents don't love children any more;
children, parents; husbands, wives ("No, Herbert, you're not just to
yourself there" and that dialogue). "Best give up all pretending those
things because it only makes matters worse." The four sons—of their
eleven children—who went off to Army and Navy and who never
write home, etc.

New the pause at noon—the siesta hour.

The Martians will die—in untragic languishing—cannot live in
atmosphere of distrust; cling for last respiration to Mrs. Bostwick
("Anybody who's had eleven children can imagine what it would be
like to have a hundred.")

The danger now of writing too much—in these interrupted
conditions. Wait until it can grow of itself. . . .

Hôtel Legris et Parc, Fontainebleau, Wednesday,
October 6, 1954.

Some fine days of quiet—only disturbed by telegrams and
phone calls from England, and their replies. . . .

Have written openings of Parts One and Two. It's all right, I
guess. Only not funny enough—and by *funny*, I mean, *appalling*.
But it's fairly appalling. And I guess I've got one thing all right: I've
placed my appallingness in the homeliest daily realm; it doesn't seem
to be taking place in the world of science fiction at all. It looks as
though this'll be a play that has to have all the *air* of "intelligence"

without a single intelligent person in the cast. Mr. Bostwick will have his highly original note, but he'll be no *raisonneur* and no coiner of phrases. This play will be all from the *entrailles*—even the Martians, who presumably have no such organs. . . .

700. HÔTEL THERMES SEXTIUS, AIX[-EN-PROVENCE,] OCTOBER 1954.
The Edinburgh Play ["The Martians"].

Arrived here—my new home—at noon today. Solemn happiness. So many things still in the way of "applying myself," but those will always be there—though I deceive myself by fancying that they will not. So I sit down now and postpone some very pressing things in order to start stirring the pot on the stove a little, to turn the fire up a degree so that the thoughts about this play can resume their *ronron*, to be interrupted from time to time, we hope, by a sudden boiling-over. . . .

I was tempted, in thought, (while sitting in the bus that brought me from Avignon this morning, past the lunar landscapes of Les Baux) to ease one problem in my exposition by some matter which I fear would rather complicate it. —No, I shall not even write it down here; it is all wrong.

But I must keep reminding myself that I won't know what I have in this play until I've really seen what Herbert Bostwick is and what possesses him. And the minute I start thinking about him I see that my Part One has not enough forward movement. In the present version we start with his decisions already taken and already revealed. One or more of them must burst on our view (perhaps, on *his*) during the Act. And if possible we must see before us the reason for his mighty decision. All right, when the play opens he has merely decided to retire with his family into a cave because of the H-bomb. He has sent for his sister-in-law; to her he announces his second decision, to embark for Mars. Photographers and press are there merely because he has retired to a cave?

Now I'd better start carrying these notes about this play over to another section of this Journal—though to do so makes me wince, for it is into just such subsections that "The Emporium" and the Opera have "dispersed" themselves. Perhaps I should not do this *written tâtonnement*, perhaps I should write only the play and leave to meditation this kind of exploration, that is to say: perhaps the fact of having written down a movement of speculative exploration renders it too concrete, robs it of the freedom of easy expungement and forgetting.

Anyway, what I got this evening—sitting over a *tisane* at Les Deux Garçons—was a picture of the sacks of mail that arrive daily at the cave. And why is the larger world so concerned with Mr. Bostwick? Because he announced that he would not allow his daughter (daughters?) to marry, adding that it was dishonest to bring a child into the world in our time. —And where is the spirit of Aristophanes now? That is not the "tone" that will permit development as comedy.[9]

702. HÔTEL [THERMES] SEXTIUS, AIX-EN-PROVENCE, DECEMBER 7,
      1954. My New Play: *The Alcestiad*.

Two weeks ago tomorrow, that is Wednesday, November 24, I picked up the fragments of my abandoned project for *The Alcestiad*, which I happened to have brought with me—by accident, by a moment's velleity. I am now accustomed, alas, to these plays that get "stuck." I know some of the reasons; those for which my own willful bad character is responsible I do not think it is profitable to analyze here; others I can affirm calmly and are external. . . . I had been reading again Kierkegaard's *Philosophical Fragments*—picked up in a French translation here. That book may have been the first-mover of this play, anyway. . . . At all events, from the first *The Alcestiad* reposed on the same group of ideas that S.K. treats so beautifully in the allegory of the King in love with the Fisher Maid—God as the "unhappy lover."

The Alcestiad had "stuck" on three difficulties: I could not see the close of Act One—Alcestis's whole-souled giving of herself to Admetus: my sketches were wooden, my Admetus was wooden. I think I have now lifted that into one of the best scenes in the play. (*Note:* by at the same time infusing it with an extension of one of the basic themes of the play—all of which I should have *seen* in the earlier writing—that the Gods come among men by implanting themselves within men.) The second difficulty was that I felt that all my sketches

---

9. The play was not completed. Notes and drafts relating to it seem to have been destroyed by the author.

for the big scene of Act Two—Alcestis's giving of her life-breath to Admetus—were meretricious. Now I think I have solved it—and yet the words are almost the same as in the first drafts. Wherein lies the difference? In the fact that Admetus has now come alive for me. Then on a walk in this glorious countryside, in this glorious weather, there came to me an unexpected (and one might say unnecessary) addition to the close of Act Two, which could have come off adequately without it—the additional motive for Hercules's journey to the Underworld: that Alcestis had forgiven him a violence. There remains the third difficulty, the last Act and the finale. That still can cause trouble, but from the moment that I foresaw that, of course, I may call on the *deus ex machina*, I felt I had solid enough ground to go forward on. . . .

703. HÔTEL [THERMES] SEXTIUS, AIX-EN-PROVENCE, TUESDAY, DECEMBER 14, 1954. *The Alcestiad.*

Last night, in an essential sense, I finished *The Alcestiad*. A night of insomnia. I had been working for days—a few hours every morning—on the Third Act, knowing that I did not have the cornerstone of the arch (*finis coronat opus*), not exactly frightened, or even worried, but uneasy and expectant. In the morning I had seen that the Third Act should open with another scene between Apollo on the roof top and Death—yet even that may not now be necessary. The motif of pestilence, which now plays so large a part, only entered the [play] five or six days ago. Last night I . . . read for a while with such smiling pleasure the youthful Proust's *Contre Sainte-Beuve**—until my eyes glazed and I turned off the light to sleep. But sleep did not come; my thoughts turned to Alcestis and the tyrant—and presently, under shaking emotion, passage after passage was "filled in." Four o'clock: I try to read or to sleep. But new material presents itself. I think I must have slept between six and eight, but I was down at

*But let me record that some of my nourishment these days has been the paper by Charles Du Bos in *Approximations V* on the last journals of Baudelaire and from that a deep taking-in of the poems of Baudelaire in Gide's *Anthologie* [*de la Poésie Française* (1949)]. The pestilence probably entered the play (*Oedipus Rex*, too) from Giono's not very good, ill-organized *Le Hussard sur le Toit*. Bedazzlement before two sonnets of Mallarmé. The Kierkegaard. And as Christmas approaches, thoughts of my mother, which have always fed it.

breakfast at nine. (The paper had predicted *nuageux* for the Bouches du Rhône, but here I am in hot sunlight under a cloudless zenith.)

Almost with amusement I ask myself: can this play be as eloquent as I now feel it to be? Is it, maybe, a great welter of grandiloquent "emotionality"? Maybe, maybe, maybe it is, at present. Remains the hope that with a cooler head I can trim and de-rhetoricize a great deal of this material without weakening its power,—a doubly difficult task when one is writing an English that is both immediately colloquial and yet adequate to these gods and lofty beings. At all events, I shall have finished this writing by tomorrow night; then the "rewriting" of the whole play should be a pleasure,—a pleasure to strengthen and enrich all those two first acts with the ground-ideas, always latent there (no, already expressed in many places) which last night showed me were the constellatory signs of the whole work. Oh, can it be possible that those statements about death and the relation to the Gods which clarified themselves to me last night *can* be as free from cant, as true without banality, as convincing without didacticism, as they have promised to be?

704. HÔTEL ALEXANDRA, LAUSANNE, THURSDAY, JANUARY 6, 1955.
Closing Work on *The Alcestiad*.

Here I am in the morning working-hours, which I have so happily re-established after so long a break, rewriting Act Three—annoyed by that tricky bit of melodrama in the middle of it, and trying to get every legitimate drop of drama out of the recognition scene. On the third from Villars we sent scripts of Acts One and Two to [Ian] Hunter, Binkie [Beaumont], and [Tyrone] Guthrie. I am expecting some kind of word from at least one of them today (though Tony [Guthrie] may not yet be back in London) and the word is, it must be said, a little delayed. It may be that the pattern will repeat itself—the difficulty my works have so often found of being "recognized" at first approach by those responsible for their divulgation. But even before being armored against that by Gertrude [Stein]'s doctrine, I was well armored by experience itself. (Armored too by the effect of the reading of this play on the group at Villars, which seemed not so much to fall into a void, as into a pool of consternation.)

January 13, 1955.

Well, the fact is the first reply I have had from those three readers came this morning. From Tony Guthrie: ". . . the play is ravish-
ing; funny, moving, wise; wonderful roles." It's been quite a wait, and
I'm still waiting for a sign from Binkie and Hunter. As I had occasion
to say in another connection: How could they be so sure that I wasn't
a vain man?

[Aix-en-Provence,] January 25, 1955.

Back at Aix after the trip to London. The play is set for Edinburgh August 22, but these entrepreneurs have not sufficient confidence in its popular drawing-power to lay on a post-Edinburgh production. That doesn't greatly worry me.

If the play were written by someone else, what would I have to
say about it?

First, that Wilder has again tried to succeed in a vast undertak-
ing and has fallen conspicuously short. The design—or, viewing it on
several levels, the designs—are prodigious. To exhibit in drama a series of actions that would tend to persuade the auditors that the supernatural order is in loving relation with us,—though the relationship is rendered difficult through the "incommensurability." Of the
lover and the beloved?—no, that was not my intention at the outset.
I had planned to do something far more difficult (and far more *honest*
on my part): to exhibit that series of actions just described in such a
way that we could never be certain that the Supernatural was, truly
speaking, hovering—nay, existing; to devise every sign and message
and intrusion of the Other in such a way that it could be interpreted
as accident, delusion, mirage: "Some said it thundered; others that a
god spoke." That would have been a beautiful play; and one that
reflected *my* present position in these high matters. It would have
been doubly difficult to fashion (how much of adroit contrivance
would have had to go into it!) because I had chosen these two Greek
myths in which the presence of the numinous is a *donnée*, and its in-
terventions in the lives of these mortals would not easily admit of being interpreted as fancied and as born of superstition. But I suppose it
could have been done and I have gone quite a ways toward doing it in
the recounting of Apollo as shepherd. What have I got now? A play of

faith which is not a very good or radiant or convinced play of faith. I have an elegiac ballad about episodes which require faith in order to lift them out of the category of mere picturesqueness. What I should have written is a play of scepticism which is continually shot through with an almost violent and demanding invocation to interpret the actions in the light of faith.

I fell short of doing this for two reasons: the silly life I have been leading since the War has dulled and dimmed my capabilities for intellectual passion. It would not have been necessary to have faith to have written the *Alcestiad* which I should have written; all that was needed was to have been decades-long urgently at grips with the problem; I should have been passionately aware of what can be done with faith and what can be done without it. Also, as artist, I have been so lazy these last years that I can no longer assemble repeatedly my total concentration—that which alone can hold the whole of a play under attention at each moment of writing, so that the whole is reflected in each of the parts. To achieve that, one must write all the time; that is a matter of practice—and the only comfort I derive from the thoughts contained in this paragraph is that I feel that I can now go on and write others, and that the *practice* in having written *The Alcestiad* will help me in its successors. The second reason why this play is not what it should be is that the old T.N.W.-pathos, the human tug, entered it so largely. There is a large place in this legend for precisely that human tug; and woe to the dramatist—a Giraudoux or a T. S. Eliot—who approaches it without that pathos; but I have allowed it (though not in Act One) to get out of hand. What strength it has would have been all the more compelling in a framework of clearer, harder intellectual structure.

Plays fail because they lack unity of tone and singleness of intention in the plot-leading. I was all too certainly reminded of that in seeing *The Matchmaker* again last week in London. All those empty seats in the auditorium are the direct consequence of the insecurity of plot-leading in Act Three. Both these plays have, I venture to say it, unity of tone—the "unity" itself being a composite of tones, but a composite in which the several tones are equally distributed, "rhythmically" emergent. . . . This play, nevertheless, may fail because I have not grasped and made visible a sufficiently deep *unity*: there should be a deeper awe surrounding the close of Act One; and the opening of Act Two is casual-episodic.

There is one aspect of the play about which I am merely curi-

ous—objectively curious. Is it possible to write a play like this—
about lofty persons in high predicaments—without more verbal
beauty? Should they—gods and men—have unlocked their throats
more often to flights of recognizably lyric and rhetorical expression? I
doubt whether any play of similar pretension has ever been written so
consistently in monosyllables. (Yet artful ones, and presenting problems for the translators: see such a simple cadence as Cheriander's
"and that here we would have great help.") My answer is that I am not
a *poetic* dramatist, but . . . I am a poetic *dramatist*. And that the collocation of what the eye sees (and *primarily* what the eye sees) and
what the ear hears bears the poetry. All is as freighted with romantic
feeling as the scenery about Aix; I keep my darks and lights in continual juxtaposition. It is a play of the ordinary stuff of life which derives
its shock of poetry through the un-ordinary situations and contrasts in
which they are embedded. Will this work? Will this save me?

Anyway, I feel reinforced for the Next.

705. HÔTEL THERMES SEXTIUS, [AIX-EN-PROVENCE,] FEBRUARY 18,
      1955. After Some Readings in Zen.

Remembering my pleasure in [Eugen Herrigel's] *Zen in the Art
of Archery*, I picked up in a Left-Bank bookstore *Essays in Zen Buddhism* (3d Series), [by] D. T. Suzuki (Professor of Buddhist Philosophy at Otani University, Kyoto), published for the Buddhist Society,
London, by Rider and Company, Hutchinson House, Stratford Place,
London, W1, 1953. This volume is a discussion of the way certain
Sanskrit *sutras* (tracts? treatises? several of them seem to purport to
be sermons by Buddha), how these *sutras* passed into China and
through the Chinese mind and were modified and became Zen Buddhism. Professor Suzuki is very busy persuading us of the consum-
mate wisdom of these works and often despairingly arguing with
Western minds that may find them unassimilable by reason, logic, or
understanding of any kind. He is an adherent of Mahayana teaching,
which holds itself responsible for the ultimate conversion of the universe and is constantly expressing itself in close relation to the daily
life, as against the Hinayana, which reflects the Hindu mind and is
chiefly concerned with the monk's private disciplines toward self-
gratification (page 82). Professor Suzuki, after having given us all the

great texts that teach us that all is vacancy, even the knowledge of vacancy, has a great task in reassuring us that in this welter of negation there is an affirmation. In all this reading one is constantly at one remove from an abstraction so total that there is nothing to see but nonsense. . . .

What does engage me in these readings, however, is my old favorite obsession, the effects on thinking (I dare not say philosophical thinking) of the grasp of multitude. Here it is as I have never seen it expressed before. A student of Enlightenment will embrace with joy the thought that he may pass through millions of years—millions of lives—in the transmigration of souls,* if only, by the accumulation of merit, he may finally discard his errors and attain Enlightenment. We are constantly hearing of worlds as innumerable as the sands of the Ganges which must be converted before Buddhahood is the property of all.

And from these readings comes, too, [the idea] that the sense of multiplicity arises not only from the all-too-visible multitude of Indians (acquired from the fact that the monks were itinerant?), but from the sharpest of all views of the misery of existence. These mighty flights into a consolatory vacancy are propelled by horror and anguish. All this is deeply congenial to me. I have long dreamed of committing to this Journal an entry on the various ways that individuals and races and civilizations react to Necessity, to that which is irresistibly given.† (An illustration—trivial in this connection though it is —is how the French are now reacting to the appalling picture of the breakdown of their political and judicial and fiscal system,—the evident occultation of the *gloire* of the greatest civilization the world has been privileged to see!—a breakdown which every day becomes more evidently not a matter of a passing crisis or a correctable deviation, but a basic datum of destiny.) The *direction* of Hindu philosophy tends to console man by saying that if you gaze long enough at the sheer vacancy of consciousness-in-things, nothing can hurt you. Yet there is something more here than mere stoicism, but it does not look as though Professor Suzuki could make it clear.

I wish I were sufficiently a philosopher to be able to make clear to myself (a thing of which I am, however, certain by intuition)

---

*[André] Malraux quotes a Chinese funerary inscription in honor of the dead enemy heroes: "In your next life, do us the honor of being reborn among us."

†Again Malraux: "*L'art est un anti-destin.*"

where, how, and why our *Weltanschauung* becomes different in *kind* when we extend the *degree*—the amount of human situations we are contemplating, where the quantitative becomes a qualitative change. If I could do that, I feel I could also understand why Christianity (though it has other contributions and greater) appears in some ways —compared to the Buddhist Way—to be local or *étriqué*. One is clear enough: Christianity comes bearing its load of reference to the Family Nexus: its solace and its ethical injunctions and its anguished striving are all projected and illustrated for us in terms of family life. There is very little, so far, of this in the *sutras*—*Prajna* (the wisdom or eye of all-knowing) "is the mother and progenitor of all the Buddhas and Bodhisattvas" (page 228), and she must be cherished by them—but no picture can be made of *Prajna*. On the contrary, Buddhism is one long harping on non-attachment, breaking away from all "empty" vain affections. Likewise, there is a striking absence of all overt or implied erotic symbolism: no embracing of doctrines, or being at one with abstractions, or merging, or even being sheltered by them, under their shadow, etc. The emphasis is on the solitude of the Way. The Masters are often shown slapping their pupils in pedagogic impatience; and yet there is much about *Karma* (love) and the compassion of the Bodhisattva, which strains to draw every mistaken being out of error.

There's something very exciting about all these extreme abstractions. And that should help me much in the Norton-Lectures [book]—especially the Whitman chapter.

This insistence on the emptiness of all things and thinking is evidence of the extreme woeful despairing life of overpopulated India —one extreme evoking the other. And when Buddhism was expelled (or replaced) from India (by Hinduism) it went to China, where it found another woeful human situation; but it came up against the more practical Chinese nature. The result is Zen, for which the mystery for me—a promising and fruitful one—is how the acceptance of so much cosmic negativity could be expressed with so much humor, vitality, and serenity. (To notice, also, against the background of all this denial of intrinsic quality, the loving appreciation of every aspect of nature, including the smallest and most ephemeral.) . . .

706. [AIX-EN-PROVENCE,] MARDI GRAS, WASHINGTON'S BIRTHDAY,
      FEBRUARY 22, 1955. The Opera.

Well, dear Diary, I guess I'd better tell you that tonight is the
night that I saw what the Opera could be. For the last two weeks
—the impulse to write being stronger and clearer than the impression what to write about—I've been flirting with the idea of picking
up the "Sandusky, Ohio, Mystery Play"—which in time I think will
come to a fine flowering. But, of course, I have on my mind the commitment to Louise Talma for the opera libretto. I have now destroyed
all the sketches I've made toward that on another *donnée*. That would
have been all right for me [in] 1940, but all my probing into it cannot
bring it into the field of ideas that occupy me now. (Like all those
other schemes it may return to me some day in another metamorpho-
sis.) All that remains from it is the strong impulsion to make a new
kind of opera wherein the singing arises from the spoken drama as an
expression of the *ja-sagende* relation to life. So tonight, . . . I saw how
that idea could be linked up with a long-abandoned project for what I
once called the "P. G. Wodehouse Play" (in fact, I had two of them:
one in a London club; one on a very worldly-worldly terrace . . . ;
—it's the latter I've picked up). . . .

I have decided that it is best not to commit to this Journal the
backward-forward movement of a work in progress, but I'd better
note here that I see the Opera as a development of that idea: of a
woman of the great world who has had a daughter (formerly it was a
son) who after prolonged illness as a child has been brought up by
governesses without any knowledge of that prowler who escapes all
our vigilance and strikes people down—from behind hedges, from
every barrier we can erect—and of that other troublemaker in life
(this is new, to this treatment), love. Her mother—probably at Palm
Beach—is entertaining friends, among them a young man, who, as
worldly and as war veteran, knows all about these intruders. So we go
on from there. A stage without scenery. Spoken drama for all the
characters including the girl, until the "realities" come into play. . . .
Now good luck to it.

707. **ALHAMBRA HOTEL, GRANADA, MARCH 20, 1955**—got here last
night. Again, the Opera.

Just a word to trace the journey—still unfinished—no, still un-
oriented—of this project. Friday, on walks in Málaga, I got excited
again. I think I see a fine new prospect, but bristling with difficulties
and maybe doomed to collapse. In Málaga, or was it in Estregona
[*i.e.*, Estremadura?], I brought to a head a long evaded decision: to
abandon entirely the Saratoga-Springs story. With it went the so-
called Palm-Beach story (the girl returning, in ignorance, from a long
illness, to the fashionable circle of her mother). I then began exploring a variety of ways of motivating parallel speech and song, and
found myself back at "The Hell of the Vizier Kabaâr." The stage a
hemicircle of cushioned seats; the arrival of the itinerant troupe; the
capocomico's address to the audience: "Do you want an opera or a
play?" (Cries for both.) "Do you want a tragedy or a comedy?" (Cries
for both.) The project to contaminate the two. This gave me [the]
difficult (and for my "modes of apprehension," highly fascinating)
problem of juxtaposing, in alternation, two stories about Haroun Al
Raschid—one tragic opera, one spoken comedy, with intra-contra-
puntal relations of theme—in which the audience would have the
disturbing experience of seeing the alternating facets of the tragic and
comic modes playing upon the same characters, not as in Elizabethan
drama through irruptions of a sub-plot, but through coalescing two totally different artistic treatments of life; and not—as in *Ariadne auf
Naxos*—interpolated, but superimposed on the same agonists. What
work!—but it could be done.

A night of insomnia, however, Friday night in Málaga (and my
ink had run out so that I could not get out of bed to set down the first
sketches) I suddenly saw how my shipwrecked castaways—of that old
Yale Literary Magazine story (though published there some five
years—seven years—after my graduation)[1] could be employed to
give us a striking use of speech-song together with the ideas so dear to
me these years of the human adventure seen on a vast scale. At present, I cannot see how after an arresting opening (the tenth anniversary of their arrival) the Opera can rise to dramatic tension. I now
take a walk in the Generalife Gardens (it is Sunday and the Alhambra

---

1. "The Warship" was printed in the *Yale Literary Magazine Centennial Number* in 1936
(sixteen years after Thornton Wilder's graduation).

may be closed; it is raining) and see what the mills of the unconscious have been grinding.

Footnote: It gives to smile that I went down to dinner last night and saw sitting opposite me Igor Stravinsky with wife and son. I called the attention of the talkative maître d'hôtel to the fact, but urged him not to tell the trio of musicians (who had been playing pot-pourris of Puccini and [Godard's] "Jocelyn") until the composer had left. The maître d'hôtel assured me, however, that the pianist of the trio was a very fine player; he dashed behind the scenes and undoubtedly overwhelmed the musicians. So poor Stravinsky had to sit through a good deal of conservatory-level Chopin earnestly hurled at him. Across the narrow room I heard him talking to his wife about George Sand.

708. SS "CRISTOFORO COLOMBO," WESTBOUND, APRIL 3, 1955.
. . . A Little Weakness of André Gide.

I've always said that the French go into great excitement, and complacent excitement, about the sins of the flesh in order to conceal the fact that they are subject to a far more deforming obsession— avarice. (All those novels in which Mauriac hounds his poor characters through the alternations of *péché* and *la grâce*, for his own savage enjoyment—an enjoyment so evident that one is unable to hear any true heartbeat in his mannequins. And then he writes a novel about avarice—*Le Noeud de Vipères*—and becomes authentic and convincing.)

A certain young American, [X], broke his leg and came to Aix to convalesce. I had met him at tea at Alice [Toklas]'s and [he] sent me a note. [X] is a sort of less vivacious Boswell, diligently and unsuppressibly cultivating Picasso and Gide and Cocteau and Marie-Laure de Noailles, and anybody who is anybody in Paris. Alice was deeply displeased that Dora Maar had brought him, uninvited, to tea; she remembered that Gertrude [Stein] had once been cultivated by [X] and had brusquely almost brutally slapped him down. I am grateful to him for . . . the following anecdote. . . .

Gide was always well off; [X] even said he was rich. One day he invited [X] and a friend to lunch in a famous restaurant. After lunch they continued talking a long while. The waiter brought the bill and laid it by Gide. They continued to talk. Finally Gide said to [X]: "I know that I asked you to lunch, but can I ask you to pay the bill? I----I----*c'est plus fort que moi.*" Those thousands of pages of self-examination in the *Journal*—all that clamorous confession—and not a word about this sorry, inglorious vice: the inability to let some money pass out of his hands. All Gide is hollow. How the French could have been taken in by that marmoreal style, which on closer examination is lathe-and-plaster. The graduate student who wished to be taken for a faun.

711.   **NORTH BRITISH HOTEL, EDINBURGH, AUGUST 14, 1955.**
       Edinburgh Play [*The Alcestiad*] and This Journal. . . .

Well, I finished that new version of Act Three, not even on the boat, but at the more-than-eleventh hour—in the Savoy Hotel during August Bank Holiday weekend. Again—as with the last chapter of *Heaven's My Destination*, the last entries of *Ides of March*, the preparation of the [Norton] Lectures—procrastination, the inability to call my wits together for a deep concentration had played their part. What astonishes me during these rehearsals is the highly effective theatricality that Guthrie [the director] is able to draw from these heterogeneous scenes. I have not yet seen those in which (so inadequately) the Idea emerges. Thank Heaven I found (how did I find it—in such harum-scarum writing conditions at the Savoy?—though the phrase lay latent subtending the whole play) Cheriander's cry: "You are sign—the sign and message, Queen Alcestis." I have not yet seen the dialogues between Apollo and Death, and shudder in advance at my share in them. I do not think, now, that they should be cut out; but they should have been written by a better hand than mine, and some more theatric device for the numenous should have been devised for their statement.

But, again, this Journal must not be the deposit of my self-reproaches. My only consolation is that I feel that now I am shaping my life more correctly toward the right conditions for writing and that my Next and my Next will give a better account of what I could and should do. And: I must emerge from this dibble-dabble in religious subject-matter; I must shake my whole self and learn what I do and do not believe, or else eschew such themes altogether. I am ashamed of this lukewarm imitative dilettante religiosity. Pfui!

712. [HÔTEL] TRIANON PALACE, VERSAILLES, SEPTEMBER 12, 1955.
Bilan.

The Edinburgh affair ended a week ago yesterday when I left Edinburgh at two and arrived in Paris at five. I have no desire to tell that story here nor my thoughts about it; the former I have recounted in many letters and very few of the latter have I told to anyone, nor do I wish to.

Let us go forward. Today is a great day: I received a letter from Elizabeth Sergeant saying that Louise [Talma] is "happy as a lark" at my suggestion that she use *The Alcestiad* as her opera libretto, instead of the one that I had planned to submit to her. That projected libretto is still rich with promise, but it would take many months to bring it to birth. Already it has consumed many, ever-changing shapes, and just today I have destroyed pages of *hors-série* entries in this Journal which dealt with it. I groaned at the thought that I would now have to return to it and work on it under extreme pressure of haste, since Louise's Fulbright year begins this month and she must have the material at once. Now I must learn once for all to enter into no "writing" projects which involve a date-line; nay, to announce no piece of work to anyone until it is finished. There lies still a large part of the coil which still involves me with this *Alcestiad*: it was finished in a hurry. I am here this week to write a new Third Act, the third; the fact that at the same time I must prepare the "singing" version of the play is a task, indeed, but compared with the other obligation, a relatively welcome one.

What shall I do in the Fall? For a while I was tempted with the thought of returning to the United States and "getting off" the Nortons [book]. Tempted also in the sense that it would fascinate me to learn just what I was going to say. I feel that there are stirring just under the surface a host of pregnant ideas, developments that precisely this lapse of time has enriched. Moreover, the fascination is blessedly doubled by the consciousness that the whole book will be also a constant freshening of the *ways of saying a thing*. Gertrude Stein's pupil will really lay a wreath on her grave. But I must not do that now: that is exposition, reflection, and "non-fiction." Another part of the difficulty that has surrounded and still surrounds *The Alcestiad* arose from the fact that I had gotten out of practice in writing—writing of the category imaginative narration. That didactic-expository year at Harvard took that toll; it brought into focus those modes of thinking that

are disturbingly incompatible with what I gropingly call symbolization. Before I return to the termination of the Nortons I must do one
more Story, in drama or novel. Then with advancing years I may with
less disturbance alternate the two.

Before I finish this note I wish to offer one more tribute to
Gertrude [Stein]. That last week in Edinburgh as I circulated at parties, as I gave parties, I was often aware, and occasionally sharply so,
that people were watching my behavior for signs that the reviews of
the play—and the worst ones began appearing (then unknown to me)
in the admired London weeklies—had crushed me, or that I was
maintaining a brave face on a turmoil of humiliation or resentment.
Finally, my last night, the hosts of the [X]s asked me to drop in after
the theatre, in a beautiful apartment in Heriot Row. I found myself in
a nest of mostly British music critics. They seemed not to have gone
to a performance that evening but to have been conversing and drinking since dinner—and expecting my arrival. I soon became aware of a
veritable barrage of alcohol-released *Schadenfreude*. One man—but
I shall not recount it. It was not until the next afternoon in the London airport that I read the review that they had been relishing.

Oh, it's to Gertrude that I owe this invulnerability to the evalu-
ations of others! Nay, I have it so deeply implanted that I can hold in
my head at one time both my confidence in what is meritorious in my
work and my real self-reproach at what is bad. I do not even oscillate
between the two reactions—between pugnacious defense and de-
jected self-flagellation. Gertrude's guidance, however, fell on a soil
already ploughed: Amos Wilder's children—and in a far subtler way,
Isabella Wilder's—were already notably well removed from being
impressed or depressed by the evaluation of the neighbors. (And it is
curious to note that Father could transmit this invulnerability with a
particular force because he himself remained toward the end not a little deferential to Place and Status—academic, governmental, and,
especially, ecclesiastical.) All the best of Maine's and Scotland's un-
worldliness was breathed in our family air; but that is not all. A thousand times in the daily life, both parents had ways of implying that the
opinions of others are a sort of nonsense. Their approbation or disapprobation does not go very far in serving as a guide. I think of the
years when we lived in Berkeley and when to an attentive youngster
it seemed odd that my mother could retain so objective and occasionally shocking a view of the acts or sayings of those friends whom in
various ways she admired—of Mrs. [W] or Mrs. [X] or of Miss [Y] or

of the [Z]s, her quick impatient or even exasperated dismissal of some reported criticism of us or of others. All this she could convey without any arrogance; there was not a measure of "Everybody's a fool except oneself." It partook rather of "Oh, people say things they don't mean" or "Oh, if we listened to everything people said, we'd be in a pretty fix!" It remained for Gertrude to elevate this self-reliance to a luminous deeply-explicated doctrine oriented primarily toward the literary life.

So it was that after the Edinburgh experience I had a sense of laughing excitement. I felt like someone who had been through a traffic accident. I listened to myself: "What? no broken bones? no strained ligaments?" No, and at once I thought of Gertrude. She protected me against such fractures—not at that low level of confirming an artist in any infatuation for his own work, but at a high laughing level, wherein one says that if one is in that kind of work at all, the only resource is to be one's first and last audience and only from oneself can one ultimately learn that one should occupy oneself with other things, or should persevere.

My behavior has been impeccable. I have neither (save here) made allusion to the fact that my collaborators were occasionally deficient nor that I was occasionally deficient. Did my behavior proceed from stoicism? No, from indifference. And from a deep-seated confidence that the work—for all its faults (which for me always seem correctable)—was sound and would prevail.

713.   [HÔTEL] TRIANON PALACE, VERSAILLES, SEPTEMBER 12, 1955.
       The Opera *Alcestiad*.

Although I no longer believe that this Journal operates for me as a constructive element in the edification of new works, I shall try it once more toward that end.

Louise [Talma]'s opera. After reflection I feel that it would not be right to employ in this work our project for a significant application of the relations between the sung and spoken word. This is heroic material and it would be out of place to call the audience's attention to the surely interesting changes one can ring on superhuman-human in this way. There are more interesting ways in which we can engage the listener. And I hope by "interesting" I can mean original—legitimately original.

(1) Is it too late for me to borrow from Cocteau's *Les Chevaliers de la Table Ronde* that *idée géniale* that he failed to express at its maximum theatricality? The evil spirit—which? of Merlin's prompting?—appears within each of the principal characters in turn, so that we see Guinevere temporarily drunken and Launcelot corrupt. Could my Apollo traverse the *dramatis personae* with the indicatory aid of the music? Think it over.

(2) Dare we have Teiresias as a woman in Act One?

(3) But if we have such cold-water-in-the-face goings-on in Act One we must have them also in Acts Two and Three, and have them aiding not diminishing the grand-style mode, the high opera-seria. *N.B.* My Act Two has always lacked the note of the numenous. We could get a little *tremendum* in there, even if it bordered [on] the morbid or horrifying. And Louise's music could always keep the stern lofty balance, however *low* I went. —A horrendous idea has just occurred to me:* that the First Herdsman–Apollo, in his scene with Alcestis and the amulet, *approaches* a physical aggression, premonition of the moment when Hercules—supposititious Zeus—confesses to the same outrage. What anthropological vistas!

[Hôtel Trianon Palace, Versailles,] the Next Day.

"Testing, just testing"—as the radio technicians say: couldn't we have two or more of the Four Herdsmen come to Alcestis's aid —in the opera? So as to heighten the interest in both those scenes. And couldn't we have—somehow—a more pictorial indication of Admetus's conviction that he is to do—his ordering, so to speak, of his own funeral? (Both these suggestions opening the way to a possibly comic effect—but none the less richening for that.)

All this is to be taking shape while I am rewriting that rather dissimilar work—the new Third Act of the play. There I must work always toward a simpler expression of its unity: to illustrate the two-way friendship of Alcestis and Apollo.

. . . Let's hope that the excogitation of these two separate pro-

---

*But in the modifications for the spoken play I had already envisaged demanding that the First Herdsman be played by the Apollo actor.

jects—the far more odd and colorful and puzzling-stupifying opera and the far more simple austere last act of the play—inter-aid one another to the benefit of each.[2]

718. HAMDEN, CT., SUNDAY, MARCH 4, 1956. Lope Work: Problems around Nicolás de los Ríos.

. . . A self-indulgent week to Lope—pure luxe.

But as never before I see the tracts of time necessary to any slight progress in this work—to which I answer that, at least, I can do it in less time than Professor X or Y, because I have certain kinds of alert perceptions for it; I can make *sauts périlleux* and then build up the supports that sustain [them]. . . .

The great importance of Ríos: for whom both Cervantes and Lope wrote.

The tracing of Ríos's personal characteristics in the role of *figura del donaire* (in what decade did the designation *gracioso* enter?—in his prefatory letter to *Parte* XIII, 1620, Lope still calls it *figura del donaire*). . . .

The characteristics are: (1) His black complexion; (2) His attitude to women: takes his pleasure; never fell in love; never gives them a cent; enemy of platonic love; (3) His many-sidedness—a characteristic which from his acting ability finds its way back into his very role-in-the-play; (4) [His] physical strength. (As to courage: he is very brave in *El remedio* [*en la desdicha*]; is he shown as conventional *gracioso* coward?)

Other things to watch: is he exceptionally accorded monologues in the form of a debate-with-himself, *i.e.*, the monologue as dialogue?—as in *Sinfimiento de honor?*

When I've traced the specific Ríos [traits], I then read the *gracioso* roles in the other (early) companies—the Porras, Pinedo, Vergara sequences.

I then show how [the] Ríos "person" (with the help of *El Viaje entretenido*) left its stamp on the *gracioso* convention.

---

2. The opera was eventually completed and was given its world première (the Wilder libretto translated into German) in Frankfurt in March 1962. Only excerpts have so far been performed in the United States.

I then show how it was built up in Cervantes's mind with (oh, dream!) its contribution to Sancho Panza.

We must remember that Ríos was not only the fountainhead of the *figura del donaire*, but, as Cervantes asserted, *all men, all roles*. And the heroic figures of heroes, kings, and saints. Is he in the *entremeseo? There* are the possibilities of this inquiry—the glory of this inquiry—and all dependent on time and patience.[3] . . .

719. HAMDEN, [CT.,] TUESDAY, MARCH 6, 1956. Bergson and the
       Beauty of Nature: . . . The American and Nature.

. . . Nature (clouds, mountains, trees, sunsets, stars) is said to be beautiful. Bergson suggests that we did not find these beautiful until Art opened our eyes to that beauty.

I held that their beauty—for the "Europeans" for example—derived from two factors: these beauties were all a part of their environment (social and psychic) and were, in addition, imposed upon the observer as beautiful because they were made by the Divine King-Father and were His House and His Dress. (This last factor admitting, however, of exceptions: that part of His Dress which was the Alps was "horrid.")

I had not sufficiently taken into account the fact that the emotion of the beauty in nature derives also from the recall (the reminder) of the sights that surrounded us when we were happy. A portion of every childhood is happy; in the majority of cases a large portion of every childhood is happy. Leaving aside for a moment the objection raised by Mrs. Apfelstrudel that there are many unhappy childhoods recorded precisely in the history of the arts, and her additional objection that Wilder has often affirmed his agreement with psychoanalysis that the infant—and particularly the infant who will devote himself to the proclamation of beauty—goes through a hellish inner life, I now declare that the beauty of nature is a qualification we confer on those things (effects of light and moisture surrounding land, sea, and air) which recall to us the surroundings of our happier hours. Natural beauty is a memory of the scenery that we scarcely noticed in our

---

3. Wilder never wrote a book on Lope de Vega, but there are more than 1,000 pages of notes, plus annotated copies of the Lope plays, among the Thornton Wilder papers at Yale.

early life during moments when we were deeply stirred. The child being taken on a walk, a drive, by the big mysterious loved one, is storing up the norms of what he will later recognize as the concomitant—the décor—of happiness. First, Eros; then the memory of the environment where Eros was aglow.

This has never been sufficiently recognized. Our twentieth-century in-spection—of which psychoanalysis is merely the scientific bulldozer—is attentive as never before to the power latent in irrational promptings. . . . chance associations in the erotic realm can build up a lifelong "pursuit." Lately reading again—on the ship—Thomas Mann's *Tonio Kröger* (with all my resistance against that ponderously signpost-planting author), I grudgingly conceded that he had indicated these subterranean drives very well: Tonio, grown up, goes on his vacation to Denmark, because a Gymnasium-student with whom he had been infatuated years before had worn a Danish sailor's cap, etc., etc. Also rereading (forwarded by a biographer of Edward Sheldon) a letter I had written to Ned: why was I so happy staying . . . at Lake Geneva, Wisconsin? Because I saw and smelled a Wisconsin lake like the Lake Mendota beside which I had passed my summers up to the age of nine—an emotion which overcame me lately when I strolled beside a very distant one, Lake Garda, at Sirmione.

All men, then, praise the world and think that its beauty is an Absolute—when basically it is merely the reminder of the only décor they have known—décor not to their infantile activities but to their infantile *émois*. As they did not, could not, wish to ascribe this reason to their emotion, they searched about for other bases: they loved it because it was beautiful *in itself*, or because it was stretched out before them by their King-Father.

The American also rejoices in the beauty of nature, but is slow to concede that it holds an *essential* beauty and, slower to concede that it is beautiful because either Privileged Beings or Repressive Fathers made it, is left with an unanswered question.

I am now almost ready to recast the whole matter in the form of a myth—to refashion that myth of mine about the Empress of Newfoundland. Here the role that reminiscence plays in her life is not that of a platonic pre-natal Absolute, but all of this world. Nor do we need any longer—except, perhaps, for the case of a "European" child—to make our little hero or heroine of royal birth; nor do we need the assumption of a "sleep and a forgetting" (though that, too, takes place in every growing-up).[4]

Let's try it.

720. HAMDEN, [CT.,] MARCH 8, 1956. Beauty of the World: The European and the American.

Tom Everedge [Everage, an American Everyman] was born of intelligent-idiotic parents of whom it can only be said that they were loving and flinty-hearted. He never forgot these traits and gradually came to ascribe them to the world itself. Right from the start his life was one catastrophe after another. He suffered from an obscure stomach complaint and made no secret of his pains. From time to time he almost starved to death. The stupidity of his guardians was beyond belief; they permitted the floor to rise up and strike him, the walls of his crib to batter his tender hands and feet, his bedclothes to stifle him, cold wet garments to chill him. Before he was a year old there developed a tormenting malformation in his mouth; no one seemed able to ease his pain and he fell into alternations of rage and despairing frustration—an emotional pattern that was to remain with him for life.

But worst of all were the miseries that beset him in his sentimental life. All his being was centered on his mother, but no words can describe the extent to which this abandoned woman trifled with his affections. She absented herself for aeons at a time; often—in the very same room—she ignored his appeals for help and comfort. Worst of all, she invited another man to share their lives and gave to *him*, in shameless dalliance, the time and attention she owed to Tom. This infidelity made her intermittent caresses seem hypocritical and from her, at a good school, he learned a whole repertory of pretense; he feigned coldness when she returned from ten-year absences; he pretended mad infatuations for other matrons. Yet her conscienceless behavior only made him love her more.

Infancy has a short memory, mercifully. In spite of and because

4. The quotation is from Wordsworth, "Ode: Intimations of Immortality . . . ," line 58: "Our birth is but a sleep and a forgetting."

of all this anguish, Tom was constantly caught up into moments and hours of delirious happiness. He could forgive and forget his mother's derelictions; he could even accommodate himself to that other man's intrusion. At times life was perfect bliss. The bliss was inward, but he gradually came to associate the sights and sounds and smells of the outer world with the inner happiness. Joy was even more acute than suffering, and though he had suffered in sunlight, firelight, under the trees and clouds of parks, many aspects of the outer world were forever after to be identified, in him, with the joys he had experienced there. It was not the beauty of foliage and sky which made him happy; it was his happiness which made foliage and sky beautiful, and later his memory of happiness experienced beneath them.

This is not an immediate confrontation with nature in itself.

He grew older.

He began to be able to distinguish between the sufferings caused by "things" (the being struck by a baseball; his fall from [a] cliff path) and those caused by intelligences (his being spanked; his being left behind on a trip); but not entirely, never entirely, did he learn to distinguish between the joys aroused in him by "things" and those aroused by minds.

The sentimental sufferings did not abate; they became more confusing. But he found a resource; he learned how to put them out of his mind. . . .

All this preamble to remind us—who are constantly needing the reminder—that although Man is the animal who has furthest developed the faculty of reason, there remain extensive tracts of his mind that he has not brought—and has not wished to bring—to rational examination.

The apprehension of beauty in nature, together with a whole repertory of gratifications and repugnances, has its source—for each individual—in the circumstances of his early life. Yet to these private relations between man's inside and the world's outside are soon added those of the community in which he lives: its nightmares, its fantasies of beatitude; its delights, frustrations, and rages; its forgettings; its history. A people crowded on a small island, a people in a hot country, a people in mountain fastnesses, a people nine centuries subject to another people, a people that has never known a civil war —such people do not all have the same views on whether the laborer is worthy of his hire, or on what you save from a burning house or what you lay by for a rainy day; nor in the presence of earth, air, water, and foliage do they find the same combinations beautiful.

The European Thomases all had one memory in common—the memory of having been duped. Together with this shameful memory was that of the gradual emergence from the deception, the longing to be duped again, and the shame of the longing to be duped again. The European peoples had believed for centuries that the Order of Being itself included the fact that a smaller number of persons were in a position of power over the mass of men and that this power was transmitted from generation to generation through the accident of birth. This was the Great Lie which had played so large a part in all human societies and, being a lie on such a vast scale, it had required for its maintenance untold expenditures of energy. Like all successful lies it had derived its strength from human weakness: it had been as much to the interest (apparently) of the unprivileged as of the privileged. It had inserted itself, as self-evident truth and as image, into every aspect of life. It had been enriched by two impressive analogies: the Privileged Man was to his people what God was to the universe; and he was what a father was to his family. Hence the emergence from the lie was an anguished passage, for it partook of blasphemy and of filial disobedience or patricide.

722. **HOTEL ALGONQUIN, NEW YORK, TUESDAY, MARCH [13, 20, or 27,]** **1956.** Nortons.

Have picked them up again. The difficulty of keeping them both meaty and light. The hope that all these pages which I write and discard, all these far-roving digressions—which so far put me in possession of the successive *idées-mères* that I can finally state them in aphoristic form and in telling condensed images—carry large burdens rapidly and airily. And I feel my instinct continually demanding of me those interruptions to the argument—the dramatic dialogue with the restive members in the audience, for example—that prevent the book from being read and appraised as one more socio-literary treatise. . . .

724. HAMDEN, [CT.,] APRIL 3, 1956. Nortons: Life of Tom
      Everage—Continued. . . .

Would it be possible to "run" this life of T.E. by instalments,
between the successive chapters, finding for each chapter its appro-
priate aspect of our hero's life, all the time playing an Old-World Tom
against a New-World? If I could do it, it would enormously unify and
support the book, as well as be a striking example of the postulated
"American" way of keeping one's eye, at the same moment, on the
Most General and on the Particular.

The instalment between Lecture One and Lecture Two (Thoreau) would include the life of all infants (the emperor in the cradle). I
would try to postpone until later (but would it be possible?) the net-
works of emotional association.

Could I—as prefatory to the Thoreau lecture—develop that
other train of ideas, so often launched by me a few years ago, about
the Humiliated Heart that turns to the Non-Human, etc.? I'll now
make some sketches for this on another piece of paper. The drawback
which I immediately foresee, with a groan, is that each of these instalments will require so much accompanying editorial direction on my
part—that is, instead of telling the Amazing Saga of Thomas Everage
(and I believe I could make a whole book of it, and an astonishing one)
straight through, obeying its own laws of subject-succession, etc., I
have to cut and trim my cloth according to the authors I am discussing and the other ideas I am unfolding. But let me now make some
sketches.

(*Later:*) Well, it's advanced. I think it can be done. Each "rewriting" of the material gets longer and better; but it's extraordinary
the extent to which my silly pen can run on, into mighty world-en-
compassing generalizations and into elevated moralizing admoni-
tions, when what I need is to be deep with lightness. But what does
most excite me about this is the form which is developing for the
book. Like *The Ides of March* it will advance by superimposed layers.
I have found a literary way of rendering that difficulty to which Gertrude [Stein] gave voice (and which I have quoted in the book): "Oh,
it's so hard, because you have to hold so many things in your head at
once." Here is a first view of the table of contents:

AMERICAN CHARACTERISTICS

Foreword.

Lecture I: Three American Predispositions of Mind.

    Interpolated Essay: On a Certain Disconnection in Americans: Essay Number One: On the Disconnection from Place.

    First Interlude: The Life of Tom Everage, American, Preparatory to a Comparision with the Lives of His Contemporaries in the Old World.

Lecture Two: Henry David Thoreau, an American who fell ill through his failure to [connect?].

    Interpolated Essay: On a Certain Disconnection in Americans: Essay Number Two: On the Disconnection from Nature.

    Second Interlude: The Life of Tom Everage, American, Continued.

Lecture Three: Emily Dickinson - - - -

I have been told that I should not ask that these "serial" essays should be printed on colored paper; it would be too expensive. But maybe —in some *de luxe* edition.

    A new serial is to be more gradually introduced for the second half—all for provoking refreshed attention, and for directing new converging "lights" on to the thick and many-layered rich subject matter—namely, Lay Sermons. I shall say—perhaps, as early as the Foreword—that the most popular and flourishing literary *genre* of the Americans, and all too congenial to them, was that sorry, now disuete,* thing, the Sermon. (*Development:* the moralizing tendency in Americans; why? etc. Its impress effect on American prose style ----) So: my obligation to furnish sermons.

725. HAMDEN, [CT.,] THURSDAY, APRIL 5, 1956. The Piano in Beethoven and Schubert.

    I can keep my peace no longer. For ages I have felt a deep uneasiness before long tracts of Beethoven's piano sonatas—all the first half and many passages in the second; and an even greater discomfort before Schubert's. At times this impression was [so] strong that I

---

*Not in *Webster's Unabridged International!*

could say to myself that I "didn't like them." The statements of themes and their developments seemed to me so *simpliste*, so easily fabricated when they were pretty and so false-grandiose when they were portentous or "rugged." I liked the development sections best, but even then the themes these masters had chosen (and I have long preferred the creation of pregnant themes to that of melodies) seemed to me to be "uninteresting." Of course, I thought the fault lay in me (there have been times when—mostly because of this very dissatisfaction—I have told myself that I was probably not musical at all), and at recital after recital I waited for the performer to "reveal" to me the beauties so celebrated in these sonatas. I didn't think that the two opening figures in the *D Minor*, the arpeggiated chords, and the anxious answer in descending steps, were awe-inspiring; nor the two that begin the *Pathétique* (and the adagio opening rises little above anyone's improvising among the minor chords). I groped around for other excuses: I told myself that I had deadened my ear to them through knowing them too well, and learning to know them in the most damaging way, *i.e.*, through fumbling with them myself. Only once did I have the sensation of hearing one of these sonatas presented in such a way that I had no difficulty with it: in Chicago I went . . . to a recital by Schnabel, who played the last of Schubert's "Three Grand Sonatas"—[the] *B Major*. But his recordings of the earlier Beethovens did not renew the miracle, nor their performance at some of the most admired hands of our time.*

Gradually I came to the view that these composers were not writing clavier music; they were "hearing" in terms of wind and strings. Their chamber music of the same periods had never given me this impression of thinness in content and thinness in statement. (I "followed," once, a trio that Alexander Schneider had organized to Hartford and heard entranced a Beethoven trio—*Opus 1*?) But finally even this explanation did not satisfy me. I felt convinced that they wrote "better notes" for other instruments than the clavier.

And that, now, is my position. The cembalo-harpsichord-pianoforte family by the time it reached the piano and for a half century thereafter was a stultifying instrument. I can understand that for

---

New York, April 13, 1956: Heard Backhaus at Carnegie Hall last night: *Sonatas Op. 2, No. 1; Op. 10, No. 1; Op. 27, No. 2* ("quasi una Fantasia")—beautiful performances, but I am still of the same mind about the first two. The third, and his last offering, the *Hammerklavier*, are another matter.

those composers and listeners it had the deceptive interest of a novelty. "*Que todo lo nuevo aplace*," as [Fernando de] Rojas repeatedly
says [in his *La Celestina*]. Invention was continually extending the
resonance of the clavier, and that was sufficiently animative for them.
As I read somewhere in the *Cambridge History of Music*, the exploration of timbre was the preoccupation of eighteenth-century music,
and the impetus continued into the nineteenth. But, for a time, the
piano could not supply what was asked of it. In the first place, these
masters thought they heard in it a capability for the continuing resonance of a long-held note. They *thought* they heard it because it was
doing so much better than a harpsichord. Only later was Liszt to show
that a sustained note in an upper-register melody must be supported
not by the Alberti bass, but by a complex of left-hand figures that set a
large range of harmonics in motion. The piano is a wretched instrument, fundamentally percussion, that must be adroitly wheedled and
cajoled into a *cantabile*. Even the slow movement of Schubert's [*B
Major*] *Sonata*, which Schnabel took more slowly than an *andante
sostenuto* (I remember feeling there was something *orientale*, something Turkish, about it), is a rank imposture—like the timpani rolls in
the first movement.

My charge is not that they wrote clavier music while their
minds were *hearing* strings and wind; but that their minds during this
awkward transitional period did not feed them very good ideas. It was
chamber-music thinking, but inferior thinking. All those themes
based on the triad, for grace or for rhetorical declamation, were ordinary ideas, artificially enhanced for them because they were hearing a
newly-invented tonal effect in the pianoforte. . . .

What it comes down to in the end is that man is a conservative
slow-budging creature. There was this clavier; its gradual "improvement" was necessary—as all innovation is necessary in the arts. So
they improved; but in a direction that impoverished the qualities of
the instrument from which they were taking their departure. Beethoven was so great that finally he not only wrote great *music* for the piano, but wrung from the piano an extraordinary new set of timbre
effects; but they were *sui generis*. It was not from them that Liszt,
Chopin, Mendelssohn and Schumann were to introduce the piano
into the *salon* and into *Hausmusik*.

Now the piano has arrived at a new state of arrest. Stravinsky
relegated it to the group of percussion instruments where it belongs,
and in that capacity it is congenial to certain aspects of the new music.

I am looking for the invention of a new musical instrument. For me even the string choir and group is an intrusion (trailing behind it the memories of the *emotion* it conveyed in its boundlessly glorious past).

The piano wandered too far from the voice, which only with difficulty (or for comic effect) can make a percussive note. The wind instruments—so rightly called—are more "vocal" than the human voice—they are nearer that of the animals. It is [by] being attentive to our voice that we will discover the instrument to carry a great new age of music.

727. **ALGONQUIN HOTEL, [NEW YORK,] APRIL 7, [AND HAMDEN, CT., MARCH 8,] 1956.**[5] The Life of Thomas Everage: Instalment Two: He Aspires to Be a Reasoning Being.

Let us return to his first, second, and third years.

As Tom grew older he began to try to be able to distinguish the sufferings caused by inanimate things from those caused by intelligent agencies.

Being bitten by a dog, spanked by his father, thrown from his baby-carriage (some passing giants bumped into it)—it was perfectly clear that those calamities were caused by wicked people who lay in wait to inflict pain upon him. However: when he was struck by a wind-blown swing, when he fell down the front steps, when he burned himself by putting his hand in the oven—what agency was responsible? One of the hardest things he was learning, and he never learned it completely, was to conceive of a non-conscious agency. He was later top-of-his-class in Physics; he was in the upper third in Logic; yet at the age of twenty-nine, when he was struck by a wind-blown door (and given a black eye by it) he turned and violently and repeatedly kicked the door. When he fell down the front steps and was laid up for two weeks with water on the knee, he found the experience "trying," a real trial, and he did not contradict his wife when she said it was a "judgment on him." When he burned himself trying to repair the oven, it was a real "blow" to him. He consoled himself with the thought that no one "escapes" hard knocks and that these are

---

5. The last three paragraphs of this entry were written originally as part of Entry 720.

"sent" to teach us patience and that it was a "mercy" that he had been "spared" a broken leg. This confusion was diffused throughout all his thinking. He ringingly told the Rotary Club that America had been blessed with three years of unprecedented prosperity (prolonged applause), though a few years later from the same banquet-table he deplored with his fellow members that our country had been the "victim" of unprecedented reverses. Each of his successive automobiles was a "she" and these young women lived dramatic lives: she was always, the hussy, breaking down—he sometimes expressed his idea more clearly by saying that "she chose to break down"—at the most inconvenient moments. Some days (but he kept this to himself) she rode beautifully; she passed all the other cars on the road "like a dream."

But returning, eternally returning, to his early days: there were these alternations of despair and ecstasy; there was this escape into obliviating activity. He began to hear the voices of the community life around him. He heard that all papas and mamas were perfect, were wise, were selfless. He must have been, surely he must have been, foolish and wicked to have harbored those distrustful thoughts in regard to his own----yet----yet----he could not control nor forget those murderous thoughts, violent thoughts. No, these problems were too difficult to cope with. The best resource was to fling oneself entirely, consumedly, into activities that had no connection with such problems.

Games were enclosed worlds, passionate but self-terminating. Later, business was to superimpose itself upon the game, for, like games, it had nothing to do with anything; each transaction effaced its predecessor; it was passionate, occupying, and null. All the rest— those alternations of bliss and humiliation—he forgot; he tried to forget; he buried. . . . And a new repertory of subjects were added to those that could always arrest his attention, that *thrilled* him. Previously these had included killing—bang, bang, bang—especially killing wicked older men; and rescuing secluded maidens; and escaping from prisons. Now to these were added stories of caves and buried treasures and the deeps of the sea and "archaeology." (Just wait till we get to Edgar Allan Poe; to Melville.)

There were also a number of secret and slightly shameful partialities. There was the color and smell of violets (but that dress had long ago been given to a charity bazaar). Years later he almost married a girl named Violet who wore that color and used that scent.

Later still he was in a bad humor all afternoon, because his son had
written an enthusiastic letter from college about a girl named Violet.
His wife had said to him: "Tom, what *is* the matter with you today?"
There was some evocative power about trees overhanging streams.
After his convalescence from whooping cough his mother had taken
him to her father's farm. Those afternoons alone together by that
willow-shaded brook—a veritable honeymoon. The farm was at a
place called Turkey Hill. All his life he wanted to visit Turkey, that
romantic land. Once in a restaurant the Turkish ambassador and am-
bassadress had been pointed out to him; he asked his wife to change
places at table with him, for a better view. All evening he was full of
buoyancy. His wife, very amused, said: "Tom, what *is* the matter with
you tonight?" Later he lay long awake trying to remember the name
of the place near his grandfather's farm. It was on the tip of his tongue
----Egypt Crossroads----Lebanon----a funny name.

He had also his peculiar detestations. He could not be persuaded to go to matinées at the theatre----they were filled with silly
women (who should be at home, where they belonged).

He was constantly forgetting the names of people named Wilson and Williams and Watson and Wilkins. In his childhood he had
loved a book about a family—the name began with W—in which the
father was stern and severe, but splendidly wise and just and unbe-
lievably capable. For a short time he had had an employee known to
him only as Mr. What's-His-Name. Mr. Weston could give no satisfaction and had to go. Tom's mind was like the face of a planet, covered with the craters of all but extinct volcanoes, with canals and
dry sea-bottoms and with mountain ranges about which very little is
known.

728. ALGONQUIN HOTEL, [NEW YORK,] SUNDAY, APRIL 8, 1956.
      Tom Everage [—Continued]. . . .

(Perhaps immediately to follow on the above.)

But returning again to infancy: the things that little emperor
was learning, their range, their influence on his later life, and the
necessity—hurrying toward him—of their being repudiated, disavowed, and buried. He was a frustrated emperor, crossed and ob-

structed at every turn. Now it is from restrictions to our liberty that we learn hatred and—as I shall have occasion to repeat and develop when we come to consider Edgar Allan Poe and Emily Dickinson—it is from the presence of hatred that we learn what death is. Most parents feel that children should be shielded from the view of death—of their relatives, or of domestic animals. Those dear little unspotted souls—"A child," Melville says, quoting Leibniz, "comes into the world like a white piece of paper"—should be allowed as many years as possible of Edenic innocence. But our little tyrants have not much to learn. It is not from the sight of dead bodies that the fact of death is first made real to us, but from the presence, rampant within us, of the death wish directed toward others. The wolves and bears and wicked stepmothers of [the] Grimms' fairy tales—and that Red Queen [of Lewis Carroll] who has endeared herself to so many nurseries, shouting "Off with their heads!"—do not introduce novel fantasies. Death is ceasing to be, is final and total removal of a hated obstacle, passionately desired.

I was once strolling on a walk beside the iron fence of a large orphanage. On the other side of the fence a group of four- and five-year-old boys ran parallel with my progress, firing imaginary guns at me. Bang, bang, bang: I was murdered a hundred times. After a time they fell silent, but continued running to keep up with me. Finally, one of them put his hand on the netting and said urgently: "Mister! Mister!" I stopped. Very gravely the boy asked: "Are *you* happy?" The connection was deep, was subterranean. Perhaps the happy do not kill. Perhaps, again, such exemption from the will to murder has never been known. Kindness is the penance we do for our crimes, but sainthood itself can never atone for that overcharged record. Fortunately there are so many forms of tolerated, nay rewarded, murder that we are not obliged to feel solitary in our cells.

Tom Everage, American, then, knew himself to be a thwarted autocratic, knew himself to be a towering criminal, and knew himself to be—as he called it—"crazy" (knew that many a decision, many a good humor and bad humor was prompted by impulses he could not explain). Did these reprehensible facts greatly trouble him? Of course. They should have. After all, man is the crown of the animal kingdom, endowed with *Reason*, and is, in addition, the last fine product of thousands of years of civilization. His judgment should be as pure as sunlight reflected through a flawless crystal. Yet he laughed about it. Shamelessly. He knew himself to be a turbid lens, and he laughed about it. When he was in a good humor, which was far oftener than he had a right to be, he would think: "Sure; I'm crazy. Everybody's crazy."

And here, at last, we must begin to describe a divergence between our man—and his sister—and their Old-World contemporaries. Millions of little thwarted emperors and empresses were growing up in the old countries too. Let us recall some of the things we said about those countries. Each walled in with its traditions; each walled in with its monuments, its language. You remember all that. Each was also walled in with its wisdom. The wisdom of England is not the same as the wisdom of France, or of Italy, of Germany, or of Spain. In each country an unbroken succession of great minds—and no less contributory: great beings, many of them unknown to fame —have built up a vast treasure-store of concepts and images by which a man lives. Occasionally one of these national wisdoms had a great influence beyond its borders, but to this day Spanish wisdom is almost as different from English wisdom as is that other wisdom we are now being told to study—"The Wisdom of the East."

Different among themselves as those wisdoms are, they all had —and still have—a number of components in common that strike us in the New World as different from our own. One of them I have mentioned already—and we shall have occasion to return to the subject again: the consequences of the long subjection to the big untruth about the deference due to the High Born. But [the] component I want to call your attention to now is the Old-World belief that on the whole the world—existence in the world—can be grasped by the reason.

Let us go slowly here.

As Gertrude Stein said: "The difficulty of thinking is that you must hold so many things in your head at the same time."

(Etc. I hadn't meant to use this Journal for this kind of "first draft of the final text"—it is rather for a "let's look around and see what we've got"—but I keep running away with myself.)

732. **HAMDEN [CT.,] MAY 2, 1956.** O'Neill's *Long Day's Journey into Night*. Yale Press. (Play apparently finished July 22, 1941, date of dedication—"our Twelfth Wedding Anniversary.")

In the dedication O'Neill says that Carlotta Monterey O'Neill gave him "the faith in love that enabled me to face my dead at last and write this play—write it with deep pity and understanding and forgiveness for all the four haunted Tyrones"—*i.e.*, father, mother, brother, and self. Papa, miser, great actor *râté*, drunkard; Mama, morphine-addict; older brother James, drunken and failure at everything; Edmund-Eugene, tubercular and incipient drunkard. Four acts of mutual recriminations under the guise of gradually probing into the "reasons" why they are so. . . .

(Here I wrote a page and a half about this play which I have torn up. Some day I must try to make clear to myself what quality it is that commands respect in this play and in *The Iceman Cometh*—in spite of the bad ear, the rudimentary thinking, the furtive untruth. But I can't now, apparently.)

736. **HAMDEN, [CT.,] DECEMBER 2, 1956.** Some One-Act Plays.

There has been a long lapse in this Journal,[6] for reasons I partly understand. While at Saratoga Springs I suddenly . . . felt the impulse to write a short play and the hope that I could write several. My plan was to do a series of Four-Minute Plays* for Four Persons as continuation of the Oberlin-Yale-and-later Three-Minute Plays,[7] the self-imposition of a schema always seen as an aid, even when as with Joyce one sees it becoming an appallingly exacting discipline.

On Friday, November 9th, I began a play reflecting my reading in Zen and Mahayana Buddhism.[8]

*The three plays so far written have far exceeded the four-minute duration; yet they are shorter than a one-act play should be for practicable purposes. But they are for an arena stage and need no investiture. . . .

6. The preceding entry (735) is dated June 20.
7. Sixteen of the three-minute plays were published in *The Angel That Troubled the Waters and Other Plays* (1928).
8. See Entry 705 (February 18, 1955).

On Monday, the 12th, I began the play of how Apollo deceived the Moirai for the life of Admetus [*The Drunken Sisters*].

On Saturday, the 17th, in Hamden, at five o'clock in the morning, I began the play now called "The Wreck on the Five-Twenty-Five."

On Friday, the 23d, at Peterboro Tavern, between 2:30 p.m. and my visiting Louise [Talma] at her studio at 4:00, I began the play now called "Bernice."

Two of these are based on ideas that have long teased me. I have salvaged literary ventures which appear to have been discards. How long I have aspired to write one of the lost plays of antiquity or to furnish (as Claudel did with his *Protée*) a satyr-play to a real or assumed trilogy. *The Drunken Sisters* is the fancied play to terminate a trilogy based on the *Alkestis* (which was itself, however, a satyr-play). "Bernice" is salvaged from the scenario I sent to Vittorio De Sica when he asked me to work with him on a movie ["Chicago"].[9] It does not use the principal idea behind that scenario (then called "Jones") —the experimental assumption of roles in life in order to discover one's essential function; but the returned convict and the Negress as adviser are from the original.

Now let me ransack the uncompleted projects of my past and see if any other motifs can be rehabilitated for the series.

"*The Emporium*." Yes, I can use the Prologue in the Orphanage, giving to its tenor and termination another existence. . . . The episode of the pleasure-loving young man, heir to the Emporium, being given pills to shrink him, etc., does not please me any more. It may "return" however in another shape.

"*The Sandusky, Ohio, Mystery Play*." I have turned over the idea of writing for this series the scene of Joseph and Mary searching for an inn at Bethlehem. In addition to not being now in the mood for that, I feel that the scene, apart from its position in the whole Sandusky framework, would be merely an exercise in "style." However —*a ver*.

"*The Hell of the Vizier Kabaâr*." That work turned on the one great scene—borrowed from Raimund's *Der Alpenkönig und der Menschenfeind*: the wicked man seeing his life "with other eyes." It needs for its force to crown a long preparatory progress.

---

9. See Entry 608 (May 9, 1952).

"The Saratoga-Springs Opera-Idea." Nothing there to our purpose, even as a one-act opera, "The Widow of Monterey"? —No.

"Geraldine de Gray or My Heart Ever Faithful." There may be
something in that.

The Gods of antiquity as surviving among us. There may be
something in this.

*Algonquin Hotel, December 13, 1956—in New York for the
One-year Birthday Party of* The Matchmaker.

On December 2d I began another [one-act] which I called "The
Attic Play" (because it's laid in the attic of a Virginia mansion, 1959).
What there is of it is wildly theatric and poignant; but it has not produced that all-shaping idea without which it is mere anecdote. (The
idea of "Bernice" arrived unexpectedly in the writing, but one can see
that it lay there latent all the time. *The Drunken Sisters* has not yet
found its idea!)

Then on December 9th I began "In Shakespeare and the Bible"
(propelled oddly enough by a story of Henry James—of which not a
motif remains except the portraits on the wall). I don't quite like
it—and the two persons I've read it to seemed merely *verblüfft* by it.
Is it the sordidness? The *idea* is splendid; something is wrong with
the carrying-out. I shall return to it and perhaps save it, through a
better treatment of the young girl.

What I particularly like about all these, including the *manqué*
ones, is the completeness of their expression as plays for a theatre in
the round. This quality is at its best in "The Wreck," precisely because it is about "looking through windows"; but in each of the later
ones I seem to acquire—without that adventitious aid—a deeper exploration of the mode. Now I want to make some more—and, oh,
Muse, I want one or two in lighter vein to go with these horrors.

Hamden, [Ct.,] January 1, 1957.

Now, after the total interruption of the holidays, I want to apply
myself to these one-act plays again, and above all to find some in
lighter vein to alternate with the others. It seems to have turned out
that "In Shakespeare and the Bible" is not right for some reason. It is
neither diversion nor significance; and I fear it must go back into the

portfolio. So as I look about for points of departure, I'm drawn to an old interest—"life below stairs." I wish Genêt in *Les Bonnes* had not used for his purposes that idea I used so long ago in "The Trumpet Shall Sound:"[1] the servants playing great folk in their master's absence.

And then—for comedy (but could so powerful an image be held to comedy alone?)—that *Rappelkopf*-mirror idea that I found so hard to work into "The Hell of the Vizier Kabaâr." So far I've turned it this way and that and do not see how I could ever get it into a one-act play. Yet the central figure is right in my immediate circle here, and his effects: the magnanimous gentleman in public, the monster in private. A martyred wife cannot persuade her doctor that her husband is a demon of avarice, jealousy, and browbeating. So she installs a tape-recorder. And sends the reels to her brother in Australia. He comes for a visit. And treats *his* wife so, in the presence of the monster?

January 16, 1957.

Unable to catch fire on any of these projects (perhaps because I am straining so hard to find one in lighter vein), I have been preparing the definitive texts of the four finished ones for the typist. And I notice an interesting thing: that several times the events of the story —and even the most important developments—came to me, were forced on me, by practical theatrical considerations. It seems to correspond to that experience of poets (Valéry delights in emphasizing it) whereby the necessity of finding a rhyme in a sonnet, for example, furnishes the idea which nourishes and even organizes the poem: a word, apparently fortuitously presenting itself, brings with it the crown of the work.

In the play "In Shakespeare and the Bible," . . . [a] principal motif of the piece . . . emerged late in the writing: that women need their wits about them to survive at all, and that the much derided curiosity is a piece of armor for the none-too-well-harnessed.

And in "Bernice" I had Walbeck on the stage alone *with nothing to do*, and it occurred to me that he might have been handed a letter from his daughter, etc. —from which the play now takes its whole di-

---

1. A four-act play, published in four issues of the *Yale Literary Magazine* (October, November, December 1919, and January 1920), and produced in New York in 1926 by Richard Boleslavsky.

rection. Mysterious are the ways of the constructive imagination. Out of that bothering exigency has come the best of these plays.

Waverley Hotel, Virginia Beach, Va., January 31, 1957.

Driving south yesterday, I turned over another subject—which had occurred to me several weeks before—the eccentric will: Joe may inherit a vast fortune if he doesn't tell anyone, not even his wife. More of that later. And I turned over another subject—derived from a novel of G. B. Stern, *The Woman in the Hall*: the adroit beggar. Here I have now begun it, have written nine pages. Am not yet quite clear as to how I can raise it from the anecdote—ah, the most engrossing, the absorbing anecdote. There's no doubt that it's interesting enough; but precisely the claim of the arena stage—the beauty and power of the arena stage—is that it diminishes all that is not in the high sense poetic. I have been working this afternoon, and only now—when I have worked too long, and must go out—the poetic image (in drama always represented by one character whose vision of life comes to large-voiced expression) is beginning to emerge. This afternoon Daphne showed signs of raising this play from the fascinating prattle of a skulduggering story to a poetic drama. —To work, to work.

In the meantime, I have been recopying the others for the typists, *i.e.*, for a definitive edition. Now I know that two of the previous four are as good as I can do, are pretty good: *The Drunken Sisters* and "Bernice" are the best of that first litter.

Why isn't "The Wreck on the Five-Twenty-Five" better? It's something in the basic organization of the play. The line is not sure enough. The audience doesn't hook on early enough to where the play is going. The elements are offered in too un-integrated a succession . . .—all too apparently heterogeneous. I should have found earlier a symbol of spiritual desperation—richer, which could carry all these divagations. It's probably too late to mend it now.*

Yes, what I want now is a theme of far more unconfinedly poetic expression. I grope. —In the meantime, I suppose the best thing to do is to write more,----to put them in the oven and to hope that two out of four (my average so far) will come out well-baked; to inform my

---

*Yet every addition has brought a clearer deeper intensification of its latent intention. . . . Maybe, all can be saved yet.

subconscious that that is what I am doing, and leave the rest to the mysterious operation.

740. ST. MORITZ, JUNE 2, 1957. Bundeskanzler Adenauer.

As I sat beside the Chancellor at lunch, I kept saying to myself: now I must remember what he says for entry in my Journal. I knew well that the conversation would not advance to statements of world-political importance; it seemed that because of language difficulties, because of his preoccupations (that morning he had reported to his parliament on the trip to Washington from which he had returned the preceding day), because of the guest on his right (a Swiss jurist, I think), etc., any contact between us would come to the barest civilities, or nothing. But we got on very finely, indeed; we even kept looking into one another's eyes and laughing. At one moment, when I had been talking to Carl Burckhardt on my left and he seemed to be well-engaged with his partner, I felt a rap on my wrist, and he picked up the thread where we had left off. And the large table of over forty must have been surprised to see that the chief and the American Benjamin were so often engaged in laughing broadly. I started out with the Yale Convocation, and my brother's degree, and the splendid impression of the speech at the Alumni luncheon in Woolsey Hall.[2] "Yes," he said, "Harvard is----but I found Yale so much warmer and nearer----I have been five times in America;" (and then with a deep glance—wonderful eyes in that big flat Slavic face;* as though he were impressing something on himself as well as on me): "One can do so much more in personal meetings. Day before yesterday, I spoke in your House of Representatives and in your Senate; *es war für mir etwas sehr rührend*, the way in which I was received----there are

---

*To the Minister of the Interior . . . I had said before we went in to lunch something about the Chancellor's wonderful face. "Yes," he said, "we call him the Old Iroquois." "I don't find it so much Indian as Slavic." "It can be," he replied; "in the Rhine valley who can say what the elements are."

---

2. Konrad Adenauer had received the honorary degree of Doctor of Laws and Amos N. Wilder that of Doctor of Divinity at the 255th Yale Commencement on June 11, 1956. Following the ceremonies, Chancellor Adenauer had addressed a special Commencement luncheon. On the American visit he was accompanied by his son Konrad Adenauer, Jr., and his daughter Mrs. Libeth Werhahn.

some great men there" (he named some, but I could not catch the English names through the German pronunciation). "I found the President well, in both health and mental grasp." (*Recalled later:* He expressed admiration for Nixon and asked why many disliked him. I told of Nixon's knowingly unfair charges against Helen G. Douglas, the immaturity of the "dog" episode, etc.; but felt that he had "grown" in office.) "America is a continent---- And think of its power to *give*; what would we have done without that?---- If we had been as rich as that, I very much doubt whether we would have so given." I said that I had just been talking to the Minister of the Interior and saying how astonishing the traffic in the Rhine under my window was. "Yes," he said, "they say that Duisberg has now the greatest commerce of any inland seaport in the world. *Sehen Sie, das ist eigentlich ein Gefahr, dass wir so bald reich werden.*" "I was delighted to see, *Herr Bundeskanzler*, that your *gnädige Frau Tochter* accompanied you again to the United States." "Yes," he said, laughing, "I like to have someone with me to take care of me; this time also I took my son— he's nineteen and studying law. I have a program all day—but the *Jungen* they go around and enjoy themselves. But" (with raised finger), "I have my *Liebereien*; in Washington I always make time to go to the National Gallery. I have always been interested in the graphic arts." "Oh, then," I said, "according to Goethe's distinction" (I do not know if it is in Goethe; for me, it is from Gertrude Stein), "you are more an eye-man than an ear-man?" He seemed to be much struck, and for the first time, by such a distinction: "I love music, but I suppose I *am* an eye-man." I cannot now see where the laughter kept coming in, but there was some about a hotel on the coast outside San Francisco (I suggested Monterey) with little cottages around it; and there was some more at the mere mention of Texans. And there was a deep sigh of concern: "I can have no vacations—with this election coming up in September. Elections are . . ." (I forget the *düstere* adjective). At one moment, suddenly from his memory, groping for the title, he pulled an expression of warm regard for *The Bridge of San Luis Rey. . . .*

All these words are nothing, but the impression of age (eighty-one) so unbored, so unweary, so ready to enter with this simplicity into a chance encounter.

745. ST. MORITZ, JUNE 8, 1957. *Die Alkestiade.*

Tomorrow Leopold Lindtberg, of Vienna, the *régisseur* of our forthcoming première,[3] comes to visit me. We are to talk over the physical production of the play. The snake; the exits through the audience; the dress of the Fates, etc.

But I don't believe in this play. It never found its way into the center of my stresses. I certainly was often under strong emotions when, in Aix, I was composing it. But there are emotions and emotions; and those were not the more commendable. The reading of Kierkegaard had not penetrated into me deeply enough. Like an ill-baked cake only portions of it are fitfully touched with heat. My embarrassment about this fact sufficiently explains my inability even to reread the text as preparation for tomorrow's visit. In ignoble fashion I trust to that old theatric faculty, and suppose that I have pulled off a succession of scenes which will arrest the attention of audiences—I even trust to the fact that the German-speaking world likes the kind of half-baked dish I serve in this case. On the other hand, a little tiny voice within me hopes that I wrote better than I know; that within those evershifting primal situations I was guided by an instinct of which I am not now the judge. Is it *Kitsch* that every woman is haunted by the possibility that there is an expression of herself superior to that of being wife and mother? No. Is it *Kitsch* that we may all be used by a life-force above and beyond the biological to serve as examples and trial-flights of where human society may advance? No. The play should say that the road on which we tread has been paved by the sufferings of innumerable anonymous souls who have been guided only by their own half-understood ethical intuitions, and those intuitions have been derived from the heart of the universe, which is an ethically oriented source. But does the text say so? In the opera text I have sharpened these intentions. If I could now bring myself to review the play-text I might incorporate some of these elements into what will take place on June 27.[4]

---

3. The revised *Alcestiad*, in German translation by H. E. Herlitschka, was first produced in Zürich on June 27, 1957.

4. The play was revised and, in German translation as *Die Alkestiade*, after various stage productions, was published in Germany in 1960. The revised English text was first published in 1977 as *The Alcestiad, or A Life in the Sun*. An acting edition, with a special foreword by Isabel Wilder, was published in New York by Samuel French, Inc., in 1980.

749. ST. MORITZ, FRIDAY, JUNE 14, 1957. Query: Another One-Act Play ["The Rivers under the Earth"]?

When did this first present itself to me? Was it before I went to Milan? . . . Yet I remember that during the agony that night—after La Scala[5]—I kept trying to take my attention off my pain by inventing material for this play. Probably it first presented itself to me about Saturday the 8th, then was suppressed for several days. Anyway, I like to think of it as having been warmed and extended by the now-famous Monday-night tantrums.

It had visited me, then, (but only as recently as I have indicated) that I could make a one-act play out of that train of thought which I was sketching for the Norton Lectures . . . :[6] that often far-reaching decisions of our life are made on the basis of irrational promptings hidden from us. And, I would add, the most powerful of these are in the erotic, and in the magnetic field of the Oedipus complex. So far this play has been developing along the lines of Tom [Everage]'s relation to his mother; I planned it to arrive at a culmination illustrating—so recurrent in me—the relations between a daughter and a father. After today's work it looks as though the boy's story will be oh! quite sufficient.

It began this morning, the writing of it. Disappointed, even mortified, by the absence of writing, real writing, in all these weeks that are passing by. And knowing that the remedy is at hand, namely, the firm intention and discipline and habit of setting myself to that kind of "writing" for an hour or two every morning on rising from breakfast—whatever the other pressing obligations may be. Filled with the vast accumulated self-discontent, I did just that this morning. I took up this *donnée*, which had quite vaguely fluttered before my view (what was clearest was the felicity for the arena stage of this nocturnal scene by Lake Geneva, fireflies, bonfires, and the "rocks" dispersed about the scene), and began: "*Mother:* I don't know where you children inherited your ability to see in the dark."

I do hope I can pull this off. I'm afraid I have lost the two others in the baking—"In Shakespeare and the Bible" and "A Ringing of Doorbells." Somewhere along the line I interfered with their finding

---

5. Thornton Wilder had been obliged by illness to leave a performance of "Iphigenia in Tauris" (with Maria Callas) at La Scala in Milan on Monday, June 10, 1957.
6. See Entries 720, 724, 727, and 728 (March 8, April 3, 7, and 8, 1956).

a relation to the universal. Had I severely established the practice of
the morning task—*"deux heures, génie ou non"*—I feel sure that I
would have fewer of these shipwrecks. I hope this comes out all right.
It seems to me now to be the promise of a beautiful and hushed and
intimative play.

   June 19, 1957.

   Well, I've about finished. And this "about" is not the same *"à
peu près"* as those for "In Shakespeare and the Bible" and "The Ringing of Doorbells"—which I could terminate any day, but which will
never be finished.
   This play presents an enormous difficulty: it must be, by its very
nature, two-thirds exposition. I have to plant all those "buried associations" which, like time-bombs, explode in rapid succession in the
closing third. The poor audience cannot foresee that this will happen;
a heterogeneous bundle of anecdotes and desultory remarks is thrown
at their heads. Is there any way that I can earlier alert their attention
to "what we are doing," "where we are going"? What are these time-
bombs? Tom has two: gerontology; Violet; and Francesca has Charlie
and the dead Robin. Could I find a title that would help the matter? I
doubt it.* I suppose a more skilled dramatist (Ibsen first acts have all
this character) would have chosen these leitmotifs so that [they] were
more closely connected with one another and the exposition of any
one of them could be conjoined with that of another. My four are separate stones that must be rolled up hill.[7]

753. **HOTEL LA PACE, MONTECATINI, [ITALY,] OCTOBER 19, 1957.** About
      the Frankfurt Speech.[8]

   So I've raised a little hornet's nest. A Dr. Rudolf Walther Leon-
hardt has a big page spread of consternation about the *Rede* in the
Hamburg *Die Zeit*, forwarded to me by a former drama critic, René
Drommert, whom I once wrote spontaneously, thanking him for a

   *"The Rivers under the Earth."

-----

   7. The play was not finished. There is an incomplete manuscript draft (twenty-three pages)
among the Thornton Wilder papers at Yale.
   8. Thornton Wilder's speech (given in German), "Kultur in einer Demokratie," was delivered on the occasion of the award to him of the Freedom prize of the Börsenverein des Deut-

beautiful review of *Die Heiratsvermittlerin*. I guess I'd better forward a short answer to all this. I'll sketch it out here:

"Dear Herr Drommert: It is a pleasure to be writing again to the critic whom I once addressed 'for the first time in my life' in spontaneous thanks.---- I thank you for sending me Dr. L.'s article and for your reasonable comments on it. And I thank Dr. L. for the reasonableness and even kindness (with the exception of one passage) which he brings to the discussion of a speech with which he is in such thorough disagreement.

"I shall briefly discuss the article—retaining the tone of a friendly letter to yourself, a continuation of our previous correspondence, though you may make what further 'open' use of this letter which you will.

"The speech was . . . short—very short indeed, considering the variety of subjects which it touched. This brevity was related to its method—already discernible within the first five minutes—speculative and, like the quotation from Walt Whitman on which it was based, largely interrogative. Its intention was not to construct logical progressions and to arrive at final definitions, but to throw out suggestions and particularly to invite a continual dialogue with attentive listeners. This aspect of the speech is largely lost on the printed page. Am I mistaken in having felt, in the Paulskirche, that the audience was entering with the most friendly participation into this manner of exposition—these emphases, pauses, and interrogations? It was not an essay but a *speech*, and by implication a conversation; and such speeches do not easily lend themselves to an examination by isolated quotations.

"I felt also—and saw—that a large portion of the audience was aware of the element of humor that lay just under the surface. Very serious, indeed, were the subjects about which we were thinking together, but I was to terminate with an invocation to hope, courage, and belief in mankind; and when I am reminded of how those qualities operate in us all, humor is never far behind. Humor delights in clarification by paradoxes, by overstatement and understatement.

---

schen Buchhandels in the Paulskirche, Frankfurt am Main, on October 6, 1957. It was subsequently published, with two other speeches, as *Drei Ansprachen anlässlich der Verliehung des Friedenspreises des Deutschen Buchhandels* (Frankfurt am Main, Börsenverein des Deutschen Buchhandels, 1957). The original English text was printed in *American Characteristics and Other Essays* (1979).

"I am astonished that Dr. Leonhardt concerns himself so little with the main subject of my speech and cites so few passages that reflect it. . . . In one instance he goes so far as to deform it. He comes very near to an act of *mauvaise foi*, that is, the conscious misuse, for polemical purposes, of the material before him. I can imagine a reader who had not heard the speech, rising in horror on finding that the speaker had wished '*sich gern dem Gemeinen, Ordinären und Vulgären verbinden.*' Dr. Leonhardt knew well that these words came in a passage that was illustrating the main theme philologically; that I had just said (in a city one of whose newspapers calls itself *Allgemeine*): '*Das Wort "gemein" müsste ein schönes Wort sein*' and that I was just [about] to say: '*Wir müssen diese Worte retten.*' If he [had] heard the speech he would have remarked the care with which I indicated the ambivalence that accompanies these words: that I said *Gemeinen* with respectful feeling; and *Ordinären* so slowly that listeners might recall that under the form *Ordinarius* it is not a pejorative; and *Vulgären* so that we might remember that one of the translations of the Bible is called the Vulgate. For those who were following the 'question that was being asked,' there was no possibility of attributing to the speaker an 'inverted snobbery.'

"I wish to thank Dr. Leonhardt and Dr. Beutler for correcting and illuminating me on a quotation from Goethe that I had made elsewhere.

"And finally I wish that the page in *Die Zeit* had been used to help me toward an answer that I seek and that we are all seeking: is it possible that conditions under a democracy can produce not only an admirable culture but a new kind of culture? And was I right in saying (in one of the passages that were added after the text had been given to the press): '*Wir wollen uns nicht zu schnell erschrecken lassen. Wir haben es hier mit unbekannten Factoren zu tun . . .*'?"

SECOND VERSION

"I am a dramatist, and, therefore, I have a preference for speeches that are not essays but speeches, and more than speeches: dialogues. My intention was not to construct logical progressions and arrive at final definitions, but to throw out suggestions and to invite a continual dialogue with attentive listeners. This living participation is largely lost on the printed page. Like the quotation from Walt Whitman on which the speech was based, my thoughts were mainly interrogatory.

". . . Such a 'conversation' does not lend itself easily to later analysis by isolated quotations. Dr. Leonhardt is not examining a congenial speculative inquiry among friends but a chilled document on paper. . . .

"I am astonished that Dr. Leonhardt concerns himself so little with the main subject of my speech and cites so few passages that reflect it. I was not vaunting boss-élites or baseball: I was talking about something close to our hearts—in Bombay and Rio de Janeiro, in Lyons and Manchester."

[November?] 1957.

After a long while—but the delay was solely due to other occupation and to indifference toward the provocation—I wrote Herr Drommert, using (from memory) some of the material above. I received other letters—mostly from students—one very indignant, the others asking for clarification. I am now amazed at some of the things I ventured to say there, especially with Dr. Schweitzer two yards beneath me: that God is not a father---- (It is a metaphor that He is a Father and also a metaphor that He is not!) At all events, nothing more confirms my "innocence" in relation to audience. I should have talked it over with Alice [Toklas] last week in Paris, and laughed about it. "I shouldn't be allowed out in public. I don't know how to behave there."

754. ON BOARD THE "STATENDAM," DECEMBER 3—SAILED CHERBOURG, NOVEMBER 30, [ARRIVE] NEW YORK, DECEMBER 6, 1957. On Closing This Journal and on the Letter Book.

755. SS "VULCANIA," APPROACHING BARCELONA, MONDAY, NOVEMBER 24, 1958. This Journal.

Almost a year has gone by since the above entry, which is no entry. As I am not given to looking backward I shall not try to give the reasons for the intermittence. As Scott Fitzgerald says somewhere, it is very easy to lose the habit of writing and thence doubly difficult to reacquire it. Among the reasons, however, was a compulsive infatuation with *Finnegans Wake*. I made great progress in it, but am now bogged down again. I begin to feel in me a glimmer of hope that I am done with it, and the paper I have almost completed for *PMLA* is supposed to be my *envoi* to that malady.[9] But one thing remains to torment me. I have always said that I could quit *F.W.* studies when I discovered the structural patterns that underlay the *Anna Livia Plurabelle* chapter. That chapter remains as beautiful but as planless as ever. I was overjoyed when I found that "*a latere dextro*" came from the collect *Vidi Aquam* and thought that I would be able to discover that the whole work came from that collect in Holy Week (and how beautiful a gloss all those *aquae* would be) but only that fragment seems to allude [to] it. Damn!

756. SS "VULCANIA," APPROACHING BARCELONA, MONDAY, NOVEMBER 24, 1958. The Seven One-Act Plays.

I see that in my Entry 749 I say that the plays "In Shakespeare and the Bible" and "The Ringing of Doorbells" will never be finished.

Soon after getting on this ship I began drawing up a list of themes that have presented themselves from time to time as possible plays for this series. Always in search of a farce subject—to vary the somber tone of two of the completed ones—I made a note about a field of experience that I call "Not before the Servants" or "Not before the Children": the quarrel or the impassioned occasion that must be repeatedly interrupted by concession to convention. I then went on to see if I couldn't save from the discard some aspect of those "Geraldine de Gray" projects. I then began one on the neurotic avarice of Massachusetts millionaires, and on the deformations in character caused by great wealth ["The Cabots," later "Cement Hands"]. During these days I have been reading a book (and an unexpectedly good one) on Joyce in the series Les Auteurs racontés par eux-mêmes. In it, the editor [Jean Paris] (I think possibly mistaken) says that four of the stories in *Dubliners* exemplify four of the Seven Deadly Sins in

---

9. Probably the article "Giordano Bruno's Last Meal in *Finnegans Wake*," published not in *PMLA* but in the *Hudson Review* (Spring 1963).

the canonical order. Since at the moment I was adumbrating a play about *Avaritia*, it suddenly swept over me that maybe all my seven could be *les péchés capitaux*. And in a few minutes I saw that I could *save* and *finish* and deepen those two plays which I thought were to be discarded, and that the three I had written could very well fit into such a series. (I then went on to see—still on a suggestion from Joyce—if I could not associate with each play one of the colors of the rainbow.) . . .

"Bernice" [*Superbia*] would require the addition of only a few lines: that the "born alone" of these two was to be born disdainful of others, superior, secret, and prideful.[1] "The Ringing of Doorbells" [*Invidia*] now comes to life and meaning and will be very strong (though at the moment I do not see its concluding moments).[2] As I groped in the extremely difficult problem of "exemplifying" *Luxuria*, there came back to my mind that notion I had long had of doing a St. Francis before the conversion: that saints are monsters of nature that have hesitated, been good and evil at their extremes. This ["Someone from Assisi"] promises to be a most extraordinary play, indeed, and full of matter not often said. I do not yet see how "In Shakespeare and the Bible" can be directed towards a statement about *Ira*; I may have to find another story, but such lies latent there: that wrath against a person is wrath against the universe; that—as I say so often of the Irish—they are grandiose before they find the pretext for the quarrel.[3] *The Drunken Sisters* [? *Golosità*] acquires a new charm when we see it in this framework.[4] "The Wreck on the Five-Twenty-Five" [*Accedia*] will require the addition of a few words to show that the type of despair into which the hero falls is, precisely, in Dante's

---

1. The play was completed. In German translation, as "Berenike, oder Der Stolz," it was produced at Congress Hall, West Berlin, in September 1957, and printed in *Die Neue Rundschau* ([December] 1960). The English text, of which there is a final typescript in the Thornton Wilder papers at Yale, has not been published.

2. The play was not finished. There is an incomplete manuscript (twenty-one pages) among the Thornton Wilder papers at Yale.

3. This play was not finished. Three incomplete manuscript drafts, the pages of one of them bearing the title "*Ira*"—which Wilder used later for an entirely different play—exist among the Thornton Wilder papers at Yale.

4. The play was eventually completed (without specific reference to *Golosità*) and was published in an acting edition in New York in 1957 by Samuel French. As a satyr play it appeared in the same volume with *The Alcestiad* (1977) and also in the acting edition of that play published by Samuel French in 1980.

sense, an unwillingness to accept the gifts of life: "Sullen we were in the bright air."[5]

Remain then to be written *"Avaritia"* ["Cement Hands"] and *"Luxuria"* ["Someone from Assisi"].

757. [HOTEL] OESTERREICHISCHER HOF, SALZBURG, SUNDAY, DECEMBER 7, 1958. The One-Act Plays.

I've been working on the two new plays, on alternate days. Going well. . . . How right I was to hit on this serial idea. The plays become *gonflé* with the concept and the author is relieved of the necessity of underscoring it.

The difficulty of "Someone from Assisi" is to carry the burden of two tremendous elements as subordinate to elements that must overweigh them—*i.e*, brief summarized sketches of the characteristics of a St. Francis and a St. Clara as merely contributive to the idea of the Erotic as Destroyer and the Erotic as Creative.[6]

Who drew up this description and position of seven mortal sins? I suppose the anonymous wisdom of the Fathers. The passing of time has necessitated many a re-modulation of their titles and contents. Dante remade *Accedia*—from an evil of monastic life to a universal "burden."

Anyway, I'm enjoying it—and very grateful to this.

759. NEUES POSTHOTEL, ST. MORITZ, NOVEMBER 10, 1959. Resumption of Journal.[7]

I should have recorded here with a wealth of commentary the immeasurably important decision that I made on or about the first week in October. I resolved to close *Finnegans Wake* for five years. I had long realized that like some will-undermining narcotic, it was

---

5. The play, in German translation, was produced at Congress Hall, West Berlin, in September 1957. The English text, of which there is a final typescript among the Thornton Wilder papers at Yale, has not been published.

6. The play was produced at the Circle in the Square Theater in New York in 1962 as one of "Three Plays for Bleecker Street." Scripts, reproduced from typewritten copy, were available from Samuel French, Inc.

7. The preceding entry (758) is dated March 15, 1959.

sapping not only all interest in any writing I might do myself, but the very springs from which come reflection, observation, and my very attention to the people and events about me. Long ago I described to myself my studies in Lope de Vega as a brightly lighted room into which I could retire at any moment and happily absorb myself in the fascinating objects with which it was furnished. I also knew, but did not permit myself to wrestle with [the fact], that Lope and *F.W.* both furnished me with the sensation of a creativity that was not a true creativity. In both researches I had the gratification of discovering new things every day. Their chief fascination was precisely that they were a progress and an unfolding journey, on which I was very often the pioneer. I was deriving from them monthly a great deal more legitimate satisfaction than many a diligent but imperceptive academic scholar gains in a lifetime. I was, for long stretches of time, happy, and that happiness would have been sufficient had I not known hours of a different sort of creativity. I cannot now remember whether I had a deep joy in writing nor what kind of joy it was. The attitude derived from Gertrude Stein—but I was well in possession of it before I knew her: to derive no satisfaction from the outside world's commendation of one's work has combined with this *Ersatz*-joy in research to erase from my mind all memory of what it is like to be "swept up" by one's own making a new thing. These new one-act plays have been written from the peripheral areas of my will and imagination—the small area left half-alive beside the bewitched devotion to Lope and Joyce. It may take a long time to re-fire the center of the mind, and I am old. And with dismay I recognize that it is not merely a matter of finding subjects and presenting them as literature; it is a matter of re-awakening the fields of observation and reflection that alone nourish and give significance to the fictions. I return as one from an illness or from a long journey into a remote territory to make my house and hearth again.

763. **HOTEL MORGANO TIBERIO, CAPRI, DECEMBER 1959.** Parolles in *All's Well That Ends Well*.

All's Well is an awful botch. Why Shakespeare persevered in it is hard to understand—probably the need to run up a show in a hurry. W.S. could not exercise his ideality on a girl of lower birth, nor a girl who seizes a technical advantage to force into marriage a man she loves and who does not love her;* and who arranges the bed-trick from *Measure for Measure*—so counter to every prompting in a Shakespeare heroine. The Old Countess: Shakespeare is not interested in older women unless they are very racy. Bertram is a botch, and it is significant that Shakespeare gives him no real "scenes" to play; his squirming and lying at the denouement are as ignoble as anything by Parolles. Perhaps the only way we are to see Bertram is in the light of the constant reference to his being *very young*. All this leaves Shakespeare working on a play without a central figure and without a prominent figure who engages his real interest. Boccaccio has betrayed Shakespeare here, for Shakespeare could not share Boccaccio's relish in mere conniving and skulduggery on the part of ladies and gentlemen. The verse is a botch, too, of his mature period, but unequal—all the manner and only occasionally the concentration. . . . The Old King has many fine things, and his submission to illness and death is very fine and, as it were, "new."

But it is Parolles who is interesting and so because of much ambivalence on Shakespeare's part. He belongs to the Osric family, whom Shakespeare hates, with the same emphasis on clothes. . . . From the opening scene Helena knows him for a liar, "great way fool," coward; old Lord Lafew "smokes" him, and Shakespeare gives scene after scene where Lafew insults him. . . Then in the episode with the lost drum, he is submitted like Malvolio to the last humiliations and exposure—lying about his benefactors and revealing war secrets. *But* Shakespeare is boundlessly indulgent about Parolles. He loves him for his self-candor. . . . And very touching is the scene (close of V.ii) where Parolles, disgraced and penniless, gets a half-contemptuous but forgiving reception from Lord Lafew. . . .

The saving grace of Parolles is his self-knowledge, and it is briefly and magnificently indicated. At the close of the scene (IV.iii) where he is . . . shown up, sneered at, and left to beggary (but with his life; he thought he was about to be killed):

> Yet I am thankful. If my heart were great
> 'Twould burst at this.

(What a reminiscence of other Shakespeare heroes!)

> Captain I'll be no more,
> But I will eat and drink and sleep as soft

---

*Yet she says to his mother (I.iii): "I follow him not / By any token of presumptuous suit." There's a howler!

> As captain shall. Simply the thing I am
> Shall make me live. . . .
> Rust, sword; cool, blushes; and Parolles live
> Safest in shame; being fool'd, by fool'ry thrive.
> There's place and means for every man alive.

If Falstaff had had no knighthood?

The Osric-motif crossed the Pistol-motif . . . and then got steeped in the lowest colors of liar and traitor (. . . [Parolles] seems to have served as pimp between Bertram and Diana, but in fact tried to warn her against him), and yet [he] won from Shakespeare this handsome pardon.

The play is placed quite near to *Measure* and belongs therefore to the Ailing Season in Shakespeare—though there is none of that season's nausea about sex. What it has of that season, however, is the mood of being fed up with Morality and "Virtue's steely bones" and "cold wisdom." That's why Helena lacks charm and Isabella almost.
. . .

764. DEEPWOOD DRIVE, [HAMDEN, CT.,] MARCH 24, 1960. The Dream-Process in Literature.

I've been writing two plays ("*Ira*" and *Childhood*) that have dream sequences, and have become very attentive to what takes place in dreaming. I'm scarcely using at all the symbol and substituted image that are illustrated in Freud's *Interpretation of Dreams* and his study of *[Jensen's] "Gradiva." Finnegans Wake* is a vast compendium of techniques to reproduce dream life, but I do not find there several on which I intend to lean heavily. There is one frequently employed in Kafka that I cannot employ because of my restriction of the number of performers in my pieces: *i.e.*, Kafka (opening chapter of *The Trial* and often in *Amerika*) introduces characters who from balconies, windows of houses across the road, etc., intently follow the action. This throws a good deal of light on Kafka—though from the letters and journals we would not need it—as *gequält* by an *eye* and by *eyes* that he cannot escape. In *Childhood*, I use something I none too clearly remember from *The Interpretation of Dreams* (and by the light of that book, observed in my own dreaming): that an important person in one's dream, whom one's censor does not wish to identify and acknowledge, appears veiled or masked, or seen from the back only. So my children's father and mother. But in *"Ira"* I wish to use the experience I know so well: "But he's *dead*----no, *she's* dead ----but *he's* alive----anyway, I'm dreaming----maybe, he's alive----I'll know when I wake up----" And then I wish to picture the effort to wake up, an effort like painfully trying to swim to the surface of the water. Can I also picture my so dignified matron trying to run to arrest a murderous assault and finding that her feet cannot move? Can I ask the actress to cling almost prone to a chair, hobbled? In fact, *"Ira"* should exhibit a sustained and continually varied picture of the dream-process; and maybe "I am trying to wake up" is the ending which I have long been seeking for *Childhood* (which would make it unsuitable for performance on the same bill with *"Ira"*).

Kafka's *Amerika* is a very strange book, pointless nonsense, and yet somehow arresting. When I read it first long ago I was merely bewildered—as I was with the other two novels [*The Trial* and *The Castle*], though never in doubt as to their grandeur. Rereading it now, consciously recognizing it as a reproduction of dream-process, I am still wearied by much of it, but see that Kafka has found a way of picturing the incomprehensibility of the world and human behavior to a sixteen-year-old. The two constant preoccupations are the frustration of trying to bring about or arrive at justice, and a very cloudy eroticism that barely reaches the surface at all. Karl is pulled in all directions by every character he meets and from the dream-process we get these long complicated episodes ever so minutely described, under a sort of powerful limelight of close attention—and so exactly reflected in the dwellings with their endless corridors and locked doors. The Occidental Hotel has five thousand guests; the halls of Pollunder's castle are unfinished and extend right into the open air. From the dream-technique comes also the woeful instability of personal relations, the constant shift from affection to rejection on the part of Karl's protectors: dreams are full of walls and obstacles and impediments. . . .

765. **DEEPWOOD DRIVE, [HAMDEN, CT.,] APRIL 2, 1960.** Rite, Ritual, in
      My Plays.

In my play "Youth," I present the initiation ceremony of a new
member into a fraternity—some Ohio college, 1912. I am going to
risk adding elements from primitive anthropology that are certainly
not thought of in our colleges. We have the gleeful cruelties of young
men to one another; I am going to have the President of the
Fraternity wear a mock white beard on his mask. Shall I have the initiate drink blood? I dare not add the (elsewhere so prevalent) threat
of castration. Anyway, I shall have no trouble with that play: all glancing allusions at a tribal initiation will only enrich it. It's the other play
that presents so many difficulties—"*Ira.*" My "*Ira*" is not a fit or burst
of rage: it is the long smouldering resentment at the world that has
not met the unbounded demands of the ego; it is pent-up murderous
impulse that breaks out into war.

My hero hates everything about him. As his wife, divorcing
him, says: "He blackens everything." For a long while I have been
bored with my own plan for this play because I felt I was merely about
to "dramatize" the Oedipus complex. The hero felt himself to have
been maimed, sapped, by his father whom we know to have been
an unusually admirable man. I was held back from writing this, not
only because I felt it to be a cliché, but because I hoped to see a still
deeper motivation for the hero's (and everyman's) murderous
prompting. . . .

. . . Could I have it that my hero in early youth did inflict death
or harm on someone else—or does that narrow it? The play has wandered farther and farther from my original plan, which was merely to
show in a "high-comedy" scene, how the idioms of our speech betray
this latent tendency ("I could have murdered him"; "Hanging's too
good for him"; "She looked daggers"; "Deadly bore"; etc.), together
with those expressions of relief at disasters to others—followed by a
scene, after the dream, with the same matter stated with hypocritical
expressions of pity and regret. Ouch! Perhaps I can get them all in
still.

766. DEEPWOOD DRIVE, [HAMDEN, CT.,] MAY 5, 1960. Veblen: The Style
of Veiled Contempt.

Albert Camus once said to me* that he owed a sort of coming-
of-age to two remarks in Dostoievski's *The Possessed*. One was: "The
trouble with me is that I don't hate everything enough." The insight
is helpful, especially if we combine it with its obverse: "I do not sufficiently love what I love." We have all ceased to grow through our inability to draw the consequences and live the consequences of our
primary intuitions.

Veblen had long *durchgeschaut* . . . (the word is better than
penetrated or *seen through*) all the received ideas of our Western
world and held them in contempt. This attitude has not the *saeva
indignatio* of Swift,[8] which arises from disappointed love and even
continuing love, nor the feline sneer that accompanies Gibbon's view
of Christianity, which takes so superior a gratification from its condition of being *désabusé*; it is indirect and veiled. Certainly it is not because Veblen is afraid of thinking these thoughts, nor afraid of the
abyss of negation into which they could lead him; nor do I think that it
is primarily fear of publishing them, though his life was rendered
difficult by his candor. I believe that something thick and viscous in
his Scandinavian blood prevented him from entering into the adventurous element in the thorough *Durchschauen*.

De Sade's point of departure for dynamiting the world was his
nonconforming sexual nature—perhaps all nihilism is. From there de
Sade passed to economic and political revolution (and meliorism).
Veblen's expulsion from the University of Chicago was at least has-
tened by the scandal caused by his going to Europe, "unchaperoned,"
with a lady. . . .

Veblen's style is viscous. He is master of the brilliant phrase, of
the electrifying word, but these float on a turbid sentence and paragraph. He is, from this point of view, at the opposite pole to Diderot
and Lessing. It seems to me that Veblen seldom says precisely what

---

*I forget now who took me to see him. He was residing at Columbia University, I think.
The whole visit has faded from my memory, probably because I did not like anything about him,
nor he about me. The other remark in Dostoevski was: "The basic problem of philosophy is why
one does not kill oneself." *Later:* Simone de Beauvoir says somewhere in *La Force de l'Age* that
Sartre was powerfully affected by the assertion in the same novel: "*If God does not exist, I am
God*."

---

8. His epitaph: "*Ubi saeva indignatio ulterius cor lacerare nequit.*"

he means and all that he means, and this inadequacy is not the result of caution or obtuseness, but of a sort of apathy. At its best it might express a view like: "Why show them the full stupidity of their minds and lives? Their reactions would only reveal their stupidity more clearly and produce still further public waste and disorder."

Now to take a passage.* Veblen is talking about how a standard of living represents a collection of habits; how, under pressure, people will retrench certain basic needs before they abandon certain "higher wants" (these retrenchments are in terms of "consumption" and "expenditure"). . . . You will relinquish nourishing meals and house-heat before you relinquish whiskey, church-dues, and paying your tradesmen's bills. These habits, he goes on (he means "higher wants" and he despises them) can be acquired very quickly and are associated with each individual's temperamental endowment. Now we get another illustrative catalogue—repute has dropped out. We get the equated "needs"—whiskey, religion, and amour: "How greatly the transmitted idiosyncrasies of aptitude may count in the way of a rapid and definitive formation of habit in individuals is illustrated by the extreme facility with which an all-dominating habit of alcoholism is sometimes formed; or in the similar facility and the similar inevitable formation of a habit of devout observances in the case of persons gifted with a special aptitude in that direction. Much of the same meaning attaches to that peculiar facility of habituation to a specific human environment that is called romantic love."

This is very funny, but it is full of holes. Veblen seems to be saying that people moving up to a higher income-bracket start going to church (and giving of their money to it) with facility . . . and, losing their money, cling tenaciously and unwisely to that habit and expenditure. Yes, there is a certain amount of façade church-attendance; Veblen doesn't know much about it and his contempt blinds his eyes to the fact that, on the large, the congregations support their churches not from a hastily acquired and facile habit comparable to alcoholism, for which certain persons are gifted, and that the money one spends on wife or mistress is called forth by something more "necessary" than a "peculiar facility of habituation to a specific human environment."

*The Theory of the Leisure Class: An Economic Study of Institutions, Modern Library, 1934, etc. (I must hurry and get The Theory of Business Enterprise, which Kenneth Burke says is his best.) My quotation is on pages 107–08.

All this has the excitement and glitter of the half-truth, the icon-oclastic half-truth. It is invigorating to hear "romantic love" thus low-ered in grade ("peculiar" does not primarily mean "odd," but he wishes it to hang in the air); he is certainly remembering Marx saying that "religion is an opiate of the people," and so is alcohol. But the glasses through which Veblen sees the world are not *durchschauend* enough. He doesn't hate enough, so that he cannot penetrate suffi-ciently deeply into the springs of illusion. And he has been super-seded. In his discussion of "predatory aggression," of the relation be-tween athletics, gambling and betting (pages 294*ff.*), one is aware of the absence of the new insights introduced by depth psychology. He hasn't the intellectual fire to probe deep enough; he doesn't hate (which is self-forgetting), he merely despises, which gives him a sort of sluggish self-satisfaction.

It is greatly to be regretted. Because we still await the heir of Nietzsche, Marx, Freud, and so many others who can orchestrate "anthropomorphic religion is a tragic burden," "property is theft," and "the libido is interlocked with the death-wish."

767. DEEPWOOD DRIVE, [HAMDEN, CT.,] MAY 16, 1960. Projects: Some New One-Acts.

Have been reading aloud *Childhood* and the three-quarters finished *Infancy*. They're all right. Have been sending out nets for the later plays:

(a) . . . "*High Noon.*" The self-sufficiency of one's prime, which I place at thirty-three. The pride that goes before the fall. A play that will have the pattern of "Queens of France."[9] A "victim" of a practical joke seen—in four successive persons—in four stages of his delu-sion. A holiday afternoon in the home of a successful surgeon in the smart residence area of, say, Westport. The surgeon, we learn toward the end, once saved the life and career and marriage of his younger brother. "He was drinking and wrecking his life. He came to me one day with a stomach ache. I examined him and deceptively gave him the impression that he had cancer. You can eat anything," etc. (A mo-

---

9. Published in *The Long Christmas Dinner & Other Plays in One Act* (1931).

tif I got from the admirable Japanese movie "To Live," which Isabel and I saw the other night.) The brother gathers he has about a year to live. He pulls himself together. (Stage Two: "Looking at everything for the last time.") He becomes formidably attentive to his wife and children. (Stage Three: Wife: "What's the matter with Joe? I can't stand it!") He comes to his brother for a last check-up. (Stage Four: "Nothing's the matter with you.") The shadow of death across the exultant prime which alone can "make a life."

Hasn't this possibilities of being arresting? . . .

I'll start it Monday.

(2) ["*Youth*"]. As I told Dear Diary—or didn't I?—I'm not pleased with "Youth" as the fraternity initiation. Can I go back to that idea I had—but now with a difference—of the confrontation of an old man and a young, whom we see, figuratively, as the same person in two stages of their life career. In my first idea we saw four deck chairs on an ocean liner (long ago). A young law student and his bride; a Justice of the Supreme Court and his wife. The Justice's wife, pretending to sleep, hears the young man sneering at her husband's distinguished career. The Justice sold himself to the "interests," etc. Then she hears the young man caught in some humiliating situation. He's lost his passport and his money. Contrive some error compounded of a young man's arrogance and, if possible, idealism: but the humiliation to tears, before his bride, in whose eyes he would wish to appear "perfect." The older woman whispers the plight to the Justice. The Justice makes a tentative overture to help the young man, and the young man in his mortification just short of insults the older, but finally must humble himself to accept the favor. And we see that the young man *is* the Justice; the Justice has been that young man. But can't I "stylize" it more? make it more poetic? transfer it into a world where the young man confronts himself as old man—as in Max Beerbohm's cartoons? I've been reading some Noh plays in the best edition I have yet seen of them (*Japanese Nôh Drama: Ten Plays. Selected and Translated from the Japanese*—apparently by a committee. The Nippon Gakujutsu Shinkōkai, 1955).

I would like this series of Seven Ages plays to be also a repertory of different kinds of plays. Could I do this "Youth" as a Noh, or as a *commedia dell'arte*, or as a Raimund *Volksstück*, and so on? Of course, this Youth-confronting-Age could take its place toward the end of the series, too.

May 17, 1960.

I have carried this project [for "High Noon"] further in my thoughts only to become dissatisfied with it.

Our surgeon is, or pretends to be, a fanatic photographer. (Isabel, Dr. [Alexander] d'Entrèves of Torino, Maude Hutchins and I went forty miles Saturday to lunch with Bobsy (Goodspeed) Chapman, and such posing before her four cameras as made conversation impossible. . . .) It would be droll, if the audience knew that there was no film in our surgeon's cameras, that he asked his friends to drop in and be photographed in order to have a pretext for getting them to talk. In addition, the cameras would tend to give the impression that the photographer had a piercing, an X-ray eye into their interiors. . . .

Before I come to the major reason why I am losing interest in this project, here are some of the secondary reasons for giving it up:

(1) Cancer is not a good symbol for the kind of *hubris*, the wasteful and galloping self-destruction of feeling perfectly wonderful in one's prime. If these victims are to be shown as taking a turn of their life at thirty-three which will be expressed in thoughtless dissipation—frequent enough—the reasons for such behavior will lie, also, in other and deeper fields than exultant self-sufficiency. I have lived too long with Freud's remark to me that it might some day be shown that cancer is allied to "the presence of hate in the subconscious"; and

(2) The Surgeon's practical joke and therapy involve so much of that attitude which I am trying to avoid in both these sets of plays, the moralizing, the admonitory. Rescuing alcoholics is a clinical matter. In so far as these problem-patients are breaking up their own homes, we must then present them as philanderers, also, which brings us into the field where Henry James has so much trouble (*The Awkward Age*, *What Maisie Knew*, and *A London Life*): the representation of scandalous goings-on. (No wonder James had to resort to dark intimations of gambling and "borrowing money"—in *The Awkward Age*—and a sort of parasitism, and of a "colored" mistress in *Maisie*, to bolster up this atmosphere of being so constantly shocked at mere adultery.)

But even supposing that, at a pinch, I could manage to make my points with the above material, the thing that bores me with the whole project now is that there's no "poetry" in it. As Dr. d'Entrèves said—across the barrier of language, also—the play *Childhood* is full of poetry.[1] And I now see that *Infancy* has even more; and both beyond any conscious intention on my part. This project for "High Noon," at the present stage of adumbration, is merely a notion, fanciful enough but not of the kind of fancy which can enlist my enthusiasm. Unless, with more meditation, a new factor enters, it must probably be relegated to that groaning wastepaper basket of mistaken departures. (But how I welcome these disappointments, how necessary it is that I explore such promptings; how nearly I abandoned *Infancy*, which bristled with factors it seemed impossible to bring to order.)[2]

Hotel Algonquin, [New York,] May 18, 1960.

Well, I've solved several of the problems, and I've got the poetry. Let's place it in Victorian England. (I've been rereading that treasurable book, Empson's *Some Versions of Pastoral*—more exactly, I was thinking about the project last night and this Victorian idea came to me, and then I began thinking about Empson's glorious discussion of *Alice in Wonderland*, and this morning I ran around to [Frances] Steloff's store [the Gotham Book Mart] and bought the book—high luck, because it's been improcurable for years and my copy has been clamorously loaned to friends who will not return it.) Note that the photographing idea was already in my head and may have "produced" Lewis[-Carroll] Dodgson by underground association.

So: The stage is set with various tripods and cameras on stumps. The distinguished surgeon is, for our overtones of worldiness, a Baronet. And we are soon informed that there is no film—there are no plates—in the cameras. It's all hoax-photographing, though accompanied with flash powder, hiding under black shawls, steel props to hold the sitter's head straight. I was happy to think that there was also a telephone on a stump in this garden with a long wire connecting it with the house, and that we were soon to learn that it was connected with nothing and that the long telephone calls our Surgeon

---

1. An acting edition of the play was published in New York in 1960 by Samuel French, Inc. It was produced at the Circle in the Square Theater in New York in 1962 as one of "Three Plays for Bleecker Street."
2. An acting edition of the play was published in New York in 1961 by Samuel French, Inc. It was produced at the Circle in the Square Theater in New York in 1962 as one of "Three Plays for Bleecker Street."

was to make were merely an aspect of his deep, deep, nature—his benevolent mystification, his non-sinister Svengali role. But of course I can't have a telephone in 1861, damn it. So the play is in the style of the *Alice* books and a sprinkling of *The Importance of Being Earnest*. That style, that language, with its primness, is already filled with innuendos, and the whole implication of wickedness is easily taken care of. . . .

This milieu permits me to leap another hurdle and to bypass another difficulty. The word *cancer* need not, in fact cannot, be mentioned. These gentlemen who have only a year to live are threatened by an illness which we do not name; while our audience surmises cancer, tuberculosis and diabetes and what-not hang in the air. And it seems to me now that the danger of sounding edifying and moralizing (the errors of over-exuberance in one's prime can be corrected by a realization of human mortality) can be both stated and played with.

Now I shall make some first sketches and see what I've got.

Deepwood Drive [Hamden, Ct.,] May 20, 1960.

And after that brief period of exhilaration, I fell into dejection again. In fact, it now seems to me that I was crazy to have imagined that I could make anything of a man who could rescue rakes by frightening them with death. In the first place, a portrait of the kind of man who would play such a joke (a humanitarian Merlin; or a cynical observing puppet-master) would absorb into himself all the interest in the play; and secondly, such a play should open with and richly illustrate the type of man, or men, drunk on their magnificent wastefulness, etc.

So I leave that among the broken bricks (always hoping that some aspects can be, somehow, salvaged) and turn to another.[3]

768. HAMDEN, [CT.,] MAY 21, 1960.   One-Act Plays: "Youth."

My first plan for this—the fraternity initiation—was relegated not because it did not promise elements of poetry, but because it did not furnish the expression of what seemed to me the principal characteristic of youth—the being torn between many aims: not merely

---

3. "High Noon," part of the Seven Ages of Man series, was not completed. There are three pages of manuscript notes for it among the Thornton Wilder papers at Yale.

Hercules at the crossroads between vice and virtue, but a wide repertory of aspirations and temptations; I wanted to show the harrowing
alternations of overweening self-confidence and self-doubt as well as
the confusion arising from the sheer excess of potential careers and
modes of living.

I think that I got it last night, between fitful waking and sleeping, and got the way of presenting it in a poetical image that is much
more than the mere poetry of its high picturesqueness. I see that
what blocked me recently was my repudiation of that little plot I had
introduced: our hero's denunciation of a fraternity man for having stolen a kiss from his girl. (How little, little plot I need in this series,
though the Deadly Sins is full of busy little plots; it appears that the
vaster the abstraction subtending the play, the smaller becomes the
demand for an illustrative anecdote.)

What I see now is that our hero, having undergone offstage
the hazing, the trials of courage and endurance, is brought into the
[room] and required to make a speech on the two edifying subjects
"What are your ambitions in life?" and "What contribution do you intend to make to the life of the College (or the Fraternity)?" Our hero
is an original—at least, he has the originality of candor. He exacts,
with great difficulty, the condition that he may be permitted to speak
without interruption. He insists on this and the members are put to
the oath. He then flings himself into his tirade: he wants to experience to the full the life of pleasure, specifically sexual pleasure, and
indicates that he has begun (tumult in the house); he wants fame and
money, or fame for money; and has begun (anecdote of an eccentric
stunt in a nearby city); but when he's got there, nothing will stop him
from going to the top places in public life, in fact he is going to give
his life for the service of mankind, and he half thinks he's going to be a
doctor in India. As for what he is going to do for the College: he is going to rid it of the damnable hypocrisy evident everywhere (tumult in
the house) and "though I have the highest grades of anyone in this
room, I'm going to expose the whole grade-system and the faculty's
slavery to grades," etc.

Several fellow members have tried to leave, but are forced to
return (laws of the Fraternity) and finally the students are caught up
in an intoxication of the reforming spirit. Now—as I saw it last night
—the "poetry" of the play arises when, by some theatrical device, I
make it clear that the one boy is all nineteen boys; that the play is a
condensation—all [the] confused, anguished, despairful, generous,

and animal in all young men. It is, in short, one whole year's bull-session crowded into one half-hour. Now let's see if I can do something with that.

Hotel Algonquin, [New York,] May 25, 1960.

Yet I am repelled by the notion of a play that turns on *one* speech, even though there be added to it this culminating symbolic tableau. I want more cross-currents. Even if I prepared a significant counter-figure—one of the students who voiced a condemnation of our hero (they all do)—that would be a non-Youth. Or had a sudden irruption of an Adult—a long-since graduated member of the Fraternity. (They are allowed to return in that way; I was invited to an Alpha Delta Phi secret meeting at Magill.) That would overweigh (and oversimplify) the piece.

Somehow I must have the play—in this case, the speech—break down of its own woeful absurdity; all its jactance (thank you, Ezra Pound) crumples like a sail with a broken mast.

Very hard.

769. **DEEPWOOD DRIVE, [HAMDEN, CT.,] MAY 27, 1960.** Other
One-Acts.

In the meantime, I've been meditating about some of the later life's stages. Elucidating some allusions in the *Pisan Cantos* [of Ezra Pound] has sent me back to the Noh plays. There I can see clearly a way of doing that odd thing I glanced at in the previous entry [767]: a young man confronting himself as an old man—or *vice versa*. But it all seems very far off still.

Bucks County Playhouse Inn, New Hope, Pa., May 31, 1960.

"Extreme Old Age." We learn (by a public announcer?) that among the Diophesians the Very Old are put to death—are given some powdered poppy seed and then a cup of hemlock. We see some of them in their last hour. It has been decided to play this in modern dress, and what we see are some delightful people—in their late forties at most—in evening clothes. They seem to have accepted the convention—no protest, not even resignation. They talk of their status. . . .

But I don't want a conversation piece. Shall I have a Young One trying to come in for the poppy-and-hemlock? Shall I have a really Old Person (who had been to another country and returns home from shipwreck or exile) join them in all the admired repulsiveness of years—wise-shrewd, repetitive, forgetful, avaricious, and dogmatical?

Shall I let the audience know that the Parliament has been sitting and, unknown to those Condemned, is about to abolish the Law of Senile Extermination? Reprieve arrives at the close of the play: dismay! The humiliation of gray hair, the trapped into "degeneration"?

I want to make sketches for this, but I fear it's a little too early to launch out.[4]

770 . DEEPWOOD DRIVE, [HAMDEN, CT.,] JULY 2, 1960. The Care and Feeding of Lies.

This was the title I planned to give to one of those essays inserted into the published form of the Norton Lectures:[5] a treatment of all the violence that society does itself by defending indefensible fictions and by forcing itself to believe principles which serve its interest, materially or spiritually. There is a sense in which no one can force himself to believe anything, but he may to a considerable extent persuade himself to a condition resembling conviction, and it is the stratagems that he employs in this process that are interesting me.

These stratagems have been much exposed in the field of religion. One of the occasions that started me on these considerations was a sentence I read somewhere long ago: "If the great minds of the Middle Ages had applied to social or scientific problems one-fourth of the intellectual power which they devoted to defending and defining the Doctrine of the Trinity [*i.e.*, defending Christianity in a kind of panic against the charge of being a polytheism], the cause of civilization would have been wonderfully advanced." (Either that author or

---

4. There is only a one-page sketch for the opening of the play among the Thornton Wilder papers at Yale.

5. The book was never published. The three Norton Lectures printed in the *Atlantic* in 1952 appear, with further revisions made by the author, in *American Characteristics and Other Essays* (1979).

myself went on to reflect that Europe fashioned its intellect—as kittens sharpen their claws—in the discipline of validating the invalidatable. Perhaps untenable positions are better training grounds for rigorous thinking.) Similarly: think of all the ink that was poured out in the Renaissance to maintain that drama must obey the law of the Three Unities, merely because Aristotle had said so, or appeared to have said so. In spite of all the energy that has been expended on exposing the misspent pains that continue to uphold the immortality of the soul, the efficacy of prayer, etc., the work has scarcely begun. It seems to me that this feeble progress has been caused by the failure of the attackers to see that it is a dissipation of strength to attempt, at one and the same time, to demolish the objects of mistaken belief and the motives and methods of erecting tenets of belief. There is a touch of hysteria in all beliefs of this sort ("*Credimus ut cognoscamus*," said St. Augustine); they suspect, but would not avow, after Kierkegaard, that they are walking over five hundred fathoms of abyss. Attack one item, even the feeblest, and they fly—as Claudel did—into furious alarm. Rare is the equanimity of von Hügel; unlike his co-religionists (who looked at him askance), he is not even *loquax*.

But it is not the problems of religion that are occupying me these days, but the dogmas of property, leisure, and social position.

I wrote my little play "Cement Hands" about avarice among the generous and philanthropic millionaires. It is a failure, and I shall probably have to tear it up; but it exhibits the beginnings of some good analysis. And, as so often, it started me thinking after the work was written.[6]

The Negroes became the hewers of wood and the drawers of water in America, not because they were conquered in war, or as punishment for having warred against us, but because their ancestors were stolen from the jungle. That is the extreme example of *born to no fortune*. The very etymology of the word *fortune* shows that the good things in life are dealt by chance; it would increase the discomfort of society (and it is the discomfort of society that I am probing) if people would say instead of "They have a considerable fortune," "They have had a considerable amount of good luck."* In *The Ides of*

---

*The word *force* comes from the adjective *fortis*, whereas *fortune* comes from the noun *fors*. It would be significant, indeed, if even our word for *strength* came from chance.

---

6. The play was not torn up. A manuscript first draft (twenty-four pages) exists among the Thornton Wilder papers at Yale.

March I already scraped the moss from the word *gifted*, with its implicit allusion to a wise rather than a blind and haphazard donor. For all the centuries those in possession* have had to *believe* (and make others believe) that the chance whereby they find themselves propertied was much more than a chance; it was a favor conferred upon them by a wise governor of affairs, or merited by them for innate superior qualifications;—that it was *right* and *just* that they be in possession. (Here we are back in my Paulskirche speech ["*Kultur in einer Demokratie*"], but I hope to see further and to draw more fruitful consequences.) Before they convinced others that they held property in right, they had to convince themselves. To have the right to property by conquest or by occupation (the Colonial system) was relatively understandable; but to have the right by luck (being born into the right cradle or of the right skin-color) required some elaborate justification (there's etymology: not the demonstration of a right but the fashioning of a justice!). Christianity set out as a consolation for the dispossessed; only by implications, slow in emerging, did it attempt to unseat those who sat before (*pos'sedentes*). It awaited the advent of the industrial civilization, when the possessors could no longer lay claim to property by birth and feudal privilege, to reveal that property lay in the hands of those (1) in the first generation who worked for it and those (2) who inherited it. In a small measure one's goods . . . were always maintained and enlarged, if not actually acquired, by working for them, but now it was writ large for all to see: property was obtainable in proportions of size beyond any conceivable relation to a man's measure of work for it. By sweat and by sagacity one can earn a house, a field, a carriage, and a few servants; but by no justifiable exertion could one man come by right to a thousand acres, five mansions, and the complete control over thousands—to more than one man can get the basic use of.

(*Later:*) We are in the season of history when the possession of more property than one can use must be justified as a man's right and reward—and this without recourse to the ancient but deflated justifications of being invested with responsibilities of leading society (feudal), of birth (God's and destiny's elect), or by specialized talents (genius for organization).

---

*My dictionary says from *sedere*, *sit*, and some old prefix meaning *before*—but here I am, trying to draw strength for my argumentation from etymologies—the thing which has so often irritated me in Alain and even Heidegger!

The strategy is to:

(1) Emphasize that society could not develop favorably without large amounts of money in the hands of persons exceptionally gifted in making money operations work to the advantage of the total community. The big industrialist is a specialized genius. This is the tenor of the capitalist propaganda.

(2) Emphasize the weaknesses and errors of the non-possessing. It is always possible to assemble, highlight, and thus exaggerate the inadequacies of any individual or group of individuals. This is the way most parents bring up their young.* Thus women were in subjection so long. Thus the Negroes are discouraged. In the South they are lazy (*i.e.*, they do all the work); they are dirty (anyway, their skins are black); they are ignorant (barred from learning anything). Almost anyone can be kept in abasement if you rub his nose in his defects frequently enough. Though it is never mentioned, I suspect that this practice played a large part in the seven centuries of Irish oppression; the Irish had their weaknesses and were only too quick to acknowledge them, and thereby lost the real élan of their recurrent rebellions. It's not by our weaknesses we fail, but by the despairful recognition of our weaknesses.

If one reads the advertising literature today one can see the implied condescension not only toward the working classes but toward the middle classes in our civilization. The middle classes, compared to the Real Right Capitalist Rich, have no taste, have no security that they are getting the things that life has to give—and they never will have; but if they buy these objects (a swimming pool, Italy-made shoes, lounge pajamas) they can struggle toward it. The possessors are bolstering their moral position by reminding the less affluent that they lack the qualifications for leadership. Veblen missed the point about conspicuous waste; it is a repressive strategy; it is designed to cow the less fortunate into believing that the privileged rich are of a different order of man and are mysteriously entitled to their outsize possessions.

(3) (The strategy is to) assure the less privileged that they are

---

*I must do a piece some day about that look on the faces of all boys from eight to twelve. In addition to the humiliation of being a male but *small* (little girls do not suffer from the corresponding deficiency; they work it [for] all it's worth), they can never be *in the right*. They make noise, break things, get dirty, and through their intense absorption in what engages them, they trample on the sensibilities of those about them. They are constantly in disgrace; no wonder they steal off to the company of one another.

not being duped. The American people is an extraordinarily unsuspi-
cious community. The Frenchman is in constant terror that he is the
victim of the knowing and a laughingstock. But even the American is
to a certain extent alert to such a chagrin. . . .

But all this is preliminary to my chief interest:

What is happening in the American mind in that realm where
the deepest motives are formed? What does the American now feel
about the situation in which he finds himself—rich-poor, handsome-
ugly, healthy-weakly, white-black? His situation was formerly accepted by him as "God's will"; his improving such elements as were
improvable was approved and even aided by God; his reverses and illnesses were sent him from Above. What goes on in his mind now
when he [is] fortunate and unfortunate, *i.e.*, victim of hazard? . . .

. . . what do the *lucky* think about their *luck*? Do they believe
themselves to be invested with a *mana*? What strategy (nearer to a
ritual) must they devise to retain and further their luck? Must they
justify their having been lucky to (1) themselves, and (2) the outside
world?

771. HOTEL SHERATON-CHARLES, NEW ORLEANS, [LA.,] DECEMBER 25, 1960. Play Projects.

I have arrived in New Orleans to lay the foundation for two
tasks. Paul Hindemith asks for another one-act opera to complete our
program over there; and Harry Buckwitz brings me the invitation to
write a play to inaugurate Frankfurt am Main's new theatre in 1963.

For the Hindemith one-act I have: (1) Just the thing—but I
can't use it. (Louise Talma is already deeply hurt that I allowed P.H.
to do *The Long Christmas Dinner*;[7] she would never forgive me if I
gave him this project also, which I once described to her as something she and I might some day do.)

But are there not some other "farces" one can unearth in the
very nature of opera itself? Or *bouffe* notions in this Creole world
around me?

(2) There's the one I can't use because it's too near De Filippo's
Questi Fantasmi!, but very good, and I could give it a wickeder twist:

---

7. Hindemith's one-act opera using the Wilder text was published in Mainz in 1961.

erring wife spreads it about that their new house is haunted so as to explain those noises at night—her irrepressible lover's jealous breaking into the dwelling. This with all the mitigatîons, however: old husband, very superstitious, etc.

What would be best would be if I could combine this task with one of the still-to-be-written playlets in the two series, Deadly Sins and Ages of Man. My first intention had been to offer each play in the series as representing, also, a different mode of playwriting: Grand Guignol, Chekhov, Noh play, etc., etc.

I then have: "*Ira*" (not suitable for comic); "*Invidia*" (ditto); "*Avaritia*" (barely). This last so hard to save from cliché: young couples turning the tables on agéd guardian, etc.

(3) However, there might be something in the other series, *e.g.*, "Youth," "Gulliver in Juventicol," or "Gullivers among the Juventibs"; but it would be most difficult to make it an action rather than a tableau.

(4) Adelina Patti *muette*.

(5) That old project: binding the King.

(6) The one that kept me awake half the night laughing—the opera in New Orleans that was blocked of its rehearsals by enemies.

(7) "Enemies of Music."

772. **NEUES POSTHOTEL, ST. MORITZ, APRIL 8, 1961.** Work in Progress.

Of the projects in the above entry I have half completed the "No. 1"—for Hindemith, and all but finished the "No. 3," "Youth-Gulliver."[8]

What occupies me now is an "*Ira.*" The previous design—the thought that tries to kill the outside world and only succeeds in killing the inside—simply won't come off. But there's something very good latent there and it will return to enrich something else. What I see now is real Grand-Guignol that re-animates that subject I had so many years ago: "The Hell of the Vizier Kabaâr." The alarming si-

---

8. "Youth-Gulliver" remained in its "all but finished" state: there are three incomplete manuscript drafts (twenty-five, twenty-six, and twenty-eight pages, respectively) and the incomplete carbon typescript (eighteen pages) among the Thornton Wilder papers at Yale.

lence of the opening: a nonchalant man dressed in surgeon's white, cleaning some instruments in the flames of lighted alcohol;* the wheeling in of the victim tied to a rolling table, belly up but head and feet hanging. Hereafter I must do everything I can to distinguish between hate and vengeance and seize on the essence they share in common: the desire not only to see the hated object annihilated but to see it understand itself as both defeated and about-to-be-annihilated; the emergence of a sort of ideality: "Oh, that my enemy might understand himself as I understand him." This relates itself to the [trial of Adolf] Eichmann [as war criminal], opening [in Jerusalem] next Tuesday, and to what Raimund was able to do with it in *Der Alpenkönig und der Menschenfeind.*[9]

Also hanging over me is Harry Buckwitz's invitation to do something to open the new theatre [in] Frankfurt am Main, *i.e.*, a big piece, in every sense and precisely in the sense where I'd never want to be big or to be caught trying to be big. Here I turn over:

"*The Emporium.*" Probably lost forever, but representing a relation to Kafka's *The Castle* that might return to me in some other form.

"*The Illinois [1905]-Small-Town-Anarchists-Reformers-Play.*" This I might well pursue, with all the more conviction that my first writing of it found it was, with very little hesitation, [thrown] into the wastebasket. As far as I offered this to Frankfurt—or to Lincoln Center!—it would be under the condition that it would certainly not be an opening-night machine: all that's best in it would be thrown out of joint under such aroused expectations; it's a big theme in a little dress.[1]

"*Geraldine de Gray.*" This is the name I have given over thirty years, maybe forty years, to an effort to find poetry, eloquence, deep meaning for the theatre in a half-ironic parody of the American Gothic—of the dime-novel of the *East Lynne* era, descended from the contemporaries of Poe. Absurd conventions of gentility that yield

---

*Stolen from the opening of De Filippo's *El Sindaco del Rione Sanità*, seen last month in Naples.

---

9. "*Ira*" (Wrath) was not finished. There are three incomplete manuscript drafts for the play (eighteen, twenty, and twenty-three pages, respectively) among the Thornton Wilder papers at Yale.

1. Wilder had apparently decided upon "The Reformers" as a final title for this "Illinois, 1905" play: various manuscript drafts (ninety-six pages) are filed under that title among the Thornton Wilder papers at Yale.

fierce ethical struggles; absurd stilted diction that permits of an infla-
tion into noble rhetoric. I have just come across a book which furnishes an extraordinary *point de départ*. I don't remember ever having read Gaston Leroux's *Le Mystère de la Chambre Jaune*, but I
have picked up here its sequel, *Le Parfum de la Dame en Noir*. Implacable hatreds and vengeances, all expressed through people creep-
ing [around] and confronting one another at four in the morning in a
ruined castle near Menton. What makes it interesting—though the
author does not seem to realize the appalling resonances he could
have derived from it—is this: there is [a] towering genius of a detective, Rouletabille, a Dupin-like master-mind; he is very young (*"mon
garçon"*), and there is nothing exotic about him, as in his prototypes,
except his genius as intellectuality; and there is a towering genius of a
criminal, Frederic Larsan, capable of every wickedness and capable
(which ruins the interest of the mystery) of every impersonation. And
the Detective is the son of the Criminal. And Mathilde, *la dame en
noir*, who throughout both novels plunges from *malheur* to *malheur*,
is *wife of the Criminal and mother of the Detective*. This is the Oedipus complex with a vengeance: Rouletabille hunting his father to the
death in order to protect his mother from her husband's cruelty.[2]

But what I'd most like to do is to write a farce-comedy, and I'm
endlessly groping for a *donnée*. Surely, surely, I ought to be able to
find one in my constant preoccupations with what I've called "The
Care and Feeding of Lies."[3] I see reflections all around me here in
Switzerland of the *loving protection of one's blindness*—Switzerland
immune for so many years from havoc and sacrifice. (Even what they
did for *Flüchtlinge* compared to what even devastated countries did.)
. . .

---

2. One of the early "Geraldine de Gray" projects produced a three-act play, of which a
typescript exists among the Thornton Wilder papers at Yale; but there seem to be no notes or
drafts for a revised version of 1961.

3. See Entry 770 (July 2, 1960).

APPENDIX I

"The Emporium"

[Journal Entries 407, 409, 410, 412–15, 417, 421, 423, 425, 428, and 429 record part of Thornton Wilder's attempt to write a play, influenced by both Kierkegaard and Gertrude Stein, combining the atmosphere of Kafka's *The Castle* with a Horatio-Alger theme—"The Emporium." He worked on the project intensively in 1948 and 1949, completing drafts of several scenes. He read at least four of these to friends in Aspen, Colo., in 1949, and at least two to other friends in Hamden, Ct., and Cambridge, Mass., in 1952. He resumed work on the play between August 2, 1953 and February 23, 1954 (as recorded in a series of entries not actually part of his Journal), but did not succeed in completing it.

His conviction (recorded in Entry 624, October 11, 1952) that he had "Two scenes . . .—solid and good" apparently continued unshaken, for the manuscripts of these two scenes are found among the Thornton Wilder papers at Yale in a separate folder along with the notes of 1953 and 1954. The two scenes are printed in this Appendix. (Note that the Horatio-Alger hero, first called Tom, then Daniel, has become John; the Emporium itself, which in 1949 was the A. and J., is now the G. and S.)]

SCENE ONE : The Amanda Gregory Foster Orphanage

[Enter MR FOSTER, superintendent of the Orphanage. He is
an excitable man of late middle age dressed in an old,
faded and unpressed cutaway. He looks like a deacon or
a small town undertaker.
He dashes out a few steps from the RIGHT and shakes
his hand imperiously at the back of the auditorium,
calling out loudly :]

MR FOSTER

Ring the bell, Mr. Conover. Ring it again. Ring it louder. I want
every child in this orphanage to be in this auditorium in
four minutes.

[He disappears as rapidly as he came.
[Enter from the same entrance MRS FOSTER, a
worn woman of her husband's age, dressed in faded
blue gingham. She also calls to the back of the
auditorium :]

MRS FOSTER

Come in, children. Come in quietly. Take your places quietly, girls.
— Boys, behave yourselves! — Girls here on my left, as usual.
Mr. Conover, are they ringing the bell out in the vegetable garden,
too? Thank you. — I wonder if the girls in the laundry can hear
it, with all that machinery going.
~~Otto Smith~~ Foster, is that you? Will you run over to the
laundry and tell all the children that Mr. Foster wants them — all of
them — here in the assembly hall.
Boys! Boys! — Don't play now. Just take your places quietly.

[Exit MRS FOSTER
[A second alarm bell starts ringing in dissonance.
[Enter MR FOSTER

MR FOSTER

That's right, Mr. Conover. Ring all the bells.
George Washington Foster, are you there? Form them into lines, two by
two. They're all pushing and crowding.
Girls on this side [LEFT]; Boys over here [RIGHT]
All children over eleven down here in front.
Very young children in the back. The blind children and the lame
children in the last rows.
Children eight to eleven up in the balconies.
[He shades his eyes and seems to be peering up to fourth,
fifth and sixth balconies. Then again to the back of the
auditorium :]
Now what's all that group late for? Oh, you've been working in
the dairy. Very well. Take your places.
[Enter MRS FOSTER. She goes up to her
husband and says in his ear:]

MRS FOSTER

Now you mustn't get excited! You remember what the
doctor said.

The first page of Scene One of "The Emporium"

THE EMPORIUM

A Play in [*blank space*] Scenes and a Prologue

The curtain of the stage is not used in this play.

Members of the audience arriving early will see the stage in half light. The six screens and the furniture and properties will be seen stacked about it at random.

Two STAGE HANDS *dressed in light blue jumpers, like garage mechanics, will enter ten minutes before the beginning and will remove these properties and set the stage for Scene One.*

The six screens are about six-and-a-half by twelve. They are like the movable walls of a Japanese house and are on rollers. They are all slightly off white, one faintly bluish, another toward buff, or green, and so on.

There is a light chair on the left front of the stage (from the point of view of the actors), by the proscenium pillar.

A few minutes before the play begins the MEMBER OF THE AU-DIENCE *enters from the wings at the left, looks about a little nervously and seats himself in this chair, turning it toward the center of the stage. He affects to be at ease, glances occasionally at the arriving audience, and studies his program. He is a modest but very earnest man of about fifty. He will be on the stage throughout the play and, except at the moments indicated, he will remain motionless, fixing an absorbed attention on the action before him.*

A screen has been placed far front in the center of the stage, parallel with the footlights. The other screens are placed as though

casually at the back of the stage though masking the entrances at the right and left. In front of the central screen is an old-fashioned "deacon's" chair. Beside it is a stand on which lies a vast Bible.
    A bell starts ringing at the back of the auditorium.

    SCENE ONE: *The Amanda Gregory Foster Orphanage.*

    Enter MR. FOSTER, *superintendent of the Orphanage. He is an excitable man of late middle age dressed in an old, faded and unpressed cutaway. He looks like a deacon or a small-town undertaker.*
    He dashes out a few steps from the right and shakes his hand imperiously at the back of the auditorium, calling out loudly:

MR. FOSTER: Ring the bell, Mr. Conover. Ring it again. Ring it louder. I want every child in this orphanage to be in this auditorium in four minutes.

    He disappears as rapidly as he came.
    Enter from the same entrance MRS. FOSTER, *a worn woman of her husband's age, dressed in faded blue gingham. She also calls to the back of the auditorium:*

MRS. FOSTER: Come in, children. Come in quietly. Take your places quietly, girls. —Boys, behave yourselves! —Girls here on my left, as usual. Mr. Conover, are they ringing the bell out in the vegetable garden, too? Thank you. —I wonder if the girls in the laundry can hear it, with all that machinery going.
Henry Smith Foster, is that you? Will you run over to the laundry and tell all the children that Mr. Foster wants them—all of them —here in the Assembly Hall.
Boys! Boys! —Don't play now. Just take your places quietly.

    Exit MRS. FOSTER
    A second alarm bell starts ringing in dissonance.
    Enter MR. FOSTER.

MR. FOSTER: That's right, Mr. Conover. Ring all the bells.
    George Washington Foster, are *you* there? Form them into lines, two by two. They're all pushing and crowding. Girls on this side [*left*]; boys over here [*right*]. All children over eleven down here in front. Very young children in the back. The blind children and the

lame children in the last rows. Children eight to eleven up in the balconies.

> *He shades his eyes and seems to be peering up to fourth, fifth, and sixth balconies. Then again to the back of the auditorium:*

Now what's all that group late for? Oh, you've been working in the dairy. Very well, take your places.

> *Enter MRS. FOSTER. She goes up to her husband and says in his ear:*

MRS. FOSTER: Now you mustn't get excited! You remember what the doctor said.

MR. FOSTER: Stragglers! Stragglers!

Yes. —Edgar Allan Poe Foster! Late as usual. Always trying to be different.

MRS. FOSTER: Remember your asthma! Remember your ulcers! You only hurt yourself when you get so excited. Remember, this has happened before and it will very certainly happen again.

> *Suddenly in irritation to a girl apparently coming down the aisle:*

Sarah Bernhardt Foster! Stop making a show of yourself; sit down and take your place quietly among the other girls!

MR. FOSTER: I want you all to come to attention.

James Jones Foster! —you may assist George Washington Foster in closing the doors.

> *Impressive pause.*

Wards of the Amanda Gregory Foster Orphanage! Of William County, Western Pennsylvania! Another of our children has attempted to run away! That makes the twelfth since Christmas!

> *He has a moment's convulsion of asthmatic coughing and sneezing into an enormous red-checked handkerchief. During this, his eyes fall on the MEMBER OF THE AUDIENCE seated on the stage at his left. He stares at him a moment, then dropping his characterization, he says:*

Who are you?

MEMBER OF THE AUDIENCE: I?

MR. FOSTER: Yes, you—who are you? What are you doing up here on the stage?

To the audience:

Excuse me a moment. There's—there's something wrong here.

To the MEMBER OF THE AUDIENCE:

What are you doing—sitting up here on stage?

MEMBER OF THE AUDIENCE: Euh—the management sold me this seat—I told them I was a little hard of hearing.

MR. FOSTER: What? What's that? I can't hear you.

MEMBER OF THE AUDIENCE: The management sold me this seat. I won't be in the way. I told them I was a little hard of hearing and they sold me this seat here.

MR. FOSTER: You certainly will be in the way. I never heard of such a thing.

He turns to MRS. FOSTER.

We can't go on with this man here.

MRS. FOSTER: Perhaps. Anyway, we'd better not stop now. We'll try to do something about it at the intermission.

MR. FOSTER: At the intermission. —I must say I never heard of such a thing. —Anyway, while you're here,—draw your chair back against the wall. You're preventing those people from seeing the stage.

The MEMBER OF THE AUDIENCE *draws his chair back.*

I hope you know enough not the distract the audience's attention in any way. It's important to us that you be as quiet as possible.

MEMBER OF THE AUDIENCE: Yes, oh, yes.

MR. FOSTER *glares at him and resumes his role.*

MR. FOSTER: Wards of the Amanda Gregory Foster Orphanage! Of William County, Western Pennsylvania! Another of our children has attempted to run away. That makes the twelfth since Christmas. He will be found.

He will be brought back to us any moment now.

I have brought you together this morning to talk this over.

You run away: to what? to whom?

Last fall *you* ran away [*fixing an orphan in the audience*], George

Gordon Byron Foster! You were brought back after a week, but what kind of week was it? You slept in railroad stations; you fed yourself out of refuse cans, or from what you could beg at the back door of restaurants. We asked you why you ran away and you said you wanted to live—to live, to live, impatience to *live*.

Joan Dark Foster, will you stop throwing yourself about in your seat! I shall not keep you long.

And you said you wanted to be free.

Every lost dog and cat is free. The horse that has run away from the stable and wanders in the woods is free.

—Do I hear talking up there—in the fourth and fifth balconies? Surely you nine-year-olds can understand what I'm saying! The five-year-olds down here are quiet enough!

Gustav Froebel Foster! —Can't you keep order among the children up there?

He waits a moment in stern silence.

This orphanage was founded by a noble Christian woman, Amanda Gregory Foster, and here—for a time—you are taken care of.

You have all been given the name of Foster, in memory of our foundress, and some of you have been given names of eminent—of great and useful—men and women.

But you are all foundlings and orphans.

These are facts. Do not exhaust your minds and hearts by trying to resist these things *which are*.

Prometheus Foster! Ludwig van Beethoven Foster! Sit down, both of you! Glaring and shaking your fists at me cannot change these matters one iota. What has to be, has to be.

But that is not the only thing which you must patiently accept in life. There is also much about each one of you which cannot be changed: your *self*. Your eyes and nose and mouth. Your color. Your height—when you have finally gained your growth. And your disposition.

Some of you are timid. Some of you are proud. We know which ones of you are lazy and which of you are ambitious.

In addition, each of you has a different store of health. Your sum of health—*yours!*

Mrs. Foster *rises quickly and points to audience, left.*

MRS. FOSTER: What's that? John Keats Foster has fainted.

MR. FOSTER: Lower his head between his knees, boys; he will come to himself.

MRS. FOSTER: Who's sitting beside him? Joseph Severn Foster and Percy Shelley Foster,—carry him out into the open air, boys. You'd better take him to the Infirmary.

MR. FOSTER: And what's that noise I hear in the back row?

MRS. FOSTER: It's—it's the blind children.

Where's Helen Keller Foster? —Oh, there you are! —Will you comfort the—? Yes.

She returns to her seat.

MR. FOSTER: There is no greater waste of time—and no greater enemy of character—than to wish that you were differently endowed and differently constituted. From these things you cannot run away.

Now one of our number, John Vere Foster, has again tried to change all this. For the third time he has tried to run away.

Ah, there he is!

Mr. Conover, will you bring John Vere Foster right down here, please. To the front row so that we can all see him.

MR. CONOVER, a shuffling old janitor, leads a boy, invisible to us, holding him by the ear, to a seat in the front row of the theatre aisle. MR. FOSTER rises, steps forward, and fixes his eyes on the boy.

Now, young man, will you tell us—tell all of us—why it is that you tried to run away?

Pause.

What! You're going to be stubborn and silent?

Pause.

You all have enough to eat. You have suitable clothing. The work is not difficult. Many of you enjoy your classes and we hear all of you playing very happily among yourselves in your recreation hours. Mrs. Foster and I make every effort to be just. There is very little punishment here and what there is is light. Many visitors tell us that this is the best orphanage in the country.

Again he has an asthmatic convulsion.

MRS. FOSTER: Take a glass of water. Sit down a moment and take a glass of water.

> *He sits down, his shoulders heaving.*
> MRS. FOSTER *comes to the front of the stage and addresses* JOHN—*more gently but unsentimentally:*

John, tell us— tell us why you have tried to run away. I can't hear you. Oh—you want to *belong*.

MR. FOSTER: What did he say? What did he say?

MEMBER OF THE AUDIENCE [*helpfully*]: He said he wanted to belong.

MR. FOSTER: Oh—to belong.

Children! —I am going to give John Vere Foster his wishes. He wishes—as you all say you do—to live and to belong.

A farmer and his wife called on me this morning. They wish to adopt a boy. Mr. Graham seems to me to be a just man. We do not usually place you—you, children—in homes until you are sixteen. John is only fourteen, but he is strong for his age—and, as you see, he is *impatient*.

John, go to Mrs. Hoskins: she will give you a new pair of shoes and a new overcoat; and she will pack your box. You are leaving with your father and mother—Mr. and Mrs. Graham—on the railway train this afternoon.

Belong!—to belong!

All of you have one thing in common: you do not belong to parents; you do not belong to homes; you do not belong to yourselves. You all *belong*.

Thousands of children have passed through this school—thousands of schools. The names of many of them you find on tablets in the corridor. The names of many of them are forgotten. The very ink has faded on our school records.

The generations of men are like the generations of leaves on the trees. They fall into the earth and new leaves are grown the following spring. The world into which you have been born is one of eternal repetitions—already you can see that.

But there is something to which you *can* belong—you *do* belong: I am not yet empowered to tell you its name. It is something which is constantly striving to bring something new into these repetitions,

to lift them, to color them, to—
It's not by running away—from place to place—that you will find
something to belong to—or that you will make yourself free—

Convulsions.

You are looking in the wrong place. —You will find it when you
least expect it.

He is shaken with coughing. His wife speaks to the children:

MRS. FOSTER: That will be all! Go back to your rooms *quietly,*
children.
Benvenuto Cellini Foster, put away your slingshot! This is no time
for play.

SCENE TWO: *The Graham farm.*

*The screens have been arranged to suggest a large room—the
kitchen of the Graham farmhouse. A gap between the two
screens at the back indicates the door into the parlor.*
*Stage left: a kitchen table. The chair at its left faces right. En-
ter* MRS. GRAHAM—*played by the actress who has just played*
MRS. FOSTER. *She now seems gaunt and stony-faced. She has
thrown a worn blue shawl over her shoulders. She carries
a farm-lantern. She comes to the front of the stage, opens
an imaginary back-door. She peers toward the back of the
auditorium.*

MRS. GRAHAM: John Graham, I want you should come in and eat
your supper before Mr. Graham comes back from prayer-meeting.
I've just heated it up for the second time and I want you should eat
it. It's eight o'clock. It's cold and it's black as pitch. But I've seen
you down by the corncrib there. You finished chores a long time
ago and there's nothing for you to be doing down at the barn, and a
growing boy should eat his food hot. It's real good. It's hominy
cooked in bacon, and greens, and it's real good. And I put some
molasses in it.

*She puts her lantern down and hugs her shawl tighter around
her.*

All right, I won't call you by your whole name; I'll just call you John. Now, John, I want you to come and eat your supper. I know you think Mr. Graham's unjust—I know that—but you ought to see that he *thinks* he's doing the right thing. In his mind he's just. When he does that,—when he whips you, John; when he whips you on Wednesday nights,—he thinks he's doing it for your own good.

And I've stewed up some of them crabapples that you picked yourself. I know what your argument is,—and I can understand it,—that, what with all the work you've done, you've got a right to take the horse and go into town nights, once in a while. It's not *that* that Mr. Graham minds so much, I think,—maybe it's that when you're in town you talk with those men down in Kramer's livery stable----and learn swear words----and----he prays to God that you don't touch liquor and learn other things. That's the truth of the matter. Now, John, I'm catching my death of cold here, and twice I've heated up that good supper for you.

She takes a step forward.

What's more, if you'll come in now, I'll tell you something—*something about yourself* that I never told you before. Something real interesting that I learned when we called for you at that orphanage. It's about where you come from, where you were found. I see now that I should've told you this a long time ago, because you're a grown-up man now, almost, and it's right you should know everything important about yourself.

> JOHN *seems suddenly to rise up in the middle aisle of the auditorium, about six rows from the stage. He is about eighteeen and wears faded blue overalls.*

JOHN [*darkly*]: You got something really to say? You're not just fooling me?

MRS. GRAHAM: I'm not fooling you. You come in and eat your supper and I'll tell you.

JOHN: You can tell it to me here.

MRS. GRAHAM: No, I can't. I'm perishing of cold. I can scarcely talk the way my teeth are chattering.

JOHN: Is it *long*—what you got to tell me?

MRS. GRAHAM: Oh, yes, it's long. I guess it'll take a whole quarter-hour to tell it right. So you come inside.

JOHN: I swore I wasn't ever going into that house again. I ain't going into any house where they call me a thief. I haven't ever stolen anything from anybody. It's him that's stolen from me: he steals from me every hour of the day, that's what he does. Maybe fathers can make their sons work for them for four years without one cent of pay,—but he's not my father and I'm not his son. He owes me a lot. I'll bet you he owes me a whole hunnert dollars. I'll bet that by now I own that whole horse and I can take it wherever I want to.

MRS. GRAHAM: I know that's your argument, John.

JOHN: You go fetch a coat or something and tell me right here what you've got to tell me,—because I'm not going into that house another night to be whipped by him.

MRS. GRAHAM: Now, John, you know he's not coming back for a while yet, and you can tell when he's come by the bells on the horses, can't you? —Until he comes back, you come inside. Whatever you do then, I can't stop you.

JOHN: Well, I'll only just come inside the door. I won't go any farther than that.

MRS. GRAHAM: You don't have to come any farther than you want to,—but scrape the snow off your shoes when you come in.

> *She opens the imagined door and returns into the kitchen. After scraping his shoes, JOHN follows her. She busies herself at the stove. He takes his stand down left center, his back to the audience, feet apart, proud and resentful.*

JOHN: Don't you worry about where I'll go. —Mr. Stahlschneider's hired man gets five dollars a week. I guess I'm worth two dollars a week—leastways, these last two years I've been. I bet I've even been worth three dollars. And Mr. Graham hasn't given me anything except that blue suit,—and even that he locks up between Sundays.

MRS. GRAHAM: Now, John Graham,—if you're thinking of running away, I can't stop you, but I've got fourteen dollars I saved making buttermilk. It's right there behind the clock in a tobacco bag. If you must go, I'm glad you should have it.

JOHN [*loud*]: I don't want no presents. I want what's *mine*. And my name's not John *Graham*. I haven't got any name,—only John.

MRS. GRAHAM: We tried to be a father and mother to you, best we could.

JOHN: I don't want no father or mother. I'm glad I didn't have any.

MRS. GRAHAM [*handing him an imagined plate*]: Here's your supper.

JOHN: Put it on the table. I don't think I'm going to eat it. —You can say what you were going to say.

MRS. GRAHAM [*putting the plate on the corner of the table, but speaking with spirit*]: And I'm not going to say one living word until you take a mouthful of that good supper while it's hot.

> *Silence. War of wills. Suddenly* JOHN *goes to the table, digs an unseen spoon into the dish and puts it in his mouth. He then resumes his former vindictive position.*

JOHN: Well, say it!

MRS. GRAHAM: When we went to that Amanda Gregory Foster Orphanage to adopt you we had a talk with that Mr. and Mrs. Foster that run it. We asked them if they knew anything about you and where you come from.

> *Pause.*

I must say I can't tell this very good with you standing there and showing hate in every muscle.

JOHN: Well, what do you want me to say? I run away three times and I'd run away again.

> *Their eyes meet. She points at the plate. He abruptly takes one more mouthful and replaces the plate on the table.*

MRS. GRAHAM: You were found in a baskit, John,—about three months old. Now maybe you'll think what I'm going to tell you isn't important, but you'll be mistaken there. That baskit, and every stitch of clothes that baby had on—and the blankits and the rattle and the milkbottle and the nipple—all of it, all of it come from the Gillespie and Schwingemeister Emporium.

> *Pause.*

Now I hope you see what that means. There wasn't a thing there that was second-rate or skimped. Somebody thought a lot of you, John—thought enough of you to get you A-number-one fittings.

JOHN [*after a short pause*]: Now I've et and I'm going back to the barn.

MRS. GRAHAM: I got something more to tell you. You eat every mouthful on that plate.

I guess you've heard of the G. and S. Emporium in Philadelphia, P.a.

There is a sound of sleighbells at the rear of the auditorium. Both listen in suspense.

That's Deacon Riebenschneider's bells.

They relax.

JOHN: Course, I have.

MRS. GRAHAM: Well, it'd be a funny thing if you hadn't, because I've noticed that you're awful interested in stores. Goodness, when we take you into town, that's all you want to see—asking me a thousand questions. I never saw anybody so interested in anything like you're interested in stores.

Well, I should think that you'd be real proud,—that all your baby-fittings come from the G. and S.

JOHN: Well, I ain't proud of it.

MRS. GRAHAM: That just goes to show how ignorant you are. I guess you think that's a store like any other store. A store that buys a lot of things and then sells 'em; a store that don't do any more than that: just does the same thing over and over, buy-sell, buy-sell. I guess you think it's that kind of store.

JOHN: Have you ever----have you ever been in it?

MRS. GRAHAM: Have I ever been in it?

Without looking at him. Brooding, with muted exaltation.

There's a kind of well that goes up the middle of it—and balconies and balconies with little white colyums. And red carpets with roses on them. And at the corners of the aisles, there's big brass cuspidors. And over the sales-ladies' heads there's wires, and when they sell something, little iron boxes run along the wires with the change. And at one side there are these elevators that go up and down taking people where they want to go.

JOHN: It's—it's only one of these stores for rich people.

MRS. GRAHAM: That shows you know nothing about it, simply nothing about it.

Again brooding.

It'll never burn up—that's what they say. Never even been a little fire in it. Of course, they keep a whole fire-fighting outfit in it—but that's just for show. Of course, if you buy goods there and bring them home—*then* they'll burn. But not in the store they won't. Why, if Philadelphia, P.a., had a fire like Chicago, Illinois, had— you go in the G. and S. and you'll be perfectly safe. That's what they say and I believe them.

JOHN: That's not reasonable.

MRS. GRAHAM: Reasonable? Ain't nothing reasonable about it. Why, there are millions of people in the world who think that the G. and S. is crazy. Why, my sister went in to buy a wedding-dress and there was one there—all fine-sewed. The most beautiful dress in the world. And it looked like it cost a hundred dollars and, of course, she couldn't pay that. But the lady sold it to her for eighteen dollars, that's a fact. Not a thing wrong with it. My sister's husband—well, one terrible thing after another happened; but it was a beautiful dress; and her daughter wore it at *her* wedding. Then on other days, little things, little everyday things cost a world of money. Nobody's ever been able to understand it—nobody. Some days the G. and S. insults the customers—there's no other way of putting it—and other days it loads you down. It's not reasonable—but it's the greatest store in the world.

JOHN: What's this other thing you were going to tell me?

MRS. FOSTER: Before I tell you, I want you to promise me----that you won't raise your hand against Mr. Graham when he----when he thinks it's his duty to punish you. Mr. Graham don't seem to notice that you're getting bigger and stronger every month. Will you promise me that?

> *John, silent a moment; then goes to back wall and takes the same pose facing the audience.*

JOHN: Say what you were going to say without making any bargains.

> *Relents.*

Depends on what he does.

> *Pause.*

Have you been in it often?

MRS. FOSTER: Have I been in it often?!----

> *Gravely she brings out locket from the neck of her dress.*

See that lockit? I got that lockit for three years' faithful service at the G. and S.

JOHN [*fascinated, peers at it*]: That says Gertrude Foster. You're name ain't Foster.

MRS. GRAHAM: 'Fore I married Mr. Graham it was.

JOHN [*backing; outraged*]: I *thought* you was like that Mrs. Foster that run the Orphanage. Are you kin of hers? Are you----*kin* of hers?

MRS. GRAHAM: Course not. Lots of people named Foster in West Pennsylvania. Lots of 'em. —Now you eat these crabapples while I tell you what comes next. You eat 'em slow----get the nourishment out of them.

> *She gives him the plate and goes back to the stove. She is again lost in thought.*

You can scarcely see to the top of it where there's painting—hand-painting on the dome. And always, way up, very faint,—there's music. Music wrote special for the Emporium. You never saw such a place.

JOHN [*now spellbound*]: And the superinten'ants and managers? Are they walking around? I mean Mr. Gillespie and Mr. Schwingemeister?

MRS. GRAHAM [*sudden scorn*]: Well, if you aren't the most ignorant boy in the world I don't know who is!! Mr. Gillespie! Mr. Schwingemeister, indeed! Why nobody's ever seen even Mr. Sordini— and he's on the fifth floor. Looks like you think the Emporium's like other stores. Huh! I wouldn't have called you in from the barn if your baby-fittings come from an ordinary store. If you want to work in any ordinary store you can go to Craigie's—yes, sir, you can go to Craigie's Deepartmental Store, that's next door to the G. and S. In Craigie's you know where you are.
You're paid regular—

> *Sleighbells at back of auditorium. Same business.*

That's Widow Ochshofer's.

JOHN: Don't they *pay* you at the Emporium?

MRS. GRAHAM: And you can see Mr. Craigie, every day, ten times a day. You're paid good and you're paid regular—and everything's perfectly clear. At six o'clock you can go home. Yes, sir, you can work there fifty years and any night you like you can go home and hang yourself. At Craigie's Departmental Store, the color's green. Everything green. What color is the Emporium color?

JOHN [*weak*]: I don't know.

MRS. GRAHAM [*whispers*]: What color do I always wear?

JOHN: ----Blue----

MRS. GRAHAM: Of *course* I do----and what color you got on?

JOHN: ----Blue!----

MRS. GRAHAM: And what color was all over that baskit you was found in? Blue. *Now*, I'll tell you something about yourself. Where was your baskit found? On the steps of the City Hall? Or the hospital, like most babies? Or at the Public Liberry? No. You were found on the steps of the G. and S. itself. You kind of belong there—that's what I think. You're an Emporium man.

But that ain't all: You know what I think? I think that Amanda Gregory Foster Orphanage—I think that orphanage is run by the G. and S.—that's what I think. I think I've seen that Mr. and Mrs. Foster before,—and I know *where* I saw 'em too.

JOHN [*excitedly*]: You look like her. That's what I always thought —that you look like her.

MRS. GRAHAM [*contemptuously*]: I don't look like her at all. But I've often said to myself: If anything happened to Mr. Graham—that's where I'd like to be. I'd like to be working at that Orphanage, help- ing some way, working with all those children. Something like that.

Sleighbells. This is it.

There he is. That's him.

JOHN [*frozen*]: I'm going to stay right here.

MRS. GRAHAM: Now remember, John. You promised.

JOHN: I never made no promise in my life.

MRS. GRAHAM: I ironed your blue suit today. It's just inside that door. And if you think you've got to go—here it is. The buttermilk money.

She goes quickly to the mantel and pushes an (imaginary) bag toward him.

JOHN: I don't need no money.

MRS. GRAHAM: Take it. Hasn't anybody ever told you that this world is a terrible place—hasn't nobody ever told you that? *Take it!*

She returns to her chair and sits down.
Enter MR. GRAHAM—*fur cap; short green coat of blanket ma-*

terial. Strides down the auditorium aisle, on to the stage; with-
out glancing right or left, goes out stage-center. They stare
motionless while he passes through the room.

JOHN [*whispering*]: What do you mean: the Emporium don't *pay*
you? —It's no good, if it don't pay you when you work for it.

MR. GRAHAM'S VOICE [*from the parlor*]: John Graham, will you come
into the parlor?

MRS. GRAHAM: Listen, now—I haven't told you the whole truth
about it: how *hard* it is. And some days you just despair. Yes, some
weeks it forgets to pay you. And some weeks it pays you too much
—like there's been a mistake in the books. And that it takes every
bit of you and don't hardly leave you any life to yourself. And that it
doesn't thank you—and it almost never gives you a compliment for
what you've done. Just the same, —it's something you can feel that
you can *belong* to. You go there! You'll see.

MR. GRAHAM'S VOICE: John!

> MR. GRAHAM *appears at the parlor door. He is holding a*
> *large stick.*

John Graham, did you hear me? You will go into the parlor and
lower your overalls. Mrs. Graham, you will go upstairs.

MRS. GRAHAM: Mr. Graham, I will stay right here.

MR. GRAHAM: Mrs. Graham, you will go upstairs.

MRS. GRAHAM: You and I, before God, adopted this boy for our
own—together.

> *She flinches.*

I'm going out on the porch, but I'm not going upstairs.

> *Hugging her shawl about her, she goes out on the porch, and*
> *stands with pursed mouth.*

MR. GRAHAM: Did you hear me, John?

JOHN [*rapidly*]: I'm coming in. But I tell you right now that you owe
me a hunnert dollars and maybe more; and that any man that's hit
by another man has a right to defend himself; and that that time the
hook fell down on you from the top of the barn and you were sick a
week—you thought it was me but it wasn't; and the only lie I ever
told you was about when the old heifer got in the lower pasture

(and that was in the second week I was here): so I guess everthing's square between us now.

> *He goes out back, center.* MR. GRAHAM *is astonished by this speech.*

MR. GRAHAM: I don't know what you're talking about. Anybody'd think you'd gone crazy. Your smoking and your drinking have made you crazy, —that's what's happened.

> *He follows* JOHN *off. His voice can be heard.*

We'll first kneel down and ask God's blessing.

> MRS. GRAHAM *slowly re-enters the kitchen: sits at the table. Sudden sounds of violence from the parlor. Stumbling. Breaking furniture.*

MR. GRAHAM'S VOICE: How *dare* you, —you young----*devil!*

> *Silence.* MRS. GRAHAM *does not move.*

Gertrude! Gertrude!

> JOHN *appears at the door, somber, and a little dazed. He is holding the stick.* MRS. GRAHAM *does not look at him.*

JOHN: I'll take my blue suit.
MR. GRAHAM [*off*]: Gertrude!

> JOHN *becomes aware that he is holding the stick. He throws it back into the parlor. He returns to the parlor and reappears with his suit wrapped in a brown-paper parcel. He starts to leave via the audience; then pauses, drops the parcel and going to* MRS. GRAHAM *leans over her with his hands approaching her throat.*

JOHN: Give me that!
MRS. GRAHAM [*in terror, defending her throat*]: John! What you doin'? What you doin'?
JOHN: I'm taking that lockit.

> *He breaks it and holds it before him.*

That's the only thing I ever stole.
MRS. GRAHAM: All right. You didn't steal it. I give it to you.

JOHN [*looking about him*]: Of all the hundreds and thousands of farms I could'a been sent to, —I was sent to this one!

MRS. GRAHAM [*proudly*]: Anyway, in this one you got one thing: you heard about the Emporium first hand.

JOHN: I'll bet it ain't much.

> *He dashes down into the audience and leaves the auditorium by the aisle.*

MR. GRAHAM'S VOICE: Gertrude----get Dr. Krueger----Go, get him----

> MRS. GRAHAM *goes slowly out back.*
> *Sound of galloping horse at the back of the auditorium.*

MEMBER OF THE AUDIENCE [*looks at the audience; smiles, rubs his hands*]: I guess that's the end of the Scene.

Notes toward "The Emporium"

[The "series of notations toward a continuation of 'The Emporium'" that Thornton Wilder began on August 2, 1953 (see Entry 655) extended to June 17, 1954. They were not made part of the Journal but are printed in this Appendix.]

655 (HORS-SÉRIE). MACDOWELL COLONY, [PETERBOROUGH, N.H.,] AUGUST 2 [1953]. "The Emporium."

As I take up "The Emporium" again, I shall begin a series of notes here. I may or may not bind them into the Journal later.

My difficulty with it was that it was going on a road all too moralizing and didactic: the choice of Hercules and the development *"par la femme l'idéalité entre dans la vie, et sans elle que serait l'homme?"** I'm not afraid of truisms; but I must believe in them vitally for myself, and I must present them tragicomically.

With that Orphanage and Farmhouse Scene the hero is certainly Everyman in Everyhome. Then I go into his Relation-to-Standards.

But what I've got now is too vast a portal for my Emporium-Craigie material; or rather, my Emporium-Craigie material is not be-

*Kierkegaard: *Etapes sur le chemin de la vie*, Gallimard, 1948. (Chapter "In vino veritas," page 54.)

ing presented by me in a large enough way to permit it adequately to
follow the Orphanage and Cleaning-Women scenes.

Later: (Thursday,) [August 6, 1953].

Thinking about time I begin to wonder whether my gropings
haven't been halfhearted merely because I've been seeing the boy's
life story wrongly from the point of view of time. A myth must be
staged as something already known. Its end must precede its beginning; or rather, its end is in its beginning and in every part of it. It
loses its force the minute it is conceived as a story-in-succession, and
unfolding-into-the-unknown; so break up, throw away any interest in
it that may depend upon chronological progression.*

Shouldn't we look into the John story as into a pit, a gulf, a cis-
tern? A myth is not a story read from left to right, from beginning
to end, but a thing held full-in-view the whole time. Perhaps this is
what Gertrude Stein meant by saying that the play henceforth is a
landscape.

(1) So today my mind has been pressing on the possibility that I
begin the play with the New-Year's-Eve-party-at-Craigie's story† (or
with some "vision" that has not yet occurred to me—John's reception
into the Emporium or his death at its doors) and then work *both backward and forward,* and close the play with the Orphanage Scene.

Friday [August 7, 1953].

How can I best show, without overt moralizing pressures, the
weakness of the Craigie Store (the inadequacy of the Ethical) and the
strength of the Emporium? Answer: by an indication of the latent
fears in the former.

(2) Suppose at the new opening scene, the Annual Party, I have
Ermengarde Craigie address the guests before her father's arrival:
"Let me remind you of two things: you know my father's displeasure

---

*Perhaps I should say, for the record, that I arrived at this by a stage (yesterday) where I
seemed to see the play as a succession of prologues: Prologue One: The Council of the Emporium founding an Orphanage; Prologue Two: The Orphanage; Prologue Three: The Farmhouse
Scene; Prologue Four: The Emporium Council preparing to baffle, repudiate, invite, etc. the
aspirant; Prologue Five: etc.

†That scene I began to write Tuesday (rewrite; earlier draft lost or destroyed) and without
conviction; *now* I could find a new spirit about it.

at any reference to *another* store in this city—let's us remember *not*
to mention any other store. And secondly, since some of you are new
here, I think I ought to tell you that my father has been in a very
nervous condition—we're all so glad that he's getting better—and I
don't want you to become alarmed if he seems----that is if he suddenly seems to be convinced that there's a flood or----or that the earth
is turning to ice, or that Philadelphia's on fire. My father every now
and then *imagines* these things." And when Mr. Craigie enters that's
what he does: inveighs against the Emporium, and has a paroxysm
lest the snow then falling will never cease. He's stored the cellars
with food. Ethics does not offer any relief to the basic fear in men;
though millions try to make themselves believe so.

This, then, can make writing the Emporium scenes easier: they
are careless of fire and thieves. And when, in the reverse-movement
of the new design for the play, we come to the scene on the Graham
Farm, Mrs. Graham can be given ([in the theater] at 10:35 [p.m.]) a
truer, briefer, surer statement of the motto of the play and the character of the Emporium: that one can only belong to that that is not
threatened with extinction.

And instead of my single Noh-theatre ideal spectator, won't I
have five people over seventy—from the Veteran Department-Store
Workers' Garden Home—one blind, two deaf—and who must sit on
the stage?

And isn't it possible that I open the play at the Craigie Party;
carry it to the moment when Mr. Hobmeyer as messenger from the
Emporium brings a summons to our young hero; then break the
scene off? The whole play then unrolls and we resume that scene
where we left off and continue to our finale. So that this play is a one-
act play with interpolated switchbacks (or what are they called?).

Saturday [August 8, 1953].

Have been writing up the scene. Haven't I found a way of expressing the abyss under the Ethical by the system of alarm bells?
The Just Man, *conscius recti*, cannot dissipate or liquidate his fears;
he can only ignore them; or, as we say, rise above them. They lie in
wait to assail him at those moments when weakness or some sudden
blow of circumstance (mis-*chance*) robs him of the will-constructed
resolution *not* to confront them. And the long-time contemplation of
the totality of experience is itself the enemy of his serenity. Many a

stoic has significant resolution to be unshaken by the ills within his own life; can he sustain it in the contemplation of the ills of all mankind? Again there is a transition from quantity to quality: to remain sincere in the presence of a few ills is stoicism; to remain serene in the face of a myriad demands faith.

Sunday [August 9, 1953].

I have reached the point where Mr. Craigie offers John the store and his daughter's hand. If this is to be the first scene in the play I am in a world of difficulties. The audience which receives this at 8:45 [p.m.] is in the presence of mere story-telling. Its only interest can be in what-will-happen-next. My dimensions are not wide and poignant enough to generate in this audience a passion to know, also, what happened before. This, then, is either not the first scene, or it is not correctly written. The play should begin with a vast reversal or a coming-to-himself.

Monday [August 10, 1953].

(3) Have begun a prologue(!): Mr. Hobmeyer addressing the crowd that's waiting to get into the Emporium's annual sale. Oh, the difficulty of it—to avoid the moralizing-didactic, to sound some large notes, and to establish the "crazy" aspect of the store.

Wednesday, August 12, 1953.

Each time I rewrite the new opening scene, it is better. To be sure, it has no explicit mention of any central aspect of John's or Laurencia's stories; but I think that from today I am free to write the plot, freed that is from that other aspect of writing which is searching for an idea.

Friday [August 14, 1953].

Now, again, I've been returning to the notion of chronological order—but this time inserting the Annual-Sale Scene after the Farmhouse Scene (taking the place of a scene I had several times written for that place: a scene in the Employment Office). The uneasiness I

have about it comes from: (1) How many times in a play can you address the audience, each time identifying them with a different public? (Query: Did Shakespeare use his audience as the Roman mob in
the scene of Caesar's funeral orations? anywhere else?) (2) Can the
higher-lower aspects of the Emporium be indicated in this way, at
this moment—do they detract from the "touches" to be added in the
next scene: the Laurencia-Hobmeyer, Laurencia-John conversations
after the store's closing-time? What I like is the introduction of John
as an unseen questioner from the audience; and a possible first sketch
of Laurencia in a relation to the waiting bargain-hunters. Let me now
try this scene again, looking for ways to build up some real give-and-
take between Hobmeyer-Bernice [(the cleaning woman)]-Laurencia.

It seems impossible to find a way to trouble the waters in this
scene by injecting doubt as to whether the Emporium is senile or
asleep or all but non-existent.

Peterborough, [N.H.,] Tuesday, August 18, 1953.

Vacillation. Insecurity in progress. But what it comes down to is
that I cannot make any decision about form or anecdote until I discover the next characteristic of the Store—the next image or merely
fact or symbol—to feed the curiosity of the audience which is the true
life of the play. And the difficulty lies in the fact that I must present
the characteristic under the form of a department store's operation.
And what I am looking for is something dealing with the fact that the
Absolute "sells" primarily to the individual and is only individually
perceived. And this I must do by presenting the contrast of this
method to the method employed over at Craigie's. The classic way of
presenting this is, I suppose, Hans Christian Andersen's story of the
King who has no clothes. Each person sees the Emporium and its
goods differently; while Craigie and all its objects are of equal valua-
tion to all its customers.

Now this I have done pretty well but only partially in John's
outburst to Laurencia ("old-fashioned----can't find the doors"): what I
need further is a figure for the relation between the customer and the
goods.

(4) (Rejected tries: to some eyes they are moth-eaten and rusty;
some claim that when you take them home the colors fade, or the ob-

jects break.) Remembering that I'm after the idea of the suitability of each object to an individual purchaser, shouldn't I search among motifs such as: the objects (claim the disparagers) are unsuitable for daily life; that they don't—in many ways—fit?*

Anyway, as I see it this motif—when I find it—should follow the motif of the has-no-doors-is-stuffy-etc. Yet I should be able to introduce it in the Mrs. Graham-John Scene (though I groan when I think of anything that overburdens that scene with overt symbolic material; so early in the play, it should catch up the spectator, mostly, as passionate human story). Now let me again go back and see if I can weave this into the Bargain-Sale Scene.

(5) For a while I have considered putting all this material (except: how can I get a job at the Emporium?) into the present "third scene" by having Bernice arriving for work, pulling a hatpin from her hat (arriving after Laurencia's discussion of the dome, the music, etc.). It is her duty to collect the complaints from the complaint boxes—to burn them. Mirthful or indignant, she reads several of them: ". . . that your wares are unsuitable for a modern American home. I regret I must transfer my patronage to Craigie's. I hope you will accept this letter in the spirit in which it is written. . . ." "Never, I repeat, never shall I put my foot in your store again . . ." (this letter is twelve pages), "to be so insulted by clerks," etc.

Yet this has the overwhelming disadvantage that it brings Bernice upon the scene before her big appearance as a cleaning woman and presents her colloquial side without intimating her sybillic quality. Besides, one could wish to do better than read aloud letters.

No, I must keep my meditations turning on the attributes of the Emporium itself—when I have those truly in hand the play will flow from them.

And to the idea of Belonging: and here I seem merely to flounder from one tiresome moralizing formula to another: you belong to what you make (or give), not to what you receive.

Later: Rewrote Laurencia resigning and first part of Laurencia-John. Raising the intensity on the realistic level; and the Bernice Scene. I think it's now all better and moving forward.

---

*To remember: that Kafka records a moment in which K., seeing the Castle for the first time, has the impression that it resembles the town in which he was born—Kafka's Castle, however, is *also* the Law.

August 27, 1953.

(6) One thing keeps worrying me: apart from what I shall do with the Member of the Audience on the stage, I seem to see in my mind's eye that this Third Scene needs to be dressed with more people. The First Scene: doesn't matter, it's an auditorium; Second Scene, comes sufficiently to life with the opening speech of Mrs. Graham; the Third opens with the liveliness of getting the customers out of the store; but we need some higher liveliness here and that could be accomplished by the (pretty soon) arrival of a third actor (that's why I tried also to introduce Bernice earlier—but that, in this last rewriting, I've disposed of). Certainly, it would be vivacious enough, if I could introduce a belated customer—an indignant insulted busybody, of the Craigie faction. To think over—but only if I can find legitimate working use for her later: just [as] I have two Seniors (Foster-Hobmeyer and Graham-Craigie) so would I be justified in having two Matrons?

(7) In this writing I have discarded the former Prologue (John-Gillespie and Dr. Abercrombie) with all its attendant business. Do I regret it? Will it ultimately find a place?

Now as to the Member of the Audience.

September 7, 1953.

Twisting and turning. Rewriting scene after scene. Forever trying to focus and define the two great problems behind this play: what is the Emporium?; and how to bring into highlight the qualities it has in common with a department store while attenuating and veiling the qualities it *hasn't* in common.

(8) These last few days I have seen that it is unsuitable that I build the Second Part on a Laurencia-Gretchen story. The framework is too big for a "simple-life lone narrative" and the point that women are catalysts of the Absolute can be made clearly without lingering too long over our illustrative anecdote (*all* Emporium girls do not shipwreck their lives in its service; and this play must see to it that it is giving a report on all). So now I think that Laurencia *quia* Laurencia has only one scene. The play approaches the form of a succession of one-act plays at the same time that it approaches the form of an oratorio or mysterium. So now I am attacking the Third Scene (first floor of the Emporium) as a one-act play. John has been "annoying" Lauren-

cia for almost a year. What is its climax? that Laurencia denounces and repudiates John? Something more.

(9) *Later:*

HOBMEYER: Sometimes I think that *this*—all this we see—isn't the Emporium at all.
JOHN [*breathlessly*]: What? What do you mean?
HOBMEYER: All this selling—all this buying and selling.
JOHN: Well, it's a store, isn't it? The Emporium's a store.
HOBMEYER: Yes, but----maybe it's only a front. A front for something else that it's doing.
JOHN: Why, that's crazy. Of course, it's a store.
HOBMEYER: But you've noticed yourself that it's not interested in selling—not interested in the same way that Craigie's is.
JOHN [*stopped for a moment*]: Then what is it interested in?
HOBMEYER: Come, it's time to lock the doors. Go down that corridor.
JOHN: Well, I know one thing: I'm never going to come here again. I don't want to work in a place that you don't know what it's doing. I'm going to stick to my job at Craigie's. At Craigie's you know where you [are].
HOBMEYER: You're perfectly right about that, boy. At Craigie's you know where you are.

So we have the scene at Craigie's party, culminating in John's mock-speech and repudiation—he will return to the Emporium.

Later: Key West, November 26, 1953.

(10) Now we're putting back the Employment-Office [Scene] (of long ago) with the whole new emphasis throughout of How do you get a job there?

November 30, 1953.

Finished the scene on the Emporium floor—now the fourth. I think the shape is coming clearer. Some vestiges of *Kitsch*, alas.

December 2, 1953.

Rewrote the former Prologue—now as a dream-sequence to open Part Two. *Later:* No, that won't do.

Deepwood Drive [Hamden, Ct.], January 21, 1954.

(11) Have been writing the Employment-Office Scene (now Scene Three), incorporating from Notion (under 2, above) the visitors from the Retired Employees' etc. Now I think it's going right. Great violence on the stage—John's manhandling of the Employment Officer. I think that, at last, this is it. And now I have the stage dressed with these disparate on-watchers who themselves are dynamic feeders of the developing tensions. And more and more Scene Four takes its shape,—getting nearer and nearer to *Das Schloss* from which I should not have departed in the first place. And all this new spurt of activity has had its point of departure from reading (through a glass darkly) an article in the latest (*Drittes Heft*, 1953) *Die Neue Rundschau:* Theodor Adorno: *"Aufzeichnungen zu Kafka"*—all the more useful too in that I cannot fully follow such thick involved German.

Saturday, January 23, 1954.

Now at last I think I'm advancing. The things that put me on the right track were seeing: (1) That the present Third Scene—the Employment Office—must all represent the terrible urgency of getting into the G. and S.—not only my hero's distrustful curiosity, but the whole world's urgency; and (2) That in the next scene Laurencia is but an episode-figure. She now has a different characterization: she is a limited little goose, but with streaks and intimations of belonging to the Great Sisterhood (young exemplar therefore of Mrs. Antrobus); now we see, with the help of the preceding scene, that John's passionate advances are a devouring urge to capture the Emporium-secret in her; and now I can *show* it without (or almost without) having to say it.

This probably means that I now discard the Boarding-House Scene (though Ruth [Gordon?] was so wild about it), unless some other use for it can be found other than developing a consecutive Laurencia-story. What I would love to do now is to introduce another girl—perhaps Ermengarde Craigie—who must be played by the same actress who has just played Laurencia;—which device will be all the more lively and theatric now that we have made Laurencia an extreme-character part. And how greatly form and pattern will be enhanced if we have our Young Actress also appearing in several roles and only John himself throughout the play.

To be sure, I now know less than ever where I am going next, but I feel less anxious about that with each new addition of a solid brick in the pavement that is leading there, and I feel pretty sure now that these first four scenes are solid and permanent bricks.

Sunday, Janaury 24, 1954.

Now I've been able to move on to Scene Four, Laurencia an episode-girl in this scene alone. Allusions to the fact that John has been hanging around girls in the other departments, too. All the John-tone is new, too,—now he is boastful. He will some day own and reform the G. and S.

Walked into town this evening: teased by a large audacity. Laurencia is an early stage, of course, in the life of Mrs. Foster—of the Mrs. Graham. How about showing that all these characters are stages in the lives of four characters? That Mr. Foster once kept an Employment Office for the G. and S.; that Mr. Dobbs (present—unsatisfactory—name for our Employment Officer) will move on to head the Orphanage. That Bertha [Bernice], the cleaning woman, was once a farmer's wife (name not given); that Laurencia will leave the G. and S. to marry a young farmer named Graham!! In which case, shall we say that she will change her name to Gertrude? That Mr. Hobmeyer will retire to take over an Employment-Agency job? —Yes, yes, yes, it would woefully confuse the audience—but when they get the point, isn't it a prodigious point to make? And what are we to make of the end of John's life?—is he to be a successful or unsuccessful G. and S. man? If the latter, couldn't we thus indicate that he will be following the Hobmeyer-Dobbs-Foster plan?

There's a cyclic drama for you. And reinforcing that image that is now stirring: department stores with their endless buying and selling are like leaves replacing leaves on trees, are like people who have children who have children; but that the G. and S. has something else and something more.

Tuesday, January 26, 1954.

Walked into town. Yes, yes, I think it can be done. Writing a letter Monday to [X], I tried to describe what I now see to be the di-

rection of the play and my efforts to describe it to him continue to operate in my mind. It is about the Wheel of Being; the endless repetitions of the life-forms; but the Emporium is, precisely, the evidence
of pressures from Elsewhere to introduce a qualitative change into
the mechanical repetitions. The wheel therefore is one of the images
of the play: Craigie's is the wheel of repetitions, and in the scene of
Craigie's Anniversary Party I must put (droll) emphasis on the Niagara of intake and outgo. And now I must find ways of adumbrating this
into the Orphanage Scene: those children (the Orphanage is "associated" with, sponsored by G. and S.) are the effort to alter and "re-
deem" the wheel. This wheel-motif, therefore, will give me the atmosphere in which to play this other game: the repetition of lives in
my characters: Laurencia will grow up to be Mrs. Graham; etc.

Now I come up against another "enlargement" of my scene: the
Emporium Girls. Dare I venture again (as in the Orphanage Scene)
the roll-call of great names: of great women who have been able to get
their men into the Emporium? Oh, how I hate "symbols" and bookish
allusions—but how in my plays I cannot escape them. Here it is doubly difficult, because the names are not so current in the average audience's field of allusion. I thought (on the walk) of such a passage as
this:

HOBMEYER: Do you imagine for a moment that these girls can get you
a job in the Emporium?
JOHN [*sullenly*]: They are sure that they can.
HOBMEYER: Maybe it has happened once or twice. I don't say that it's
impossible. In the Emporium we can never say that a thing is im-
possible----eh. For instance, do you know that Eyetalian girl that
works in the dress-fabrics department, Beatrice her name is----
calls herself *Beatrice*—or those other two Eyetalian girls, Laura
and Vittoria. Couldn't they perhaps bring a man to himself? And
that way, somehow, get him a job here?

I shrink, but maybe I must do it. And follow it by a catalogue:

HOBMEYER: Oh, we have some fine girls here: Monica and Aspasia,
that Greek girl, and Teresa and Clara and Magdalene and [*blank
space*]—oh, I won't say they couldn't bring a man into the G. and
S. if he were ripe for it.

Digression: Several things about these developments have an
almost comical effect upon me. I have been writing this piece on the

theatre for Rosamond Gilder and the European anthology on décor[4] (weeks behind on it, as usual) and toward the close I have been trying to describe what the play of the future might be like, and I have (in my notes—it may not appear in the final draft) described just such a play as this: the realism in the specific detail subtended by the largest arcs of time and place and custom. Secondly, I see that this play which took its point of departure from Kafka's *Castle* is drawing into itself more and more modalities of *Finnegans Wake*. Maybe this play will have originality, will be original. It has always been quite clear to me that the other two [*Our Town* and *The Skin of Our Teeth*] were not. The other two were *calqués*.* It may be possible that by now my possession of my time concepts, my human-situation concepts is so deep-digested and so all-permeating that I may be permitted to write a really original play—original not in the sense that it is filled with novel devices, but that it makes people see for the first time things that hitherto they had known without being aware that they knew them.

February 9, 1954.

It's all in a ferment. But I see that out of my Member of the Audience seated on the stage I must derive elements still lacking from my play: there must be fear and awe and----somewhere there must be melodrama. And yet every nerve of me revolts at introducing any more of those devices that erupt in the Second and Third Acts of *The Skin of Our Teeth*. Oh, Heaven help me not to have to make the *dramatis personae* emerge from their roles, or members of the audience, further, intrude themselves into the play. And yet!—when the play is about Everybody, isn't it legitimate and functional that Everybody should be drawn into the unfoldment of the play? So if I have to do it, Heaven help me to make it irresistibly real and spontaneous.

Now what is the active enemy of the Emporium? Not Craigie's, which merely rages impotently and enviously. There are two ene-

---

*I see the dictionary gives *calquer* as *copier servilement*. I don't mean that. I mean merely superimposed upon a variety of molds and prior achievements in theatrical art. They derive their air of originality from the facts that: (1) Very few persons knew (or profoundly knew) the great originals; and (2) The variety and disparateness of the models concealed the indebtedness; and (3) The indebtedness was one of admiration and love—which is seldom the case in such borrowings.

---

4. See Entry 667 (January 18, 1954).

mies: for those "in it" there is doubt; for those outside it (in addition to doubt), there is the thing that prevents them entering, the deference to the opinion of the market place, the inability to think alone. (I have just written that into Laurencia's scene, groaning because I had to state it so explicitly). So the Journey of John is the journey to self-as-authority; and the stadia are: (1) His outburst at the Employment Office; (2) His revolt and final acquiescence before the charges of Bertha [Bernice]; and (3) His consciousness that Craigie's is precisely the servile adherence to the market place and his release. But where can I get melodrama into that? And how introduce my sitters-on-the-stage? Well, I shall take a walk into town in an hour and see what the walk can bring me.

February 13, 1954.

Well, nothing came of that walk into town. Then I went to New York.* Another lacuna in the play has been glaring me in the face: I haven't found any way to express what it is in the G. and S. that has been attracting John. So far I have merely stated it in the shape of that he is puzzled by it: and that's not enough. While I had the so-called dreamed episode, the former "Prologue," I could convey sufficiently to the audience that he belonged there by divine inheritance. Now, I have nothing but Mrs. Graham's assertion. So the elements I must bring up and coalesce are the magnet-pull, the *Schaudern*, and the audience seated on the stage.

I have been phantasizing long scenes in which the actress playing Bertha (*ossia* Bernice) recognizes among the actors-on-the-stage some old long-lost friend—or enemy. And some such thing may well develop, but the whole raison d'être of such an encounter must be that it illustrates an aspect of the Emporium; and also that it contributes to our matrix-form of repetitions. Say she recognizes Mrs. Frisbee (of the Veteran Department-Store Workers):

---

*It's well to name here what I have been reading and seeing that has contributed: more and more Hölderlin; Ezra Pound's translation of Sophocles's *Trachiniae* [*The Women of Trachis*], comparing it line by line, in laughing amazement with old [Richard C.] Jebb's); some ineffable passages of Balanchine's choreography of Mendelssohn's Scotch Symphony; and "tea" with Alma Mahler [-Werfel]—an Emporium girl, genre *viennois*, who flatters me to the last limits: "*Mein Herz hat' so geklopft, als wäre es einen König den ich erwartete.*" As "tea" were champagne, caviar, and pâté de foie gras.

BERTHA: What are *you* doing here?! And what are *you* doing as an actress?

MRS. FRISBEE: They didn't tell me this was about the Gillespie-Schwingemeister. Oh, I won't stay a minute. I'm going right out to sit in the bus. The G. and S. killed my husband.

Then big fracas as she tries to draw all her companions out "to sit in the bus." All that could work—but oh! I cannot, must not, place it there, at the Cleaning-Women's Scene—can I? I'll draw up some sketches and see.

February 15, 1954.

The sketches I then drew up are not final (doubly distressing, since they inevitably overemphasize the aspect of "theatrical tricks," tiresome *Wiederholung* of the non-actors' intrusion into the play, that I must render completely vital and organic or else discard), but they perhaps point the way.

To encourage myself, let me put the fairest possible face on what I am doing: my "instinct" urges me to do two things (two things at the same time—perhaps more than two—in the simultaneity of several operations is the health and reassurance of the measures), to break up and frustrate any interest in mere anecdote, in mere individual life story; and to make converge upon my action-idea as many and as diversified a series of pertinent elements-of-life as possible. One of the reasons that this play has been so long a-writing is, of course, that I have not been able to make fiercely clear to myself what the Emporium is,—what I am saying; the other is that my will-to-work slackens, my faith fades, when the daily task (*i.e.*, the pages I am at work on) do not bristle, sparkle, dance, with representations of life's diversity, time's achroneity, and any idea's *Vielseitigkeit*. All that is what kept me interested in *The Ides of March*.* No view of life, then, is real to me save that it presents itself as kaleido-scopic,—which does not mean essentially incoherent. (The very children's toys of that name show us always a beautifully ordered though multi-fragmented pattern.)

---

*Was that long a-borning? I don't know. That is the kind of thing I blandly, balmily forget. I kept no Journal then. My impression is that it went quite blithely on, interrupted only by my ever-reprehensible enjoyment in distractions and by the everpresent interruptions caused by the mismanagement of my life's *corvées*.

In my plays, and last novel [*The Ides of March*], there is this constant interruption. The more I seek to exhibit an idea about life, the more I must make sure that the tumult of sheer existences be introduced, pertinent and impertinent (perhaps it is my fault that I do not sufficiently introduce the confessedly absurdly impertinent, as Gertrude Stein does), and the more I start out to give an instance of some character's individual action, the more I lift it from the specific-unique into the realm of the typical and the idea-expressive. It is natural, therefore, that in a play I should not rest content with the actors moving only in their fictional play: my *dramatis personae* are characters in the fiction, *and* representatives of an idea, but they are also men and women engaged in an impersonation. More than that, the members of the audience are not inert intelligences. Since my play is about Everybody, everybody is in my play. Even in *The Skin of Our Teeth* I went so far (in introducing the captain of the ushers, etc.) as almost to introduce characters who were not intent upon the play. *This* play is also about the man and woman who are passing by the theatre, in the street outside: why not introduce them?

So let me reassure myself that there is an organic, legitimate way to introduce these intrusions and interruptions, and when I have found and expressed that way correctly I shall be able to overcome my diffidence. And one sign that I shall be getting it correctly will be laughter—the right kind of laughter: the recognition that it is wildly disproportionate that these members of the audience seated on the stage should be caught up into the fiction, but that that *disproportion* is not in contradiction with the fact that they move in a real relation to the drama.

Now to get down to specific instances: what precisely do I want Mrs. Frisbee to carry in this scene? Why,—as I said in the previous entry—the magnet-pull, the fascination of the Emporium. And this I can do—as I have done so often—*in reverse*. She can warn the audience against the fascination. And if through her warnings, I can also intimate the *Schaudern*, so much the better. It has ruined her life and that of her husband.

Now let's go back and try that.

February 16, 1954.

But what my play above all lacks is passion—which, in all the forms that passion could take, is here the *movement* of the passion of people seeking the "Right Way." I feel that it is present in the first scenes, but it slips away, somehow, between the scenes. The figure of John must be a hot-winging arrow that carries the whole play with it. And it seems to me that the reason I've lost it is that I haven't been clear in my head as to what obstacle it is that prevents his being invited to enter the Emporium. I shy away from facing this problem because every side-glance at it seems to lead toward moralizing *platement*: he lacks humility; he refuses to renounce worldly success, etc.

But we decided—didn't we?—that the qualification of the Emporium-worker was that he could "do a thing alone"—nay, that nothing worthwhile was done save unaided (whereby G[ertrude]. S[tein]. enters the play). There too all the pitfalls of eupeptic moralizing lurk, but less flagrantly; this introduces, rather, the pitfalls of the sentimental and pathetic. So that John can be represented as desiring the G. and S. and yet incapable of seeing that success, etc. are forms of dependency. Now it would seem that for this we need a *raisonneur* or *raisonneuse*, probably several.

Let me return now to the text and see what I can do.

Walked downtown.

Now it seems to me that we can follow this line: Scene One: Orphanage; Scene Two: The Graham Farm; Scene Three: First Floor of the Emporium; Scene Four: The Employment Office; Scene Five: First Floor of the Emporium (terminating with John's dream).

Certainly very dangerous seems the plan for placing *two* scenes in the same Emporium corridor; but out of our dangers let us make us successes. In this way, I can make ever more *serré* the inner intensity of John's "hunt"—hunter and hunted. I want John (and the audience) to get into their consciousness that Laurencia-Hobmeyer dialogue about the vast traditions of the G. and S., before we see the scene at the Agency. I want a first stage of a flirtation with Laurencia, and I want a complete first picture of Hobmeyer kicking John out of the store. All this, too, will give me more space in which to develop all the other motifs which have been developing.

In this new lay-out, do I have the Cleaning-Women's Scene in the first or the second of the Emporium scenes? And can I give Mr. Hobmeyer four big scenes in a row: Hobmeyer-Dobbs (the Employment Officer)-Hobmeyer-Dr. Abercrombie? Or should I assign Mr. Dobbs (as a feeble member of the G. and S. community) to the actor who has just died offstage as Mr. Graham?

Both the Emporium scenes begin in the same way: floorwalker's injunction to the customers to leave the store.

Let's write at it all and see what happens. (I now can restore that first entrance of John into the store: "Fifth-rate store----air bad----no doors.")

February 18, 1954.

Yes, it's going forward. I'm pretty sure it's on the right tack. And several of those boldest tricks with time seem to have found their way with naturalness into the text; and I've found a place to insert the figure of the Wheel. Of course, it's all just first draft still. The best sign that it is moving correctly is that it is beginning to indicate its further development; but more of that later.

What I want in it now is richness, not as ornament, but as expressive force. And one of these richnesses is more humor—precisely because it is so heaven-reaching a subject,—hence, a disconcerting humor. I want [it] in Laurencia; her role is so important because it shows us that the G. and S. does not mean an intellectual élite. A few of my touches so far relate her to Sabina [in *The Skin of Our Teeth*], but she is not a Sabina, she is a Mrs. Antrobus at twenty-one. I don't want much more humor from the Ex–Department-Store Workers; they are in danger of being too funny as it is. Then, too, I want a sort of splendor in Scene Five—the material's all there, but I want it better: Laurencia's cry for more life; the love scene; the Cleaning Women; the dream. Oh, I must have John threaten not only to stay in the store all night, so as to glimpse the Higher-Ups (that I have already), but his threat "to go up to the offices on the fifth and sixth floor"—an echo of Kafka (K. to the Innkeeper's wife: "*Was fürchten Sie also? Sie fürchten doch nicht etwa . . . für Klamm?*"). Somehow I must get into that scene—at the climax; it is the close of Part One, preceding the only intermission—a big rebellion or reaction from the persons seated on the stage.

Now as to the impediment in John: my Mr. Hobmeyer must again serve as *raisonneur*. Here so hard not to bore us with the moralizing-didactic. It is John's craving for success, and his boasting; to which Hobmeyer points out----how? how avoid the most abysmal sententiousness?—the craving for success is a dependency. John's surprised answer. Can I somehow swing it up into the splendor? Can I give [it] to the cleaning woman as laughing derision?

How can my one lone cleaning woman give the impression I want? I wish I could have fifteen. At least, thank Heaven, I have the benefit of the stage-picture dressed with those members from the audience. Now to involve them. The first little man no longer demands the Prologue. What else does he do at his first appearance?

February 23, 1954.

A succession of interruptions: dinners, guests, concerts. Not this time so distressing and harmful, because they have been confined to a few days—delimited and clearly terminated last evening, leaving few engagements before me now. (Though that other interruption, the real enemy, is there forever without intermission: correspondence, manuscripts submitted, etc. From that there's no surcease, and talking about it is no alleviation.) This time I return to this problem here, after the interruption, with renewed spirit.

What the play needs is a larger deeper happier immersion on my part in what it's all about. Today the emphasis is on *happier*, for the sign that all is going well in this portentous and often painful subject matter will be that it will be permeated with the comic.

Oh, the form isn't bold and splendid and revolutionary enough. That's why I'm so inhibited and tentative and scratchily groping.

Now let me put down some of the fancies that have been crossing my mind in this matter of form,—not because they are the *eureka*, but because they give me imaginative practice in bold form-shattering invention.

(Before I put them down I want to add another thing: when I find the right form—the right statement for this cosmological comedy—wouldn't it be wonderful if I could do it without those names of celebrated orphans—those names of the painters and music-makers of the Emporium? To other people—but not to me—they bring in the smell of professor and historian. Not to me, because "culture" is in me a second nature. Hitherto it has always seemed to me that the "comic" aspect of their introduction into the play—the anachronistic game, for instance,—saved them from the academic stink—but *even* I, as I have expressed it several times in the Journal, am aware that in those names, through those names, is felt the hated didactic formal-symbolic strain. After all, Kafka did it without names.)

So to return to formal liberation, enlargement:

(1) Maybe that first Member of the Audience seated on the stage, —maybe he objects:

MEMBER OF THE AUDIENCE: This scene in the Orphanage, —I heard that that scene was the last scene in the play. Why—excuse me—are you playing it *first* tonight?

MR. FOSTER: If you make interruptions you must go back and sit down in the audience. It's not important *what you've heard*. We on the stage are doing what we have been instructed to do.

MEMBER OF THE AUDIENCE: Well----, but isn't it true that this scene in the Orphanage used to be last?

MR. FOSTER: This is very tiresome. We can't go on, if this is going to happen.

MRS. FOSTER [*to* MR. FOSTER]: Since he's brought the matter where the whole audience can hear him, we might as well explain. [*She addresses the man:*] We have been instructed—I mean, the author says—that the order of the scenes in this play should be changed every performance. Some nights this scene comes first and some nights it comes last. Some nights we begin at the Fourth Scene and go through the whole play and end at the Third Scene. Some nights we begin at the Sixth Scene and end at the Fifth Scene.

----Would I stop the *explication* there? Anyway, something like. There's an advance notice of the Wheel-motif.

(2) To resort, as I did in *The Skin of Our Teeth*, to a parodic (the dictionary also allows *parodical*) allusion to old-fashioned kinds of playwriting. To return more closely to what was the initial departure of this play, the Horatio-Alger novel—via the theatre contemporary to Horatio Alger. All this would involve throwing away the Orphanage Scene. I could here launch upon a long essay to show that one of the livelier expressions of our time (of collapse of old modes, of bewildered helplessness before new frights and new grandeurs) is the mock-heroic and the parody.

Now let these notations (and here is the benefit of the Journal) start a train of opening up and encouraging the imagination to all but anarchical freedoms, —whatever the cost of time and effort.

June 17, 1954.

(That was almost six months ago. . . . Here I am back with some new impulses toward "The Emporium"—and at a moment when so many other *corvées* and projects surround me----nevertheless:)

It's the Hero I haven't got right—the Hero and the Girl. Since the play, by very reason of its mode of staging, to say nothing of the vast implications of the theme, the wrestling with the Absolute, is about the type Hero, let's do the eternal Hero myth. I have been too much drawn into the Kafka hero, the frustrated pre-condemned struggler. That's not my bent; I'm not the stuff of which nihilists are made; I'm not even sympathetic toward the broken-winged; all that derived from a mimetic sympathetic admiration for the Kafka vision, perhaps merely for the Kafka art, the virtuosity with which he could present his maimed soul. I want to liberate myself from the Kafka hero—and can we call Hero the man who dies *"wie ein Hund"*?—while at the same time retaining that element in Kafka which is real to me, the seduction and the ambiguity and the terror of the Absolute?

So back to the Hero.

Let us bear in mind the eternal myth-patterns of the Hero—viewed not only as the Exceptional Man but as the potential in every man. His birth is surrounded with mystery. At first all he knows is the beatific, timeless, effortless floating in the womb. Then he is separated from that nirvana—the ego emerges as he becomes aware of an Outside which is not the self. He has two mothers: the benignant goddess of all living and the baleful enemy-mother who wishes to retain him in nirvana, to draw him back to the chaos of instinctual life. He has two fathers: the warrior-worker-creator to emulate; and the jealous old man who wishes to restrain and maim and kill him. He sets out on the quest for a treasure: the treasure is a virgin. He must win her through trials and perils.

At once I see that I have wasted time over the choice between Emporium and Craigie. (Yes, there is a play there, a theme there, but it is secondary to the more basic theme of the Hero's journey—and it has led me all this time into a resort to the tiresome moralizing side of my "formation.")

Let us say that our Hero does get into the Emporium at once, but at the ground floor: he is a package-wrapper in the basement.

The Girl is the daughter not of Craigie's but of the Emporium.

She is guarded against young heroes, because even Excellence becomes tyrannical and conservative-petrified. The Emporium is old-fashioned and airless; the Hero wins the daughter of the Emporium and the power to refresh and renew it.

Now I can play with this business of the Older Actress playing the successive Good and Bad Mothers; and the Older Actor playing the Good and Bad Fathers. The Orphanage-Mother is Good, but against John's being sent away. The Orphanage-Father is Stern-Justice. The Farmer's Wife is in one scene both Good and Bad. (Can that be done?)

There is in the first Emporium Scene (this is just groping now) no Laurencia? John comes up at closing time from the bowels of the Emporium and inveighs against its airlessness, etc., and hears, again, about the Virgin-Princess.

It also sounds (1) excruciatingly schematized and (2) oriented toward a sunburst of a happy-ending; but let's see what can be done with it.

Now for some random ideas that accompany this new project:

In the Orphanage Scene: Mrs. Foster constantly asking the children have they eaten—dare I have her insisting that they each eat their mid-morning apple, and their mid-morning glass of milk. Their after-lunch nap.

In the Farmhouse Scene: John: "He's always swinging that scythe" (or sickle—Hell, you run into symbols at every turn). Mrs. Graham alternately urges him to stay and incites him to the Emporium----. There's no more about *not* seeing Gillespie or Schwingemeister----, but isn't it run by an old woman?

Where on earth is our *Padre Nobile?* Can it be indicated (as I did rather well in *The Skin of Our Teeth*) that the repressive action of the fathers is a pure delusion in the young men's minds?

Now we can do the scene that was formerly the Craigie Annual Party with a whole new effect. It is the Emporium Annual Party. Old Mr. Gillespie—invalid, and fearful—is the Decrepit King. He no longer throws his daughter at the young Hero—he resists him at every turn.

It's now not so much a question as to whether it can be done, as one of whether I can catch fire from it. And whether the Opera-libretto cannot also be fed from some of these notions.

Where shall I begin to write on it? Not at the beginning, but at the (first) Emporium Scene. And here rises the question that if there's no Laurencia, how do I get that background-conversation in? Does Miss Gillespie visit the store at closing time to call for her father? Is Mr. Hobmeyer still with us? And can we now "work" the members of the audience who are seated on the [stage]?

Index